Learning Microsoft Power Apps

Building Business Applications
with Low-Code Technology

Arpit Shrivastava

Beijing · Boston · Farnham · Sebastopol · Tokyo

Learning Microsoft Power Apps

by Arpit Shrivastava

Copyright © 2024 Arpit Shrivastava. All rights reserved.

Published by O'Reilly Media, Inc., 1005 Gravenstein Highway North, Sebastopol, CA 95472.

O'Reilly books may be purchased for educational, business, or sales promotional use. Online editions are also available for most titles (*http://oreilly.com*). For more information, contact our corporate/institutional sales department: 800-998-9938 or *corporate@oreilly.com*.

Acquisitions Editor: Andy Kwan
Development Editor: Rita Fernando
Production Editor: Beth Kelly
Copyeditor: Penelope Perkins
Proofreader: Piper Editorial Consulting, LLC

Indexer: nSight, Inc.
Interior Designer: David Futato
Cover Designer: Karen Montgomery
Illustrator: Kate Dullea

July 2024:   First Edition

Revision History for the First Edition
2024-07-17:   First Release

See *http://oreilly.com/catalog/errata.csp?isbn=9781098150426* for release details.

The O'Reilly logo is a registered trademark of O'Reilly Media, Inc. *Learning Microsoft Power Apps*, the cover image, and related trade dress are trademarks of O'Reilly Media, Inc.

978-1-098-15042-6

[LSI]

Table of Contents

Preface

Greetings from the world of Microsoft Power Apps, the low-code, no-code app development platform. Thanks for choosing this book, where I will introduce you to many techniques that will simplify your app development process. In today's fast-paced world, organizations aspire to boost their abilities by developing apps quickly with low-code, no-code development platforms. Not only does this lower the development costs, but it also allows even nontechnical people to design business applications. In this book, I'll take you through the fundamentals of Microsoft Power Apps and show you how to develop new applications quickly using drag-and-drop controls like those used in PowerPoint and formula-based expressions like those used in Excel. I'll also touch base on some complex aspects, such as how to integrate Microsoft Power Apps with external data sources, write code to perform advanced business logic, and leverage AI capabilities to extend the app's functionality.

Who This Book Is For

By reading this book, both technical and nontechnical folks can begin developing mobile, tablet, and web applications using many of the Power Apps built-in capabilities. This book covers both the features of canvas apps and the components of model-driven apps to provide a thorough understanding of Power Apps.

Nontechnical folks, those who are not programmers but have a need to develop apps (such as functional consultants, presalespeople, business analysts, and so on), will learn how to quickly build an app using Power Apps' built-in features so that you can immediately show your customers what Power Apps can do. Once you understand the basics, you are introduced to more advanced topics.

Technical folks (such as full stack developers, solution architects, and so on) will learn how to quickly put together an app, but also extend the app's functionality by connecting it to external data sources, developing custom components, writing JavaScript and C# code, using Web APIs, and so on.

You don't need to have any prior knowledge of Microsoft Dynamics 365 and Power Platform to get the most value out of this book. However, because you'll be working with a variety of Microsoft products as we build our apps, it's recommended that you have a basic understanding of Microsoft Power Apps, and the Microsoft 365 apps Excel, PowerPoint, Teams, SharePoint, etc., because Power Apps uses Excel-like formulas to write business logic and drag-and-drop controls similar to PowerPoint to design the app.

Why I Wrote This Book

I've published many articles and delivered many trainings around the world, and my favorite topics to discuss have always been Power Apps and Power Pages. Despite all the articles and trainings, I've never felt like I've been able to cover Power Apps and Power Pages to the fullest, especially its fundamentals. There's so much to cover, and there are so many things that are underutilized. There are many excellent publications that discuss Power Apps, but none that cover it to its full extent. In this book, I'll take the opportunity to go into detail about the foundation of Power Apps, Microsoft's goal of introducing a low-code, no-code development platform and how it differs from previous app development technologies, and how anyone with basic computer skills can create business apps. Although specific features and components may change over time, the basics of how they work will likely stay the same. Thus, I believe that it is important to learn fundamentals via real-world examples so you gain a practical understanding that can be applied, even if the features and components change in the future.

In this book, I get to talk about my favorite topic and share my enthusiasm and knowledge with more people than before. I'll take you through examples that are based on real-world scenarios. I believe that hands-on experience is the best way to learn about features and capabilities. It is my hope that this book will help people, regardless of their technical experience, learn how to take advantage of this powerful tool and build amazing apps.

What This Book Covers

This book covers everything related to Microsoft Power Apps, from its evolution to its fundamentals to advanced topics with real-world examples, over 15 chapters. This book has been written in a way that anyone who has worked with Power Apps or who intends to begin working with Power Apps can benefit from it.

You will enter the Power Apps world by first learning about the evolution of Power Apps in Chapter 1. In this chapter, you will learn how Microsoft released its first CRM product to the market and subsequently expanded its features by releasing new versions. And finally, turned an entry-level CRM product into a low-code and no-code application called Power Apps, empowering everyone to create business apps, not just developers but even nondevelopers (citizen developers).

After learning about the evolution of Power Apps, you will learn about the Microsoft Power Platform, a low-code and no-code development platform, and its various components in Chapter 2. These components play a key role in Power Apps development as they enable both developers and citizen developers to extend Power Apps' functionality and create complete business solutions. Additionally, you will learn Microsoft Dataverse, which dynamically stores Power Apps data and metadata in a scalable and secure environment to meet ever-changing business demands.

You will go deeper into the Power Apps ocean in Chapter 3 by learning how it empowers application development and makes it easier for organizations to rapidly design and deploy enterprise-grade business applications by using Excel-like formula expressions and PowerPoint-like drag-and-drop controls. In this chapter, you will also learn about Power Apps' various types and how they vary from one another, as well as its licensing options, building blocks that connect you to various Power Apps features and components, system requirements for launching the Power Apps on your desktop/laptop/tablet/mobile and in browsers, and different options for configuring your Power Apps environment so you can begin creating apps.

After you have a basic understanding of Power Apps and its building blocks, you must be aware of the many database choices that Power Apps can use to communicate with data. In Chapter 4, you will learn the fundamentals of data sources and how different types of Power Apps use different types of data sources. After reading this chapter, you will understand how Power Apps can interact with the data stored in either Microsoft-provided data sources (such as Dataverse, SharePoint, OneDrive, and Excel) or non-Microsoft-provided data sources (such as Salesforce, DocuSign, and Adobe). In this chapter, you will also learn about a variety of connectors that enable you to establish communication between Power Apps and data sources without writing code by serving as an API wrapper.

Once you know the different types of Power Apps and which database they use to store the data, you must know which type of Power Apps is best suited to meet your business needs. Chapter 5 will show you the difference between various types of Power Apps, when to use each type, and their real-time use cases.

When determining whether to use a canvas app or a model-driven app to fulfill your customer's needs, data source is not the only factor to consider. The various features and components of each app type might assist you in picking the most suitable app for your business requirements. Therefore, you must know about each app type's features and capabilities. So in Chapter 6, you will learn about every feature and component of model-driven apps. However, there are instances when creating custom components and writing code to an application is necessary to make it a fully functional business solution. As a result, Chapter 7 will cover every option available to you for extending the model-driven app's capabilities. And in Chapter 8, you will learn the built-in features, controls, and components of canvas apps.

After you are familiar with all aspects of Power Apps, in Chapter 9 you will learn how to write business logic in Power Apps using an Excel-formulas-based low-code programming language called Power Fx. It was previously limited to use in canvas apps, but it quickly spread throughout the Power Platform as a common programming language.

Once your Power Apps solution is developed, it must be moved to a different environment for testing and live usage. In Chapter 10, you will learn about Dataverse Solutions, including their types, deployment methodologies, and approaches to automate the deployment process.

Chapter 11 focuses on Microsoft Copilot and other AI features in Power Apps to increase app users' productivity. In this chapter' you will learn how Microsoft Copilot in Power Apps enables you to build an app, including the data behind it, just by describing what you need in natural language through multiple steps of conversation.

Chapter 12 discusses how to increase business users' productivity by integrating Microsoft Dataverse and Power Platform into Microsoft Teams. In this chapter, you will learn how Dataverse for Teams enables business users to quickly create custom applications, workflows, and chatbots in Teams by leveraging Power Apps, Power Automate, and Copilot Studio, along with Dataverse with limited capabilities to automate day-to-day manual and repetitive activities.

In Chapters 13 and 14, you will learn about real-world case studies and how to implement them using Power Apps. Chapter 13 focuses on how to plan your Power Apps implementation, including the various implementation methodologies, phases, and types, before kicking off the Power Apps development. In this chapter, you will create a model-driven app called "Book My Service" to help a retail company overcome their customer service-related challenges. While in Chapter 14, you will create a canvas app called "Service at Home" for field service agents to provide on-site support.

Finally, in Chapter 15, I will wrap up the book by sharing some useful tips and best practices based on my own experiences.

After reading all 15 chapters, you'll be in the driver's seat and have the steering wheel in your hand to enjoy the beautiful journey of Power Apps. Remember that you are responsible for adhering to all traffic rules and safety guidelines (Power Apps best practices) during this journey. Despite this, you will come across many potholes and bumps on the road, but with continuous learning, following the right path, and enjoying your journey, you will eventually reach your destination.

Power Apps Case Study

At the end of this book, I'll take you through the development of a cost-effective Power Apps-based low-code, no-code solution for a retail company that is currently facing many business challenges like lack of automation, security, and mobility when it comes to offering customer service to its clients.

This Power Apps solution will have the following two apps:

Model-driven app
> I will create a model-driven app named Book My Service for the support agents who are working in the stores and handling customer queries and complaints over the phone, email, or in the stores.

Canvas app
> I will create a canvas app named Service at Home for the field service agents who will visit customer locations to install the devices, fix their issues, and collect feedback.

You can see the solution code in the book's GitHub repository.

Microsoft Power Apps Updates

Microsoft Power Apps are updated frequently, and as a result, there may be instances where the data or graphics in this book aren't current. Also, it's possible that some of the features you learn will become obsolete in the future. There may also be more features that Microsoft discloses in the future, so to stay updated, keep an eye on the release notes that Microsoft posts following each release plan.

Regardless of what else occurs in the realm of Power Apps, the approaches and thought processes that I describe in the book are likely to remain the same, even if the features change. Therefore, the goal of this book is to address the foundations of developing Power Apps-based applications rather than relying on each feature's specifics.

Conventions Used in This Book

The following typographical conventions are used in this book:

Italic
> Indicates new terms, URLs, email addresses, filenames, and file extensions.

`Constant width`
> Used for program listings, as well as within paragraphs to refer to program elements such as variable or function names, databases, data types, environment variables, statements, and keywords.

Constant width bold

Shows commands or other text that should be typed literally by the user.

Constant width italic

Shows text that should be replaced with user-supplied values or by values determined by context.

 This element signifies a tip or suggestion.

 This element signifies a general note.

 This element indicates a warning or caution.

Using Code Examples

Supplemental material (code examples, exercises, etc.) is available for download at *https://github.com/arpitpowerguide/LearningPowerApps/tree/main/PowerApps-CaseStudy*.

If you have a technical question or a problem using the code examples, please send email to *support@oreilly.com*.

This book is here to help you get your job done. In general, if example code is offered with this book, you may use it in your programs and documentation. You do not need to contact us for permission unless you're reproducing a significant portion of the code. For example, writing a program that uses several chunks of code from this book does not require permission. Selling or distributing examples from O'Reilly books does require permission. Answering a question by citing this book and quoting example code does not require permission. Incorporating a significant amount of example code from this book into your product's documentation does require permission.

We appreciate, but generally do not require, attribution. An attribution usually includes the title, author, publisher, and ISBN. For example: "*Learning Microsoft Power Apps* by Arpit Shrivastava (O'Reilly). Copyright 2024 Arpit Shrivastava, 978-1-098-15042-6."

If you feel your use of code examples falls outside fair use or the permission given above, feel free to contact us at *permissions@oreilly.com*.

O'Reilly Online Learning

 For more than 40 years, *O'Reilly Media* has provided technology and business training, knowledge, and insight to help companies succeed.

Our unique network of experts and innovators share their knowledge and expertise through books, articles, and our online learning platform. O'Reilly's online learning platform gives you on-demand access to live training courses, in-depth learning paths, interactive coding environments, and a vast collection of text and video from O'Reilly and 200+ other publishers. For more information, visit *https://oreilly.com*.

How to Contact Us

Please address comments and questions concerning this book to the publisher:

O'Reilly Media, Inc.
1005 Gravenstein Highway North
Sebastopol, CA 95472
800-889-8969 (in the United States or Canada)
707-827-7019 (international or local)
707-829-0104 (fax)
support@oreilly.com
https://www.oreilly.com/about/contact.html

We have a web page for this book, where we list errata, examples, and any additional information. You can access this page at *https://oreil.ly/learning-microsoft-power-apps*.

For news and information about our books and courses, visit *https://oreilly.com*.

Find us on LinkedIn: *https://linkedin.com/company/oreilly-media*

Watch us on YouTube: *https://youtube.com/oreillymedia*

Acknowledgments

To hold this book in my hands is a dream realized, a journey completed, and a milestone achieved. I never imagined that my words would find a home on the shelves of readers around the world. I am deeply grateful to all those who supported me along this path.

To my wife: This book stands as a testament to the unwavering support and boundless inspiration provided by my beautiful wife. Your encouragement ignited the spark within me to embark on this writing journey. Your unwavering belief in my abilities and your steadfast support sustained me through the highs and lows of the creative process. Your patience, understanding, and endless love have been the cornerstone of this endeavor. Your presence by my side, offering words of encouragement and wisdom, has been my guiding light, propelling me forward even when the path seemed daunting. Thank you once again for standing by me, for believing in my dreams, and for always being my biggest cheerleader.

To my parents: This book is dedicated to my parents, who have dedicated their lives to the noble profession of teaching. Your tireless commitment to education has been a source of inspiration for me. From you, I have learned the importance of patience, empathy, and the power of knowledge to transform lives. Thank you for instilling in me a passion for learning and for being unwavering pillars of support throughout my journey. This book stands as a tribute to your tireless efforts and the profound impact you have had on countless lives.

To my mentors: I can't forget to extend my heartfelt thanks to all my mentors, Sapan Jaiswal, Manoj Chauhan, Karan Ojha, Ashish Shukla, Harish Shinde, Pranav Shroti, Sachin Lade, Malini Johri, Razwan Choudary, and many more, whose wisdom, guidance, and unwavering support have been instrumental throughout my career. Your mentorship has not only shaped my professional journey but has also inspired me to reach greater heights.

To my friends: I am indebted to my friends Aman Ghuraiya and Manju Gurjar, who graciously took on the role of reviewers for this book. Your insightful feedback and words of praise have immensely enriched its content and clarity. Your encouragement and motivation have been invaluable, spurring me on to give my best.

To my book editors and reviewers: A heartfelt thank you to my dedicated book editor, Rita Fernando, and reviewers: Nishant Rana, Aman Ghuraiya, and Connor Ingram, whose insightful feedback and thoughtful critique helped shape this book into its final form. Your time and attention are deeply appreciated.

Finally, to the readers who embark on this journey with me, your interest and support are the ultimate reward. I hope this book resonates with you and adds value to your lives.

CHAPTER 1

Evolution of Microsoft Power Apps

Today, Microsoft Power Apps is an incredible suite of apps that empowers everyone to build custom business applications. As they say, Rome was not built in a day, and neither was Power Apps. In this chapter, you'll learn about the history of Microsoft Power Apps and how it evolved into what it is today. Figure 1-1 illustrates the progression of each product rather than a full replacement of the preceding one, just as we humans have grown from the day of our birth to the present.

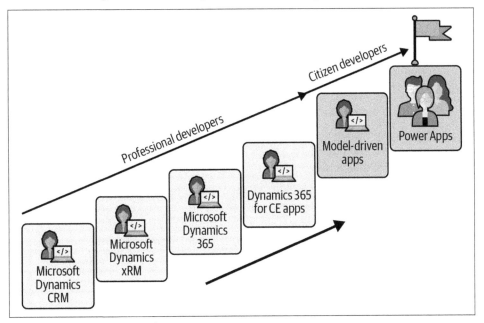

Figure 1-1. Power Apps evolution

Microsoft Dynamics CRM

All businesses, whether they are large or small, local or global, rely on customers to survive and thrive. The success of each business depends on managing its customer base. Therefore, every industry must try its hardest to manage the relationship with the customer by effectively utilizing its people, processes, and products. And this is what *CRM* (customer relationship management) is all about.

Good customer relations are largely dependent on how well you manage and use your customers' data within an organization. Without reliable and accurate data, organizations cannot make well-informed decisions about how to engage with their customers, how to improve the sales and service experience for them, or how to use resources for more targeted marketing. For these reasons, data management is the heart of CRM, and any organization's ability to succeed also depends on how well it manages its customers' data. In today's fast-paced digital world, every customer expects their sales and service experience to be as seamless as possible. For effective management of customer data and to store that data in a centralized database, companies have developed CRM software. The most common advantages of using any CRM software are:

- It facilitates quicker deal closure, more effective cross- and up-selling of products, and better lead management for the sales team.

- It enables the customer support team to respond to inquiries from customers in a more effective manner.

- It aids the marketing team in targeting the right customers for campaigns and advertising.

- It helps organizations to do the analytics, which helps sales managers to track sales performance and make smarter business decisions.

- It improves communication between customers and companies by centralizing customer data and automating tasks like emails and follow-ups, ensuring timely and consistent interactions.

- It enables businesses to develop AI capabilities by using their customers' data (compliant with GDPR (*https://oreil.ly/WoqGf*)) to make wiser business decisions. For instance, if customers are automatically notified by text or email whenever a discount is available on a product, they buy more frequently.

CRM became popular in the 1990s, and, as a result of its success, we now have many CRM products offered by different companies such as Oracle, Salesforce, SAP, Freshsales, Zoho, Pipedrive, and Monday Sales. You can find the complete list on Wikipedia (*https://oreil.ly/Bt7r1*). In response to the rising demand for CRM products, Microsoft released Microsoft CRM 1.2 in 2003 as its first CRM offering. This product had a basic sales and service module, and developers could add their own custom fields and use JavaScript code to augment its capabilities. In 2005, Microsoft released Microsoft Dynamics CRM 3.0, which had a marketing module as well and allowed users to add custom tables and store additional information regarding sales and service activities.

So now, Microsoft Dynamics CRM has three core modules: Sales, Service, and Marketing. This is significant because sales, service, and marketing operations form the backbone of customer relationship management in medium to large industries (Figure 1-2). Let's look at how sales, service, and marketing are part of the customer relationship management process.

Marketing is critical to every business in the world, no matter how big or small, because it helps customers become aware of your products or services, and helps you engage with those customers and influence their purchasing decisions. Businesses use a variety of media to promote their products. Email, SMS, newspapers, billboards and banners, commercials, and events are a few examples that make up a marketing campaign.

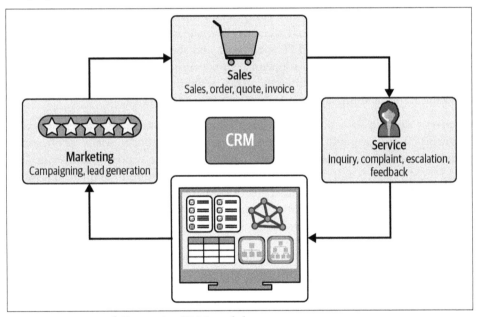

Figure 1-2. Microsoft Dynamics CRM modules

As a result of a marketing campaign, a customer may show interest in purchasing a business's product, either from a physical store or from an online shop. This is now part of the Sales domain. The success of any organization is mostly dependent on the sales department. The crucial function of sales is to close the gap between the needs of a potential customer and the goods or services that the company provides that can meet those needs.

Customers who purchase your product might have inquiries about it as they use it, want to offer feedback, or have issues while using it, in which case they might need to submit a complaint or get in touch with the business for assistance. This is part of the Service domain, which covers post-purchase customer support.

At first, Microsoft's only goal when it launched the CRM product was to manage customers, sales, service, and marketing. However, to maintain market leadership and stay ahead in the competition, Microsoft sought to make its CRM product *dynamic* so that businesses could expand their functionalities, combine it with other Microsoft products/applications, and create their own CRM apps to suit their business requirements.

xRM

Today, every company wants to improve, broaden, and customize the CRM system to meet its unique business needs. Manufacturing businesses want to use CRM software to manage their assets, health care businesses want to use CRM software to manage their health care staff and patients, colleges and universities want to use CRM software to manage their faculty and students, IT businesses want to use CRM software to manage their employees and IT operations, and some companies need CRM software to manage their vendors, compliance and governance, suppliers, insurance policies, and the list goes on infinitely. Also, each business sector has its unique procedures for handling sales, marketing, and customer service.

Microsoft decided to extend the CRM product capabilities under the name xRM (Figure 1-3) and promoted it under the slogan "One Platform, Many Applications, Infinite Possibilities" in response to the demand for the creation of numerous apps using CRM products and their extension based on business needs. Similar to how x is used to represent any value in mathematics, Microsoft introduced X into its CRM product, envisioning that the software could adeptly manage various business applications through its extension capabilities, including:

- Extend the data model made available by Microsoft.
- Use a CRM product as a web-based application.
- Customize the user interface.
- Write workflows to automate processes and tasks.
- Let developers modify the platform using their own C# and JavaScript code.
- Build custom modules (or applications) on top of Dynamics CRM to suit business needs.

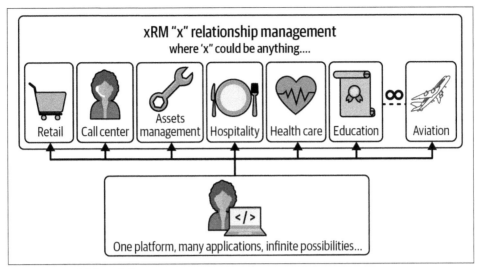

Figure 1-3. xRM modules

Following the popularity and positive customer feedback of the CRM product, Microsoft continued the concept of "One platform, Many applications" and released four ERP (enterprise resource planning) applications onto the market: Microsoft Dynamics Great Plains (GP) (*https://oreil.ly/3ovPq*), Microsoft Dynamics Navision (NAV) (*https://oreil.ly/xHut6*), Microsoft Dynamics Axapta (AX) (*https://oreil.ly/_7TOM*), and Microsoft Dynamics Solomon (SL) (*https://oreil.ly/iP_z2*).

Although CRM and ERP are connected and have similar goals, the two products serve different purposes, as shown in Figure 1-4. CRM, as previously mentioned, is all about managing customers and their sales, marketing, and services to increase business profit; whereas ERP focuses on managing finances, supply chain, accounting, resource planning, and handling operations that save costs while boosting profits.

CRM focuses on and attempts to improve external customer interactions. Businesses must provide excellent customer support since customers are the major drivers of success. ERP focuses on the business's essential operations. It includes streamlining processes to reduce costs, supplying workers with information to keep them focused on their jobs, and completing a certain process or production as quickly as is feasible. Hence managing front-office activities is the sole responsibility of CRM, whereas back-office tasks are the sole responsibility of ERP.

Every industry needs ERP and CRM systems to run its business. So let's say if your car were a company, the car's engine would be a CRM, and the car's steering wheel would be an ERP. As it boosts sales and boosts profitability, CRM will be your company's engine and driving force. The ERP system will act as your precise compass and steering wheel. Both the employees and the customers benefit from the integration of CRM and ERP.

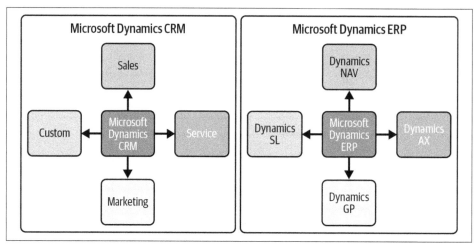

Figure 1-4. Microsoft Dynamics CRM versus Microsoft Dynamics ERP

Microsoft wanted to develop CRM and ERP together. In contrast to Microsoft CRM, the major challenge with ERP products was that they were ill-suited to offer cloud-based solutions and to create unique line-of-business application solutions. As a result, compared to CRM software, the rise of ERP applications was slower.

Between 2005 and 2015, five new versions of Microsoft Dynamics CRM were released with a variety of new features and capabilities. Table 1-1 illustrates the multiple iterations and releases of Microsoft Dynamics CRM with improved capabilities from 2003 to 2016. I will discuss product updates beyond 2016 in the next section.

Table 1-1. Evolution of Microsoft Dynamics CRM

Microsoft CRM versions	Release date	Mainstream support end date	Extended support end date
Microsoft CRM 1.2 (*https://oreil.ly/60G9V*)	31 October, 2003	09 January, 2007	—
Microsoft Dynamics CRM 3.0 (*https://oreil.ly/YNKd4*)	01 December, 2005	12 April, 2011	12 April, 2016
Microsoft Dynamics CRM 4.0 (*https://oreil.ly/ZUPQj*)	29 February, 2008	09 April, 2013	10 April, 2018
Microsoft Dynamics CRM 2011 (*https://oreil.ly/LRuCY*)	18 May, 2011	12 July, 2016	13 July, 2021
Microsoft Dynamics CRM 2013 (*https://oreil.ly/NiNS1*)	12 January, 2014	08 January, 2019	09 January, 2024
Microsoft Dynamics CRM 2015 (*https://oreil.ly/THn6e*)	11 February, 2015	14 January, 2020	14 January, 2025
Microsoft Dynamics CRM 2016 (*https://oreil.ly/mAIyF*)	30 November, 2015	12 January, 2021	13 January, 2026

You can find information about the difference between Mainstream and Extended Microsoft Support on the Microsoft website (*https://oreil.ly/uwTOH*).

Microsoft prioritized migrating their ERP systems to the cloud. Out of their four ERP applications, only Microsoft Dynamics AX and Microsoft Dynamics Navision were found suitable for cloud solutions. However, to the general public, having a mix of different cloud-based CRM and ERP applications might seem confusing.

Dynamics 365

In November 2016, Microsoft Dynamics 365 was released to incorporate the capabilities of Microsoft Dynamics CRM and Microsoft Dynamics ERP.

Microsoft Dynamics 365 came about because the Microsoft marketing team suggested that since their primary goal was to provide a single platform or cloud-based solution, why couldn't they merge all of the Microsoft CRM and Microsoft ERP applications into a single cloud-based solution? They also brought up that the nomenclature of all these products appeared to be a bit muddled because all ERP and CRM applications shared the same name (Microsoft Dynamics), but each one had a different appearance. They should have a single name for all groupings of business applications, regardless of whether they come from CRM or ERP.

Microsoft consolidated its ERP and CRM business applications under the unified brand Dynamics 365. This initiative involved renaming Microsoft Dynamics CRM to Dynamics 365 for Customer Engagement (CE), transforming Microsoft Dynamics AX into Dynamics 365 Finance and Dynamics 365 Supply Chain Management, and rebranding Microsoft Dynamics NAV as Dynamics 365 Business Central. Despite these updates, Dynamics GP and SL have maintained their original branding and remain independently supported by Microsoft as ERP solutions, receiving ongoing updates and support.

And it was time to say goodbye to Microsoft Dynamics CRM, AX, and Nav…

As of this writing, Dynamics 365 is a large collection of CRM and ERP-based business applications that enables all-in-one solutions so you don't have to pick and choose from the plethora of application options.

And, in short, and as illustrated in Figure 1-5, Microsoft Dynamics 365 = Dynamics 365 Customer Engagement Apps (Microsoft Dynamics CRM) + Dynamics 365 ERP Products (Microsoft Dynamics ERP).

Additionally, Dynamics 365 includes a number of new apps that address a variety of business functions. A single integrated solution contains all the necessary components for managing client relationships, finances, logistics, and human resources.

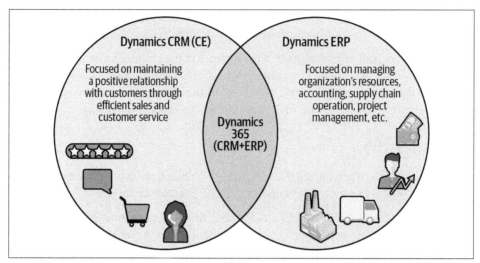

Figure 1-5. Dynamics 365 is the combination of Microsoft Dynamics CRM and Microsoft Dynamics ERP

Dynamics 365 launched the following CRM and ERP business applications:

- Dynamics 365 Sales (CRM)
- Dynamics 365 Customer Service (CRM)
- Dynamics 365 Customer Insights or Marketing (CRM)
- Dynamics 365 Field Service (CRM)
- Dynamics 365 Finance (ERP)
- Dynamics 365 Supply Chain Management (ERP)
- Dynamics 365 Project Operations (ERP)
- Dynamics 365 Business Central (ERP)

Since the major objective of all the CRM applications is to attract customers and build a strong relationship with them over time by making sure they want to do business with your organization, all CRM-based apps were later renamed as Dynamics 365 Customer Engagement (CE) Apps.

From that point on, users didn't have to keep track of as many Microsoft Dynamics CRM and ERP application names. I'll refer to them collectively as Dynamics 365. Obviously, this was a significant product release from the previous years. However, the product continued to be updated and innovated after this point.

Important Note About Names

You've had to deal with a lot of application names up to this point, but it's about to get easier.

After this point, I will use the collective names for the following:

- Dynamics 365 = Microsoft Dynamics CRM and ERP applications
- Dynamics 365 Customer Engagement (CE) apps = Microsoft Dynamics CRM
- Dynamics 365 ERP products = Microsoft Dynamics ERP

I won't go into further detail about Dynamics 365 ERP products because they are outside the scope of this book.

The Start of Low-Code, No-Code Development

In the past, only professional developers could customize software or business applications by writing code to meet business requirements. As a result, there was a high demand for professional developers and technical experts to build business applications. At the same time, organizations all over the world were embracing digital technologies as a result of a rise in demand for new business apps and modernization as well as a shortage of development resources. These organizations are now turning to low-code enterprise solutions to lead their digital transformation initiatives.

This was made evident during the COVID-19 pandemic, when businesses needed to supply their services to customers despite having a reduced workforce, international conflicts, less production, supply chain disruptions, a slow economy, and a reshuffling of their workforce. At that time, the demand for developing websites, online business applications, mobile apps, and chatbots rapidly increased to enable organizations of all sizes to build the digital capability required to address these challenges.

Here are the most common business challenges that enterprises face today:

Evolving demands of the workforce
> With rising digital transformation, organizations continue to shift and evolve. They want their processes to be automated and digitalized. They want to build more and more custom applications, websites, mobile apps, and collaboration tools to boost productivity and customer satisfaction. Additionally, they need a scalable system that can be transformed to fit every business need and flexible applications that can be easily adapted with minimal development effort. This demands the adoption of technology that keeps up with the speed at which the world is changing.

Costs for developing custom applications have gone up

Costs associated with developing software and applications are currently a problem for the majority of industries. Companies wish to create software and modify business applications in accordance with their requirements, which requires hiring qualified developers. This can be expensive and time-consuming. The cost of maintaining the application after it has been developed is another expense.

App development must be scaled up

Due to the present surge in digital transformation, where every industry tries to digitize its business processes, the demand for business application development has increased. Depending on IT professionals and developers for the creation of apps can be risky and time-consuming. Thus, organizations want to reduce their dependency on professional developers and, instead, want everyone to be able to develop apps, creating a trend toward hybrid development teams that enable the expansion of the entire organization.

A need for increased agility

In software development, *agility* refers to a quick, iterative development process. Historically, it took years to build and release software to end users. And if there were any problems, suggestions, or requests for changes, it would take months to resolve them. But in today's fast-paced world, that privilege is no longer available. Organizations must be able to quickly develop solutions based on fast-changing business strategies and demands.

Customer expectations

In today's rapidly changing digital industry, customers expect their business demands and requirements to be rolled out as soon as possible in the form of a live application. Additionally, they need a highly extensive and scalable development platform to rapidly customize the live applications to meet future demands in less time. So, if a particular development platform doesn't meet their business requirements and deliver the expected outcome within agreed timelines, they will simply move on and choose a different product or technology to build the application. As a result, in order to satisfy customer expectations, technology must be advanced, and the software development cycle must be efficient and quick.

To overcome these challenges, Microsoft decided to alter its perspective and process for creating software. This began with Satya Nadella's appointment as the new CEO in 2014.

He said in this interview given to CNET (*https://oreil.ly/Ol7yE*): "You join [Microsoft] not to be cool, but to make others cool." This quote may seem simple at first, but there is a lot to unpack. Nadella went on to explain that many years ago, Microsoft was known for being a product-based company that always wanted to "be cool" by only selling products (Windows, Microsoft Office, Visual Studio, Surface, XBOX, etc.) and squeezing the maximum number of sales from each customer, rather than focusing on innovation and advancing its technology and making it available to everyone.

So how is it beneficial to put an emphasis on "making others cool"?

As per Satya Nadella, "Together we can do more, and people naturally gravitate toward you and your brand when you concentrate on serving others and adding value." He encouraged a collaborative working style rather than a competitive one to empower individuals to achieve more in their personal and professional lives. Hence, with partnerships and collaborations with other software giants Salesforce, LinkedIn, GitHub, OpenAI, and others, Microsoft generated more income than ever in the second quarter of 2024, exceeding $62 billion, and aims to reach $500 billion by the 2030 fiscal year.[1]

With the vision of "making others cool," Microsoft has modernized its software development process and updated its technology and products in such a way that everyone, whether an employee or a customer, may profit from it. This is how the low-code, no-code development platform came about, and it's quickly becoming an integral part of the business world. Because of this, Microsoft has emerged as a global leader in technology innovation, advancing not just its CRM and ERP products, but also Windows, Visual Studio, GitHub, Microsoft 365 Apps, and other products.

Microsoft wanted to extend its "One Platform, Many Applications" concept to "One Low-Code, No-Code Platform, Many Applications" (Figure 1-6), with the primary objectives of:

- Enabling anybody to create an application based on business requirements without relying on professional developers.
- Reducing development cost and time.
- Providing simple interfaces and drag-and-drop features to expedite app development.
- Integrating seamlessly with a wide range of other Microsoft applications. This includes robust compatibility with SharePoint for document management and collaboration, Teams for communication and teamwork, and other applications within the Microsoft 365 suite such as Word, Excel, and Outlook.
- Developing greater flexibility so that team members can readily step in and assist if professional developers aren't available.

---

1 Jordan Novet, "Microsoft CEO Satya Nadella Set Goal of $500 Billion in Revenue by 2030, Court Filing Shows," (*https://oreil.ly/J-lm_*) CNBC, June 26, 2023; Microsoft, "Earnings Release FY24 Q2," (*https://oreil.ly/YbnN3*) January 30, 2024.

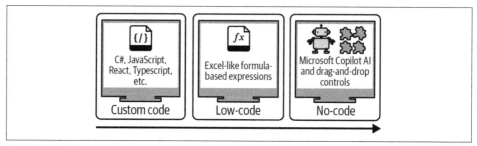

Figure 1-6. Transition of app development from custom code to low-code and no-code

Birth of Power Apps

It's important to understand that everyone has a different perspective about how Power Apps evolved and changed over time, and I truly respect and appreciate that. But only the Microsoft product team, which actually worked on the development of Power Apps and Dynamics 365, knows exactly what happened at Microsoft. So a lot of what I am going to describe to you probably did not happen exactly with Power Apps; the details have been provided to better portray the story in a more compelling way, similar to what you read in celebrity biographies. And for this story, I am inspired by famous Power Platform experts Nick Doelman and Scott Durow.

With the vision of developing a low-code, no-code app development platform to allow *citizen developers*, or nondevelopers, to build business applications, Microsoft put together a project team to develop it. The low-code, no-code app development project team launched its first low-code, no-code tool/product on the market called Microsoft Power Apps (later called Power Apps) with the objective of allowing users to design web- and mobile-/tablet-based apps without writing a single line of code. The goal was to provide a platform where everyone can simply drag-and-drop controls, similar to the experience of using PowerPoint, to design business applications and use Excel-like formula expressions to write the business logic.

Parallel Development of Dynamics 365 Customer Engagement Apps and Power Apps

After launching Power Apps, the project team held a demo to showcase the product's low-code, no-code capabilities to other Microsoft project teams. To their surprise, team members discovered that the Dynamics 365 CE team had also been developing business applications for the past few years. The teams were unaware of each other's work, and, although their intentions of developing business application development software were similar, their development approaches and app features were different.

The major advantage of Power Apps at the time was that it had low-code and no-code development features. However, it lacked many of the pro-code features and components that Dynamics 365 CE had been utilizing for the past few years. (*Pro-code* refers to the use of advanced coding techniques or languages, such as C#, JavaScript, or TypeScript, to extend the functionality of Power Platform applications beyond what can be achieved through low-code or no-code methods alone.) For instance, Dynamics 365 has a built-in database with several prebuilt tables, enables developers to design their own data models, and provides a strong security approach to give business apps a granular level of authorization. The business application components can be packaged, deployed to multiple environments, and much more using its solution management features.

Dynamics 365 CE, on the other hand, was derived from Microsoft Dynamics CRM. Additionally, its features and components were all designed with professional developers in mind.

So, both project teams separately created useful features and components. However, if they worked together, it would be a huge success for Microsoft to develop a standard business application development platform.

Handshakes Between Dynamics 365 Customer Engagement Apps and Power Apps

The Microsoft marketing team came to the rescue by recommending that Dynamics 365 CE apps be combined with Power Apps as a single offering and advised developing a new product name that would be simpler for customers to understand. As a result of the collaboration, illustrated in Figure 1-7, all Dynamics 365 CE apps are now model-driven apps, as they were largely driven by data models, and Power Apps have been transformed into canvas apps, because they offer a way to create business apps utilizing any data sources from a screen that looks like a blank canvas.

And that is how the Power Apps we have today originated. It is a common misconception that Power Apps are just canvas apps, but, in reality, they are a combination of model-driven apps and canvas apps and offer everyone the ability to develop business applications with distinctive features using various low-code, no-code and pro-code components. In the subsequent chapters, you will dive deeply into each feature and component with practical examples.

 After this point, I will be referring to Dynamics 365 Customer Engagement apps or Dynamics 365 CE apps as model-driven apps.

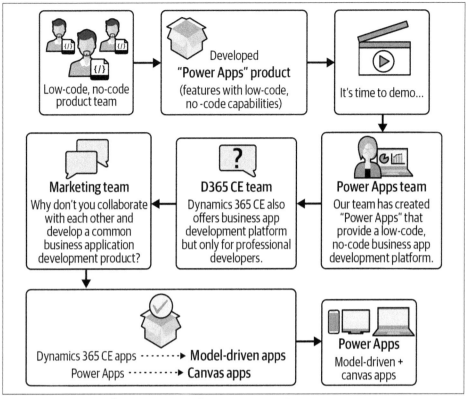

Figure 1-7. Merger of Power Apps and Dynamics 365 CE apps

Summary

In this chapter, you learned how Microsoft transformed its basic CRM product into low-code, no-code apps so that anybody, not just professionals but also citizen developers, could create business applications. Also, you discovered that all prior Microsoft Dynamics CRM applications were transformed into Dynamics 365 CE apps, later referred to as model-driven apps, and combined with canvas apps to form a new product called Power Apps.

In the next chapter, I will discuss Microsoft's ongoing innovation in the low-code, no-code development platform known as Microsoft Power Platform to expand the capabilities of Power Apps. Additionally, I will discuss Microsoft Dataverse, which dynamically stores Power Apps data and metadata in a scalable and secure environment.

CHAPTER 2

Introduction to Power Platform and Dataverse

The goal of this chapter is to provide you with an understanding of the capabilities of Microsoft Power Platform and Dataverse. Power Platform helps you create innovative end-to-end business solutions with low-code, no-code tools. Power Apps is one of those tools, while Dataverse is a robust, cloud-based database that stores business data in a secure and compliant manner, along with providing various components to write complex business logic.

By the end of this chapter, you'll understand the business value of Power Platform and Dataverse and their integration with Power Apps and other Microsoft services.

The Power Platform

In the last chapter, you learned about Microsoft's ambition to develop a low-code, no-code development platform and that one of the initiatives to accomplish that purpose was Power Apps. It works well for designing business applications. Nevertheless, there are situations where creating a business application's user interface alone is insufficient to create a complete business solution. You often need the following features as well:

- Complex business logic for different database integration and data activities
- Business analytics for dashboards and reports for data visualization and business decision making
- Conversational chatbots that can respond to customer inquiries
- A customer-interactive, self-service website for online use

So, the innovation and advancement of low-code, no-code development platforms didn't stop with the development of Power Apps. Microsoft continued to invest in the platform and launched four new low-code, no-code products in the market: Power Automate, Power BI, Copilot Studio, and Power Pages. These products, including Power Apps, are collectively referred to as Power Platform.

I'll go through each of its components in more depth in the next section.

Power Platform Key Products

The Power Platform is Microsoft's low-code, no-code application development platform, which is designed to work seamlessly with other Microsoft cloud services, including Microsoft 365, Azure, and Dynamics 365, with the goal of fulfilling Microsoft's mission to offer "One platform, Many applications, Infinite Possibilities." It allows you to convert an idea into reality. Sounds amazing, doesn't it? Professional and citizen developers alike have countless options when creating business apps using the Power Platform.

The Power Platform is composed of the five key products shown in Figure 2-1, and some additional tools that enhance the solutions you create on the Power Platform.

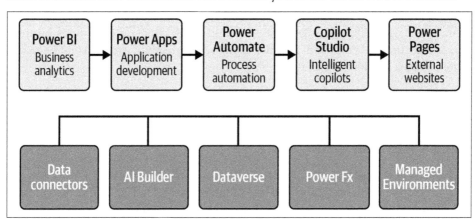

Figure 2-1. Power Platform key products and additional tools

Each key product of Power Platform is a standalone product that can be purchased and used separately to suit your business needs. For instance, if a company only wants to create a business app to display the data stored in Microsoft Dataverse that its employees can access via a mobile app or web browser, it can license only Power Apps without licensing any other parts of the Power Platform.

Let's discuss each Power Platform component and its usage in more detail.

Power Apps: A business app development tool

As previously discussed, Power Apps, a key member of the Microsoft Power Platform family, offers an efficient low-code development environment for creating tailored business apps. Power Apps makes it possible to build cross-platform web and mobile applications that can run on all modern devices.

Using Power Apps features and capabilities, you can design apps for every possible business requirement, including helpdesk, budget tracker, site inspection, service desk, leave request, booking, and product showcase apps. Other examples are shown in Figure 2-2. In addition to making apps with the provided templates, you can also make your own custom app that is tailored to your business requirements.

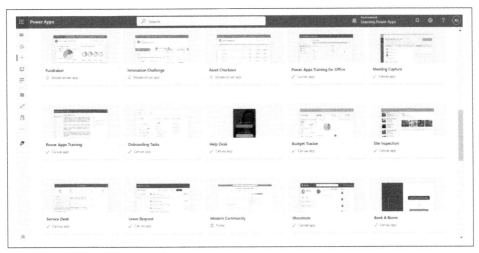

Figure 2-2. Power Apps templates

Power Apps has many prebuilt connectors, controls, components, and AI capabilities that allow both professional and citizen developers to design a full-fledged, cloud-based business application.

I will go through its features and capabilities in depth in the subsequent chapters.

Power Automate: A business process automation tool

Power Automate (sometimes referred as Power Automate flow) is one of the key products of the Power Platform family, which empowers both developers and business users to automate routine operations, tasks, and business processes. It includes cloud flows, which automates tasks online, connecting various cloud-based services and applications. And another type is desktop flow, which automates tasks directly on your computer, interacting with desktop applications and performing repetitive tasks locally. Both are types of workflows you can create with Power Automate.

A flow consists of one trigger and a number of actions. A *trigger* is the Power Automate entry point that starts the logic when a specific business event, such as create, update, delete, and so on, takes place in the database. An *action* specifies the data source operations you wish to carry out. For example, I have created a simple Power Automate flow that triggers when a new contract is created in Dataverse (see Figure 2-3). Then, it uses a variety of connectors to carry out a series of actions: Teams Connector is used to send and receive finance team approval via Teams; DocuSign Connector is used to send the contract to the customer for a signature; SharePoint Connector is used to upload the signed contract to a SharePoint site; and, finally, the Outlook Connector is used to send the finance team and customer a confirmation email.

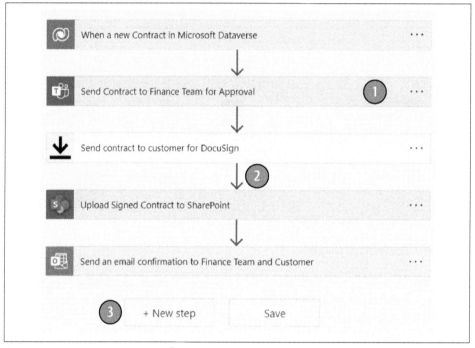

Figure 2-3. A Power Automate flow

In Figure 2-3:

1. You can modify the properties of the trigger or action step by clicking on the three dots (...) next to it.

2. You can add a new action step by clicking on the (+) icon below each step.

3. You can add a connector to perform additional actions by clicking the New step button.

Power Automate enables both professional and citizen developers to swiftly integrate Power Apps with external data sources and automate business processes by supporting various prebuilt connectors (*https://oreil.ly/2N0vj*) to data sources, thousands of templates, and a variety of AI capabilities.

The automation capabilities on desktop, mobile, web, and Microsoft Teams are expanded by Power Automate. Depending on the business requirements, a flow can be trigger-based, schedule-based, or executed manually (on demand) to perform business logic.

 Power Automate is one of the Power Platform key products for automating tasks. Within Power Automate, cloud flow automates online tasks between cloud services, while desktop flow automates tasks on your computer using desktop applications. Both are types of workflows you can create using Power Automate.

Power BI: A reporting tool

Data is the heart of any organization, and the business world is becoming more and more data-driven. Businesses rely on data to make decisions on sales, service, marketing, recruiting, goals, and all other areas. Some common business questions are: How much did we earn in sales last financial year? Which product feedback is not up to the mark? How is my sales team performing this month? Which sales region is doing best? Who are our top customers? These questions can be answered by checking the organization's data in the form of graphs, reports, charts, and dashboards.

Sometimes, data is not stored in a single data source; it might come from social media and various external sources as well. In this case, the disparate data sources need to be transformed into coherent, immersive graphics and interactive insights. That's where Power BI (business intelligence) comes into play.

Power BI is a business intelligence tool that provides low-code, no-code capabilities to quickly create insights and analytics of business data. It provides plenty of ways to create data visualizations, built-in AI capabilities, and prebuilt data connectors that allow professional and citizen developers to quickly create dashboards and reports for your business applications. Power BI uses Data Analysis Expressions (DAX) to solve simple calculations and perform data analysis. In the near future, Power Fx might take its place, but there is no plan or official announcement yet, so keep an eye on Microsoft's release plan.

Power BI can be embedded within other Power Platform components like Power Apps and Power Pages (which we discuss later in this section) to display charts, reports, and dashboards. For example, a standing meeting for reporting on business KPIs (key performance indicators) like sales data, target progress, or staff performance may be replaced by a Power BI dashboard, such as the one shown in Figure 2-4.

Figure 2-4. Power BI dashboard

Copilot Studio: An AI-based chatbot development tool

Nowadays, customers expect everything to be at their fingertips, from sales to service. In today's age of AI, companies across all industries use chatbot capabilities to quickly resolve customer issues and utilize AI to provide the best service to their customers in less time and in a cost-effective way. With Copilot Studio (announced on November 15, 2023 (*https://oreil.ly/mxDyT*)), shown in Figure 2-5, you can build robust AI-powered chatbots called *copilots* for a variety of tasks, such as answering basic questions and resolving problems that don't require complex conversations, without needing a human agent. These bots can be designed quickly without using professional developers or data scientists. Some of the real-world examples of copilots are:

- Sales and support assistance
- Common employee questions for businesses
- Employee health and vacation benefits
- Store opening hours and information
- COVID-19 vaccination updates and tracking information

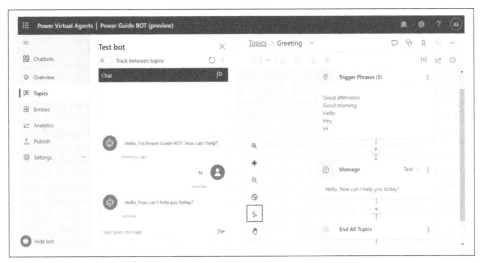

Figure 2-5. Copilot Studio

Copilot Studio provides seamless integration with other Power Platform components as well. You can embed copilots in Power Apps to provide chatbot capabilities in business apps or integrate with Power Automate to bring in data from external data sources and Dataverse. They can also be embedded in Power Pages (discussed in the next section), allowing customers to resolve their queries or issues directly on your website. Additionally, copilots can be embedded into any external-facing website to extend its capabilities.

Microsoft collaborated with OpenAI to provide AI capabilities in Copilot Studio. With generative AI and large language models, Copilot Studio empowers professional developers and business users to build conversational AI bots using natural language. It also uses the Boost Conversation feature to understand the user's intent by parsing what they type to determine what they are asking, along with finding, collating, and parsing relevant information from various external sites based on URLs you specify.

You will find more information about generative AI and Copilot features in Chapter 11.

Power Pages: A business website development tool

Power Pages is an enterprise-grade, low-code, no-code, software as a service (SaaS) platform for developing, hosting, and managing modern, external-facing, business-centric professional websites (see Figure 2-6). Whether you are a professional developer or a businessperson with no coding skills, it empowers you to quickly design, configure, and publish websites that run on a variety of web browsers and devices.

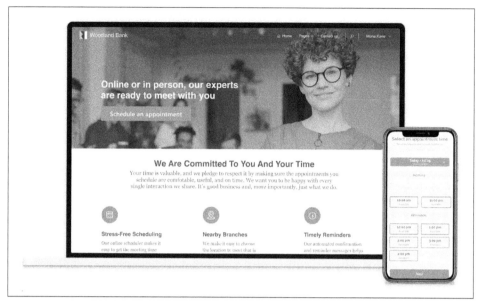

Figure 2-6. Power Pages website

Power Pages evolved from a product called Adxstudio Portal, first developed in 2009 by Canada-based company Adxstudio. The company was acquired by Microsoft in 2015, and the product was rebranded as Dynamics CRM Portals. In 2019, it was rebranded again as Power Apps Portals to better align with other Power Platform products. Finally, in 2023, it was added into the Power Platform family and introduced as a standalone product named Power Pages.

While a lot has changed since the product was first released in 2009, the core has remained the same. Power Pages provides many built-in components and features to rapidly create secure, low-code, no-code business websites. As a Power Platform product, it tightly integrates with Power Apps, Power Automate, Copilot Studio, Power BI, and Microsoft SharePoint. Business data that website users interact with is securely stored in Microsoft Dataverse. And you can bring in data to your Power Pages site through various connectors through cloud flow integration, APIs, and virtual tables.

Power Pages lets internal and external users (anonymous and authenticated) access Dataverse data through external-facing websites. Therefore, it also provides enterprise-grade security and various security components for administrators and website makers to harden data security and protect business data. Please refer to the Power Pages security white paper (*https://oreil.ly/V97ew*) before implementing a Power Pages site for your client, to avoid accidentally exposing your customer data.

To learn more about Power Pages, watch my *Power Pages 30 Days Learning Challenge* (*https://oreil.ly/WvOaD*) video series on my YouTube channel (Arpit Tech Show (*https://oreil.ly/Pv-Mx*)). Here I explain everything about Power Pages from the basics to advanced topics with demonstrations of practical examples.

Additional Power Platform Tools

Apart from Power Platform's key products, there are some additional tools and services that extend the capabilities of Power Platform. These tools support businesses that not only have a hard time developing solutions to modernize their systems, but also lack the resources necessary to keep up with the rapidly evolving needs of modern business. Power Platform's key low-code, no-code products and enterprise-level application development tools enable professional developers and citizen developers to develop targeted solutions that are based on the daily needs of the users of these applications.

Microsoft Dataverse

Microsoft Dataverse lets you securely store and manage the data used by business applications. Some of the Power Platform components, such as model-driven apps and Power Pages, use Microsoft Dataverse as their primary database. Other components, such as canvas apps, Power Automate, Copilot Studio, and Power BI, are not tied to it; they can use other external data sources such as SharePoint, SQL Server, OneDrive, and Excel as their primary database. You will learn more about Microsoft Dataverse later in this chapter.

In this book, the terms *primary database* and *primary data source* refer to the main database of a given product, which contains the core components (tables, fields, forms, views, dashboards, etc.) needed to configure and customize business applications. The term *secondary database* refers to an external data source (Microsoft or non-Microsoft) such as SharePoint, OneDrive, Excel, or SQL Server that you can use to import data into your primary database through various components (Power Query, virtual tables, Power Automate, custom connectors, custom APIs, etc.).

AI capabilities

Power Platform supports many built-in AI capabilities to optimize the business process. With AI Builder, you can leverage the power of AI without having any coding or data science skills. You can either choose a prebuilt AI model that is suitable for many common business scenarios, or you can develop custom AI models that are tailored to your needs. A few prebuilt AI models available in Power Platform include a business card reader, text recognizer, form processor, and sentiment analysis.

Microsoft announced the collaboration with OpenAI (*https://oreil.ly/tSAsP*) on January 23, 2023, and it was a game changer for the IT industry. It has brought many AI capabilities not only to Dynamics 365 CE Apps, but also to Power Platform components and Microsoft 365 applications (including Word, Excel, Teams, and Outlook). Today, the convergence of large language models and chat interfaces has made it possible for you to ask questions in natural language, and business applications are now intelligent enough to respond, generate content, or take action.

I will discuss more about the use of AI in Power Platform in Chapter 11.

Data connectors

Connectors are used to integrate the Power Platform components with external applications and data sources to extend the platform's capabilities. Connectors can be grouped into three categories:

Standard connectors
> These are the most commonly used connectors and are available for use in all the licensing plans of Power Platform. These connectors include Microsoft Dataverse, Teams, SharePoint, OneDrive, Outlook, and Microsoft Forms.

Premium connectors
> These connectors are used to connect to external or third-party applications from companies like Adobe (Adobe PDF Services, Adobe Acrobat Sign, etc.), Amazon (Amazon S3, Simple Queue Service), DocuSign, Google (Google Drive, Google Contacts, etc.), and Salesforce.

Custom connectors
> These connectors are custom built by professional developers to call external services and APIs for which there are no built-in connectors available.

Additionally, Microsoft provides an *on-premises data gateway* that serves as a bridge to enable quick and safe data transfer between on-premises data sources (data that is not in the cloud) and various Microsoft cloud services such as Power Apps, Power Automate, and Power BI.

As illustrated in Figure 2-7, a cloud service such as Power Apps uses Gateway Cloud Service to encrypt and store on-premises data source credentials and on-premises data gateway details. Whenever any new request is made from a cloud service, Gateway Cloud Service encrypts that request and sends it to an on-premises data gateway. The on-premises data gateway decrypts the request and connects to an on-premises data source to perform the operation (create, read, update, delete, aka CRUD). Once the operation is performed, the results are sent from the data source back to the data gateway and then to the cloud service via the Gateway Cloud Service.

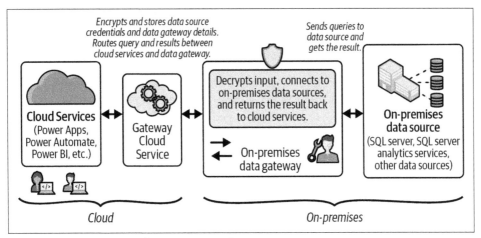

Figure 2-7. On-premises data gateway architecture

In Chapter 4, I'll go into more detail on data connectors.

Power Fx

Power Fx is a low-code programming language provided by Microsoft for use across the Power Platform. The "low" in low-code is due to the concise and simple nature of the language, which makes programming tasks easy for citizen developers. Power Fx uses Excel-like, formula-based expressions to write business logic. It can be considered a first step toward an AI-based programming language, where you can write business logic in human-friendly text.

For example, the output of the Power Fx expression:

```
Concatenate("Arpit", " ", "Shrivastava" )
```

would be:

```
Arpit Shrivastava
```

In Chapter 9, I'll go into depth about this topic.

Managed Environments

As the name indicates, the Managed Environments feature is used to manage environment resources. Organizations that use Power Platform's low-code, no-code assets need governance tools to enable them to thoroughly monitor and control how assets or components are used. From a security, compliance, licensing, and governance perspective, this is extremely important.

Using Managed Environments, you can manage the visibility of and control your environment's resources in the following three ways:

Limit sharing

> After creating a canvas app that solves a business problem, you can share it with other employees in your company, giving them access to run, edit, and even re-share the app. You can specify the names of specific users, choose a security group in Microsoft Entra ID, or share the app with the entire organization. Sometimes IT admins need to set a limit on who an app can be shared with; using the Limit Sharing feature in Managed Environments, an admin can restrict how widely users can share canvas apps to help lower risks.

Usage insights

> Managed Environments offers insights on how Power Apps and Power Automate are used, the most influential app developers, and the state of inactive and active resources so that you can take appropriate action to clean them up to conserve database memory.

Data policies

> As previously mentioned, there are a large number of data connectors that let Power Platform resources talk with a wide variety of external applications for data exchange. Your company may need to protect its business data by limiting the connectors. This is where data policies come into play; they specify and regulate the list of connectors with which particular data can be shared.

Why Power Platform Is Important for Power Apps

You might be wondering why learning about Power Platform and its components is necessary to learn Power Apps, which is the focus of this book. This is because Power Apps, one of the foundational components of Power Platform, seamlessly integrates with all the other components to develop an end-to-end business solution. The relationship between Power Apps and Power Platform components is depicted in Figure 2-8.

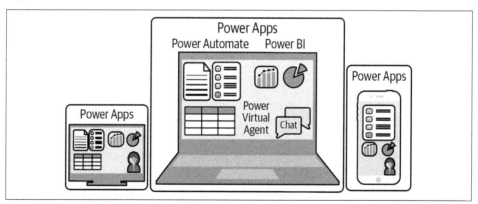

Figure 2-8. Relationship between Power Apps and Power Platform components

With Power Apps, business applications are created for internal users with data that is either held within Dataverse or integrated from external data sources. Apart from that, it uses data analytics and chatbots. Power Pages, on the other hand, is used to create external-facing websites for external users, while using similar elements like data, analytics, and chatbots. The business data for both apps is stored in Microsoft Dataverse.

Solutions can make extensive use of Power Platform components. Although individual components can be used alone, they are more powerful when combined and used to drive action, analyze data, assist in business, and automate tasks. Figure 2-9 shows the four ways that they can work together.

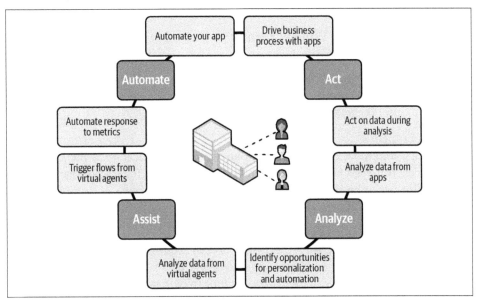

Figure 2-9. How low-code tools are related to each other

Let's look at each of these in more detail:

Act

Any business solution development starts with app development to drive business processes and *act* on data stored in databases. Business users can use business applications (developed using Power Apps) through a mobile, tablet, or web interface to interact with UI controls to perform various actions (CRUD) in Dataverse.

Automate

It is required to *automate* the business process used in the app and perform various data operations based on business events (CRUD, etc.) triggered by business apps. Power Automate can be used to create the flow to automate the process, bring the data from various data sources, and perform trigger-based actions in Dataverse.

Analyze

Data captured by business apps needs to be *analyzed* so your organization can make decisions. Power BI analyzes the data stored in Dataverse or other external data source to generate reports and dashboards.

Assist

The business app needs to *assist* users and customers based on the data captured by the apps. Copilot Studio provides customers and users with chatbot-based assistance to address their questions.

Power Platform Real-World Example

Let's look at a real-world example to demonstrate how the features within Power Platform work together to create solutions. Imagine that you need to create an event management app for your client. You've determined that to offer a complete solution, you need to meet the following business requirements:

Requirement 1: UI

The first and most crucial feature of any business application is the UI or look and feel. You need to create an event management app for event organizers and coordinators to be able to manage events. You must create a responsive application for your client because it might be web-based, mobile, or tablet-based.

Requirement 2: Business logic

Writing business logic is the next most crucial requirement for the app to function. You need to write business logic for event data validation; communication; integrating your app with other Microsoft or third-party applications like Microsoft Teams, SharePoint, Outlook, Facebook, and Twitter; automating session approvals and event check-in processes; generating QR codes; creating event banners, etc.

Requirement 3: Analytics

Analytics is the third crucial requirement of the event management app so that event organizers and coordinators can track and monitor the event's data. You need analytics to track how many participants have registered for a particular event, how many speakers have submitted their sessions, how many sessions have been approved/rejected, which are the top-rated sessions and most-attended events, etc.

Requirement 4: Self-service

By giving customers self-service options, businesses today aim to empower both their customers and their employees. Thus, there is a demand for a website or self-service portal so that participants can view events and track their registrations, speakers can submit sessions and track approvals, and sponsors can submit and track requests for event sponsorship.

Requirement 5: Chatbot

Organizations often need a digital assistant or chatbot to free up employees to focus on more productive work and avoid keeping customers waiting. Managing thousands of participants at once can be a very tedious task for event organizers and coordinators. You can create a chatbot and embed it into your event management portal so that it can answer queries from participants and speakers related to events, sessions, registrations, etc.

Requirement 6: Integration

Organizations often need to integrate business apps with third-party applications like Facebook and Twitter and with Microsoft 365 applications like Teams, Outlook, and SharePoint. The app also requires connections with social media for event marketing, SharePoint to store event-related documents, Outlook for email communication, and Microsoft Teams for creating meeting invitations.

Requirement 7: Advanced features

Event organizations often need some advanced features, like sentiment analysis, to determine whether event feedback is positive, negative, or neutral; predictive analytics for event planning; and QR code scanner to verify participant details and event entry.

The Power Platform can address the initial five business requirements with the following products:

- Power Apps can be used to create responsive web, mobile, and tablet-based applications (requirement 1).

- Power Automate can be used to write expression-based business logic and automate repetitive tasks (requirement 2). In Power Apps, you can directly write business logic using the low-code language called Power Fx (covered in 9). This language enables you to create formulas, validate data inputs, perform calculations based on user inputs or data from various sources, and automate processes within your applications with ease.

- Power BI can be used to design reports, analytics, and dashboards using a variety of prebuilt visualizations and importing data from more than 1,000 different data sources (requirement 3).

- Power Pages can be used to quickly design low-code, no-code business websites (requirement 4).

- Copilot Studio can be used to create low-code, no-code conversational bots that can be embedded in websites or applications (requirement 5).

To meet requirement 6, Power Platform offers a large number of data connectors that provide seamless integration with a wide variety of external data sources. I will discuss more about data sources and connectors in Chapter 4.

And finally, for requirement 7, Power Platform has a variety of built-in AI features, including a business card reader, document processing, text recognition, receipt processing, and sentiment analysis. In Chapter 11, we'll go into more detail regarding the potential of AI.

Power Platform for Developers

Power Platform, by offering low-code, no-code, and AI capabilities for end-to-end business solutions, doesn't replace professional developers, but rather encourages collaboration between them and citizen developers, allowing everyone to contribute to the solution's development. This development approach is called *fusion development* (*https://oreil.ly/i1Iw3*) (see Figure 2-10).

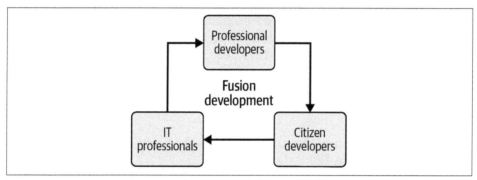

Figure 2-10. Designing fusion applications with fusion development

The fundamental objective of Power Platform is to bring together professional developers, citizen developers, and IT administrators/professionals to create an end-to-end business solution. The basic goal of this fusion development strategy is to integrate low-code, no-code capabilities with code components to produce *fusion applications*.

Sometimes the built-in features of the Power Platform key products fall short of meeting business requirements, and professional developers either need to expand the built-in capabilities or create custom components. Hence, the following Power Platform products offer custom components (shown in Figure 2-11), enabling developers to expand their capabilities.

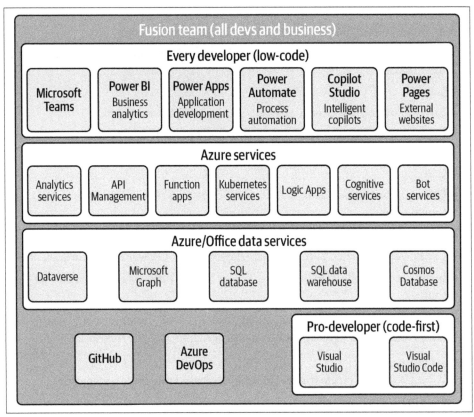

Figure 2-11. Various tools and products to extend Power Platform features

Let's look at these products in more detail:

Power Apps
- Build custom UI components using Power Apps component framework (PCF).
- Create custom Dataverse business events and custom APIs.
- Write plug-in code to write trigger-based custom business logic.
- Write JavaScript to perform complex client-side business logic.
- Design HTML pages using HTML web resources.

Power Automate
- Create custom connectors to call external APIs.
- Call Power Automate by custom applications/code.
- Develop custom workflow activities in C# and invoke them from Power Automate.

Copilot Studio
- Embed Copilot Studio in external websites and apps.
- Extend chatbot capabilities with Bot Framework Composer (*https://oreil.ly/-c-u8*).

Power BI
- Embed Power BI reports in external websites and business apps.
- Create custom visuals using an open source SDK, React, JavaScript, and other programming languages.

Power Pages
- Create custom pages using HTML, JavaScript, CSS (Cascading Style Sheets), and Liquid code.
- Perform operations in Dataverse using portals Web API.
- Use Power Platform CLI to automate deployment of Power Pages components.
- Invoke a cloud flow to integrate Power Pages with over 1,000 external data sources.

Apart from that, sometimes you might also need to create custom Azure and C#-based components to meet your business needs, such as the following:

Azure Functions
Write C# code to create trigger- or schedule-based integration scenarios.

Azure API Management (APIM)
Create, secure, and analyze custom APIs to provide seamless integration between Dataverse and external systems.

Microsoft Graph API
Allow Power Platform components to interact with other Microsoft 365 Platform applications such as Microsoft Teams, OneDrive, OneNote, Microsoft Entra ID, and Outlook.

Cognitive services
Enable developers to add AI capabilities to your business apps. Using cognitive services-based APIs, developers can embed the ability to see, hear, speak, search, understand, and accelerate advanced decision-making features into your apps.

C#-based web applications
Create a custom web application and display Dataverse data to it, such as a single-page, web-based ticketing tool that enables non-CRM users to create tickets in CRM and view their resolution.

C# console applications
Create a C# console application to perform bulk operations in Dataverse using the Dataverse SDK.

This is just an overview of the custom code components that can be used to modify or customize Power Platform components. In subsequent chapters, I will give more in-depth information about each component.

Microsoft Dataverse

In the previous section, you learned how Microsoft developed Power Platform as a low-code, no-code development platform that offers one platform to design numerous cloud-based business applications. Now let's consider where these applications will store their data.

All web-based applications, regardless of the technology or platform used for development, need two basic components to operate: the *client* and the *server*. The client sends a request to the server, and the server responds to the client request. Here, "client" refers to any client-based application (whether web, mobile, or tablet) that users interact with, while "server" refers to the database that stores data and provides the information to the client application. Power Apps uses a similar mechanism, as shown in Figure 2-12.

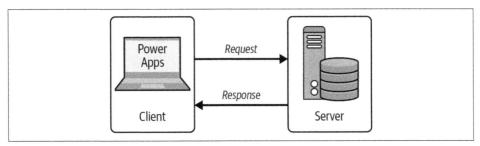

Figure 2-12. Power Apps as a client application

Both model-driven and canvas apps are considered clients, and they need a database on the server to store the data.

As you learned in previous sections, Power Apps uses Microsoft Dataverse to safely store and manage the data used by various business applications. Let's take a closer look at Dataverse.

Evolution of Microsoft Dataverse

Microsoft Dynamics CRM is the source of Microsoft Dataverse. At first, Dynamics CRM had some of the same fundamental database elements and features as other databases, such as tables, columns, keys, and relationships. More features have been added to this database over time, yet due to the absence of a common data model, it lacked complex integration and had problems with data ambiguity. As a result, Microsoft combined all business-related entities, such as accounts, contacts, and activities, created a common data model in Microsoft Azure SQL, and renamed the database the "Common Data Service." Soon, it became an integral component of the Microsoft Power Platform (as discussed in previous sections), and in November 2020, Common Data Service was rebranded to "Microsoft Dataverse."

Birth of the business application layer

From the beginning, Microsoft Dynamics CRM apps have used Microsoft SQL Server as their database. SQL Server has all the features found in other databases: tables, fields, relationships, queries, etc.

Imagine, though, if you gave someone complete access to the database, how easily it might be compromised and used without adhering to any rules. Also, it's possible that it will fail to fulfill the original intent of its creation. That's why, to eliminate the need to connect directly with the database, Microsoft built middleware called the *business application layer* between the application (client) and database (server) (see Figure 2-13).

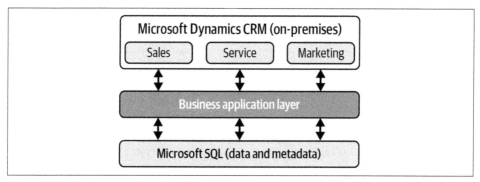

Figure 2-13. Business application layer

If you are using Microsoft Dynamics CRM's on-premises version, where you are able to set up and install all components on your own server, you are permitted to see what the actual database looks like, how the data model has been designed, and to run your SQL queries to view the data directly without even signing into the CRM application.

But if you use the cloud version of Microsoft Dynamics CRM, you won't need to worry about setting up your infrastructure, such as installing SQL Server. Microsoft handles all infrastructure setup and hardware prerequisites, and automatically updates the features, released version, bug fixes, and security patches for its products. As a result, unlike the on-premises version of Microsoft Dynamics CRM, you cannot directly interact with the SQL Server or database on Microsoft Dynamics CRM cloud. Communication between the client (CRM applications) and server (SQL Server) must be established using the business application layer.

The goal of the business application layer was to provide some additional features on top of SQL Server in a more user-friendly way so that even citizen developers could understand the basic concepts of a database and easily design a data model, including creating entities (tables), attributes (fields), relationships, and so on, referred to as *business objects*.

The business application layer had two major challenges, ambiguous data and complex integration.

Ambiguous data. Every new feature also brings new challenges. The business application layer was no different. The difficulty was that it did not adhere to a common data model, which led to data ambiguity and redundancy in the database. To understand this, let's look at a simple example.

Imagine that you have two business apps—one each for customer service and sales. It's likely that each app was created independently, with different structures to represent an entity, such as Contact, but not necessarily used in the same way. Each app might have its own set of fields, relationships, and form elements. However, some fields, such as first name, last name, and email address, would be common to both apps. Regardless of the app, the Contacts table will still serve the same purpose—to hold contact information. If a standard data model is not followed, each developer will create an individual table with distinct fields for a common purpose, which will result in the database holding a lot of ambiguous data.

Complex integration. If you need to develop a third app for marketing purposes, where you require the contact information for sales and customer service app users, you must bring in the data from two different tables. And if the data is dispersed over several data sources, this task becomes even more difficult.

As you can see in Figure 2-14, if the same customer information is distributed across multiple tables, it will be complex to create apps and reports using that data, which is stored in various tables, fields, and formats. It will require complex integration with various data sources or tables.

Don't you think there ought to be a standard data model that all businesses must adhere to regardless of the number or type of business apps? For example, an Account table should contain information about the company, a Contacts table should keep information about individuals, and so on. Having a common data model allows you to focus your development efforts on business logic rather than navigating sticky transformations and muddled data.

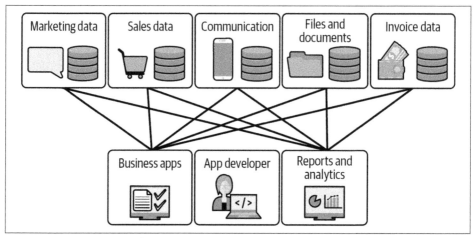

Figure 2-14. Business application layer challenge

Common Data Service

A common data model (Figure 2-15) is required to mitigate the data ambiguity and complex integration issues. So that everyone could develop business objects using the same model, Microsoft developed the *Common Data Service* (CDS), a brand-new, user-friendly database based on Azure SQL. The CDS included predefined, commonly used data objects like Account, which is used to store company information; Contact, which is used to store contact information for people or customers; and Activities, which is used to store customer interactions such as emails, phone calls, faxes, appointments, letters, and so forth.

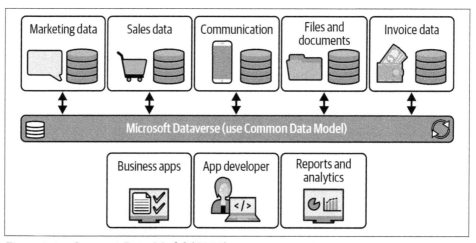

Figure 2-15. Common Data Model (CDM)

The sole purpose of creating this database was to adhere to the Common Data Model (CDM) (see Figure 2-16). As the name implies, the CDS was built to be a service, which means that you may connect to it via APIs, connectors, and other web services regardless of the platform or application from which you are connecting. Using connectors and APIs, all Power Platform components can establish a connection to this database.

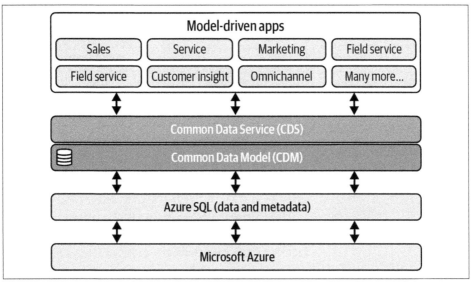

Figure 2-16. Common Data Service (CDS) based on Common Data Model (CDM)

Birth of Dataverse

In November 2020, Microsoft migrated the CDS to Microsoft Dataverse (*https://oreil.ly/f2FFs*) and gave it some low-code, no-code capabilities. Microsoft also changed some common terminology used in the database to increase the platform's accessibility and appeal to a wider audience. For instance:

- *Entity* changed to *Table*
- *Attribute* changed to *Field*
- *Option Set* changed to *Choice*
- *Boolean Field* changed to *Yes/No*
- *Record* changed to *Row*

This is how Microsoft Dataverse evolved. Now, Microsoft Dataverse is the common database that is used across Power Platform components to design cloud-based business applications. While some Power Platform components can work independently of Dataverse, others are closely tied to it (see Figure 2-17). We'll discuss this later in this chapter.

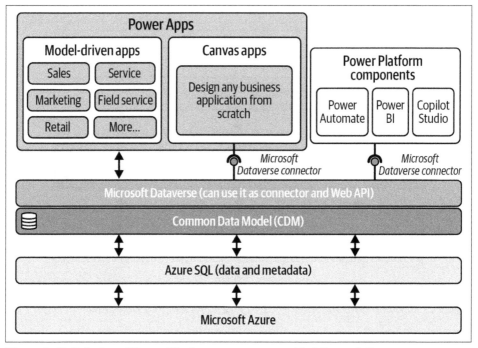

Figure 2-17. Relation of Power Platform components with Microsoft Dataverse

Microsoft Dataverse Connector

Dataverse is more than just another database like SQL, Microsoft Access, or Oracle. It has other capabilities and the ability to store business objects like tables, fields, relationships, and data. It also provides a connector that other components can use to communicate with it.

A Dataverse connector is not necessary to establish communication between model-driven apps (including Dynamics 365 CE apps) and Dataverse (see Figure 2-18).

Figure 2-18. How model-driven apps communicate with Microsoft Dataverse

Other Power Platform components, such as canvas apps and Power Automate, developed separately from Dynamics 365 and were later integrated (as you learned in the previous chapter). So these Power Platform components need an API, or connector, to communicate with Microsoft Dataverse (see Figure 2-19).

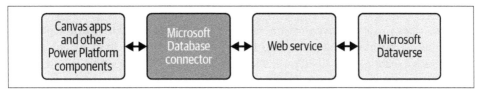

Figure 2-19. How canvas apps and other power platform components communicate with Microsoft Dataverse

APIs act as a mediator between systems or databases that are unable to communicate with one another because they are running on separate platforms or languages. It's similar to how two people who do not share the same language need an interpreter to communicate. In software development, when two applications running on different platforms want to communicate data to one another, they need an API that establishes communication using a common language like JSON or XML.

Power Platform offers a wide range of data *connectors* (which are wrappers around APIs) to connect with different data sources without having to use code to call an API. There is a connector for Microsoft Dataverse as well, which you can use to conduct data operations in Dataverse from various Power Platform components.

I will discuss more about the connectors in Chapter 4.

Microsoft Dataverse Security

Microsoft Dataverse comes with built-in, platform-level security features, which control all aspects of security, including user authentication and authorization, enabling users to interact with data and services. Ideally, security in Dataverse should allow users to complete their tasks with the least amount of hassle while safeguarding the information and services. Dataverse security ranges from a basic security model with wide access to an extremely complex security model that can be used to build up security in Dataverse and give users specific record- and field-level access.

There are two main components to any application's security: *authentication* and *authorization*. Authentication is the process of proving that the user is who they claim to be, typically with a username and password. Authorization is the process of controlling what a user is allowed to do, such as having the ability to create, update, and delete data.

Power Platform integrates with Microsoft 365's most sophisticated data protection and compliance tools and makes use of the same security stack that earned Azure the right to host and safeguard the most sensitive data in the world. Hence, it uses Microsoft Azure for user authentication and uses security roles for authorization to data stored in Dataverse.

Microsoft has made massive investments in Power Platform security in the past few years due to businesses speeding up their migration to the cloud by integrating cutting-edge technologies like Power Platform into their daily operations and strategic decision making. Additionally, Power Platform has earned the confidence of government security agencies, financial organizations, and health care providers.

Protecting client data is a key concern for any firm. Starting with new user setup and ending at the field level, Microsoft Dataverse offers comprehensive security, as shown in Figure 2-20. I refer to these levels as *security gates* for better understanding.

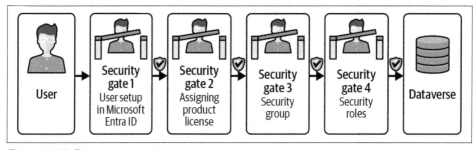

Figure 2-20. Dataverse security

Security gate 1: User setup in Microsoft Entra ID

First, a user needs to be set up in Microsoft Entra ID to start using the Dynamics 365/ Power Platform or any Microsoft cloud-based application like SharePoint, OneDrive, or Microsoft Teams.

Real-life example: When you join an organization, the first thing that happens is your onboarding process, where the HR department collects your details, verifies them, and generates your employee ID card that you'll use to enter a specific office location.

Security gate 2: Assigning product licenses

Licensing serves as a kind of security gate: The organization assigns an appropriate license to the user based on the user's position within the organization; for example, a Power Platform license or a Dynamics 365 Apps license like Sales App or Field Service App. Based on the license, users will be able to access a specific application or its features. I will be discussing licensing in more detail in Chapter 3.

Having an appropriate product license may not be directly related to Power Platform security, but it's a great way to control or protect your Power Platform resources and applications from unauthorized access.

Real-life example: Once you have your employee ID, it doesn't mean you can do anything in the organization; you still need to show your ID card either to the security person at the gate or tap it on the login device to enter the building that you are permitted to enter.

Security gate 3: Security groups

Once you have the appropriate license for a product or application, then you can log in to the platform to start developing your application. However, let's imagine a scenario where you want to group users based on their job or role and responsibilities. For example, developers will create and customize the components in the platform; testers will create test data, run test cases, and test the application; and end users (live users) will access the application in real time. Sometimes grouping is required when you are using the same platform for multiple vendors or partners, and sometimes it is required when the organization has multinational business, where Country A needs different resources and roles than Country B.

In all these scenarios, grouping of resources is handled with *environments*. Environments are a kind of container in Microsoft Dataverse that groups resources like business data, apps, chatbots, Power Automate, tables, forms, and views. You can create multiple environments based on your business, organization, and project requirements. For example, let's say I want to create three environments in my tenant. One is for developers (called dev environment), one is for testers (test environment), and one is for end users (production environment). I can then control who will have access to which environment by using *security groups*. So, security groups are basically used to control which licensed users can be a member of a particular environment.

Real-life example: Once you enter your office building (that you have permission to enter), you only have access to use the facilities of the organization based on your job role. For example, if you are part of HR, then you will have access to HR-related applications like managing talent and acquisition, recruitment, and onboarding. Employees with other job roles, such as developers, salespeople, and so on, cannot access those applications. Some organizations also control this by setting up separate premises and infrastructure based on the client or domain you are working for. For example, client A project team, which works in the banking domain, has a different work location than client B, which is a project team working in the insurance domain. And each team doesn't have access to the other's work location unless given access by the organization.

Tenants

A *tenant* is a dedicated, isolated instance of Microsoft cloud services, tailored specifically to your organization. When you create a new tenant in the Power Platform (or more broadly, a new Microsoft 365 tenant), you specify a primary region or location for that tenant, which determines the data center region (e.g., United States, United Kingdom) where your organization's data and resources will primarily be stored and where required services will be hosted. Although the tenant has a primary region (e.g., United States) set during its creation, environments within that tenant can be created in any supported region (e.g., Europe, Asia, Australia), offering significant flexibility for global operations, regulatory compliance, and performance optimization.

If we understand this with a real-world example:

Tenant
> The HQ of an IT company that oversees all operations, resources, and policies for the entire organization.

Environment
> Branch offices of the IT company located in different regions, focusing on various projects or operations (such as development, production, or testing). It's not always necessary for the branch offices to be in different regions; they can also be in the same region, depending on the organization's needs.

Security gate 4: Security roles

Once you have access to a particular environment, the resources of that environment are controlled by security roles. Security roles are one of the most important security features of Power Platform and provide a granular level of security for your Microsoft Dataverse data. Security roles enable you to control who can access what. Power Platform has many resources and components like Power Apps, Power Automate, and connectors. You can control access to all of these components with security roles.

Real-life example: Once you enter the work location to which your organization has provided access, you will see other people who have different roles at your project level such as project manager, team leader, developer, and tester, or if your project is Agile based, then you will see a scrum master, product owner, and others. Each person has their own job roles and responsibilities.

Using security roles, you can configure a granular level of security in your Microsoft Dataverse:

Environment-level security

> Using security roles you can control access at the environment level. For example, the System Administrator and Environment Administrator roles can perform all administrative actions in the environment, while the Environment Maker role only has permission to create resources within the environment.

App-level security

> Users will have access to apps based on the security roles they're assigned. For example, using security roles you can assign User A access to Dynamics 365 Sales App, but not Dynamics 365 Customer Service App, while User B can access Dynamics 365 Customer Service App, but not Dynamics 365 Sales App.

Table/record/data-level security

> Users will have access to tables and their data based on the security roles they're assigned. Table/record-level security determines the level of access a user has to a specific record of a particular table, such as the ability to create, update, or delete data.

Form-level security

> A Power Apps form is the collection of fields that you use to either take user input or display Dataverse data. Sometimes, you might need to create multiple forms for a particular table depending on business requirements. You can apply security roles to the form to only allow users with that security role to see the form.

Column-level security

> At the table level, data-level permissions are granted; however, you can have some columns connected to a table that hold data that is more sensitive than the other columns. For example, say you are designing an application for a banking domain and it has a policy stating that sales managers can only have read-only access to the customer's debit card field, the vice president will have full access to that field, and the salespeople can't even read that the field. This kind of security can be managed by column-level security.

Microsoft Dataverse Business Logic

Business logic is an integral part of any business application development. Here are some of the most commonly used tasks that require business logic when designing a business application:

Perform Dataverse data validation

> Validate whether the user's input is in the correct format. For example, format of phone number, email address, Social Security number (SSN), etc.

Perform Dataverse data migration

Extracts the data permanently from an external system, transforms it into Dataverse format, and loads/stores it in Dataverse. This process is also called ETL (extract, transform, and load). This is also applicable when you have to migrate the data from Dataverse to an external system.

Perform Dataverse data integration

Brings the data from various systems together and provides a consolidated view of it. Sometimes in data integration, if we don't want to physically store that data in the Microsoft Dataverse, we can use either virtual tables or API integration to display the data virtually.

Automation logic

Sometimes, you need to write logic to automate operations; for example, automatically send birthday wishes or shipping notifications.

Calculation logic

Used when you need to write business logic for performing complex calculations; for example, calculating the estimated sales revenue for a particular customer or total sales revenue generated in a year.

Trigger-based logic

Some business logic only needs to trigger when a particular operation occurs in the database; for example, send an email to a customer only when a new lead is created or create a follow-up task for the sales team when a new lead is created in the system.

Scheduled logic

Used for recurring events that need to trigger on a scheduled basis (once a day, per minute, hourly, weekly, monthly, yearly, on a specific date, etc.). For example, you could send a sales report to the sales manager every day at 6 P.M.

Dataverse provides many built-in components that can be used to write custom business logic. Some of these are low-code, no-code, such as business rules and business process flows, while others are code-based, such as plug-ins, PCF controls, and so on.

In Chapters 6, 7, and 8, I will dive deeper into each component with some practical examples.

Microsoft Dataverse Data

Data is the heart of any digital transformation. And, without having customer and organization data managed properly, a business can not run its operation. This data can be stored in different formats and distributed across various systems. As a result, every industry looks for secure and scalable database options. Microsoft Dataverse is the backbone of the Power Platform, whose primary objective is to store the data needed to build thousands of business applications, flows, analytics, and intelligent bots in a secure and scalable environment. In addition to storing data in a variety of formats, it has a wide range of built-in tools for bringing in data from various external systems and an API for securely exposing data to third-party applications.

What type of data can be stored in Microsoft Dataverse?

Microsoft Dataverse can store both *structured* and *unstructured* data, as shown in Figure 2-21.

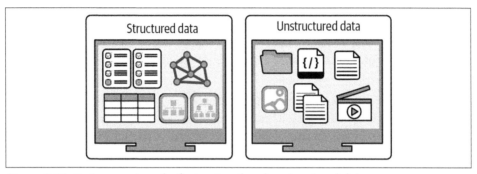

Figure 2-21. Dataverse stores both structured and unstructured data

The term structured data comes from SQL (Structured Query Language), the programming language used to manage structured data, which is also the language and database behind the Microsoft Dataverse.

Structured data is highly organized, readable, and properly stored in tables in predefined formats. This type of data represents real-world business objects like lead, opportunity, customer, employee, product, and contact. Additionally, this type of data can have relationships with other table data and users can interact with it by providing input or by searching. For example, you can store a phone number or search on home address in the Contacts table.

In contrast, unstructured data is not organized or readable and doesn't have any predefined formats. Examples of unstructured data are audio files, image files, documents, and PDF files.

How are business objects created in Microsoft Dataverse?

The database business model used by Microsoft Dataverse is equivalent to other databases available in the market. It has tables, fields of various data types (such as text, number, decimal, image, etc.), relationships, and keys. For citizen developers, it adds some low-code, no-code features on top of that, allowing them to construct a data model without any prior database experience.

Microsoft Dataverse comes with predefined common data models so that someone who is creating a data model doesn't need to set up everything from scratch. For example, Account, Contact, and Activities are the most common tables you need to design any business application. If you are designing an application for the banking domain, you can use Contact to store customer information; if you are designing an application for the health care domain, you can store patient information; if you are designing an application for a college or university, you can store student details, and so on. Hence, Contact is a table that can be used to store any contact details, no matter what domain you are designing the application for.

You may be aware of what a costly and time-consuming operation it can be to combine data from several systems and apps. Each application or data integration project needs a custom solution because it is difficult to exchange and interpret the same data.

Using the predefined common data models from Microsoft Dataverse makes it easier for organizations to manage data. These models provide a common language for different business and analytical applications. This means data can be easily shared and understood across tools like Microsoft Power Apps, Power BI, Dynamics 365, and Azure.

Microsoft Dataverse has the following business objects, which are also referred to as *solution components* because Dataverse uses *solutions* to hold all these business objects or components. Keeping all these components in a solution (single or multiple, depending on your project needs) is also necessary to deploy them to other target environments. (I will talk more about solutions in Chapter 10.)

There are some more advanced components in the Microsoft Dataverse that you will learn about in Chapters 5 and 6.

Tables. Tables are used to store business data (also referred to as *records* or *rows*) such as contact, account, leads, etc. You can either use default tables provided within a CDM or create your own custom tables based on your business needs.

Columns. Columns (also referred to as *fields* or *attributes*) are used to store different types (text, choice, lookup, etc.) of data in a table. A record is made up of the data gathered in the fields along a single row.

Column data types. In Dataverse you can create columns of various data types. Some common data types are Text, Multiline text, Date and Time, Autonumber, Currency, Decimal number, Whole number, File, URL, Choice, Lookup, Power Fx, and more.

Additionally, Dataverse supports a special type of lookup field called *polymorphic lookups*, which can reference records from two different tables. For instance, an owner of any Dataverse table's data can either be User or Team; therefore, the Owner column of any table is called a polymorphic lookup, which can refer to both the User and Team tables. Similarly, the Opportunity table's Customer column can refer to both the Account and Contacts tables.

There is one more special type of lookup field called *party list*, which is used in activity-type entities (for example, email, appointment, tasks, and phone call) to reference multiple records from different tables in a single field. This is useful for scenarios like tracking participants in an email or meeting, where participants can be contacts, accounts, or users.

Relationships. Relationships define how one table is related to another table in Dataverse. For example, a single company will have multiple employees; hence, a one-to-many relationship needs to be created between the Company and Contacts tables. There are three types of relationships: one to many, many to one, and many to many.

Keys. The data in Dataverse is uniquely identified via keys. There are two types of keys in Microsoft Dataverse: *primary key* and *alternate key*.

The primary key, often known as a Globally Unique IDentifier (GUID), is a 32-digit unique identifier that upholds the component's or the data's global uniqueness within Dataverse. For instance, any component or data you create in Dataverse will have a GUID with the format XXXXXXXX-XXXX-XXXX-XXXX-XXXXXXXXXXXX; for example, C12EF73E-1234-684D-BE34-F7B22C4F0EH8. As the primary key is internally managed and immutable, it uses the GUID only for uniquely identifying the data. If you need a unique key or wish to identify data with a different column value, you can create an alternate key. You can generate several alternate keys for every table if necessary, but you cannot have multiple primary keys. For example, you may designate SSN, Email Address, and Mobile Number as alternate keys for the Contacts table to prevent someone from entering the same SSN, email address, or mobile number while creating a contact in Dataverse.

Alternate keys are often used for external data integration with Dataverse. When you need to integrate with an external data store, you might be able to add a column to the external database tables that contains a reference to the unique identifier in Dataverse. This allows you to have a local reference to link to the Dataverse record. However, sometimes you can't modify the external database. With alternate keys, you can define an attribute in a Dataverse table to correspond to a unique identifier (or unique combination of columns) used by the external database. This alternate key can then be used to uniquely identify a record in Dataverse in place of the primary key.

Forms. Forms in Dataverse are the collection of multiple fields that you show to the user to either collect their input (insert mode) and save it to Dataverse or to display the existing data (edit or read-only mode).

Views. Views in Dataverse are used to display a list of Dataverse data. You can apply filters, such as active contacts or inactive contacts, to limit what is displayed (see Figure 2-22).

Figure 2-22. Dataverse's table view

In Figure 2-22:

- My Active Contacts is a view that displays only contacts created by me (the person using the account in Dataverse), and the status is active.

- Contact is a table that stores the contact information using multiple fields or columns.

- The list of contacts in the My Active Contacts view is called Contacts Rows (sometimes referred to as data or records).

- Full Name, Email, Company Name, Business Phone, etc., are the columns (fields) of the Contacts table.

- Full Name is a Text type column, Email is an Email type column, Company Name is a Lookup type column, Birthday is a Date type column, Description is a Multiline text type column, and Gender is a Choice type column.

- To prevent contacts with the same email address and business phone number from being duplicated, you can define the Email or Business Phone column or both as an alternate key.

- The Company Name column relates to the Account table, which establishes the one-to-many relationship between the Account and Contacts tables and stores the company of the relevant contact. Since these types of fields look up the data from different related tables, these kinds of columns are known as *lookup fields*.

- You can open the Contact record in a form and read the complete information if necessary. Depending on your security role, the form will either be in edit or read-only mode.

What is the difference between data and metadata in Dataverse?

Data represents the piece of information, such as an email address, associated with either customer or employee and used by business applications. Data in Dataverse is stored within a set of tables.

In contrast, *metadata* is data about data, which means that it represents the properties of the data itself, like properties of column or table. When you use the customization tools to create or edit tables, columns, and table relationships, you're actually editing their metadata, as shown in Figure 2-23.

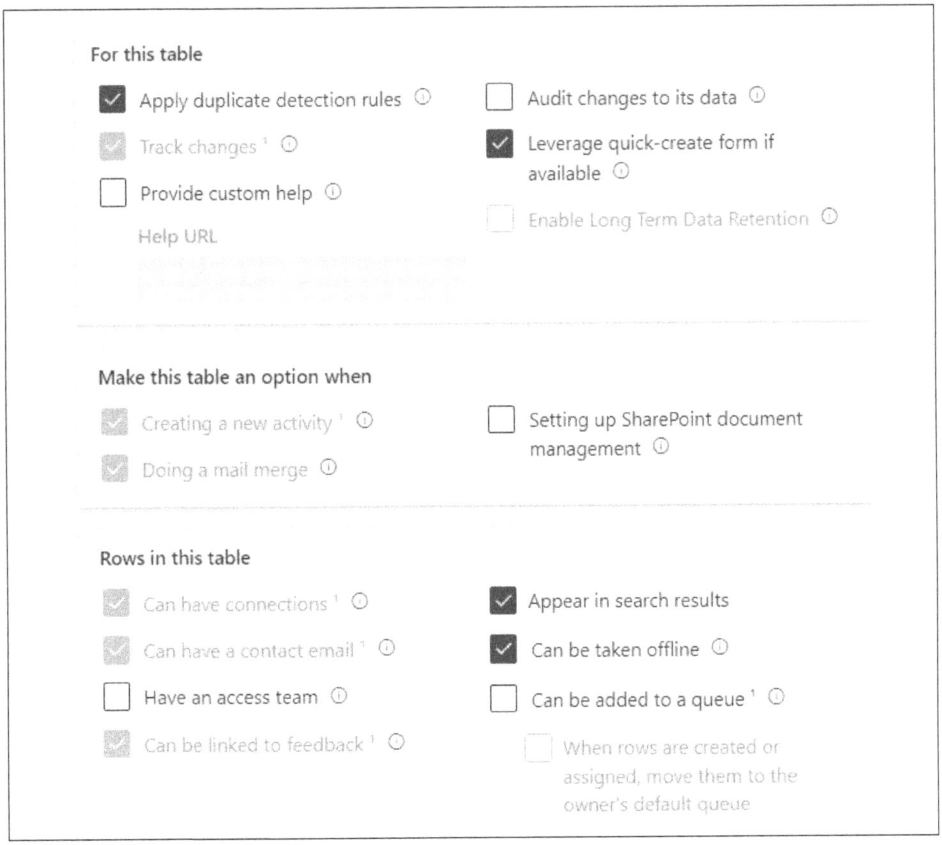

For this table

☑ Apply duplicate detection rules ⓘ   ☐ Audit changes to its data ⓘ

☑ Track changes ¹ ⓘ   ☑ Leverage quick-create form if available ⓘ

☐ Provide custom help ⓘ

Help URL   ☐ Enable Long Term Data Retention ⓘ

Make this table an option when

☑ Creating a new activity ¹ ⓘ   ☐ Setting up SharePoint document management ⓘ

☑ Doing a mail merge ⓘ

Rows in this table

☑ Can have connections ¹ ⓘ   ☑ Appear in search results

☑ Can have a contact email ¹ ⓘ   ☑ Can be taken offline ⓘ

☐ Have an access team ⓘ   ☐ Can be added to a queue ¹ ⓘ

☑ Can be linked to feedback ¹ ⓘ   ☐ When rows are created or assigned, move them to the owner's default queue

Figure 2-23. Metadata of table

Summary

This chapter covered the foundations of the Microsoft Power Platform and Microsoft Dataverse and their connection with Power Apps. You learned that Power Platform and its components are required to combine with Power Apps to develop an end-to-end business solution, while Dataverse offers a Common Data Model for storing the customer and company data generated by various business applications.

From the next chapter onward, I will dive deep into various Power Apps building blocks, features, and components.

CHAPTER 3

Getting Started with Power Apps

You learned about the evolution of Power Apps and its relationship with Microsoft Power Platform and Dataverse in the previous chapters. In this chapter, I'll go into more depth about Power Apps.

Introduction to Power Apps

Power Apps is a cloud-based app development platform that was developed to empower software developers and make it easier for organizations to rapidly design and deploy enterprise-grade business applications. To accomplish this, Power Apps uses low-code, no-code software development techniques that empower not only professional developers but also citizen developers to create and design responsive business applications for the web, mobile devices, and tablets by dragging and dropping components and using various other methods that I will discuss in later on.

It's important to know that model-driven apps and canvas apps are collectively referred to as Power Apps. Each type of app has its own features, benefits, and use cases. Using Power Apps, you can connect to the data that is stored in either Microsoft Dataverse or a variety of other online or on-premises external databases and services, such as SharePoint, Azure SQL, Oracle, Adobe, DocuSign, Microsoft Excel, and SQL Server. Depending on your needs, you can create Power Apps-based business applications from either ready-made templates offered by Microsoft or from scratch. Power Apps offers a wide range of functionality, including drag-and-drop controls and custom code components, to allow anyone to design apps, regardless of programming experience.

With Power Apps, everyone on your team can contribute to app development instead of depending on professional developers. Imagine you are a business owner whose primary responsibilities are to understand business processes and models closely, but you do not know how to write code. You spend most of your work time using Microsoft PowerPoint and Excel to create business proposals, data tracking, estimations, request for proposals, and slide decks. You can use your existing familiarity with these programs to create a business application with Power Apps (see Figure 3-1).

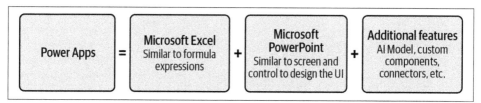

Figure 3-1. Power Apps are similar to Microsoft Excel and PowerPoint

Power Apps supports fusion development (see Figure 3-2), allowing everyone in your organization to contribute to app development without relying on professional developers. Anyone in your team or organization, regardless of coding experience, can kick off the app development with built-in, PowerPoint-like, drag-and-drop controls, such as text boxes, labels, buttons, and icons, along with Excel-like, formula-based expressions to write business logic. Later, developers can add further functionality to the app by calling external APIs, building custom connectors, and writing custom code.

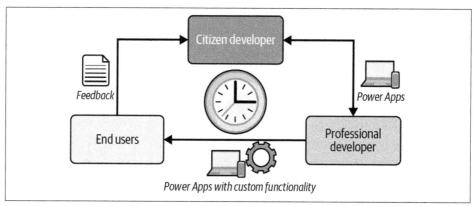

Figure 3-2. Power Apps fusion development

By combining low-code, no-code tools with the capabilities to use enterprise-level application development tools, Power Apps enables a collaborative development approach in the organization, where professional developers and citizen developers can work together to create an end-to-end business solution based on the requirements of the clients. It reduces the overhead on professional developers who used to be the only person responsible for designing and developing things in an organization.

Using Power Apps, any business application can be designed in three steps (Figure 3-3):

1. Connect to a data source, whether it's external or internal, cloud-based or on-premises. This step is necessary only when creating a canvas app. For model-driven apps, connecting to a data source is not required, as they always store data in Dataverse.

2. Create an app using default controls, forms, views, etc.

3. Use the app on mobile, tablet, or web browsers.

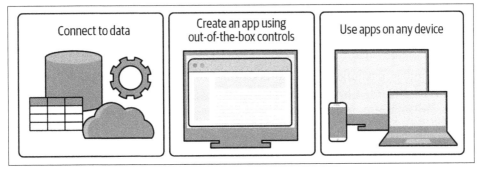

Figure 3-3. High-level steps to designing a Power Apps-based business application

System Requirements

Power Apps supports multiple platforms and browsers, and can be run on Android, Windows, and iOS. Tables 3-1 through 3-3 list the system requirements needed to run Power Apps on various devices and platforms.

Table 3-1. Supported platforms for running Power Apps on mobile devices

Platform	Version
iOS	Latest version of iOS is recommended to run Power Apps mobile.
Android	Latest version of Android is recommended to run Power Apps mobile.
Windows	Windows 10 version 17763.0 or later is required to run Power Apps for Windows.

Table 3-2. Supported browsers for running Power Apps

Browser	Supported version	App type
Google Chrome	Latest three major releases	Model-driven, canvas, and Power Apps designers
Microsoft Edge	Latest three major releases	Model-driven, canvas, and Power Apps designers
Mozilla Firefox	Latest three major releases	Model-driven and canvas
Apple Safari	13 and later	Model-driven and canvas

Table 3-3. Supported operating systems for running Power Apps

Operating system	Supported version	App type
Windows	Windows 10 or later	Model-driven, canvas, and Power Apps designers
macOS	10.13 or later	Model-driven, canvas, and Power Apps designers
iOS	iOS 13 or later	Model-driven (using the web browser on a phone to run a model-driven app isn't supported) and canvas
Android	10 or later	Model-driven (using the web browser on a phone to run a model-driven app isn't supported) and canvas

Later in this chapter, I will go through how to use Power Apps on various devices.

Why Power Apps?

Power Apps has revolutionized the process for developing apps for organizations. But aside from that, it has had some economic impacts on the market and many organizations, which is why, in recent times, it has been a top choice for app creation.

As per the "The Total Economic Impact of Microsoft Power Platform Premium Capabilities" (*https://oreil.ly/BDrvV*) study by Forrester in 2022 and the feedback received from Power Apps customers (*https://oreil.ly/qxXal*), the following are the major advantages of using Power Apps over other app development platforms:

Reduced development cost
 Application development requires a significant investment, starting with finding and hiring technical resources with the required skills, followed by the acquisition of external tools, software, and third-party apps to customize the application, as well as the cost involved in maintenance and support of that application. With Power Apps, you can reduce development costs by 74% by reducing the developer dependencies in app design and support. It comes with many built-in tools, components, features, and connectors that allow everyone to extend the app capabilities with minimum cost.

Reduced development time
 Previously, you had to rely on professional developers to jump-start app development, resolve production problems, and carry out minor change requests. To cut down on development time, Power Apps allows even citizen developers to create a simple prototype of an application using PowerPoint-style drag-and-drop controls and business logic written in Excel-style formulas. Later, when professional developers join the team, they can update the app with more advanced features. As a result, Power Apps reduces the amount of time needed for app development, bug fixes, and feature changes compared to other platforms available on the market.

Increased employee efficiency

Power Apps improves productivity for everyone involved in the company, including site visitors and field employees who can now easily access information using a range of tools and devices. Regardless of whether they are online or off-line, field employees can use a mobile app on the job site to update information immediately in the system. Office employees can access the information using web-based apps, and businesspeople can access it through Microsoft Teams-based embedded Power Apps (we will discuss this more in Chapter 12).

Facilitates better and faster decisions

By accelerating the app development and review processes, Power Apps empowers both app designers and clients to make smarter decisions more quickly. With the help of Power Apps' prebuilt templates and built-in controls, citizen developers can rapidly design a proof of concept (POC) that allows clients to see the features of the future products. Also, clients can have early access to the app so they can begin using it, provide feedback, and accelerate business decisions. Just a few years ago, a similar process would often drag on for months, causing considerable exhaustion and stress. Due to the delayed response, many projects ended up being suspended or postponed.

Seamless integration with other Microsoft products

Power Apps provides seamless integration with all other Power Platform components and other Microsoft products. For instance, it supports SharePoint integration for document management; Outlook integration for emails and meetings; Microsoft Teams integration for chat, call, screen sharing, and other communications; Power BI integration for reporting and data analytics; Power Automate integration for automating the business logic; and Copilot Studios for chatbot integration. Additionally, it provides integration with Azure components as well to design custom APIs and call trigger-based business logic using Azure Functions. Power Apps also supports 1,000+ data connectors that extend its capabilities to communicate with data stored in external data sources.

More secure than other platforms

Power Apps comes with built-in platform-level security features. It controls all aspects of security, including user authentication and authorization, enabling users to interact with data and services. While security roles are in charge of handling data authorization, Power Apps security is linked to Microsoft Entra ID for managing user identities and authentication. The IT staff can simply manage data authorization at the environment, table, form, and field levels. The data is additionally protected from being shared with unauthorized individuals or apps through several governance- and compliance-related features. The list of connections with which certain data can be communicated is specified and regulated by data policies in Power Apps. To reduce risk, IT administrators may limit how extensively users can distribute Power Apps canvas apps using the Limit Sharing option in Managed Environments. Also, all Power Apps created with Microsoft Dataverse adhere to GDPR requirements.

Increased customer satisfaction

There was a time when customers had to wait months, and perhaps years, to receive functional apps. And it took even longer if they needed to integrate feedback or modifications. Power Apps has expedited the app development and operation process by providing low-code, no-code tools, by enabling everyone in the team to work collaboratively, and by increasing agility in the app development process, all of which increase customer satisfaction.

Reduced need for third-party applications

Previously, to design an application you had to purchase or rely on some additional software or third-party tools for development, testing, code writing, deployment, etc. These third-party tools required additional licenses and ongoing maintenance. Power Apps comes with many built-in tools that enable not only professional developers but also citizen developers to use them effectively. Power Apps includes Power Apps Studio, which allows users to design an app using drag-and-drop controls, along with many other built-in features. Test Studio can be used to automatically write test cases for you. Power Apps supports integration with Azure DevOps Pipelines, which brings application lifecycle management (ALM) and continuous integration and continuous delivery (CI/CD) capabilities to the app. There are many other free tools and thousands of business applications you can get from Microsoft AppSource (*https://oreil.ly/VR318*) to extend Power Apps' capabilities.

Support for built-in templates

A quick and simple approach to developing an app is by using templates in Power Apps. You can find a wide variety of built-in templates in the Power Apps template gallery, such as site inspection, budget tracking, meeting scheduling, document viewing, and reservation booking. For example, imagine you have a customer who wants to create a helpdesk app that would enable employees to submit questions about vacations, compensation, appraisals, the resignation process, filing income taxes, etc. Instead of starting from scratch, you can use the helpdesk app in the Power Apps template gallery, customize it to match the branding of the company, connect to the necessary data sources, and display it to your customer.

Support for natural language (Microsoft Copilot)

Power Apps can automatically generate a usable app for you in less than a minute after you explain the concept you have in your head. If you articulate the requirements in your own natural language, Copilot in Power Apps can turn your concept into a functioning app (we'll discuss this in more detail in Chapter 11).

Due to the limitless opportunities and advantages provided by Power Apps, a vast number of organizations—both private and public, including government entities—are harnessing its capabilities to fulfill their business requirements. According to Forrester, as of 2022, when using Power Apps:

- Organizations increased ROI by 140%.
- Organizations saved USD 14.25 million through enhanced business outcomes and reduced business and development processes.
- Organizations experienced a cost reduction of 45% for application development.

This is the reason behind the widespread adoption of Power Apps by industry titans across all sectors, including energy, retail, education, finance, insurance, aviation, manufacturing, health care, media and communications, professional services, public sectors, travel, transportation, and hospitality.

Types of Power Apps

As previously mentioned, you can create two types of apps when using Power Apps: canvas apps and model-driven apps.

Pages or Custom Pages

When designing business apps, you have an additional choice: Pages, also referred to as Custom Pages. Pages brings the power of canvas apps into model-driven apps. It is used to design full pages, dialogs, or side panes within model-driven apps using Power Apps Studio (discussed later in this chapter). Since it uses the same designer that we use to design canvas apps, this option is also available while creating a new app under Solutions → New → App option list, as shown in Figure 3-4. I discuss Pages in more detail in Chapter 7.

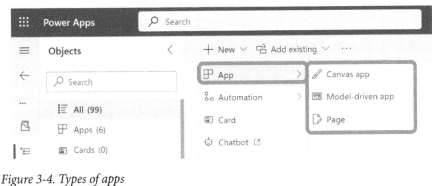

Figure 3-4. Types of apps

Model-Driven Apps

Model-driven apps are tightly coupled with the data models housed in Dataverse; thus, we refer to them as model-driven apps. These kinds of apps are especially well suited to creating data-dense, process-driven applications that make it easy for users to switch between related data. Model-driven apps are a great choice for managing a complex process, such as onboarding new employees, managing a sales process, handling customer service, setting up omnichannel integration, and maintaining a complex hierarchy or relationship in a business like a bank.

Model-driven apps can communicate with any external data sources by bringing the data into Dataverse before using it in the app (as depicted in Figure 3-5). But sometimes you don't need to save the data in Dataverse, as you can connect to external data sources directly via APIs or virtual tables.

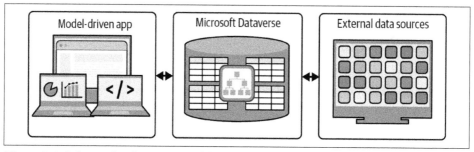

Figure 3-5. Relationship between model-driven apps and data sources

These kinds of apps are also well-suited for business scenarios where complicated business processes, complex business logic, sophisticated security implementations, and complex data relationships need to be established. Model-driven apps have a pre-built UI that makes it possible to quickly create apps without the requirement for UI design knowledge. Therefore, these kinds of apps are also the best choice when a company wants to concentrate on implementing business processes, logic, and security rather than improving its user interface and overall design.

Model-driven apps come with a variety of built-in features and components that help companies satisfy their business objectives:

- Business process flow
- Business rules
- Classic workflows
- Plug-ins
- Calculated and rollup fields
- JavaScript and Dataverse Web APIs

- Custom APIs
- Dashboards, reports, and charts
- App designer, forms, and views
- Command bar
- Web resources
- Security roles

...and many more. In Chapters 6 and 7, we'll explore these components in more detail.

Figure 3-6 shows the evolution of model-driven apps. Microsoft first merged Microsoft Dynamics CRM and ERP to create Microsoft Dynamics 365. After being combined with the Dynamics 365 product, all Microsoft Dynamics CRM apps became Dynamics 365 CE apps, and later, Microsoft integrated them into Power Apps and called them model-driven apps. As a result, Dynamics 365 CE apps are now model-driven apps. Moreover, several new model-driven apps have been released throughout time, and more might be on the horizon.

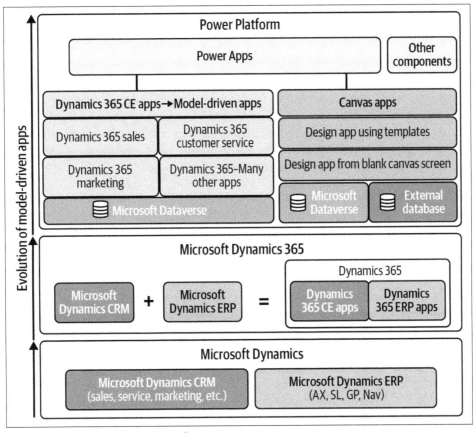

Figure 3-6. Model-driven app evolution

Let's take a look at some business requirements where a model-driven app is the best fit to design the application:

- Create a sales app that can handle the end-to-end sales process of an organization, including manage campaigns, marketing, leads, opportunities, contacts, accounts, orders, quotes, invoices, etc. It should be able to handle all customer interactions, including phone calls, emails, and appointments, and associate them with customer data in the form of activities. This sales process should have guided steps for the salesperson to ensure that the data is being captured consistently and in the correct manner. There should be a proper security hierarchy in place so that sales data can't be seen by unauthorized users or teams. For example, the vice president can see data for all sales managers and salespersons, sales managers can view only salesperson data, and each salesperson can view only their own data.

- Create a customer service app for an organization to track its customer issues, queries, escalations, complaints, feedback in the form of cases (tickets); manage conversations across various channels (SMS, email, chat, phone calls, meetings, etc.); provide case routing and escalation; support collaborations with other support agents through Microsoft Teams; manage service-level agreements (SLAs); and provide knowledge articles and FAQs.

There are numerous business cases where model-driven apps are the best option to satisfy the demands of the company. All of these requirements call for handling intricate business processes and building a security hierarchy, rather than putting more of an emphasis on improving the application's UI and overall look and feel. The complete list of model-driven apps, as of writing, is shown in Table 3-4.

Table 3-4. Model-driven apps (first-party apps) provided by Microsoft

Model-driven app	Description
Dynamics 365 Business Central	Manages, adapts, and streamlines operations like finance, manufacturing, sales, and more, across your small or medium-sized business
Dynamics 365 Commerce	Delivers unified, personalized, and seamless buying experiences for customers and partners
Dynamics 365 Contact Center	A Microsoft Copilot-first contact center solution that delivers generative AI to every customer engagement channel.
Dynamics 365 Customer Insights	Helps your organization deliver exceptional customer experiences by creating personalized, responsive, and connected customer journeys across sales, marketing, and service teams
Dynamics 365 Customer Service	Offers a suite of capabilities to ensure your business can deliver the best customer service experience possible to your customers
Dynamics 365 Customer Voice	Creates surveys and captures customer feedback that you can use to easily keep track of the customer metrics that matter the most to your business
Dynamics 365 Field Service	Handles world-class onsite services at customer locations

Model-driven app	Description
Dynamics 365 Finance	Monitors global financial operations in real time, predicts outcomes, and makes data-driven decisions to drive business agility and growth
Dynamics 365 Fraud Protection	Protects your organization from serious threats of fraud through several innovative and advanced capabilities
Dynamics 365 Guides	Provides on-the-job guidance by enhancing remote collaboration and empowers employees with step-by-step holographic instructions to use where the work happens
Dynamics 365 Human Resources	Provides a suite of human resources capabilities to connect people and operations data to help optimize workforce costs and take care of your employees
Dynamics 365 Intelligent Order Management	Offers a suite of capabilities that helps your organization coordinate, standardize, and optimize orders captured in a mix of channels and systems through a single point of order orchestration
Dynamics 365 Project Operations	Connects sales, resourcing, project management, and finance teams in a single application to win more deals, accelerate project delivery, and maximize profitability
Dynamics 365 Remote Assist	Empowers technicians to collaborate more efficiently by working together from different locations on HoloLens, HoloLens 2, Android, or iOS devices
Dynamics 365 Sales (Premium, Enterprise, Professional)	Enables you to build strong relationships with your customers by providing smooth sales experiences, take actions based on insights, and close deals faster
Dynamics 365 Supply Chain Management	Builds an adaptable, resilient supply chain that automatically reacts to challenges using real-time visibility, agile planning, and advanced insights

The list may include other apps in the future. You can keep an eye on the Dynamics 365 documentation. (*https://oreil.ly/BFhif*)

Canvas Apps

Another kind of Power Apps is the canvas app, which enables citizen developers to create their own apps from scratch, like an artist's canvas. While designing a canvas app, the app maker has full control over where each control is placed on the screen to suit their business needs. These apps are the best fit for the business scenario where a company wants to change the look and feel of the app as per their company branding.

Unlike model-driven apps, canvas apps are not tightly coupled with Microsoft Dataverse. Canvas apps do not require data to be stored in Dataverse, but may be designed to use data from different databases, including SQL Server, Microsoft Excel, SharePoint, OneDrive, Azure SQL, and Oracle (Figure 3-7).

With the built-in templates, anyone can begin designing an app using canvas apps. For example, there's a template for a "Product Showcase" app, which can be used to develop an app to show customers the products your business sells. Or you can connect end users with support staff in a user-friendly manner by developing an app with the "Helpdesk" template.

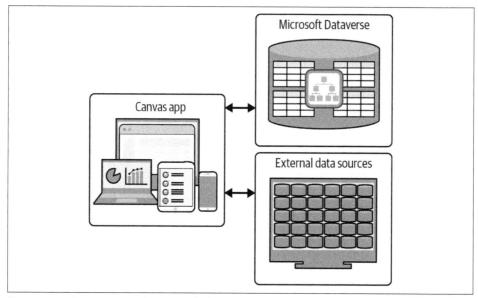

Figure 3-7. Canvas app relation with data sources

Apps created from templates come with a sample data source, data, and controls; however, they require a small amount of setup, such as connecting to appropriate data sources and customizing the controls to suit your needs.

Templates can help you create the app quickly, such as when you need to develop a POC or prepare a demo. Then, once decisions have been made, you can modify the app to meet the client's needs. Canvas app templates can also be useful to jump-start the app development process and for training purposes, such as to learn about default app behaviors, best practices to write the expressions, and use of default controls.

Canvas apps contain many built-in AI capabilities, drag-and-drop controls, components, and functions, as well as the ability to create formula-based expressions similar to Microsoft Excel. We'll discuss that later, and in Chapter 5, I'll go through numerous possibilities and business scenarios to help you decide what kind of Power Apps to create to suit your business needs.

Power Apps Building Blocks

Power Apps is more than just a tool to create business apps and let you view your business data. It is a collection of many components, services, apps, and connectors that work together to expand your app capabilities. These resources and components form the building blocks of Power Apps (Figure 3-8).

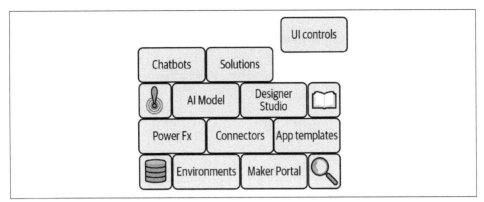

Figure 3-8. Power Apps building blocks

In the subsequent chapters, you'll delve into each building block in detail. This chapter will show you how to access them. All of the building blocks can be accessed via the Power Apps home page (*https://oreil.ly/oCd-g*) and Power Platform admin center. (*https://oreil.ly/Apq-Y*)

Power Apps Home Page

The *Power Apps home page* is the entry point for Power Apps. Every time you build a new app or manage an existing app, you start from the Power Apps home page, also referred to as the *Power Apps Maker Portal*. To access it, go to *make.powerapps.com* and log in with your Microsoft Entra ID user account that you created when you set up the Power Platform environment.

On the home page, you get all the options to start building your app either from a blank screen, Dataverse, or sample app templates. Let's have a look at the Power Apps home page.

It mainly consists of the following 10 elements (more elements may be added in the future):

- Left navigation panel
- Search bar
- Environment information
- Notifications and Settings
- App build options
- Learn hub
- App list
- Get help from a virtual agent
- App templates
- App designer tools

Let's look at each of these in turn.

Left navigation panel

The first area I'd like to call to your attention is the left navigation panel, as shown in Figure 3-9.

Figure 3-9. Options in the left navigation panel

You'll find the following options in the left navigation panel:

Home
> Redirects you to the Power Apps home page, where you can discover a comprehensive overview of all elements connected to Power Apps.

Create
> Shows options to create apps, including canvas apps, model-driven apps, websites, and other components such as chatbots and AI models. You can:

> - Create an app from a blank screen.
> - Create apps using data sources (Dataverse, SharePoint, Excel, SQL, etc.).
> - Create an app from the image of an app or form.
> - Create an app from a sketch generated by Figma UI Kit.
> - Create an app from a template.

Learn

This directs you to the Learning Hub, where you can find Power Apps manuals, courses, articles, videos, training materials, support from the Power Apps community, and other tools to assist you in developing Power Apps.

Apps

List all the apps built within the environment. Here you'll find both prebuilt applications that are created when the environment is set up and your own custom applications.

Tables

Shows all the tables in the Microsoft Dataverse that are connected to your environment. You can add, edit, and delete tables, their data, and their metadata to configure the data model.

Flows

Shows all Power Automate flows that exist in your environment. You will find three categories of flows: *cloud flows*, *desktop flows*, and *shared with me*. When you want your automation to be performed automatically, instantly, or on a predefined schedule, create a cloud flow. Desktop flows are used to automate processes on the web or the desktop. "Shared with me" shows the list of flows that are created by someone else in your team and which have been shared with you.

Solutions

Shows all the solutions that exist in your Power Platform environment. Solutions are used to package all the resources and components you create to build an app and move them to another environment; we'll talk more about them in Chapter 10.

More

Allows you to tailor the left navigation items to your needs. This enables you to *pin* your most frequently used items, such as tables, flows, and chatbots, to the left navigation. The items that you don't want to appear in the list can also be *unpinned*, as shown in Figure 3-10.

You can also reorder the list items by clicking on the three vertical dots next to the item and choosing "Move up" or "Move down," as shown in Figure 3-11.

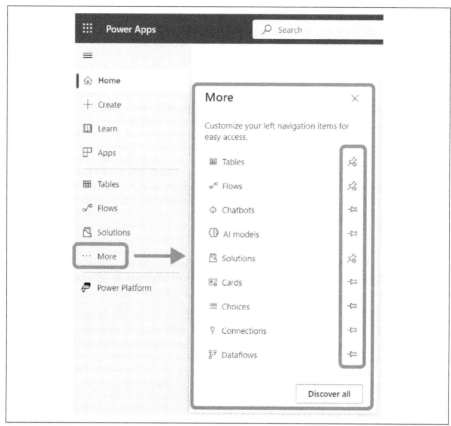

Figure 3-10. Pinning and unpinning items in the left navigation panel

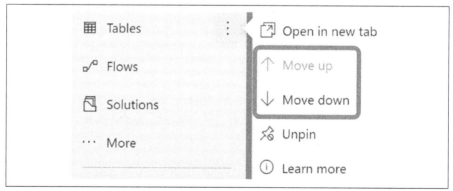

Figure 3-11. Reordering items in the left navigation panel

Power Platform

All of the Power Platform's components are available here, along with a link to the admin center where you can control them. To expand the app's capabilities, you can integrate these components into your apps (Figure 3-12).

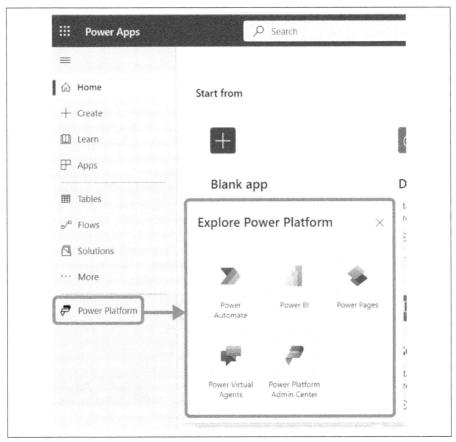

Figure 3-12. Power Platform components

Search bar

As depicted in Figure 3-13, the Search bar can be used to:

- Find your Power Apps (under the "My apps" section)
- Create a new app (under the Create section)

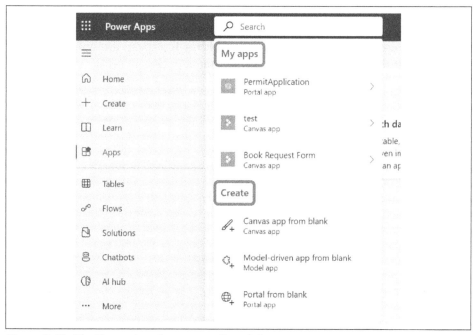

Figure 3-13. The Power Apps home page Search bar

You may have many apps in your environment, either created by you or someone else and shared with you, and you may have difficulty finding them. Use the Search bar to quickly find the apps by simply typing one or more characters (Figure 3-14). Once you find the app you want, you can Browse (play), Edit, or Share it directly.

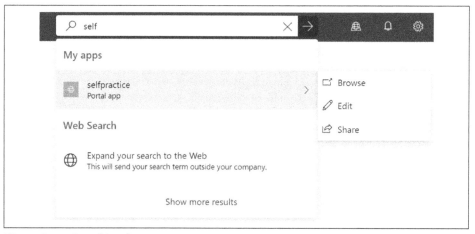

Figure 3-14. Searching for an app

Environment information

An *environment* is a container of resources (apps, chatbots, flows, connectors, tables, etc.), which is used to separate your app components for audiences that might have different roles, responsibilities, and security requirements. You can choose to create multiple environments, depending on your needs. For example, you can create separate environments:

- For development, testing, and production (live usage)
- For different regions of your company
- That correspond to specific teams or departments in your company
- To try out different features and keep different components in each environment

For example, Figure 3-15 shows three environments: Arpit Power Guide - DEV, Arpit Power Guide - UAT (user acceptance testing), and Arpit Power Guide - PROD. The Arpit Power Guide - DEV environment is for developers and is used to develop and customize the app and its related components. Arpit Power Guide - UAT is for testers and is used to create testing data and test the app and its related components. Arpit Power Guide - PROD is the environment used by actual users.

The environment icon in the toolbar can be clicked to view and switch between environments (as shown in Figure 3-15).

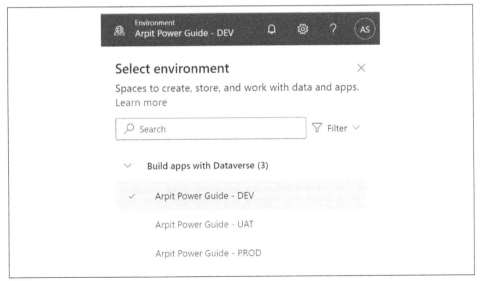

Figure 3-15. Power Platform environments

Notifications and Settings

When you click the bell icon, it opens a panel that displays the list of all notifications related to your Power Platform environment. Unless you dismiss them or until they expire, notifications remain in the notification center (Figure 3-16).

Figure 3-16. Notifications panel

When you click the gear icon, you can access the Settings panel, where you can carry out administrative operations. You will find four sections under the Settings area, as shown in Figure 3-17.

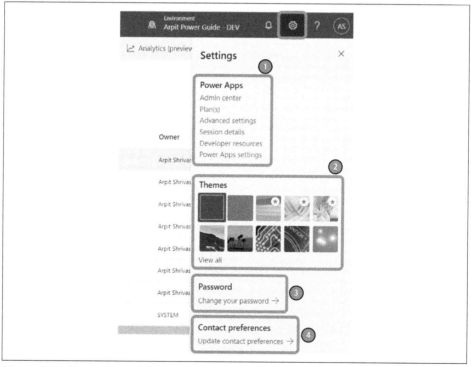

Figure 3-17. Settings panel

In the first section, Power Apps, you will find following options:

Admin center
Takes you to the Power Platform admin center, where you can manage all environment-related admin settings. I'll go into further detail about the admin center later in this chapter.

Plans(s)
Shows your current license or licenses.

Advanced settings
Directs you to a page where you can control all settings connected to your environment, as shown in Figure 3-18. Since many options also pertain to administrators, they are gradually being moved to the Power Platform admin center; it's possible this page won't exist in the future.

Figure 3-18. Advanced settings

Session details
Displays Power Apps session details such as session ID, tenant ID, environment ID, and more, as shown in Figure 3-19.

```
Timestamp: 2023-09-05T11:27:33.165Z
Session ID: 206d2c80-4bdf-11ee-8fbe-f7ec8fd8c7f4
Tenant ID: 72ad288c-64a9-465c-b076-7d2bb19db75a
Object ID: e4a63062-e609-4ae2-a35d-a081421d19b9
Build name: 0.0.20230823.3-2308.3-prod
Organization ID: 9b42a57d-b4da-ed11-aed0-002248282d11
Unique name: unq9b42a57db4daed11aed0002248282
Instance url: https://org2f1b6a85.crm.dynamics.com/
Environment ID: 826b9d17-8256-e8f3-b783-5075cc19da14
Cluster environment: Prod
Cluster category: Prod
Cluster geo name: US
Cluster URI suffix: us-il103.gateway.prod.island
```

Figure 3-19. Session details

Developer resources
Displays development-related resources or information that developers frequently use when building code to perform Dataverse operations; for example, the endpoint for a Web API, the endpoint for a discovery service, the environment's unique name, and so on (see Figure 3-20).

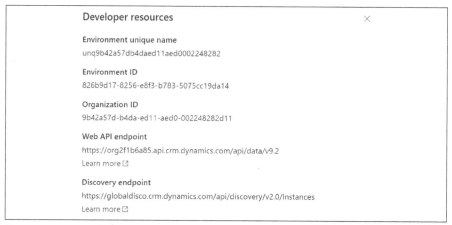

Environment unique name
unq9b42a57db4daed11aed0002248282

Environment ID
826b9d17-8256-e8f3-b783-5075cc19da14

Organization ID
9b42a57d-b4da-ed11-aed0-002248282d11

Web API endpoint
https://org2f1b6a85.api.crm.dynamics.com/api/data/v9.2
Learn more ☐

Discovery endpoint
https://globaldisco.crm.dynamics.com/api/discovery/v2.0/Instances
Learn more ☐

Figure 3-20. Developer resources

Power Apps settings

Lets you manage your language, time, notifications, and directory-related settings. Under "Language and time," you can view or update your language and time settings. Under Notifications, you can subscribe to Microsoft's newsletter for a particular region and get updates, tips, and offers about Power Apps feature releases. Directories shows current directory information associated with your Power Platform environment (see Figure 3-21).

Figure 3-21. Power Apps settings

In the second section, you'll find the option to change the Power Apps theme. You can modify the ribbon color that appears in the Power Platform environment by using the theme option, as depicted in Figure 3-22. This is not the place to alter the branding, user interface, or look and feel of your Power Apps.

In the third section, you'll find the option to change your password. It takes you to the page where you can change your Power Apps account's password.

In the fourth section, you will find the option to change your contact preferences. It redirects you to the My Account page, where you can update your contact information.

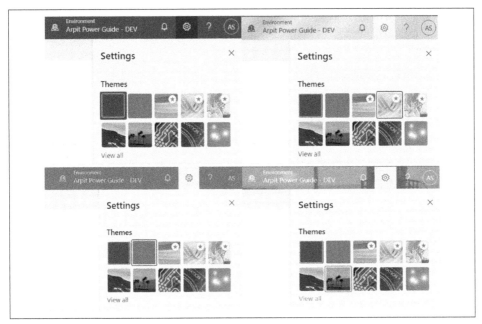

Figure 3-22. Themes

App build options

In the build options area of the home page, you can find all the possible ways to create an app, as shown in Figure 3-23:

Start with Copilot
You can create an app by describing your requirements, such as what it should collect, track, list, or manage, in your natural language or everyday words. For example, you might type "Create an app that collects reader feedback on the Power Apps book and stores it in Dataverse."

Start with data
You can create an app using data stored in either Dataverse or another supported database, such as SharePoint, Excel, or SQL. Here, you will find the following options to start creating your app:

- Upload an Excel file.
- Start with a blank table.
- Select an existing table.
- Select external data (SharePoint, SQL Server, etc.).

Start with a page design

You can create an app by selecting a design from the list of available designs and layouts:

- Gallery connected to a table
- Gallery connected to external data
- Blank canvas or screen
- View and form (to create a model-driven app)
- Blank page with navigation (to create a model-driven app)
- An image or Figma file (*https://oreil.ly/-lWNv*)
- Split screen
- Sidebar
- Header, main section, footer
- Dashboard (to create a model-driven app)

Start with an app template

You can create an app from a list of fully functional business app templates that you can use either as is or customize to suit your business needs. These templates are available for both canvas apps and model-driven apps.

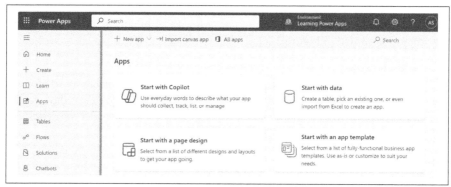

Figure 3-23. App build options

Learn hub

In the Learn hub, you can find Power Apps manuals, courses, articles, videos, training materials, support from the Power Apps community, and other tools to assist you in developing Power Apps. You can also suggest an idea if you believe that any topics are missing from the learning list (Figure 3-24).

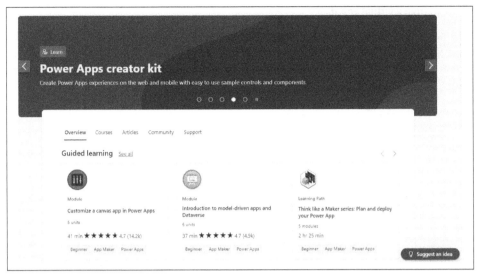

Figure 3-24. The Learn hub

App list

A list of all the apps built within the environment can be found in the Apps area. You can play with or edit any of the apps on this list, whether you made them yourself or someone else shared them with you. Here you will find three options to filter out the apps: "My apps" displays the apps created by the logged-in Power Apps user; "Shared with me" displays apps that were created by someone else in your team and have been shared with you; and "All" displays all apps created by you and shared with you (Figure 3-25).

Figure 3-25. App list

Get help from a virtual agent

You can ask a virtual agent for assistance if you run into any problems locating the stuff you need to begin building your app. The virtual agent is an AI-based conversational chatbot that can assist you in finding pertinent responses to your questions about the development of Power Apps.

For example, as depicted in Figure 3-26. I have asked the chatbot to provide me with information about creating an app from Dataverse.

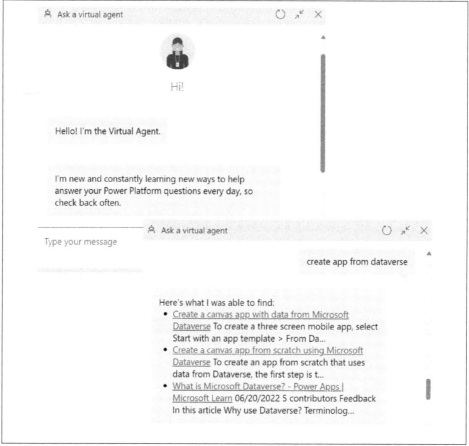

Figure 3-26. Getting help from a virtual agent (chatbot)

App templates

You can quickly get your app development off the ground by using app templates, as shown in Figure 3-27. Microsoft has released ready-to-use app templates based on common use cases. You can either use these templates as is or customize them to suit your needs. In the future, more templates can be added to this list.

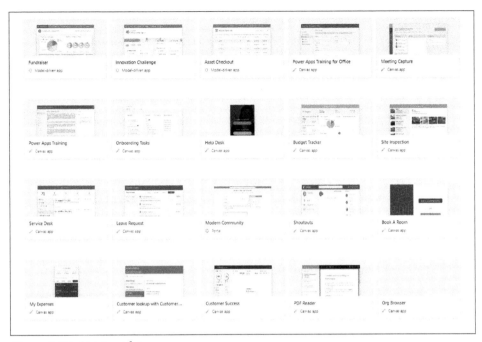

Figure 3-27. App templates

App designer tool

To create, edit, and manage your business apps built on Power Apps, you'll need *app designer tools* (also called *app builders*). There are two kinds of designer tools: one is called *Power Apps Studio* for canvas apps, and the other is *app designer* for model-driven apps. Select the app from the Apps list and click the Edit button on the toolbar to launch the corresponding designer tool (see Figure 3-28).

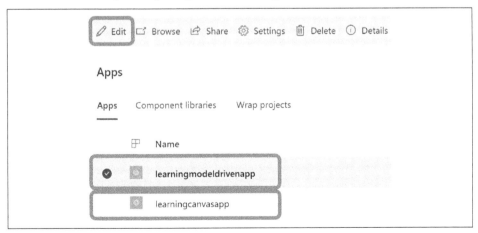

Figure 3-28. Opening app designer tool

Let's discuss each designer tool in more detail:

Power Apps Studio

This is a UI designer tool that is used to design canvas apps. It offers a user interface experience similar to PowerPoint, which makes building an app feel like creating a slide deck. It has four primary panes, as shown in Figure 3-29:

- The left pane (1) in Figure 3-29) shows the tree view of all the controls added to the screens or thumbnails of each screen in the app.

- The middle pane (2) shows the screen that you are working on.

- The right pane (3) shows the properties of the controls you are adding to the screen, such as font color, screen background color, control's height and width.

- The top pane (4) shows various options for adding controls to the screen, along with the formula bar to write Power Fx expressions (which I'll discuss in more detail in Chapter 9).

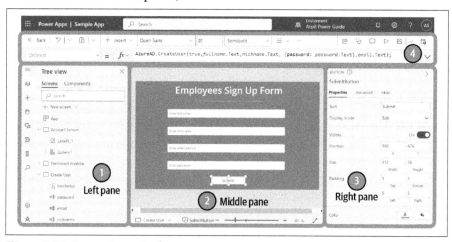

Figure 3-29. Power Apps Studio

App designer

App designer is a UI tool to design model-driven apps. The UI is similar to that of Power Apps Studio, with a left, middle, and right pane, with some additional properties, features, and controls related to model-driven apps (Figure 3-30):

- The left pane (1) in Figure 3-30 shows the grouping of various components added to the model-driven app: Pages to display the Dataverse table; Dashboards; Web resource; Data to manage Dataverse tables; and Automation to manage business process flows added to your app.

- The middle pane (2) shows a live preview of the app as it will be seen by users after the app is published.
- The right pane (3) is used to change the properties of the elements you are adding to the left navigation panel.
- The top pane (4) is used for managing various app settings, as well as adding comments, saving, and publishing the app.

Figure 3-30. App designer

I discuss these tools and their components in more detail in Chapters 6–8.

 The tool used to edit websites or Power Pages sites is called Power Pages design studio. You can find more details about it in the documentation (*https://oreil.ly/kc6wh*).

Power Platform Admin Center

The Power Platform admin center provides a unified portal for administrators to manage environments and settings for Power Apps and other Power Platform components. You need to have either the Environment Admin role or the System Administrator role to manage admin-related settings from the Power Platform admin center (*https://oreil.ly/FzLxY*).

The admin center provides the capabilities to administrators shown in Figure 3-31.

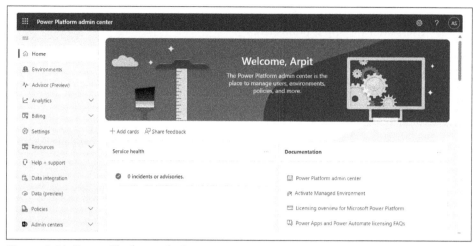

Figure 3-31. Power Platform admin center

Let's go over these capabilities in more detail:

Home
> You can personalize your home page by navigating to the Settings menu and selecting a theme, language, and time zone. To personalize your dashboard, select "Add cards" at the top of the home page and drag any of the following cards to the desired location on the dashboard:
>
> - Monitor service health
> - Message center
> - Resources for documentation and training
> - Advisor

Environments
> View, create, and manage your environments and their users, teams, and security roles. You can also enable new updates released by Microsoft.

Advisor
> View recommendations for issues that may be impacting the health of your tenant. You need to activate Managed Environments (*https://oreil.ly/guXhU*) to get recommendations.

Analytics
>View key metrics for Power Apps such as usage, location, performance, and errors.

Billing
>View a summary of environments in your tenant requiring licensing attention.

Settings
>Shows tenant-level settings that are applicable across your organizations. For example, you can enable preview features, add-on capacity assignments, etc.

Resources
>View and manage resources such as Dataverse capacity.

Help + support
>Create a support ticket to get technical support or get a list of self-help solutions.

Data integration
>Integrate data from external data sources into Dataverse.

Data
>Set up data transfer between on-premises data and cloud services.

Policies
>Create and manage data loss prevention policies.

Admin centers
>Shows other admin centers, including Microsoft Entra ID, Microsoft 365 admin center, and Power BI admin center.

From the Power Platform admin center, you have the ability to modify environment-specific settings (see Figure 3-32), which were previously accessed through the Advanced Settings option in Dynamics 365 CE. To do that, from the Power Platform admin center (*https://oreil.ly/bEdhD*), select Environments from the left navigation panel, select your environment (I have selected Arpit Environment DEV), click on Settings from the command bar, and it will take you to the Settings page where you can expand various categories to change the settings.

For example, to change the "Maximum file size for attachments" setting, expand the Email category, scroll down to the Attachments heading, and change the file size in kilobytes, as shown in Figure 3-33.

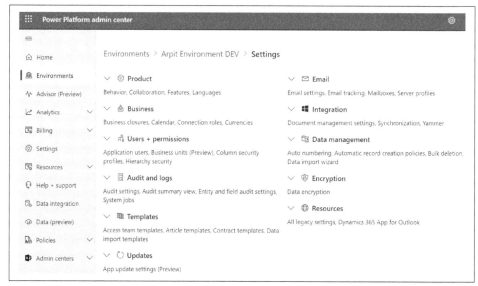

Figure 3-32. Power Platform admin center settings page

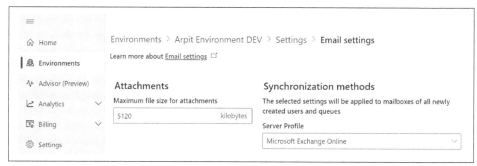

Figure 3-33. Change email attachment file size setting

Power Apps Collaborative Development

The low-code, no-code platform's goal is to make it possible for anyone to create business apps, as you learned in the previous chapter.

Let's use a simple, real-world example of how Power Apps facilitates collaborative development to better understand this. Imagine that we need to develop an event management app that will showcase information about events, sessions, speakers, etc.

The following six personas will be used in this example:

- Raz, business analyst
- Deepali, citizen developer

- Arpit, professional developer
- Aman, IT administrator
- Malini, tester
- Manju, app user, who will use the app in real time

Power Apps Is for Business Users

Raz is a business analyst who is in charge of interacting with clients to gather requirements for creating an event management app; for example, how many apps need to be built, what features they should have, how the UI should appear, where the data will be stored, who the users are and how they will access the apps—via mobile or web—and so forth. Raz can quickly design a POC using Power Apps templates or from scratch using default controls, depending on the requirements, and show how the app integrates with other low-code, no-code components like Power Automate, chatbots, Power BI reports, and Power Pages-based websites. He can seek Arpit's help if he wants to demonstrate any advanced functionality that requires coding or technical expertise, like calling an external API.

Once the app requirements are finalized and the client gives the go-ahead, Raz can pass on the detailed requirements to the citizen developers, the low-code, no-code developers.

Power Apps Is for Citizen Developers

Deepali is a citizen developer who lacks technical experience but is well-versed in Microsoft products including Excel, PowerPoint, Teams, OneDrive, Outlook, and SharePoint. She is in charge of building up the data model required for the app development, creating an app with built-in controls similar to PowerPoint, writing expressions similar to Excel, and other tasks. Based on the business needs, she will also be responsible for building and creating numerous tables, fields, relationships, forms, views, dashboards, etc. She has the ability to use Power Apps Studio and app designer to customize the menu, toolbar, and site map in addition to writing basic field-level validations using business rules, flows to automate tasks, and business process flows to ensure consistent data submission in the app.

Once she is done with the basic app design and data model setup, she can hand over the app to a professional developer.

Power Apps Is for Professional Developers

Arpit is a professional developer and will be in charge of writing the custom code and adding complex features to the app. For example, he may need to write JavaScript to conduct complex form validations that need to query related tables, write plug-ins to make synchronous calls to external APIs, and develop custom controls based on React and TypeScript to improve data visualization.

Developing the app is not the only thing required to start using the app in the live environment. There are many configurations and settings that need to be in place to control and manage the visibility of the app and its related components like user creation, security role assignment, sharing the app, monitoring app performance, setting up a new environment, managing the storage capacity of the environments, setting up app sharing limits, and setting up data policies. Once these admin settings are in place, the next step is to deploy the app components from one environment to another.

To manage the admin-related settings, the IT administrator comes into the picture.

Power Apps Is for IT Administrators

Aman, an IT administrator (Power Platform admin or global administrator) whose responsibilities begin when the project kicks off and continue until the project is successfully delivered to production. He will be responsible for setting up and configuring the Microsoft 365 tenant and environments, ensuring proper security and compliance policies. During the project, he will also be responsible for managing product subscriptions, licenses, data storage, and backups, while monitoring environment health and app performance. At the project's end, he also needs to review compliance, decommission unnecessary environments, and document configurations and lessons learned.

Additionally, he will be in charge of setting up an Azure DevOps CI/CD pipeline or a Power Platform-based pipeline to automate the deployment of the app and any associated components to the target environment, such as UAT or production.

Once the app development is complete, the app is available for distribution to end users. Aman will also be in charge of sharing the app with the appropriate individuals, groups, or the entire organization, depending on the situation, with the necessary rights and privileges.

Power Apps Is for Testers

Malini, a tester in the team, will be in charge of creating and executing automated test cases (using the Power Apps Test Studio tool; this will be covered in Chapter 8) to make sure the app performs as intended before delivering it to end users.

Power Apps Is for App Users

Manju is an app user who will run and use the app in real time, either via a web browser, tablet, or mobile device, and share feedback.

Based on the feedback received from the actual users, Deepali will make the changes to the app without involving Arpit unless code or complex features need to be added or modified.

Power Apps Is for Everyone

This was just a simple illustration of how your project team can work together to develop an app.

Raz, the business analyst, is responsible for contact with clients, highlighting the benefits of the product, and generating revenue for the organization. He can still contribute to the development of the app despite having no programming experience. He doesn't need to rely on Deepali or Arpit unless the client requests to see some advanced features of the app during the POC. This shortens the decision-making process that used to be required to close a deal.

Deepali previously used PowerPoint to make eye-catching presentations for client demos and Excel to enter business data and perform simple calculations. She can contribute to the design of the application's UI by using her Excel expertise to create Power Fx expressions and her PowerPoint expertise to create screens using drag-and-drop controls. She doesn't have to wait for Arpit to start the application development.

When Arpit takes over the app, he won't need to worry about creating its fundamental functionality because the team's citizen developers have already done that using low-code and no-code methods. As a result, reliance on professional developers will be reduced, allowing them to concentrate on activities such as research and development, investigation, and custom development.

While this is going on, Aman from the IT admin team can handle configuring environments, app settings, and configuring deployment pipelines without needing assistance from other team members.

After doing extensive end-to-end testing using the automated test cases created by Malini, the app will then be pushed to production.

Power Apps Licensing and Cost

To use the Power Apps tools, you must have a license. Since there are several factors to consider when deciding which license option best fits your business needs, your primary deciding factor should be which Power Apps capabilities you want to utilize in your business applications.

Limited Capabilities

If you do not need to use all of the features in Power Apps, you can use Dynamics 365 and Microsoft 365 licenses, which provide Power Apps as an additional product or service and allow you to use Power Apps with limited capabilities.

Dynamics 365 license

With this license, limited Power Apps use permissions are provided within the same environment(s) as the licensed Dynamics 365 application(s) to enable users to modify and expand licensed Dynamics 365 applications. The licensed Dynamics 365 application must be used only in the same environment as the Power Apps features that come with that license. Usage permissions differ depending on the Dynamics 365 license type (as depicted in Table 3-5).

Table 3-5. Power Apps capabilities with a Dynamics 365 license

Features and components	Dynamics 365 license	Dynamics 365 Enterprise license
Build and run custom apps	X	✓
Power Pages use rights	X	✓
Data connectors or data sources	Allowed to use all prebuilt standard, premium, and custom connectors	
On-premises connectors and gateway	Allowed to use on-premises connectors and data gateway	
Store and manage data	Only 15 custom tables per D365 application Perform CRUD operations	No restriction on custom tables Perform CRUD operations
Use Microsoft Dataverse	✓	✓
Executive Power Automate Flows	Allowed to use Power Automate (only within app context)	
Business process flows	Can create business process flows (only within app context)	
AI Builder capabilities	Need to purchase AI Builder add-on	

Microsoft 365 license

With Microsoft 365 (formerly known as Office 365) licenses, you have restricted Power Apps use rights. These rights enable users to customize and expand Microsoft 365 applications for productivity scenarios, and they provide Microsoft Teams with a robust low-code extensibility platform (see Table 3-6).

Table 3-6. Power Apps capabilities with a Microsoft 365 license

Features and components	Microsoft 365 license
Build and run custom apps	Unlimited (Canvas apps only)
Data connectors or data sources	Allowed to use only Standard connectors
Use Microsoft Dataverse	Provides Dataverse for Teams with limited capabilities compared to standard Dataverse. Allows only 1 million rows or 2 GB space.
Create Power Automate flows, chatbots	Within the context of Dataverse for Teams

Full Capabilities

To take advantage of all the Power Apps features and capabilities, you will need to get a standalone Power Apps license. The options are:

- Subscription plan:
  — Power Apps per app (per user per app)
  — Power Apps Premium (per user)
- Power Apps per app pay-as-you-go plan

Let's go over these options in more detail:

Subscription plan

A pre-paid subscription plan is the best fit for organizations that want predictable costs based on the predicted number of users who are going to use the app. It allows users to run an unlimited number of apps or only one at a time. There are two categories:

Power Apps per app (per user per app)

In this license plan, you will get only one app, per user, per month. This one app can be either a model-driven app, a canvas app, or a portal. This is a *stacking license*, which means you can purchase multiple per app plans for an environment, based on your business needs. For example, initially you might purchase a per app plan for one user and then after a few months, two more users want to use the app, and so you need to purchase two additional per app plan licenses for them.

Power Apps Premium (per user)

In this license plan, you will get unlimited apps (model-driven, canvas, portal, or a combination), per user, per month.

Power Apps per app pay-as-you-go plan

A pay-as-you-go plan allows you to use Power Apps by using your Azure subscription. It enables you to start creating and sharing apps without making any upfront purchases or commitments to licenses. This plan is the best fit for organizations that want the flexibility to only pay when a user uses an app within a certain month. That is, you have to pay per user, based on the number of unique apps they run per month. A meter counts the total number of distinct users that launched the app at least once in a given environment over a given month. Regardless of how many people have access to it, you are only billed for the unique users who actually launched the app. Users who run many apps in a given month will be counted as active users for each of those apps.

Table 3-7 compares the various plans. Note that the prices listed in the tables are current as of the time of writing. Please check the Power Apps website (*https://oreil.ly/s70fa*) for updated pricing.

 Due to changes in local currencies, countries, and regions, prices provided by Microsoft are only for marketing purposes and may not represent actual prices. Your precise price will be displayed at the time of checkout.

The rates shown in the tables are based on the Power Apps licensing scheme as of writing. Pricing and licensing may change at any point in the future if a new feature or component is introduced. Don't make the decision to buy the Power Apps license based on the price stated in the book! Always check with Microsoft for the most recent prices and product costs.

You get a lot of other features and components along with the Power Apps standalone license based on what type of license plan you purchased.

Table 3-7. Power Apps subscription plans

Features and components	Subscription plans		
	Power Apps (per user per app) $5 user/app/month	Power Apps Premium (per user) $20 user/month (or $12 user/month with 2,000+ new user licenses)	Power Apps per app (pay-as-you-go) $10 active user/app/month
Build and run custom apps	1 model-driven app, 1 canvas app, or 1 website	Unlimited apps and websites	1 app
Data connectors or data sources	Allowed to use all prebuilt and custom connectors		
On-premises connectors and gateway	Allowed to use on-premises connectors and data gateway		
Store and manage data	Allowed to create and access custom entities		
Use Microsoft Dataverse	50 MB database capacity 400 MB file capacity	250 MB database capacity 2 GB file capacity	1 GB database capacity 1 GB file capacity
Execute Power Automate flows	Allowed to use Power Automate (including Premium connectors) in the context of app		
Execute Dataverse workflows	Can write asynchronous and custom real-time workflows		
AI Builder capabilities	250 service credits	500 service credits	Charges based on usage

How Do I Decide Which License Plan to Choose?

Which license plan to choose will largely depend on the app usage and app users. If you already know your user base (who is going to use the app) then the subscription plan is best; if the user base is not known or is unpredictable, then pay-as-you-go is a good fit.

Let's talk about a few scenarios.

Scenario 1: You know that you'll have limited apps with limited users

Let's say my client only wants to use one model-driven app for a salesperson for handling sales processes and one canvas app for a sales representative for creating leads in the system. Then, I can go with the Power Apps per app plan, because I already know that the number of apps and number of app users are only two.

Figure 3-34 depicts the Power Apps licensing estimate for the next three months. Only one canvas app and one model-driven app had to be made for two distinct app users in months #1, #2, and #3. The total licensing cost for three months would therefore be $30 ($10/month).

Active users	Month #1	Month #2	Month #3
Model-driven app 1	👤	👤	👤
Canvas app 1	👤	👤	👤
Total active users	2 users use 2 different apps in a month. Per user/app/month = $5×2 Total cost: $10/month	2 users use 2 different apps in a month. Per user/app/month = $5×2 Total cost: $10/month	2 users use 2 different apps in a month. Per user/app/month = $5×2 Total cost: $10/month

Figure 3-34. Power Apps licensing example 1

Scenario 2: You want to use unlimited apps

Let's take an example where my customer wants to create two model-driven apps, one for managing the sales process for sales users and the other for managing the service process for service users. The customer also aims to provide business users and sales managers the freedom to develop as many applications as they like. In this scenario, the Power Apps Premium plan is a better option and less expensive in comparison to the per app plan because there is no restriction on how many applications can be developed. (See Figure 3-35.)

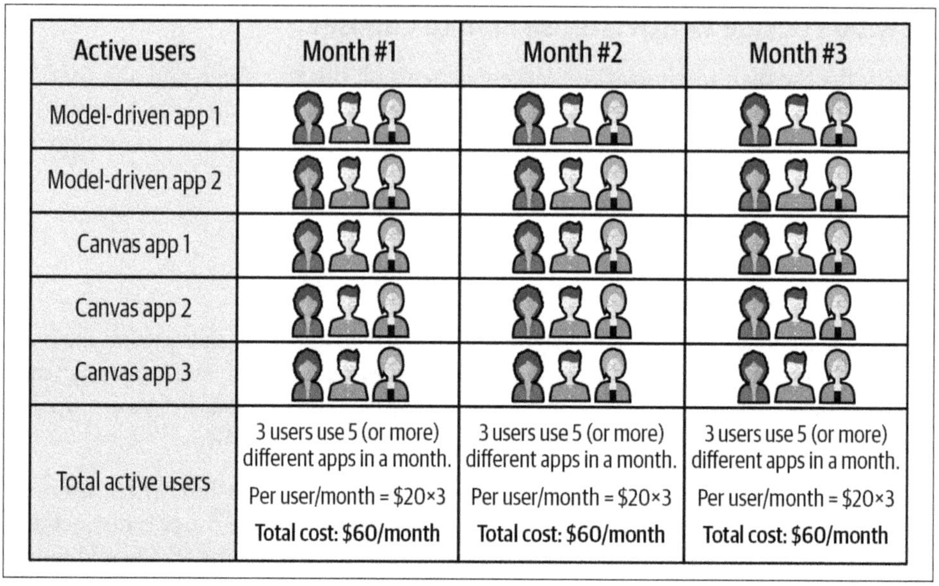

Active users	Month #1	Month #2	Month #3
Model-driven app 1			
Model-driven app 2			
Canvas app 1			
Canvas app 2			
Canvas app 3			
Total active users	3 users use 5 (or more) different apps in a month. Per user/month = $20×3 Total cost: $60/month	3 users use 5 (or more) different apps in a month. Per user/month = $20×3 Total cost: $60/month	3 users use 5 (or more) different apps in a month. Per user/month = $20×3 Total cost: $60/month

Figure 3-35. Power Apps licensing example 2

Scenario 3: The app's user count is unpredictable and fluctuates

Let's say my client wants to design an appraisal app that will allow appraisers to submit their goals and achievements as well as share feedback and ratings twice a year. There is no limit to the number of employees who will use this app. For some months, the app usage will be high, and for some months, it will be less. In such a situation, where the apps need to be used/shared by a large user base with infrequent and/or unpredictable use, you should use pay-as-you-go. (See Figure 3-36.)

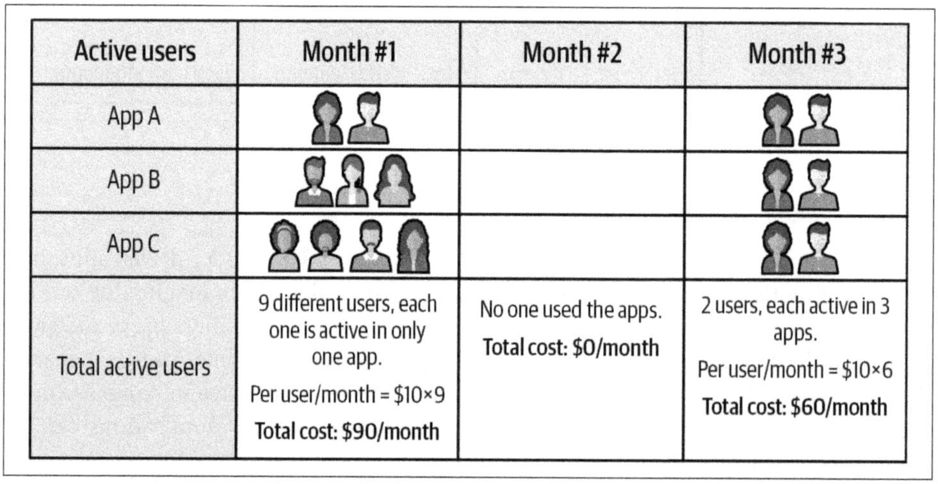

Active users	Month #1	Month #2	Month #3
App A			
App B			
App C			
Total active users	9 different users, each one is active in only one app. Per user/month = $10×9 Total cost: $90/month	No one used the apps. Total cost: $0/month	2 users, each active in 3 apps. Per user/month = $10×6 Total cost: $60/month

Figure 3-36. Power Apps licensing example 3

Scenario 4: You want to use your Azure subscription without purchasing an additional license

Pay-as-you-go is the best fit for scenarios where you already have an Azure subscription and do not want to purchase an additional license for Power Apps.

Scenario 5: You want to have flexible purchasing

The pay-as-you-go plan is the best fit when you are looking for flexible purchasing options and want to reduce the license procurement overhead every month.

Let's use mobile's data recharge plans, which include pre-paid (same as a Power Apps subscription plan) and post-paid (same as a Power Apps pay-as-you-go plan) options, as a practical example to better understand the Power Apps license plan. If you purchase a pre-paid plan to recharge or refill the internet data on your mobile device, you are already aware of who will use the internet data—you or a member of your family—and how much data will be consumed. And if it runs out, you have to recharge it again in the middle of the month.

But post-paid plans are purchased if internet data needs to be used on a larger scale, such as in a company with thousands of employees, as you are unable to predict how much internet data will be consumed by how many users each month. And unlike pre-paid plans, you want to reduce the plan procurement overhead every month.

Understanding Power Apps Licenses

Regardless of your role in your project team, you should have a basic understanding of licensing for the products you are using. Before starting app development, you should plan the licensing costs and convey them to your stakeholders so that you will have clarity regarding the features and components you are allowed to use.

Lack of Power Apps license knowledge can lead to the following issues:

Expensive app design
> One of the major reasons why people choose Power Apps is because it's cheaper than other products on the market, but a lack of knowledge of Power Apps licenses can lead to creating an expensive solution. For instance, say you want to build a canvas app that will enable salespeople and sales managers to track their sales data. Both groups will utilize features in the app that are essentially identical, with the exception that the sales managers will have access to all salesperson data and a screen to view sales performance. If you make two distinct canvas apps, one for salespeople and one for sales managers, your organization will have to spend money on two Power Apps per app plans: one for the app used by the salesperson and one for the sales manager.
>
> But, if you are aware of how building multiple apps would affect licensing, you can merge them into a single canvas app and save money by not needing to buy a second Power Apps per app license.

Additional development efforts and rework

If you use any features or components that don't add significant value for the business and are outside of your client's budget, the client may ask you to remove the features from the live app. This takes more work and development efforts. For instance, your client has a Power Apps per app license that allows them to use a single model-driven app to manage customer requests. They now want to develop a single-page external application that will allow their customers to submit questions and feedback, without having to buy any more licenses. You already know that Power Pages, which is used to develop websites for external customers, will be the best fit for this purpose. Without understanding the licensing and associated costs, you set up the portal in the environment. It will take too much work to remove all portal components from the environment if your customer refuses to use it since using it requires an additional Power Apps per app license.

Paying extra

It is occasionally more cost-effective to purchase components as a bundle or as part of a shared platform than to purchase them separately. You can use Power Automate within an app, for instance, if you have a Power Apps license. Yet, if you are unaware of this, you might buy a second license for Power Automate, paying extra for something that was included in your current license.

Losing business

Power Platform is a very large platform with a wide variety of tools, services, and applications that offer seamless connection with one another. The wrong licensing choice might cause you to lose business. As a result, you should choose licenses wisely depending on your company's needs. For instance, your customer wishes to enable unlimited application creation by users within the company. Unfortunately, you buy a per app license, which is inappropriate given the circumstances. Hence, in order to establish more Power Apps for the organization, you either need to modify the license type and make users wait while this is done, or you need to buy more Power Apps per app licenses.

For further information, read the Power Platform licensing FAQs (*https://oreil.ly/4JuG2*), which contain answers to common licensing questions.

Power Apps Trial and Developer Plan

Microsoft provides a free Power Apps trial environment to let developers and customers create and test Power Apps along with other components like Power Automate, Microsoft Copilot Studio, Power BI, Power Pages, Microsoft Dataverse, and many AI Builder capabilities.

There are many scenarios where you might need a Power Apps trial environment:

- You need the trial environment to create a POC for your prospective client. A POC or demo is usually required to allow the client to test the features that they wish to see in the final product. Knowing the product's limitations will also help you communicate those to the customer.

- Creating a trial environment is also beneficial for app developers who want to test new Microsoft updates and features before using them in a licensed environment.

- Trial environments are also beneficial for learning and sharing. You can learn about Power Apps and other components before starting to develop with them in a licensed environment. Additionally, you can also use a trial environment for training and other knowledge-sharing activities.

Microsoft provides two types of trial plans for Power Apps developers:

- Power Apps Plan Trial
- Power Apps Developer Plan (earlier known as Power Apps Community Plan)

Power Apps Plan Trial

Power Apps Plan Trial (*https://oreil.ly/QouCk*) is a free trial that gives you the Power Apps Premium plan for 30 days to explore the full capabilities of Power Apps with unlimited app creation. This trial allows you to try all the premium capabilities that are available with a Power Apps licensed plan. This trial expires after 30 days. However, if you need more time, you can extend the trial twice more for 30 days each, with a maximum trial length of 90 days.

Unlike Power Apps Developer Plan, Power Apps Plan Trial allows you to directly convert the trial to a production or licensed Power Apps Premium plan (as shown in Figure 3-37).

Figure 3-37. Convert Power Apps trial to production

Additionally, the trial plan is useful if you have already been using Power Apps with limited capabilities with an Office 365 or Dynamics 365 license (as discussed earlier) and want to try out the premium features or full capabilities of Power Apps before making the decision to purchase the Power Apps Premium plan.

Power Apps Developer Plan

Power Apps Developer Plan (*https://oreil.ly/pFvS3*) is the extended version of Power Apps Community Plan. It gives you access to all Power Apps capabilities, as does the trial plan, including Dataverse and Power Automate. Unlike the trial plan, Power Apps Developer Plan is meant for development and test environments only. It cannot be converted to production like the trial plan can.

You can view the type of your Power Platform environment by heading to the Environments area of the Power Platform admin center, as shown in Figure 3-38.

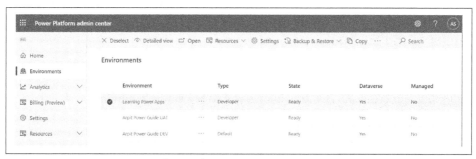

Figure 3-38. Power Apps Developer Plan

Power Apps Developer Plan's license doesn't expire after 30 days. You can keep using it without charge as long as components in the environment are being actively used. You should refrain from abusing the plan by developing apps for production usage or using more storage than is allowed by default. If a developer plan has been idle for 90 days or has not been used, it will be terminated automatically.

Furthermore, as the names suggest, the Power Apps Plan Trial and Developer Plan are not intended for your customer's actual project implementation, testing (sandbox), and live usage (production). Their main objective is to provide hands-on experience or experimentation with the Power Apps features, allow you to create POCs that show off the capabilities of the product to your clients, and for your own learning. For actual project implementation, you need to have the appropriate Dynamics 365, Microsoft 365, or Power Apps licenses based on your business needs, as mentioned in the previous section.

Once you have purchased an appropriate Power Apps license, you will require a separate environment for developing and testing your application. This environment type is known as a *sandbox environment*. Once your development and testing are completed, you will need another environment called the *production environment* for live usage, when your actual user will begin using your application.

 You don't get any Dynamics 365 apps (model-driven apps) as part of any of the Power Apps trial plans. Check out the Dynamics 365 trial plan (*https://oreil.ly/3eWfM*) if you wish to test out Dynamics 365 apps.

Power Apps Mobile Apps

You can run the Power Apps (model-driven and canvas) from your mobile/tablet devices by installing the Power Apps app from either the Google Play Store or the App Store (Figure 3-39).

You need to follow these instructions to install and access the apps on a mobile device:

1. Find Power Apps in the App Store or Play Store and install it. You'll find the Power Apps icon on your mobile device's home screen.
2. Log in to Power Apps with your Microsoft Entra ID account.
3. You will find a list of all the model-driven and canvas apps that you either own or that have been shared with you.
4. Open an app to start using it.

Figure 3-39. Installing the Power Apps mobile app on your mobile device

You can install the Power Apps app from the Microsoft Store as well for your Windows devices (as shown in Figure 3-40), same as for Android and iOS devices (Figure 3-41).

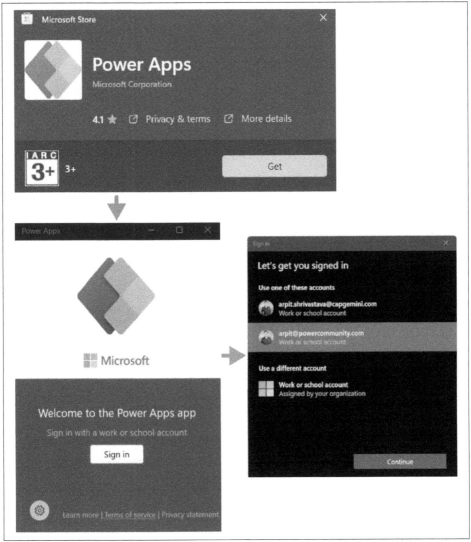

Figure 3-40. Download, install, and log in to Power Apps on a Windows device

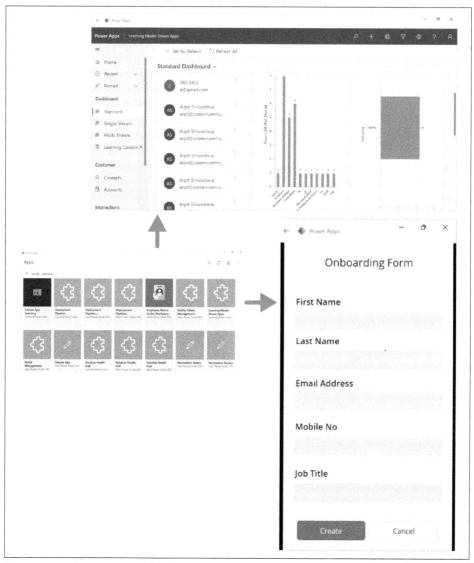

Figure 3-41. Opening a model-driven app and canvas app

Microsoft has provided a common mobile app (available in the App Store, Google Play Store, and Microsoft Store) to access all types of applications built on Power Apps. However, for a few Dynamics 365 customer engagement apps, like the Sales and Field Service apps, there is a separate mobile app (for example, Dynamics 365 Field Service mobile app, Dynamics 365 Sales app).

Table 3-8 lists the types of mobile apps you can download based on your business needs.

Table 3-8. Other types of mobile apps

Mobile app	Types of Power Apps you can run
Power Apps mobile	Model-driven apps Canvas apps Dynamics 365 Marketing Dynamics 365 Customer Service
Power Apps for Windows	Model-driven apps Canvas apps
Dynamics 365 for phone	Microsoft Dynamics 365 Customer Engagement (on-premises) Note: Dynamics 365 for Tablets is deprecated
Dynamics 365 Sales mobile	Dynamics 365 Sales
Field Service mobile	Field Service (Dynamics 365)

Summary

This chapter gave you a thorough introduction to Power Apps, its licensing, and its economic impact on diverse enterprises. You also learned about the collaborative development capabilities of Power Apps for the entire team, and, lastly, the Power Apps building blocks, which connect you to different components and resources so you can develop apps.

It's also very important to understand that Microsoft can change the naming conventions and branding of Power Apps screens and its components at any time. So, instead of relying on the app navigation and components depicted in various figures, please visit the Power Apps home page for the most up-to-date navigation options.

In the next chapter, I'll talk about fundamentals of data sources and connectors to explain how Power Apps communicates with various internal and external data sources via connectors.

CHAPTER 4

Data Sources and Connectors

Any business application needs a database, also known as a data source, to store the data. OneDrive for Business, Microsoft SQL, Excel, and Oracle are a few examples of frequently used databases. Power Apps uses Microsoft Dataverse to store data and also provides a variety of connectors that enable you to connect to various external data sources. In this chapter, you will learn the fundamentals of Power Apps data sources and connectors, their architecture, and their various types based on Power Apps types.

Introduction to Data Sources and Connectors

Data is the heart of any organization that stores information about its customers and employees. This data is needed by many business applications in your organization to make business decisions. Therefore, it needs to be stored and centralized somewhere so that various business applications can talk to it and perform various transactions like create, read, update, and delete.

The location or database where the business data is kept is referred to as a data source or database, and the channel or link via which that data source communicates with business applications is referred to as a *connection*. This connection between your business software and the data source is established using an API, which serves as middleware or a bridge and is referred to as a *connector* (see Figure 4-1).

Let's understand this using the LinkedIn app as an example. LinkedIn is a business- and employment-focused social media platform that stores its customer and business data in the LinkedIn data source. It doesn't let you view any data unless you provide valid credentials and log in. In the background, as soon as you log in, the LinkedIn App first makes a connection with the LinkedIn data source to validate your identity and then provides you access to view data through the LinkedIn app. The connection between the LinkedIn app and LinkedIn data source happens through APIs or middleware that takes the input from the LinkedIn app and passes it to the LinkedIn data source and then takes the response from the LinkedIn data source and passes it back to the LinkedIn app.

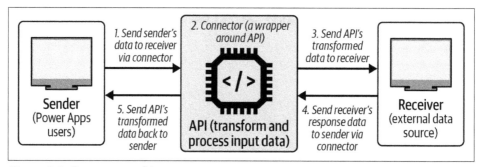

Figure 4-1. Connector architecture

APIs are typically used to establish communication between two different systems that are on two different platforms and don't understand each other's language. The most popular and well-known data formats that APIs use for data transmission are XML (Extensible Markup Language) and JSON (JavaScript Object Notation).

JSON is more widely used and accepted than XML since it is lighter in weight, has a simpler, easier-to-understand syntax, and transfers data more quickly.

Microsoft developed a new component called a *connector*, which is a wrapper around an API that encapsulates all API functions and provides an easy UI to send and receive data. Now you simply need to use the connector of the applicable data source, send the input data, and get the output data; you don't need to worry about how the API is developed and operates (see Figure 4-2).

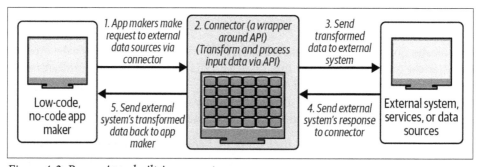

Figure 4-2. Power Apps built-in connectors

Power Apps distinguishes between primary data sources and secondary data sources. The *primary data source* is the main database on which any Power Apps run and where their business data is stored. For example, Dataverse is a primary database for a model-driven app. A *secondary data source* is an additional or external database that is often used in integration scenarios, where you need to bring external data into the primary data source. In some scenarios, there could be multiple primary databases. For example, canvas apps can use SharePoint for document management and SQL Server for contact and account data.

Data Sources for Model-Driven Apps

Model-driven apps can store data only in Microsoft Dataverse. Model-driven apps don't need a connector to connect with Dataverse because they are tightly coupled with Dataverse (see Figure 4-3).

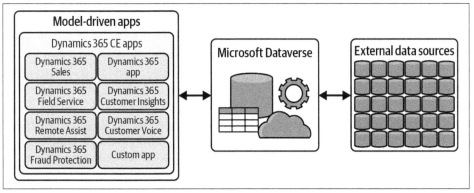

Figure 4-3. The primary data source of model-driven apps can only be Microsoft Dataverse

You can also integrate model-driven apps with external (secondary) data sources via various connectors like Oracle, SQL Server, Salesforce, Twitter, Facebook, Adobe, and Google. These connectors bring the data from external data sources into Microsoft Dataverse. In some cases, you don't need to store the external data in Microsoft Dataverse, but can directly retrieve it in your business app on the fly.

Data Sources for Canvas Apps

In canvas apps, you have the flexibility to choose your data source to store your app's data. The primary data source can be either Microsoft Dataverse or an external database such as Oracle, SQL Server, Salesforce, Twitter, Facebook, Adobe, or Google, as shown in Figure 4-4.

Data sources for canvas apps are grouped into three categories: tables, AI models, and connectors.

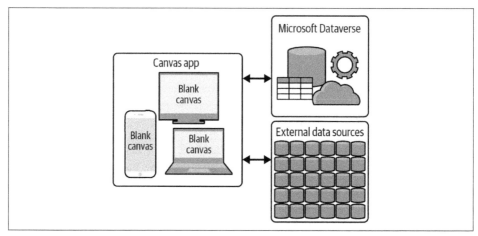

Figure 4-4. Primary data source of canvas app can be either Dataverse or another data source

Tables

You would choose the tables type of data source when you want to use Microsoft Dataverse as your primary data source. Tables display the list of all tables contained in Microsoft Dataverse for the environment, such as Account, Contact, Opportunity, Phone Call, Appointment. You can create a new table as well by clicking on "Create new table" from the "Select a data source" panel, as shown in Figure 4-5.

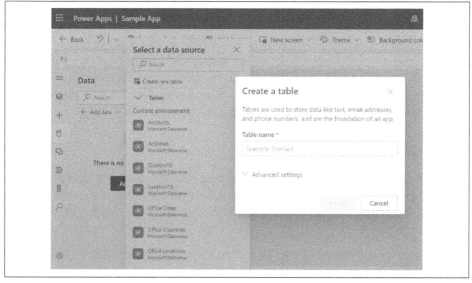

Figure 4-5. Table as data source in canvas app

Once you choose a Dataverse table from the list, such as the Account table shown in Figure 4-6, it will be added to the data source list (in the left panel). Then you can use it in your app to play around with its data.

Figure 4-6. Data source panel

You can now use the Account table as a data source for the Items property of the gallery to display the account data in the app, as shown in Figure 4-7.

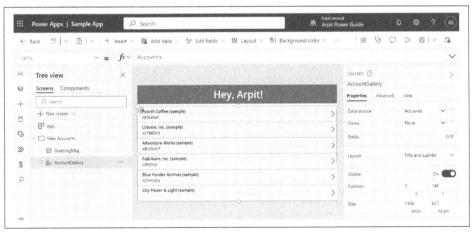

Figure 4-7. Using the data source in a canvas app Gallery control

AI Models

The AI Models feature gives apps AI capabilities such as a business card reader, sentiment analysis, and form processor. AI models also behave as data sources, processing the incoming data from your app to produce the appropriate results using a variety of built-in algorithms and machine learning capabilities. For instance, an AI model for sentiment analysis is trained to understand written text and translate it into appropriate sentiments. Hence, it will return positive if I write, "I had a fantastic day at the office today," and negative if I write, "I am not well today."

In Figure 4-8, there are lists of AI models available to use as data sources in a canvas app. I have added a "Sentiment analysis" AI model to the app for demonstration purposes.

Figure 4-8. Available AI models in a canvas app

I've added a new screen in the app along with a few text boxes, labels, and icons, as shown in Figure 4-9. The text boxes will allow users to enter the event's feedback, labels will be used to display the outcome of sentiment analysis, and icons are used to display the emoticons based on the feedback.

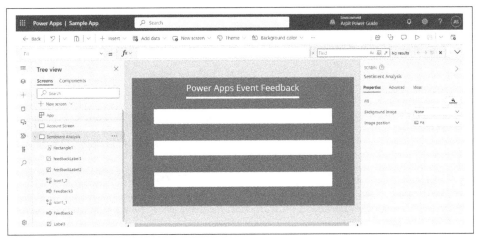

Figure 4-9. Sample app screen designed using textbox and label controls

I have used the following Power Fx expression on the Icon property of the Icon control to change its type based on the sentiment analysis outcome, as shown in Figure 4-10:

```
If(
    !IsBlank(Feedback1.Text),
    Switch(
        feedbackLabel1.Text,
        "positive",
        Icon.EmojiSmile,
        "negative",
        Icon.EmojiSad,
        Icon.EmojiNeutral
    )
)
```

This expression says that if the user-provided input is not blank and is positive, show a smiley emoticon 😃; if negative, show a sad emoticon ☹; otherwise, show a neutral emoticon 😐.

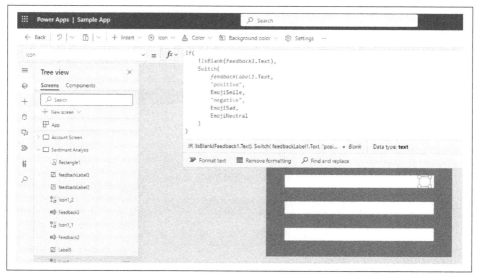

Figure 4-10. Power Fx expression on Icon control to change its type based on sentiment analysis outcome

I have used the following Power Fx expression on the Text property of the Label control to change its label message based on the sentiment analysis outcome, as shown in Figure 4-11:

```
If(
    !IsBlank(Feedback1.Text),
    Lower(
        'Sentiment analysis'.Predict(
            Feedback1.Text,
            {Language: "en-us"}
        ).Document.TopSentiment.Name
    ),
    "feedback not shared"
)
```

This expression says that if the user-provided input is not blank, then display sentiment feeling (positive, negative, neutral, etc.); otherwise, display "feedback not shared."

You will learn more about Power Fx expressions in Chapter 9.

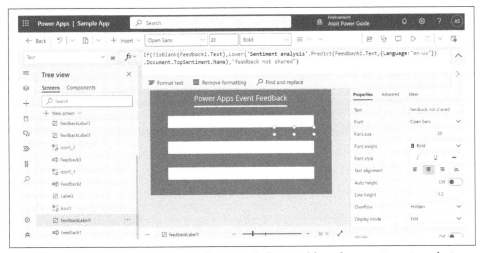

Figure 4-11. Power Fx expression to change Label control based on sentiment analysis outcome

And, finally, when I run the app from Power Apps Studio on a web browser, it displays the outcome, as shown in Figure 4-12.

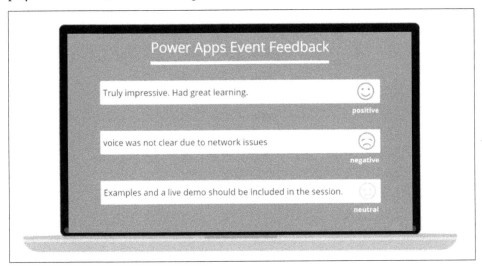

Figure 4-12. Canvas app output screen

Connectors

Canvas apps need connectors when they need to talk to any external data sources like Oracle, SQL Server, or Salesforce. As depicted in Figure 4-13, there are various connectors available that you can use.

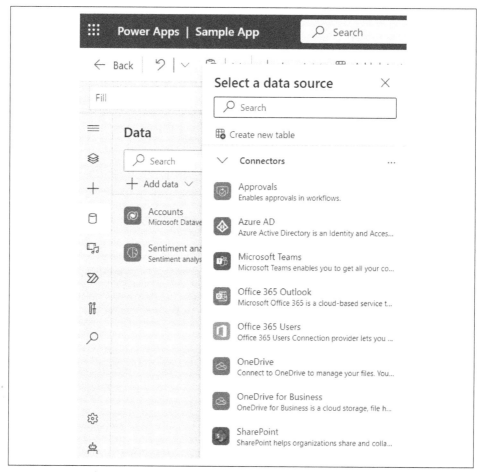

Figure 4-13. Built-in connectors available in Power Apps

For this demonstration, I have used the Microsoft Entra ID connector to create a new user in a Microsoft Entra ID (formerly Azure Active Directory) data source, as shown in Figure 4-14.

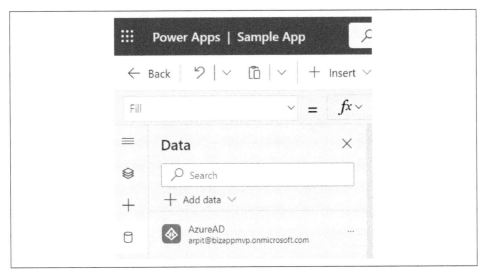

Figure 4-14. Adding a Microsoft Entra ID connector to the canvas app

To create a new user in Microsoft Entra ID, I have added a new screen, along with a few controls including a text box to take the user's input, a label to display header text, and a button to perform an action and submit data to the Microsoft Entra ID data source, as shown in Figure 4-15.

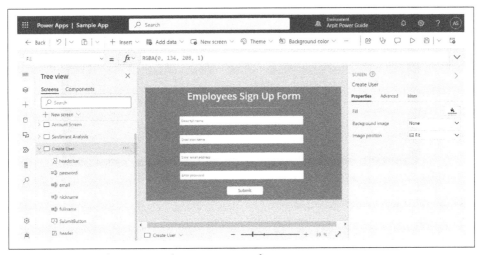

Figure 4-15. Sample screen to design a sign-up form

Then, I added a Power Fx expression to read values from the text box controls and create the user in Microsoft Entra ID, as shown in Figure 4-16.

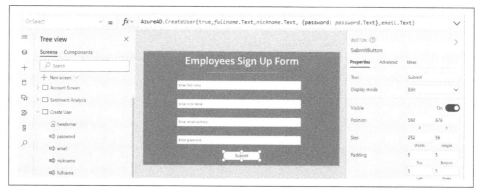

Figure 4-16. Power Fx expression on button control to create user in Microsoft Entra ID

Figure 4-17 shows what the app's screen looks like when I run the app through the Power Apps Studio in the web browser.

Figure 4-17. Canvas app output screen

In Figure 4-18, you can see that a new user has been created in Microsoft Entra ID with the specified details.

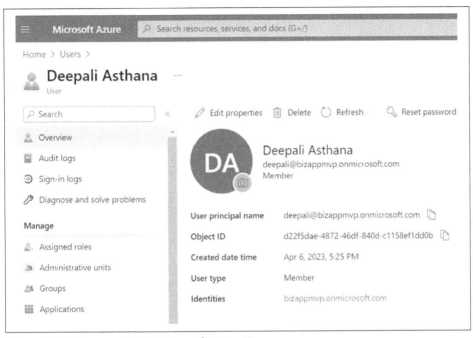

Figure 4-18. User created in Microsoft Entra ID

The Architecture of Power Apps Connectors

Connectors in Power Apps are SaaS-based components. That means you don't need to bother about what things are going on in the background to get your things done; everything is managed by the service provider, which is Microsoft Azure. You only need to pass the required input parameters to the connector and receive the output from it to further process it. How it makes the connection with the data source, how it stores the connection details, how information is being passed between your app and data sources—everything is taken care of by Microsoft Azure. See Figure 4-19 for the difference between IaaS, PaaS, and SaaS service providers.

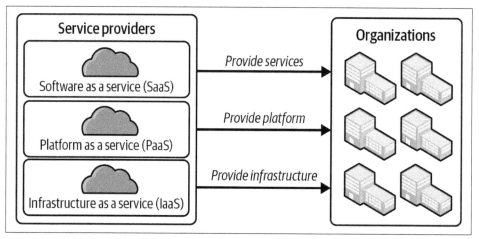

Figure 4-19. Types of cloud service providers

There are three main architectural components of connectors, as shown in Figure 4-20.

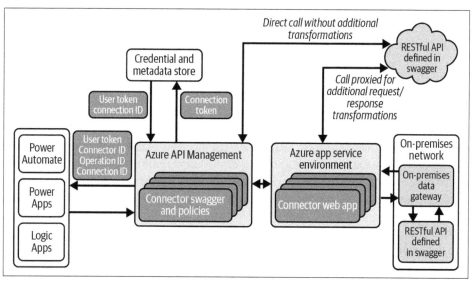

Figure 4-20. Connector architecture

Let's review these components in more detail:

Credential and metadata store

This essentially stores the connection information between your Power Apps and data source. For instance, for Power Apps to communicate with a Salesforce data source, you must first provide the relevant connection details of Salesforce. Depending on the platform or security architecture of the specific data source, these connection details may change. Some data sources require a URL, username, and password to connect, while others require API keys, client IDs, secret keys, etc. The credential and metadata store keeps track of your data source connection information so that Power Apps can communicate with the data source without your having to repeatedly enter the same connection information.

We previously used the LinkedIn app as an example. It only asks for your credentials the first time to connect your app to the LinkedIn data source. Your login information is stored locally going forward, so you won't have to enter it again. The credential and metadata store works in a similar fashion in the case of connector.

Azure APIM

This is the entry point of the connector. Each time a new request is made through the connector by Power Apps, the credential and metadata store is consulted to verify the connection information. If the information is accurate, it receives a *connection token* that Azure APIM uses to call the external data source API to execute the necessary operation in the data source. Any database will grant access to read its data based on your connection token, which is similar to a valid ID.

App service environment

By calling the external APIs, Azure APIM can execute actions directly in the relevant data sources. However, sometimes it is necessary to transform the data transferred between Power Apps and data sources to make it readable in corresponding data source formats. Additionally, there are occasions when Power Apps needs to communicate with on-premises data sources. So, there was a need to have a platform where developers can write their custom business logic and make custom web apps for the connectors (connector web apps). The result is Azure App Service (*https://oreil.ly/gt7wS*), a platform as a service (PaaS) offering that provides a way for developers to:

- Create custom apps based on ASP.NET, ASP.NET Core, Java, Ruby, Node.js, PHP, or Python

- Connect with on-premises data sources via data gateway (*https://oreil.ly/QfzOy*), Hybrid Connections (*https://oreil.ly/xLAfu*), or Azure virtual networks (*https://oreil.ly/FONbC*)

Types of Power Apps Connectors

Connectors are divided into three categories based on their usage, license, and publishers: standard, premium, and custom.

Standard Connectors

Standard connectors are used to connect with the most commonly used data sources (*https://oreil.ly/zZmNO*), such as Microsoft Entra ID, SharePoint, OneDrive, Dropbox, Google Drive, and Microsoft Teams (see Figure 4-21). Publishers of Standard connectors can be either Microsoft; a non-Microsoft entity such as Google, Adobe, or Facebook; or an individual. Some of the Standard connectors are also Premium in nature like Microsoft Dataverse. However, with all plans of Power Apps licensing, these connectors are completely free and open to use.

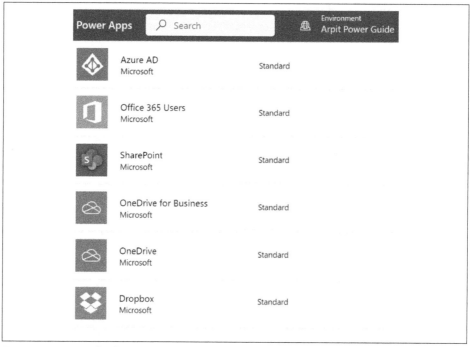

Figure 4-21. Standard connectors

Premium Connectors

Premium connectors (*https://oreil.ly/XBDLL*) are only available if you have a Power Apps Premium, Power Apps per app, Power Apps per app pay-as-you-go, or Dynamics 365 Professional and Enterprise license. Publishers of these connectors can be either Microsoft, non-Microsoft entities, or individuals, and include Microsoft

Dataverse, SQL Server, Salesforce, Adobe PDF Services, DocuSign, and Amazon. In Power Apps, all the connectors are in one list, but you can identify the Premium connectors by the "Premium" stamp next to the Publisher name (see Figure 4-22).

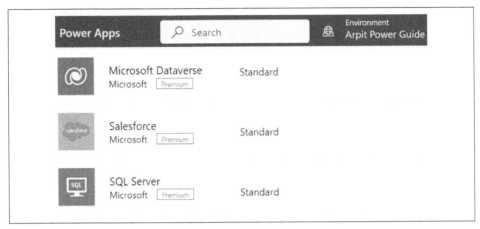

Figure 4-22. Premium connectors

Custom Connectors

Microsoft provides a wide variety of connectors. As of writing, the count is over one thousand, but it continues to increase. What happens when the available Standard and Premium connectors don't fit your needs? Sometimes, you might need to call an API or service or connect to a system that is not available as a prebuilt connector. In this situation, you can create your own connector, a *custom connector*. You can send your own connector to Microsoft for certification. If the connector satisfies certification requirements, Microsoft will examine it and give it the go-ahead for publication, making it publicly accessible for all users in Power Apps.

Custom connectors are a premium feature of Power Apps. So, if you wish to develop and use one, you must have a Power Apps Premium license.

For example, I want to create an app to make use of the COVID-19 APIs that my government has made available to allow the employees of my company to schedule vaccination appointments. The first API will accept a cellphone number as an input and return a one-time passcode to register a new user. The user's postcode will be entered into the second API, which will then display available vaccination slots nearby and reserve the appointment once the user approves the slot. To fulfill this requirement, I need to create a custom connector to call this API, as there isn't any prebuilt connector for it (Figure 4-23). Also, after it has been reviewed and authorized by

Microsoft, you can publish and make this connector publicly available for other companies.

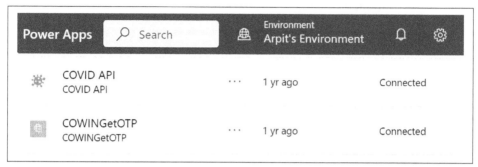

Figure 4-23. Custom connectors

Using Connectors Versus Calling an API

You might be wondering why you need to build a connector each time you need to call an API. Why can't you just use the API directly? There are two advantages of using connectors over directly calling an API:

Low-code, no-code capabilities
   Using connectors, even citizen developers can connect Power Apps with external systems without writing a single line of code. Remember the early days, when it used to require weeks or months to test a simple API provided by your client? You first had to prepare input parameters in the appropriate format (XML or JSON), then write code to send the input parameters to the appropriate API, and finally write code to parse the API's response, returned in either XML or JSON format, to make it available for your business apps. Now, instead of worrying about building code to parse and process the data, you can test the API using connectors and use it within business applications in less than an hour.

Reusability
   Connectors are an integration component that can be used by Azure Logic Apps, Power Automate, and Power Apps. Moreover, Power Automate and Logic Apps are trigger-based components that can be triggered by other Power Platform components like Power BI, Copilot Studio, Power Pages, and Azure components like APIM and Azure Functions. This means that once the connector is created, it can be used on both the Power Platform and Azure, as shown in Figure 4-24.

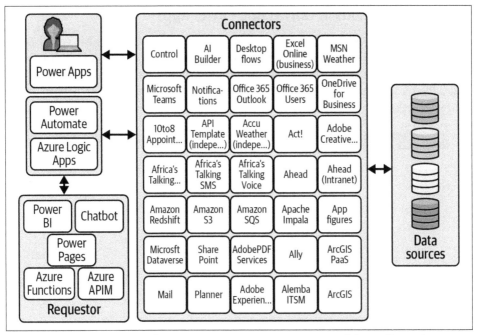

Figure 4-24. Connectors with Power Apps, Power Automate, and Azure Logic Apps

Components of Power Apps Connectors

You learned that connectors are used to establish the communication between your business apps and data sources. But *when* the connector should talk to the data source and *what* transaction or operation it should perform in the data source are described by its components.

Triggers and *actions* are the two primary components of any connector, as shown in Figure 4-25. Trigger specifies when the data source operation should be carried out, and action specifies which operation (create, update, delete, etc.) needs to be made in the data source. For example, in Figure 4-25, "When a new contact is created in Dataverse" is a trigger of the Dataverse connector, while "Send an email to the contact" is an action of the Outlook connector.

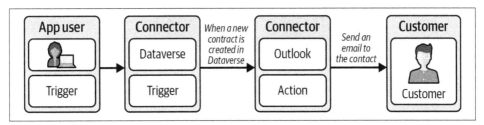

Figure 4-25. Trigger and action in connectors

Triggers and Actions in Canvas App Power Apps

As shown in Figure 4-26, in the left navigation panel, I have added a Microsoft Dataverse connector to create a contact in Dataverse and an Office365 Outlook connector to send an email to the customer. In the middle panel, I have added a blank screen and added a form to it. In the right navigation panel, I have set Contacts as a data source in order to create data in the Contacts table in Dataverse.

Figure 4-26. Adding a form to the canvas app screen

I have added the following Power Fx expression on the `OnSelect` property of the Button control, as shown in Figure 4-27:

```
SubmitForm(ContactForm);
Office365Outlook.SendEmailV2(emailTextInput.Text,"Contact Onboarding
    Confirmation","Dear User, Your onboarding is successfully completed");
```

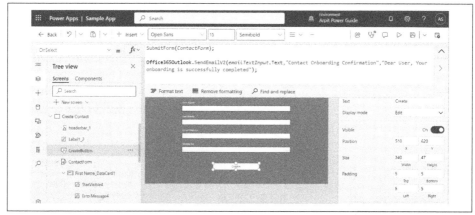

Figure 4-27. Power FX expression on Create button to perform operation (action) in data source

So here the trigger is when the user clicks on the Create button, and the action is to create data in Dataverse and send an email to the customer.

Triggers and Actions in Power Automate

As shown in Figure 4-28, I have added a Microsoft Dataverse connector that will trigger a Power Automate flow when a new contact is created in Dataverse, and an Outlook connector will perform an action by sending an email to that contact.

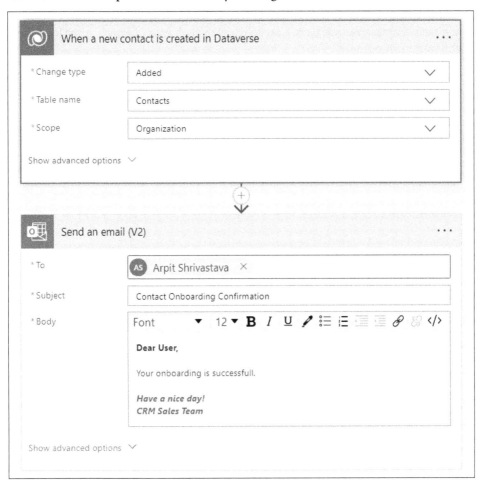

Figure 4-28. Trigger and action in Power Automate

Summary

In this chapter, you learned the fundamentals of the data sources and connectors used by Power Apps, as well as how different types of Power Apps interact with different data sources using various connectors. Additionally, you gained knowledge of the components, connector types, and architectural design of the connector.

This chapter demonstrated using Power Fx expressions to write business logic in a canvas app; however, I will dive into more depth in Chapter 9.

In the next chapter, you will learn how to decide which type of Power Apps is the best fit for your business needs.

CHAPTER 5

Determining Which Type of Power Apps to Make

As you learned in the previous chapters, model-driven apps and canvas apps are the two Power Apps options for building business applications. Each has unique features and advantages, so it is crucial to know which application is best for your organization.

The following are the considerations you have when designing an end-to-end business solution:

- How do I want the app to look and function?
- Should I use a canvas app, a model-driven app, or a combination of both?
- How will data be stored and retrieved from data sources?
- Where should I write business logic and store my data?
- Will I need to implement advanced features?

I'll go over several factors and business use cases in this chapter to help you decide whether to use a canvas app, a model-driven app, or a combination.

When to Use Model-Driven Apps

As discussed earlier, model-driven apps are best suited for process-driven and data-dense business apps that let users quickly navigate between related records. Apart from that, you should consider the following factors when deciding whether to use a model-driven app.

Data Stored in Microsoft Dataverse

Where the data will be stored is the first concern that arises before building the application. There are two potential solutions:

- Set up an entirely new database and store data in Dataverse.
- Use the client's existing database or any database other than Microsoft Dataverse, such as Oracle, SQL Server, Microsoft Entra ID, Microsoft Excel, SharePoint, or OneDrive.

While creating a new database, you can choose to use Microsoft Dataverse as the common data model. This gives you complete control over the data's structure, including how many tables and columns to construct, how the data will be connected to one another, etc. You can additionally make use of Power Query, data connectors, or custom APIs to bring in data from a variety of external data sources.

Model-driven apps are the ideal option for designing business apps using data stored in Dataverse since they are closely tied and significantly rely on the data model stored in Dataverse. No additional configuration is required to establish communication between the apps and Dataverse.

Model-driven apps, however, are not the ideal option if your customer wishes to build an app on top of a database other than Microsoft Dataverse (such as Excel, SharePoint, or SQL Server). A model-driven app gives you many options and provides components to build the app by bringing data from numerous data sources into Dataverse, but it does not provide you the option to substitute Dataverse with any other data sources.

Complex Business Logic

As you learned in earlier chapters, model-driven apps, which were initially created for professional developers, evolved from Dynamics 365 Customer Engagement (CE) apps. As a result, they offer a variety of native logic and code components for professional developers to help with writing business logic, including business rules, JavaScript, Dataverse Web API, plug-ins, real-time workflows, business process flows, calculated and rollup fields, WebHooks, service endpoints, command bar designer, custom pages, and data import/export via Excel.

Hence, model-driven apps are the best option to meet your needs whenever you have to write complex business logic that requires writing server-side code, client-side script, custom pages to display external system data, HTML, JavaScript-based pages, heavy business data transformation, and complex business logic writing.

Design Web-Based Apps for Internal Employees

Model-driven apps are best suited for designing web-based applications that run in the browser. Employees who work in offices and use desktop or laptop computers to manage complex business processes and customer data are best suited to use these apps. For example, to manage sales processes, the sales team needs to:

- Enter data in a consistent manner using a business process flow in forms
- View and filter sales data using views
- Associate different types of sales data, such as leads, opportunities, customers, quotes, invoices, orders, and products
- Track sales performance using dashboards
- Assign or share data with other salespeople or managers
- Secure data across business units using security roles
- …and much more

That doesn't mean model-driven apps can't be accessed by mobile devices. It's just that you can't alter their layout and user interface quite as much as you can with canvas apps, so the mobile version of a model-driven app (Power Apps mobile) will offer the same controls, navigation, and features as a web browser.

Limited App Layout, UI, Look and Feel Requirements

Model-driven apps are not UI extensible. That means all model-driven apps, whether custom or out of the box, offer a similar UI experience and layout. For instance, you can only put navigation controls on the left navigation panel (also known as the site map), the command bar (toolbar/menu) on the top navigation panel, and a company logo in the left top corner.

So, model-driven apps are a great option if you need to develop an app that is more focused on business processes and handling complicated logic than on customizing the UI and app layout.

As shown in Figure 5-1, you can customize your model-driven app as follows:

1. You can add navigation options in the left navigation panel.
2. You can display either views, a dashboard, custom pages, or external URLs in this area.
3. You can customize the toolbar and write your own business logic using either Power Fx or JavaScript. You can customize the similar toolbar in the model-driven app forms as well.
4. You can add a company logo using Themes (*https://oreil.ly/_ZqzA*).

5. You can change the navigation bar color and the colors of other form controls, like business process flow stages, hyperlinks, etc., using Themes.

Figure 5-1. Model-driven app layout

Moreover, Microsoft offers Power Apps component framework (PCF) controls, which enable professional developers to build unique components using TypeScript, React, HTML, and CSS. These elements can also be used to expand the model-driven app's user interface while adhering to the predetermined layout. To see all the custom controls made by different people to enhance the model-driven app Interface, see the PCF Gallery (*https://pcf.gallery*).

Automatically Responsive Apps Design

Model-driven apps provide a uniform user experience across a variety of devices, including desktop and mobile. Hence, these apps are automatically responsive. Tables, forms, views, charts, dashboards, and fields all adjust their appearance to fit the screen size of the device being used.

In contrast to canvas apps, model-driven apps don't require the use of containers or the writing of extra expressions to make them responsive. So, a model-driven app is the ideal option if you need to create a responsive app that can be used across all devices without the need for additional effort.

Complex Dataverse Security Requirements

As Microsoft Dataverse is the foundation for model-driven apps, it comes with built-in Microsoft Entra ID-based authentication and Dataverse security for business data authorization. When a user logs in using a Microsoft Entra ID account, different levels of security are made available, including at the environment, app, form, data, and column level (discussed in Chapter 2). In addition, Dataverse contains several additional security features and components, such as access teams, hierarchical security, and data loss prevention (DLP) rules. Model-driven apps are the best choice if you need such a granular level of security in your app.

Nevertheless, this doesn't mean that the canvas app is not secure or unfit for scenarios in which securing user data is crucial. All of the security features offered by model-driven apps are likewise supported by canvas apps if they also use Dataverse as their data source. However, other data sources, such as Excel, SQL Server, and SharePoint, don't have the same safety features as Dataverse.

Use Customer Engagement Apps

Model-driven apps have evolved from Dynamics 365 Customer Engagement (CE) apps, as you learned in Chapter 1; therefore, all Dynamics 365 CE apps are now model-driven apps. So, model-driven apps are the ideal option if you have needs that can be readily addressed by existing Dynamics 365 CE apps. You can use any of the model-driven apps listed in Table 3-4.

When to Use Canvas Apps

Canvas apps are best suited for mobile and tablet-based apps where you want to have complete control over the app's UI and UX, flexible data storage options, and use intuitive UI controls like barcode scanners, audio, cameras, galleries, and components, among other things, as well as for component-based collaborative development.

Unlike model-driven apps, canvas apps are also the best option for low-code, no-code citizen developers.

Apart from that, you should consider the following factors when deciding when to use the canvas apps.

Design an App from Scratch or Blank Canvas

In many business scenarios, the client wants to build an app from scratch and wants complete control over the UI, placement of controls on screen, and storage location of the data. Canvas apps are the best option in this case.

In contrast to model-driven apps, canvas apps can be created from scratch or blank screen and provide you the freedom to integrate different UI features in accordance with your organization's branding. Canvas apps' adaptable architecture prevents them from being automatically responsive. To make controls responsive, you must modify their characteristics (height, width, X/Y coordinates) and use controls like vertical and horizontal containers to make the app responsive for different devices.

Data Storage Flexibility Other Than Dataverse

If your customer wishes to store data somewhere other than Microsoft Dataverse, such as Microsoft Excel, SharePoint, OneDrive for Business, Microsoft Entra ID, or SQL Server, canvas apps are the ideal option. Over 1,000 data connectors are supported by canvas apps, allowing you to develop an app using data from other data sources. The various types of connectors have already been covered in Chapter 4.

To reuse data across app screens, canvas apps also offer temporary data storage locally called *collection*.

Control Over the App UI

Sometimes your customer is more concerned about the UI, the look and feel, and the layout of the controls displayed in the app, or wants to match the app branding with other apps in the company. Some common UI requirements are:

- Change the company logo alignment on the screen.
- Add a welcome screen, greeting message, and additional login or verification screens.
- Use icons for navigation instead of labels and buttons.
- Align the app's themes, font colors, control properties, etc., with those of other apps being used in the company, whether they are Power Apps-based or not.
- Create split screens to display left and right navigation panels.
- Display different types of controls on the same screens. For instance, you could need to show the sales target, to-do task list, appointments, and recent company news/announcements on the home screen.

The canvas app is the best option for fulfilling such requirements.

Template-Based App Development

There are numerous occasions when you need to create an app for which Microsoft has already provided a template. Instead of having to design the app from scratch, you can develop the app from the template, and then edit the controls, change the branding, and connect to the right data source to quickly adapt it to your needs. These templates are also helpful for learning about canvas apps, understanding how to use controls, and designing screens.

Some of the most common templates are shown in Figure 5-2.

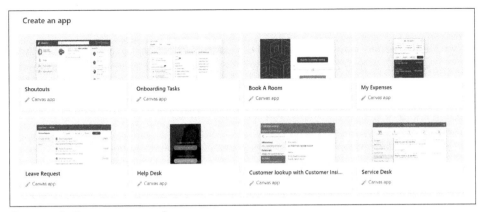

Figure 5-2. Canvas app templates

Design Mobile Apps for Internal Employees

The ideal option for designing mobile apps if you want complete control over the UI and layout is a canvas app. Then, why do we sometimes choose model-driven mobile apps (Power Apps mobile) over canvas apps?

Because model-driven apps work well on mobile devices and tablets when you want to reuse an existing model-driven app feature that you might not want to re-create in a canvas app. Some of these features, which come out-of-the-box when you use model-driven apps on mobile devices, are:

- Site map
- Search
- Relationship assistant
- Out-of-the-box views
- Out-of-the-box forms, tabs, sections
- Quick Create option
- Subgrids
- Custom controls
- Dashboards and charts
- Record actions (export to Excel, assign, merge, delete, deactivate, unfollow)
- Work offline without any additional customization
- View recently visited rows
- Pin rows
- App selector to switch between different apps

When to Embed a Canvas App in a Model-Driven App

As you have learned from our previous discussions, there are several types of Power Apps, and each one may be used to create a business solution. You might occasionally wish to integrate a canvas app with a model-driven app to take advantage of the functionality of the canvas app (but vice-versa is not possible). These are some scenarios where it could be necessary to integrate a canvas app with a model-driven app:

- Display data from external systems and perform the CRUD operation.
- Display Dataverse-related table data and perform CRUD operation without navigating away from the original screen.
- Create rich visual areas on a model-driven app form and display data from a variety of sources right next to data from Microsoft Dataverse.
- Enhance the data visualization of the Microsoft Dataverse data. For example, using an embedded canvas app, you can display related contacts of any account in hierarchical format by displaying their profile images along with other details (as shown in "Steps to Embed a Canvas App in a Model-Driven App Form" on page 132) instead of using native subgrid control.
- Reuse data or show the same data or content across several forms—integrating a canvas app is a preferred option.
- View data from child tables by doing deep level nesting on the form, without leaving the current screen. For instance, you wish to view the connected contacts of an account, opportunities linked to a particular contact, products related to a certain opportunity, and so on.
- Use a control or feature that is not available in a model-driven app, such as a PDF viewer or a timer.

Guidance on Embedding Canvas Apps

The following are tips to remember when embedding canvas apps:

- In the left pane of Power Apps Studio, you'll see a unique ModelDrivenFormIntegration control, as shown in Figure 5-3. Contextual information is transferred to the embedded canvas app by this control from the host model-driven form.

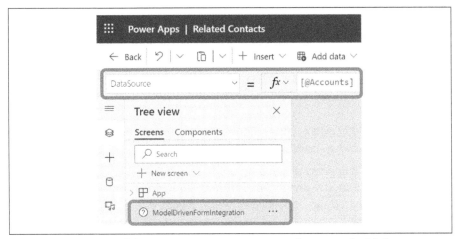

Figure 5-3. Using ModelDrivenFormIntegration control in an embedded canvas app

- The embedded canvas app has full access to read from the host model-driven form via `ModelDrivenFormIntegration.Item`. For example, `ModelDrivenForm Integration.Item.accountnumber` or `ModelDrivenFormIntegration.Item.'Ac count Number'`.

- The `ModelDrivenFormIntegration.Item` object is read-only. You must make use of the Microsoft Dataverse connector to write data back to Dataverse.

- The ModelDrivenFormIntegration control doesn't provide a value for columns of a related table. For example, when the ModelDrivenFormIntegration control is connected to the Accounts table, using `ModelDrivenFormIntegration.Item. 'Primary Contact'.'Full Name'` will not return a value. To access columns of a related table, you can use one of these expressions:

```
LookUp(Accounts, Account = GUID(First(ModelDrivenFormIntegration.Data).
            ItemId)).'Primary Contact'.'Full Name'
```

or

```
LookUp(Accounts, Account = ModelDrivenFormIntegration.Item.Account).'Primary
            Contact'.'Full Name'
```

- Although there can be multiple embedded canvas apps added to a form, only three can be enabled at once for web clients and only one at a time for tablet and phone clients. If there are more than three embedded canvas apps enabled with the web client type, the following error message will display: "The maximum number of canvas apps you can have with the Web form factor is three. Three canvas apps are available for the web and one each for the tablet and phone form factors."

- Any modifications you make to the embedded canvas apps must be published separately from the host model-driven forms.

- Always use a required column that's guaranteed to have a value when adding an embedded canvas app to a model-driven form. If your column is empty, any data changes made to the host model-driven form won't cause your embedded canvas app to refresh.

- Since embedded canvas apps require a row context to be passed to them, they are not displayed when creating a new row or record.

- If the error "It appears that you do not have access to this app" displays when you are viewing a model-driven form with an embedded canvas app, make sure the author has shared the embedded canvas app with you.

- Modifications made in the embedded canvas app are not saved when a save event is made from a model-driven app, such as selecting the Save button on the main form command bar. Use the Dataverse connector to save changes made in an embedded canvas app.

- The option to embed a canvas app into a model-driven app is only present on forms for model-driven apps. You must use the canvas app URL to open the app if you want to embed it in other places in the model-driven app, such as the dashboard, or if you want to open it in a pop-up or dialog upon clicking the command bar.

- The model-driven app and the embedded canvas app are collectively recognized as one app. As a result, using an embedded canvas app with a model-driven app does not require having multiple Power Apps per app plan (as discussed in Chapter 3).

Steps to Embed a Canvas App in a Model-Driven App Form

The canvas app can be embedded in a model-driven app form using either the modern form designer or the classic form designer. The modern form designer is a new form designer based on modern UI within Microsoft Power Apps that enables users to design and customize forms for model-driven apps, while classic form designer is part of a legacy interface used for designing forms in the Dynamics 365 platform.

The only difference between the two while embedding the canvas app is that the customize option in the classic form designer allows you to directly create or edit a canvas app in the Power Apps Studio from a model-driven app form. When using the modern UI form designer, you don't get this option; therefore, you must manually copy the canvas app's ID and name to embed it in model-driven app forms.

Figure 5-4 shows an example of an embedded canvas app on the Account main form used to display the Contacts of an Account in a rich, interactive visual gallery format.

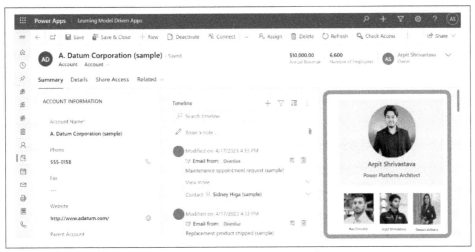

Figure 5-4. Embed canvas app to display related contacts of an account

Perform the following steps to embed a canvas app in a model-driven app using classic form designer (the first three steps are shown in Figure 5-5 and the next five steps are shown in Figure 5-6):

1. In the classic form designer, select the section on the form where you want the embedded canvas app to appear (see Figure 5-5).

2. Using the Column pane, add a required column, such as Account Name.

3. With the column selected, on the Home tab go to the Edit group, and select Change Properties.

Figure 5-5. Choosing the required column on the form where you want to add canvas app control

4. In the Column Properties dialog box, select the Controls tab (see Figure 5-6).

5. On the Controls tab, select Add Control.

6. In the Add Control dialog box, in the list of available controls, select "Canvas app" and then select Add.

7. In the Column Properties dialog box, in the list of controls, select "Canvas app" and then select the Web option.

8. If you are creating a new canvas app or editing an existing one, select Customize to create or edit a canvas app. This opens Power Apps Studio in a new tab.

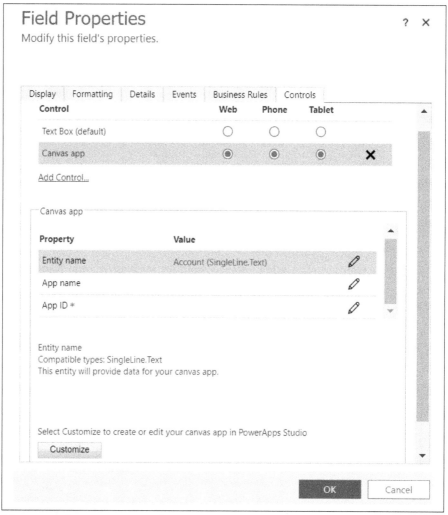

Figure 5-6. Canvas app control

9. In Power Apps Studio notice that there is a special *ModelDrivenFormIntegration* control in the left pane, as shown in Figure 5-3. This control is responsible for bringing contextual data from the host model-driven form to the embedded canvas app.

10. Add a new screen and the following controls to display Primary Contacts and other associated contacts of a particular account, as shown in Figure 5-7:

Image (1)
　　To display the primary contact image

Rectangle (2)
　　To set the background color

Text label (3)
　　To display the primary contact name

Text label (4)
　　To display the primary contact job title

Horizontal gallery (5)
　　To display all associated contacts

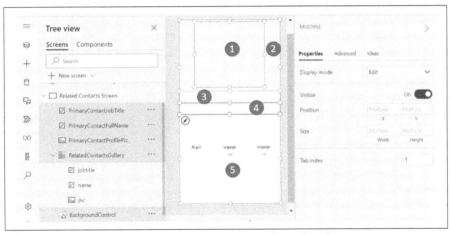

Figure 5-7. Designing a canvas app screen to visualize related contacts

11. Change the gallery layout to the "Title and subtitle" (*https://oreil.ly/YUHO3*) type, as shown in Figure 5-8, and set the following:

- Image: `ThisItem.'Entity Image'`
- Title: `ThisItem.'Full Name'`
- Subtitle: `ThisItem.'Job Title'`

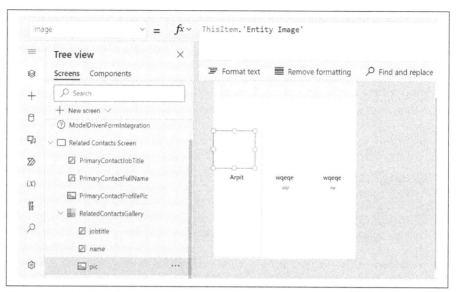

Figure 5-8. Adding a horizontal gallery to display related contact details

12. Use the following Power Fx expression, as shown in Figure 5-9, to display the primary contact image:

```
LookUp(Accounts, Account = ModelDrivenFormIntegration.Item.Account).'Primary
        Contact'.'Entity Image'
```

Figure 5-9. Using a Power Fx expression to retrieve an account's primary contact image

13. Use the following Power Fx expression, as shown in Figure 5-10, to display all associated contacts of an account:

```
Filter(Contacts, AsType('Company Name',[@Accounts]).Account =
        [@ModelDrivenFormIntegration].Item.Account)
```

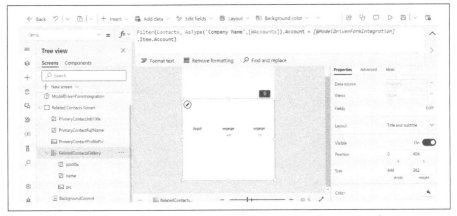

Figure 5-10. Using a Power Fx expression to retrieve related contacts of an account

The Power Fx expression `ModelDrivenFormIntegration.Item` gives you the current account record context, through which you can get the column's values available on the form. For example, `ModelDrivenFormIntegration.Item.Account` gets the current account record GUID.

However, you can't retrieve the related table data using `Model DrivenFormIntegration`. You need to either use a `Lookup` or `Filter` expression. In our case, Primary Contact is a lookup column that refers to the Contacts table. To retrieve the value from columns Entity Image, Full Name, and Job Title of Primary Contact, I have used a `Lookup` expression.

14. Select the File tab, and then select Save.

15. Select the Cloud tab, provide a unique name for the app, and then select Save located on the lower right.

16. Publish the app.

17. Select the browser tab that has the classic form designer open. Observe that the App ID and App Name properties of the canvas app control now have a value automatically filled in, as shown in Figure 5-11. You'll notice a Customize button located at the bottom of the dialog, which is currently exclusive to the classic form designer. This feature enables developers to edit the canvas app directly from the classic form designer, bypassing the need to navigate to the Power Apps home page. Click OK to save the details, close the dialog box, and return back to form designer.

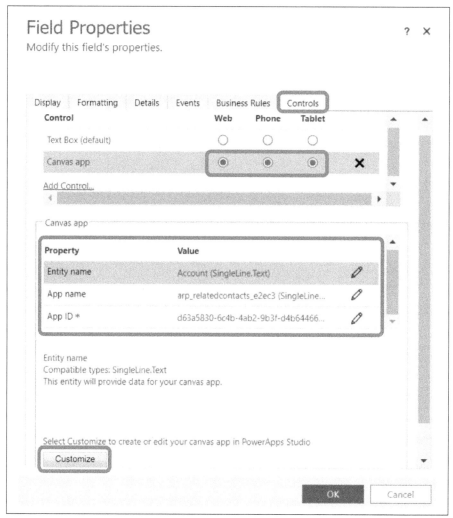

Figure 5-11. Canvas app control autopopulated with App ID and App Name

18. Save and then Publish the model-driven app form.

19. Press Ctrl + F5 to refresh the app page/form to view the embedded canvas app on the account form.

20. Once you've successfully published an embedded canvas app onto your model-driven form, proceed to share it with other users. For further details, refer to the documentation on how to share an embedded canvas app (*https://oreil.ly/WMNbE*).

In my experience, embedding a canvas app with a model-driven app may put limitations on the size of the app, branding, and the ability to pass complex data as parameters from the current form and associated tables. Additionally, the ID of the embedded canvas app must be stored somewhere in your configuration table or in an environment variable, or changed manually each time it is deployed to a different environment.

In this situation, you should use either custom pages or iframe-based integration. As of this writing, custom pages doesn't support embedded features the same way that canvas app and iframe do; it can only be displayed as a side pane or dialog box.

An iframe-based control is the best choice for complex integration scenarios that require the ability to send contextual data from the current form and related tables using the Dataverse Web API, as well as the display of external application content or pages within a model-driven app form. You should add inline frames (iframes) to a form (*https://oreil.ly/cwFg9*) to integrate content or a page from another website within the form. You can also open an iframe on demand from the command bar using openWebResource (Client API reference) (*https://oreil.ly/KgL03*).

Power Apps Decision Tree

The Power Apps decision tree shown in Figure 5-12 is a summary of what we discussed when deciding which app type is the best choice to meet your business needs. You can get the full-sized version of this image from the book's GitHub repo (*https://oreil.ly/pvoZI*).

Apart from that, you should also look through the Power Apps features before making your final decision about the app selection. Canvas apps provide some features that don't exist in model-driven apps. These include collections, AI Builder, Test Studio, component library, GitHub-based collaborative development, page templates to change the app layout, and the ability to create apps using Figma design, sketches, and natural languages. I will be discussing these features in Chapter 8.

Conversely, some features supported by model-driven apps are not available for canvas apps. These include single- and multi-stream dashboard, custom pages, web resource, JavaScript, business process flow, real-time flows, plug-ins, actions, routing rules, SLAs, complex table relationships, connections roles, email templates, duplicate detection, and bulk deletion job. Additionally, because model-driven apps originated from Dynamics 365 CE apps, there are already many apps available that provide processes, features, and components to meet your requirements.

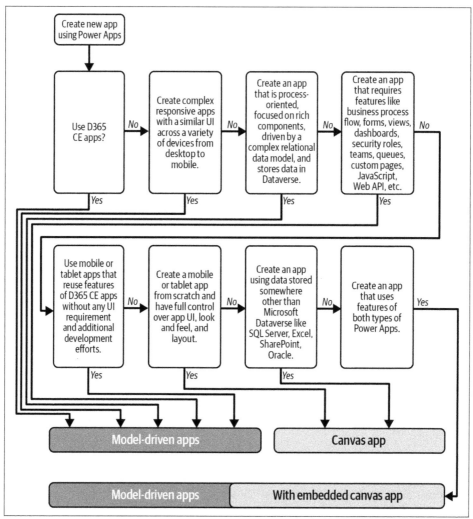

Figure 5-12. Power Apps decision tree

Sometimes choosing between a canvas app and a model-driven app depends on the distinctive features that each app provides. So you might not always want to replicate a feature in your custom app that is already present in a different kind of app.

Switching App Types

When starting your app creation, you should pick the most suitable app type by carefully reviewing the requirements. It's difficult to switch between app types later because they use different UI controls, layouts, and features. That said, if you do have to switch app types, you must categorize your work as follows:

App UI

Because controls in model-driven apps differ from those in canvas apps, the UI cannot be reused across different apps. In canvas apps, some model-driven app controls are not available and vice versa. As a result, you will need to redesign the entire app and may even need to make your own controls.

App storage

If your data is structured and kept in Microsoft Dataverse, app storage can be reused. Nevertheless, to perform Dataverse activities in the canvas app, you must use the Microsoft Dataverse connector. If the canvas app uses a different data source, it cannot be transformed to a model-driven app until the data is synchronized with Dataverse, as Dataverse is the only data source that can be used as the primary data source for model-driven apps.

Business logic

There are some similar and some different approaches to building business logic in both types of apps. Model-driven apps allow you to develop business logic using many different components, including Power Fx, JavaScript, Dataverse Web API, custom pages, form-level business rules, business process flow, plug-ins, flows, and a lot more. Power Fx expressions, connectors, and Power Automate are used by the canvas app to provide business logic. When using Microsoft Dataverse to store the data, canvas apps occasionally leverage the same logic components as model-driven apps, such as plug-ins, and flows. All the logic components must be checked once more to ensure they are still supported by the individual app before writing the same business logic from scratch.

Power Apps Patterns

With Microsoft Power Apps, you can easily create apps tailored to the particular requirements of your company. Your needs may be unique, but there are common patterns in the apps that businesses frequently develop to address their most pressing requirements. Let's look at examples of the most common use cases for Power Apps.

Event Management

Businesses can use Power Apps for event management. These events could take the form of trainings, bootcamps, conferences, hackathons, seminars, or knowledge-sharing sessions, or they could be anything else that requires a host, organizers, speakers, trainers, coordinators, and volunteers. Such events often require an end-to-end solution where attendees can register for the event, organizers and administrators can manage the event, and so on.

Event coordinators, organizers, and admin departments often use model-driven apps to handle internal data processing and event administration, with a dashboard for monitoring and tracking the event data. Speakers, attendees, and volunteers may use the canvas app for a variety of purposes, such as sharing event feedback and tracking the status of submitted sessions. Figure 5-13 shows a sample event management app.

Figure 5-13. Sample event management app

Where can I use model-driven apps?

In creating an event management app, tables (entities) store essential data like event details, attendees, and venues. Forms provide interfaces for inputting and accessing this data, ensuring smooth user interaction. Business rules enforce validation and automate processes such as attendee registration. Dashboards offer visual insights into event metrics and attendance trends. Business process flows streamline workflows, guiding users through event planning and execution. Security roles ensure data integrity by controlling access levels, while charts visualize data for comprehensive analysis, aiding in decision making and optimization of event management processes.

Where can I use canvas apps?

Canvas apps offer diverse controls and features to build an event management app. Use galleries for displaying event lists, forms for attendee registration, and calendars for scheduling. Leverage features such as data connectors to integrate with calendars, notifications for event updates, and geolocation for venue mapping. Implement QR code scanning for check-ins and payment processing for ticket sales. Through these elements, the canvas app facilitates seamless event planning, attendee engagement, and logistical management within an intuitive user interface.

Lifecycle or Workflow Management

You can use Power Apps to track and follow a well-defined process such as employee onboarding, employee promotion evaluation, request management, helpdesk ticket management, contract lifecycle tracker, and expense reporting. Figure 5-14 shows a sample workflow management app.

Figure 5-14. Sample lifecycle or workflow management app

Where can I use model-driven apps?

In a lifecycle workflow management app for project managers and team members, tables (entities) store project details, tasks, and team member information. Forms facilitate data entry and updates, while business rules enforce project guidelines and automate task assignments. Dashboards provide a comprehensive view of project progress and resource allocation. Business process flows guide users through project stages, ensuring adherence to protocols. Security roles control access levels, safeguarding sensitive project data. Charts visualize project metrics, aiding in performance analysis and decision making, enhancing collaboration and productivity within the project lifecycle.

Where can I use canvas apps?

Canvas apps offer a range of controls and features ideal for building a lifecycle or workflow management app. Leverage galleries for displaying tasks, forms for data entry, and drop-down lists for selecting project stages. Utilize features such as data connectors for integrating with project management tools, notifications for task updates, and timers for tracking task durations. Implement swipe gestures for task management and barcode scanning for inventory tracking. Through these elements, the canvas app streamlines project workflows, enhances collaboration, and improves efficiency for project managers and team members.

Scheduling

You can use Power Apps to show resource (assets, people, tools, etc.) availability, allow users or customers to book appointments, and schedule resources based on calendar availability—all common business requirements. Additional requirements might include booking meeting rooms, vehicles, doctor appointments, apartment inspection appointments, building and construction site inspections, and so on. Figure 5-15 shows a sample meeting scheduling app.

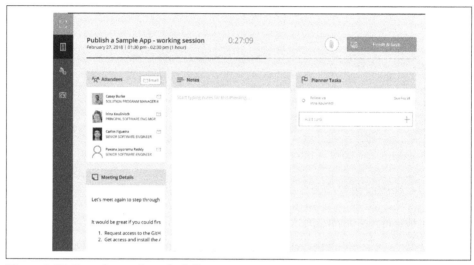

Figure 5-15. Sample meeting scheduling app

Where can I use model-driven apps?

In creating a scheduling app, tables store data on appointments, resources, and availability. Forms enable users to input and manage scheduling details, while business rules ensure data accuracy and enforce scheduling constraints. Dashboards provide an overview of upcoming appointments and resource utilization. Business process flows guide users through scheduling workflows, from appointment creation to confirmation. Security roles control access to scheduling information. Charts visualize scheduling data for insights into trends and optimization. Workflows automate notifications and reminders. JavaScript enhances app functionality, allowing for customization and integration with external systems.

Where can I use canvas apps?

Canvas apps offer versatile controls and features for developing a scheduling app. Use controls such as calendars for visualizing appointments, drop-down lists for selecting time slots, and buttons for booking or canceling appointments. Leverage data connectors to integrate with calendars or scheduling systems, notifications for reminders, and GPS for location-based scheduling. Implement drag-and-drop for rescheduling appointments and barcode scanning for check-ins. Through these elements, the canvas app streamlines scheduling processes, enhances user experience, and ensures efficient appointment management.

Approvals

You can use Power Apps to manage single-level and multi-level approvals. Examples include leave requests, employee travel requests, overtime requests, time sheets, and desk or computer bookings. Figure 5-16 shows a sample leave request app.

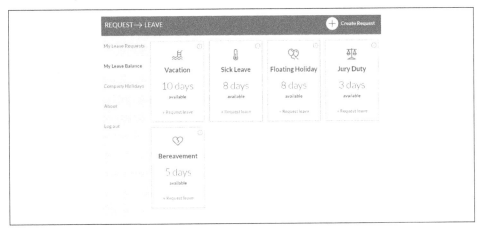

Figure 5-16. Sample leave request app

Where can I use model-driven apps?

To create an approval app, tables store data on requests, approvers, and approval statuses. Forms enable users to submit requests and review pending approvals. Business rules validate request data and enforce approval criteria. Dashboards provide an overview of pending and completed approvals. Business process flows guide requests through approval stages. Security roles control access to sensitive approval data. Charts visualize approval metrics for analysis. Workflows automate notification of approval actions. JavaScript can enhance app functionality, such as dynamic form behavior or custom approval workflows.

Where can I use canvas apps?

Canvas apps offer diverse controls and features for building an approval app. Use forms for request submission, galleries for displaying pending approvals, and buttons for approving or rejecting requests. Leverage data connectors to integrate with approval systems, notifications for alerting users of pending actions, and timers for tracking response times. Implement conditional visibility to show relevant information based on approval status and drop-down lists for selecting approvers. Through these elements, the canvas app streamlines approval processes, enhances user productivity, and ensures efficient decision making.

Asset Management

Power Apps can be used to manage inventory or other assets in the organization. Examples include asset checkout, asset rollout, supply order management, and inventory management. Figure 5-17 shows a sample asset checkout app.

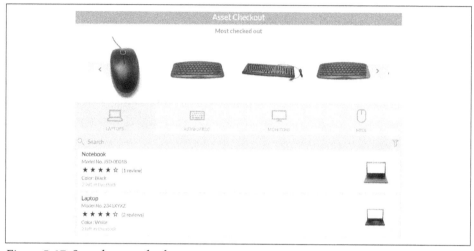

Figure 5-17. Sample asset checkout app

Where can I use model-driven apps?

To develop an asset management app, tables store data on assets, maintenance records, and user assignments. Forms facilitate data input and updates, while business rules enforce validation and automate asset tracking processes. Dashboards provide visual insights into asset utilization and maintenance schedules. Business process flows guide asset lifecycle workflows from procurement to disposal. Security roles control access to sensitive asset information. Charts visualize asset data for analysis and decision making. Workflows automate notifications for maintenance tasks and asset status changes. JavaScript enhances app functionality, enabling customizations and integrations with external systems.

Where can I use canvas apps?

Canvas apps provide an array of controls and features for building an asset management app. Use galleries to display assets, forms for data entry and updates, and barcode scanners for asset identification. Leverage data connectors to integrate with asset databases, GPS for tracking asset locations, and notifications for maintenance reminders. Implement image controls for visual asset identification and drop-down lists for categorizing assets. Through these elements, the canvas app streamlines asset tracking, improves maintenance efficiency, and enhances overall asset management processes.

Calculation/Transformation

You can use Power Apps for complex calculations and transforming data. Examples include cost estimation, project estimation, calculating discounts, and tracking monthly sales goals. Figure 5-18 shows a sample budget tracker app.

Figure 5-18. Sample budget tracker app

Where can I use model-driven apps?

To create a calculation or transformation app, tables store input data and calculated results. Forms allow users to input data and view outputs, while business rules ensure data integrity and enforce calculation logic. Dashboards provide visualizations of calculated metrics and trends. Business process flows guide users through transformation workflows. Security roles control access to sensitive calculation data. Charts visualize data transformations for analysis. Workflows automate calculation processes and notifications. JavaScript enhances app functionality, allowing for custom calculations and dynamic interactions.

Where can I use canvas apps?

Canvas apps offer a range of controls and features ideal for building a calculation or transformation app. Use input fields for user input, labels to display calculated results, and buttons to trigger calculations. Leverage formulas to perform calculations, variables to store intermediate results, and galleries to display transformed data. Implement sliders for adjusting parameters and charts for visualizing transformation outputs. Through these elements, the canvas app facilitates dynamic calculations and transformations, providing users with a streamlined and interactive experience.

Communication/Announcement

Many companies use Power Apps for communication purposes like publishing or announcing news to employees or customers. Examples include corporate news management, announcement viewer, HR communicator app, product catalogs, and learning catalogs. Figure 5-19 shows a sample shoutout app.

Figure 5-19. Sample shoutout app

Where can I use model-driven apps?

In developing a communication or shoutout app, tables store data on shoutouts, user profiles, and message logs. Forms facilitate shoutout creation and interaction. Business rules ensure proper message delivery and adherence to communication policies. Dashboards provide insights into shoutout engagement and user participation. Business process flows guide the shoutout communication process. Security roles control access to sensitive data. Charts visualize shoutout metrics. Power Automate automates shoutout delivery. JavaScript and plug-ins enhance app functionality, allowing for customization and integration with external systems.

Where can I use canvas apps?

Canvas apps provide versatile controls and features for building a shoutout or communication app. Use controls like text inputs for composing messages, galleries for displaying shoutouts, and buttons for sending or reacting to messages. Leverage data connectors to integrate with communication platforms, notifications for alerting users of new messages, and timers for scheduling shoutouts. Implement swipe gestures for navigating through messages and image controls for sharing multimedia content. Through these elements, the canvas app fosters real-time communication, collaboration, and engagement among users in an intuitive and interactive interface.

Inspection/Audit

There are many business use cases where Power Apps are used for auditing and inspection purposes that require you to create standardized questionnaires that need to be filled out and acted on. Some common use cases are building site inspection, incident reporting, IoT-based monitoring, safety and compliance audits, store audits, supply tracking, and quality control checklists. Figure 5-20 shows a sample site inspection app.

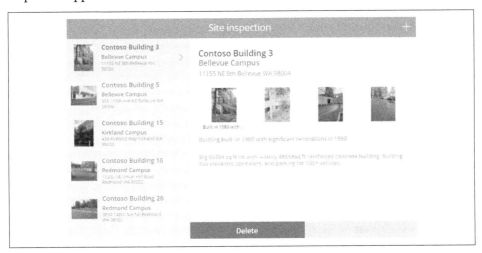

Figure 5-20. Sample site inspection app

Where can I use model-driven apps?

In creating an inspection or auditing app, tables store data on inspection reports, checklists, and audit findings. Forms facilitate data entry and review processes. Business rules enforce compliance standards and automate validation checks. Dashboards provide insights into inspection metrics and compliance status. Business process flows guide inspection workflows from initiation to resolution. Security roles control access to sensitive audit data. Charts visualize inspection trends and findings. Power

Automate automates notification of inspection tasks. JavaScript and plug-ins enhance app functionality, allowing for custom features and integration with external systems for comprehensive auditing capabilities.

Where can I use canvas apps?

Canvas apps offer a range of controls and features to develop an inspection or auditing app. Use controls like forms for data input, galleries for displaying inspection records, and drop-down lists for selecting audit criteria. Leverage data connectors to integrate with auditing databases, GPS for location tagging, and photo controls for capturing evidence. Implement checkboxes for marking compliance and buttons for submitting reports. Through these elements, the canvas app streamlines auditing processes, enhances data accuracy, and ensures regulatory compliance in an intuitive user interface.

Project Management

Power Apps can also be used to track a project from inception to completion, along with all the project management-related activities that the project manager needs to do. Some common project management use cases include task management, timeline management, resource management, and tracking task completion time. Figure 5-21 shows a sample project management app.

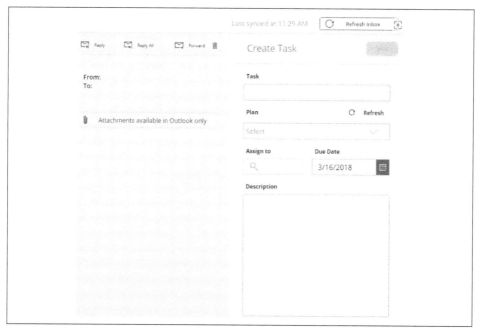

Figure 5-21. Sample project management app

Where can I use model-driven apps?

In developing a project management app, tables store data on projects, tasks, and team members. Forms enable users to input and manage project details, while business rules ensure data integrity and enforce project protocols. Dashboards provide visual insights into project progress and resource allocation. Business process flows guide project workflows from initiation to completion. Security roles control access to sensitive project information. Charts visualize project metrics for analysis. Power Automate automates task assignments and notifications. JavaScript and plug-ins enhance app functionality, allowing for customizations and integrations with external project management tools.

Where can I use canvas apps?

Canvas apps provide a diverse set of controls and features ideal for creating a project management app. Use controls such as galleries for displaying tasks, forms for data entry and updates, and calendars for scheduling. Leverage data connectors to integrate with project management platforms, notifications for task reminders, and timers for tracking project timelines. Implement drag-and-drop for task management and drop-down lists for assigning resources. Through these elements, the canvas app facilitates streamlined project planning, enhances collaboration, and improves overall project efficiency.

Summary

You learned many aspects and business use cases of Power Apps in this chapter that can help you determine when to use canvas apps and when to use model-driven apps. In short, if your data is stored in Dataverse and you want to use its features, and you need to design an automatically responsive application with minimal UI requirements, a model-driven app is the best option. Alternatively, canvas apps are best suited for creating a mobile or tablet application from scratch when you want complete control over the user interface and layout, including how and where to position controls on the screen. Moreover, canvas apps allow you the choice to store the data in various data sources in addition to Dataverse.

In the following chapter, you will learn about the model-driven app's built-in features, building blocks, and components so you can get started with development.

CHAPTER 6

Model-Driven App Components and Features

Although model-driven and canvas apps share common elements, they are best discussed separately. I will talk about model-driven app features in this chapter and canvas app features in Chapter 8.

As discussed in Chapter 3, model-driven apps are tightly coupled with Dataverse. The primary goal of model-driven apps is to design a data model, which involves creating tables and columns, and adding forms, views, charts, dashboards, and relationships to ensure easy data navigation and data reuse. As such, there are many different building blocks you can use to create a model-driven app, as shown in Figure 6-1.

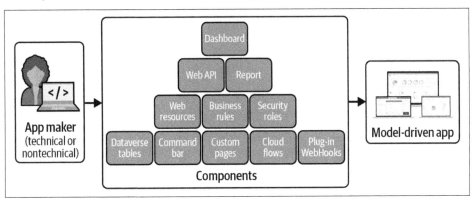

Figure 6-1. Model-driven app components

Model-driven apps are made up of a variety of components and features that allow anyone to create an end-to-end business application. In this chapter, I'll go through the most significant and commonly used components of model-driven apps from a citizen developer's perspective. Let's get started by creating a basic model-driven app solution.

Creating a Solution

Before you build a model-driven app, you need to first create a solution to hold your app and its related components. A *solution* is a container that holds all the components that you use to customize your application. Solution components can be things such as plug-ins, Dataverse tables, forms, views, columns, dashboards, and so on. I'll go into more detail on solutions and using them during deployment in Chapter 10, but for now, just know that you must create a solution to hold the components of your model-driven app. By creating a solution, you can keep track of all your components in a single place and easily move them to different environments.

To create a new solution, go to the Power Apps home page (*https://oreil.ly/WlAha*) and select the environment in which you are going to create your application. Select Solutions from the left panel and click "+ New solution" from the toolbar, as shown in Figure 6-2.

While creating the solution, you also need to create the publisher to provide the owner/publisher details along with the "prefix" for the solution components. You can create new and find any existing solution's publisher information in the Power Apps Maker Portal (*https://oreil.ly/WlAha*) by selecting the Solutions option from the left navigation panel.

The solution publisher provides the details about the ownership, or publisher, of the components in a particular solution that you are creating within an environment to uniquely identify your own components. For example, when you install an app on your mobile device from app store or play store, you can see who owns it, what features it provides, version of the app, app creation date, etc.

A component is considered to be owned by the publisher of the solution where it was generated. The owner of a component decides what modifications other solution publishers are permitted to make or prohibited from making. Within the same publisher, but not between publishers, it is feasible to transfer ownership of a component from one solution to another.

Each publisher has the following details:

- Basic details about the publisher, like its unique name and display name.
- Prefix to avoid name conflicts between components. Assume that you are using the same Power Platform environment for various vendors and that each one is

---

developing its own components. There's a chance that their component names will conflict with those of other vendors. This can be avoided by giving each publisher its own unique prefix, which must be added to each component you create as part of that solution.

- Prefixes must be two to eight characters long, can only consist of alphanumeric characters, must start with a letter, and cannot start with "mscrm" (because Microsoft uses that prefix for its internal components that are used in your environments).

- Contact details of the publisher like phone number, email address, website and address.

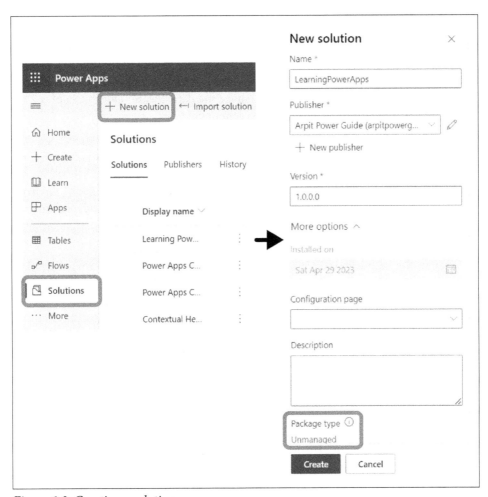

Figure 6-2. Creating a solution

After creating and selecting the publisher in the solution creation pop-up window, choose the package type for the solution. Typically this is "unmanaged" since an unmanaged solution is intended for ongoing development, and you're creating this solution to create new components to design the application.

Once your solution is created, you are all set to begin designing your app by either creating new components or adding existing components available in your environment to your solution.

Now let's go through the various types of components that are required to build the appearance and functionality of the model-driven app.

Data Components

In a model-driven app, the data components determine how the data will be stored. As discussed in Chapter 2, Dataverse serves as the primary data source for model-driven apps and houses the data there. Tables, columns, relationships, keys, and other data components are used to store and manage the data. Please refer to Chapter 2 for further information about Dataverse data components.

One additional feature that I want to talk about is *data localization*, also called *language translation*. Data localization is a feature that displays the content or configuration of your model-driven app in the user's preferred language. To allow any additional languages (other than the one that you specified at the time of environment setup) in a model-driven app, you first need to enable that language in your Power Platform environment by going to Environments, selecting an environment, then selecting Settings → Product → Languages.

By default, the language translation of all out-of-the-box tables and their metadata (columns, views, forms, etc.) gets changed automatically as soon as you change your preferred language in your Personal Options (*https://oreil.ly/U6Ieh*). However, for custom components and metadata, you need to perform the following steps to change the translations:

1. Export the localizable text. You can export the localized text available in your environment by opening your unmanaged solution and selecting Translations → Export Translations from the command bar. When the export is completed, save the translations ZIP file. The file is named something like *CrmTranslations_{0}_{1}.zip*, where {0} is the unique name of the solution and {1} is the version number of the solution.

2. Get the localizable text translated. You can send the translation file to a linguistic expert, translation agency, or localization firm to do the translation:

    a. Extract the ZIP file that you exported, and you will see that it contains two XML files: *<Content_Types>.xml* and *CrmTranslations.xml*.

b. Open the *CrmTranslations.xml* file with Microsoft Excel and go to the Localized Labels tab. Any custom tables or columns will have empty cells for the localizable text where you can add the translated text. The file contains columns only for the languages enabled in the environment, identified by their locale identifier (LCID). You can see a sample file (*https://oreil.ly/9uPQz*) on GitHub or examine the file (*https://oreil.ly/pvoZI*) that is part of the app you'll develop in Chapters 13 and 14.

3. Import the localized text. After changes are made to the *CrmTranslations.xml* file, you can use any zip tool to zip that file together with the *<Content_Types>.xml* file. To use the built-in Windows tool, just select both files and right-click to open the context menu. Then choose Send to → Compressed (zipped) folder. Now, go back to the unmanaged solution that you exported the translations from and choose Translations → Import Translations. Select the file that contains the compressed translated text and select Import.

After the translated text is imported, you should publish all customizations to see the changes in your apps.

User Interface Components

In a model-driven app, the UI components determine how the data will be displayed in the app and how the user will interact with the app. Model-driven apps provide built-in low-code, no-code UI designer tools that anyone can use to configure the app UI, toolbar menu, side navigation panels, forms, view, etc.

Model-driven apps are not advised for scenarios where extensive UI customization is required. Only the following UI elements are customizable in model-driven apps (see Figures 6-3 and 6-4):

Left navigation panel (1)
    Shows various navigation options to display different pages/content to the main screen. Site map designer is used to customize the left navigation panel (site map) of the app.

Right panel (2)
    Displays the types of pages/content based on the option you select in the site map. As shown in Figure 6-3, I have shown the view My Active Accounts to display the list of account data.

Home page command toolbar (3)
    Displays a toolbar or commands on the app's home screen. Command bar designer is used to manage the commands on the main screen.

Figure 6-3. *The main screen of a sample model-driven app*

Design and layout (4)

When you open any record from the view (in item 2), it opens the associated table form to display detailed information about the record. The forms in the table are designed using a form designer that I'll discuss in the next section.

Command bar (5)

Displays the toolbar or the commands on a particular form. Command bar designer is used to manage the commands on the form screen.

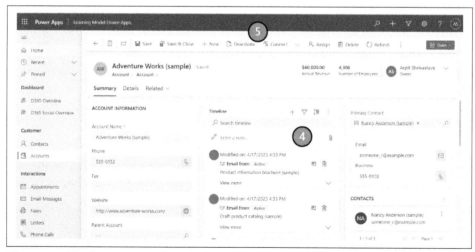

Figure 6-4. *The form screen of a sample model-driven app*

You should use the app designer to customize all of the listed UI elements. Let's talk about each UI component in more detail

App Designer

App designer is the primary tool used to design the overall UI of model-driven apps. To get to the app designer, go to the Power Apps home page (*https://oreil.ly/WlAha*), choose the appropriate environment, then choose your app from the app list, and click Edit from the toolbar (see Figure 6-5).

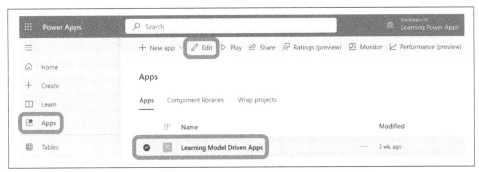

Figure 6-5. App designer tool

You will now see the app designer, as shown in Figure 6-6.

Figure 6-6. App designer

Let's explore each area of the app designer in more detail:

Navigation bar (1)

This is where you see the grouping of various elements that you want to show on the model-driven app pages:

Pages

Displays a list of all the pages that are used in model-driven apps to display the following controls: Dataverse table, Dashboard, URL, Web resource, Custom page.

Data

Displays all tables that you've added to your app and their respective environments.

Automation

Displays a list of business process flows added to the app along with the option to add a new business process flow.

Panes (2)

This panel allows you to configure the elements of the group selected in the left navigation pane. For example, as shown in Figure 6-7, if you choose Navigation from the Pages list, then you can configure the app's left navigation panel; if you choose Data, then you can create/update tables in your app/environment; if you choose Automation, then you can create business process flows (BPFs) for your app (which I will discuss more in the next section).

App preview pane (3)

Shows a live preview of the form as it will be seen by users after being published.

Property pane (4)

This is used to change the properties of the elements you are adding to the left navigation panel. For example, if you add a dashboard to the left panel, then from this section you can change the properties of the dashboard like title, icon, and type.

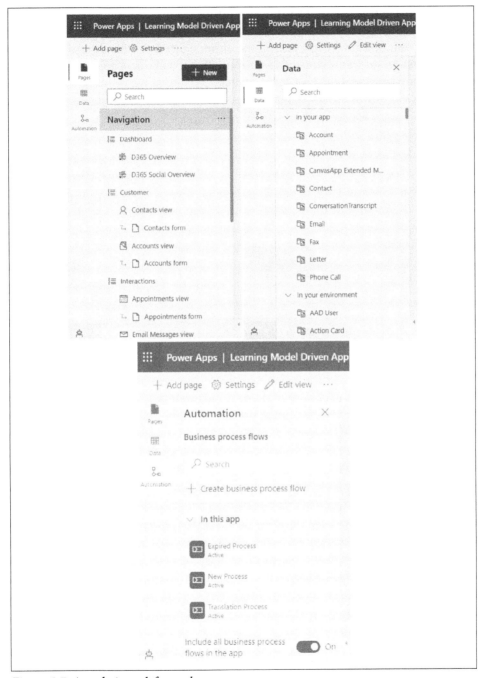

Figure 6-7. App designer left panel

Settings button in the command bar (5)

Takes you to the app Settings page, where you can change the app's name, logo, description, welcome page, etc., as shown in Figure 6-8. This page also displays the preview features (discussed in Chapter 3) that you can enable to start exploring it in your nonproduction environments.

Figure 6-8. Model-driven app Settings page

The right-most options in the command bar (6)

These allow you to add comments if multiple app developers are working on the same model-driven app, save your app configuration to Dataverse, publish app changes so they are reflected in the live app, and play the app directly in the web browser.

Site Map Designer

Site map designer is part of the app designer tool that is used to design the left navigation panel (site map) of your model-driven apps. To get to the site map designer, go to the Power Apps home page (*https://oreil.ly/WlAha*), choose the appropriate environment, then choose your app from the app list and click Edit from the toolbar. You can then customize the site map by selecting Pages from the app designer's left navigation panel, as seen in Figure 6-9.

From the site map designer, you can display content from a Dataverse table, dashboard, URL, web resource, and custom page in the left navigation panel of the model-driven app.

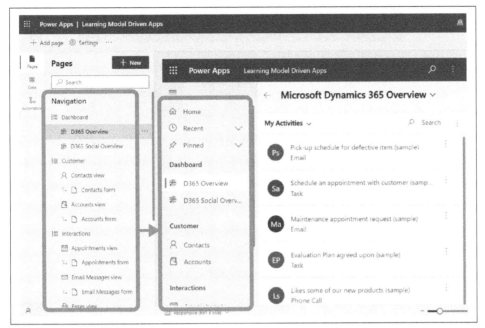

Figure 6-9. Site map designer

Form Designer

A model-driven app can have multiple forms of various tables, where the user enters information, which is saved to Dataverse. To create these forms, you need to navigate to the *form designer* (also referred to as the *form editor*) for the desired table. This designer provides a real-time, WYSIWYG (what you see is what you get) preview. Changes to the form are immediately reflected in the preview, allowing you to see how it will appear to users once published.

To open the form designer, first you need to open your model-driven app in the app designer, click on any table's form from the site map designer panel (for demonstration I will edit the Contacts form), and click the pencil icon next to the form, as shown in Figure 6-10.

Figure 6-10. Editing a form from site map designer

Once you open the form, you'll see the form designer, similar to the one shown in Figure 6-11, with the areas that follow.

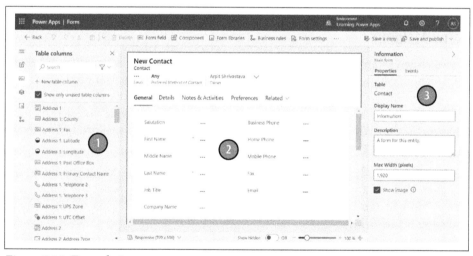

Figure 6-11. Form designer

Left panel

The left panel (number 1 in Figure 6-11; shown in more detail in Figure 6-12) enables you to add the types of components to the form that are shown in Table 6-1.

Table 6-1. Form components

Component	Purpose
Layout	Components used to design the layout of the form, like tabs and sections
Grid	A subgrid and an editable subgrid that are used to display related table data in read-only and editable modes, respectively
Display	Components to display advanced controls like calendar, HTML page, embedded canvas app, external website using iframe, quick view, timeline
Input	Components to change the visualization of the input data, such as pen input, rich text editor, toggle
Media	Media-related components, such as images and maps
AI Builder	AI Builder-related components, such as a business card reader
Power BI	Power BI report control used to embed Power BI reports in the form
More components	Components you've created and can import to the form

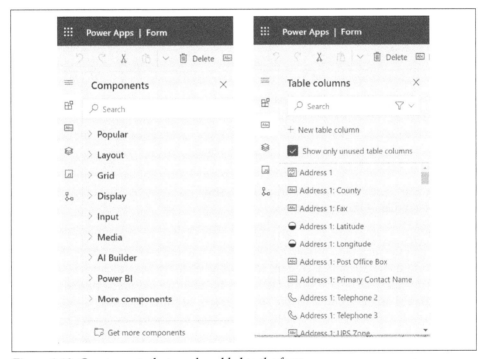

Figure 6-12. Components that can be added to the form

As shown in Figure 6-13, along with adding components to the form, you can add two more types of controls to the form from the left panel:

Form libraries

To add JavaScript libraries (web resources) to the form. These contain various JavaScript functions that can run on onLoad of the form, onSave of the data, and onChange of the form columns. I will discuss this in more detail in Chapter 7.

Business rules

To write client-side validations, which can also be run on the server side, depending on their scope. I will discuss this more in "Logic Components" on page 171.

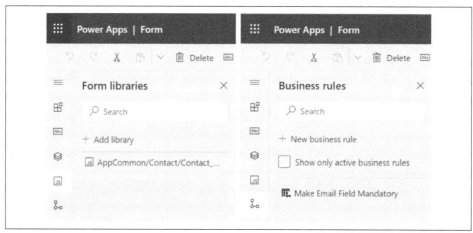

Figure 6-13. Form libraries and business rules to write business logic on the form

Middle panel

The middle panel (number 2 in Figure 6-11) shows a preview of the form.

Right panel

The right panel (number 3 in Figure 6-11) mainly manages the metadata properties and event handler of the components:

Properties

Manages the metadata properties of the form and the form's components, including form name, form description, control's label, hide the control's label, hide the control, make the control read-only, hide the control on mobile phone, and lock the control on the form so that it can't be removed from the form.

Events

Manages when a JavaScript function will be triggered as written in the form libraries' component. For example, it might be triggered by onLoad, onSave, onChange, tabStateChange, etc. I've shown how to set up the form's On Load event in Figure 6-14. The onChange event for fields and the tabStateChange event for tabs can be configured in a similar manner.

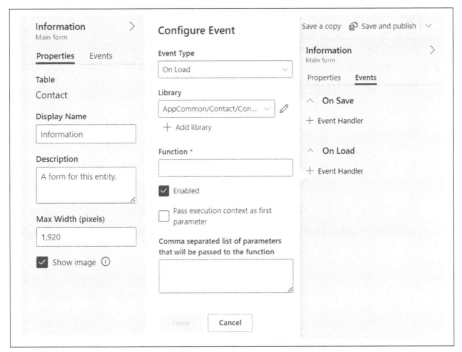

Figure 6-14. Form properties and events

View Designer

Views are used in model-driven apps to specify how a list of records from a particular table should be displayed for the user. You can create multiple views for a table and display filtered data. For example, you might have a view to show draft emails and a view to show sent emails. There are three types of views:

Personal views
> These belong to each individual and are only visible to the person who created them unless that individual shares them with others.

System views
> These exist for system tables or are created automatically when you create custom tables. These views have specific purposes and some additional capabilities and can only be modified by users with the System Administrator or System Customizer security roles.

Public views
> These are all-purpose views that you can edit as needed. When made available, all app users can access them by using the view selector.

You might need to make any of the following changes to the views:

- Add/remove columns
- Reorder columns
- Alter the width of columns
- Sort the data
- Filter the data

The *view designer* is used to customize a view. You can open the view designer of a particular table directly from the site map designer, as shown in Figure 6-15.

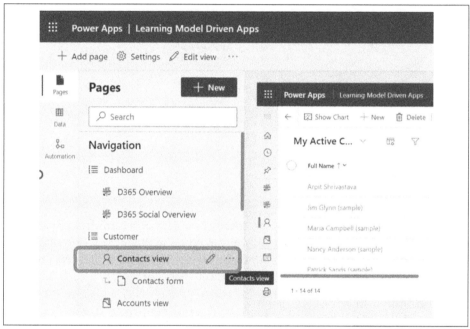

Figure 6-15. Editing the view directly from the site map designer

When you edit a table's view in a model-driven app, you are shown three panels, as shown in Figure 6-16:

Left panel (1)
Shows the table and the column for which the view is being created or edited, along with its related table and its columns. You can drag a column to the middle panel and add it to the view.

Middle panel (2)
Shows the preview of the view.

Right panel (3)

Allows you to change the properties of the view, such as label and description. In addition, you can:

- Configure the column based on how you want to sort the view data, either in ascending or descending order. For example, you can use the Created On column to sort the contact records based on their creation date.

- Filter the data to only show records that fit certain criteria. For example, in Active Contacts view, you display only contact records whose Status is Active.

Figure 6-16. View designer

Command Bar (Toolbar) Designer

In model-driven apps, the command bar is also known as the *toolbar and ribbon*. It serves to personalize the toolbar options of a model-driven app's main grid, main form, subgrid view, and associated view. Using the command bar designer, you can create custom commands, drop-down menus, and split buttons as well as write Power Fx expressions to control their visibility and actions when a command (also known as a button) is clicked.

To open the command bar designer of any table, you first need to edit your model-driven app in the app designer, click on the three dots (…) next to the table view in the left panel, click on "Edit command bar," and select "Edit in new tab" (as shown in Figure 6-17). I chose to modify the command bar of the Contacts table, so I clicked on the three dots next to the "Contacts view."

Once you choose the option you want to customize (main grid, main form, subgrid view, or associated view), you'll be directed to that command bar page.

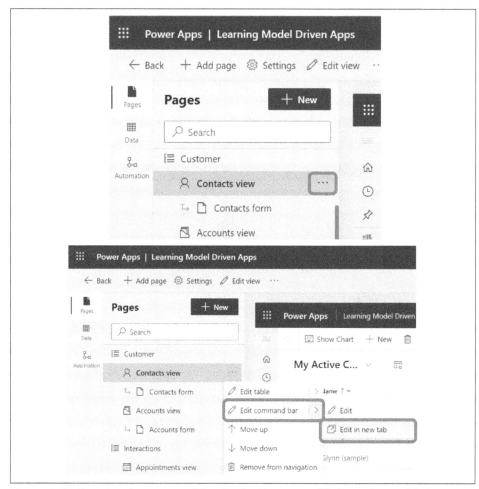

Figure 6-17. Opening the command bar for the Contacts table from the model-driven app designer

After creating your command (which appears as a menu option on the toolbar), you have two choices for executing the action you want to happen when the user clicks on the command: you can either trigger a JavaScript function or a Power Fx expression. Power Fx had limited capabilities at the time this book was being written. In upcoming releases, new features and capabilities will be added. Consequently, it is currently used to perform basic CRUD operations in Dataverse. JavaScript is required to create advanced and complex business logic. You'll learn more about Power Fx in Chapter 9.

Custom Page Designer

Custom page is a low-code, no-code canvas app-based page that uses similar features, components, data sources, and controls as a canvas app. It also uses Power Apps Studio to design the pages. I will discuss more about custom pages in Chapter 7.

Logic Components

In a model-driven app, logic components play a pivotal role in shaping its business rules, automation logic, and overall business processes. Various design approaches are employed, tailored to the specific type of business rule or process. Let's delve deeper into each logic component and its corresponding logic designer.

Business Process Flows

In model-driven apps, a *business process flow* (BPF) is a guided, predefined set of steps to accomplish a specific business objective. A BPF makes sure that users are entering data consistently and following the same steps. It consists of multiple stages, and each stage is a group of fields that needs to be completed before moving on to the next stage.

Consider an example where you want to manage the sales process in your company by developing a BPF (see Figure 6-18.) First, a lead is created for the potential customer. If the customer expresses interest in purchasing the product, the lead is converted to an opportunity (qualify stage). Next, the user identifies the detailed customer needs, the stakeholders (who may or may not be members of the organization), other colleagues who will work on the opportunity, and potential competitors who may be selling a similar product to develop a proposal (quote) for the customer, and then sends the proposal to the customer. The customer may ask to revise the proposal, and then finally the salesperson closes the opportunity once the customer places the order and pays the invoice.

Figure 6-18. Business process flow and its stages

Some BPFs are available in prebuilt model-driven apps (Dynamics 365 CE apps). For example, Lead to Opportunity Sales Process is available in the Sales app and Phone to Case Process is available in the Customer Service app.

Creating a business process flow

To create a new BPF, you need to open your solution, click on +New from the toolbar, and select Automation → Process → Business process flow, as shown in Figure 6-19.

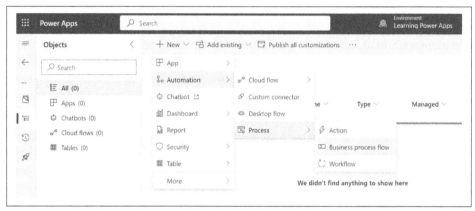

Figure 6-19. Creating a business process flow

On each BPF creation, a new table gets created with the same name as the BPF to hold the information about the current active stage of a particular table's record on which the BPF is used.

For example, as shown in Figure 6-20, I have two records in the Lead table, Lead A and Lead B. I am using the Lead to Opportunity Sales Process BPF on the Lead table. Lead A is at the qualify stage and Lead B is at the develop stage. To track this, the BPF will also create two records (BPF A and BPF B) in the business process flow table, along with the active BPF stage of the respective lead record. That means BPF A will link to Lead A with the Active Stage field value set to "qualify," and the BPF B record will link to Lead B with Active Stage set to "develop."

You can create multiple BPFs for a single table, if there are different users following different processes to enter the data.

Lead ⌄	Active Stage ⌄	Process ⌄	Created On ⌄
Lead A	qualify	Lead to Opportunity Sales Process	9/6/2022 12:50 PM
Lead B	develop	Lead to Opportunity Sales Process	9/6/2022 12:52 PM
Lead C	develop	Lead to Opportunity Sales Process	9/6/2022 12:53 PM
Lead D	qualify	Lead to Opportunity Sales Process	9/6/2022 12:55 PM
Lead E	qualify	Lead to Opportunity Sales Process	4/22/2022 2:10 PM
Lead F	qualify	Lead to Opportunity Sales Process	6/13/2021 3:27 AM
Lead G	qualify	Lead to Opportunity Sales Process	7/13/2021 1:17 PM

Figure 6-20. Business process flow table

Business process flow designer

The business process flow designer enables you to do the following (see Figure 6-21):

1. Specify the BPF name and description.

2. Add stages, conditions, data steps, workflows, and flows.

3. Set the BPF order (if multiple BPFs are enabled).

4. Enable security roles for the BPF, so that only authorized users can see the process flow.

5. Activate the BPF to reflect on the forms. (This option is a toggle; Figure 6-21 shows an activated BPF, so you see the Deactivate option on the toolbar.)

Figure 6-21. Business process flow designer

If you click the Add button, you can add new or conditional stages to the business process flow, call workflow (Dataverse classic or real-time workflow), action step (custom actions), or flow step (Power Automate), as shown in Figure 6-22.

Figure 6-22. Performing actions on the BPF

When you design a BPF, note the following limitations:

- One table can have a maximum of 10 activated BPFs.
- Each BPF can have a maximum of 30 stages.
- One BPF can be used on up to five different tables.

I discussed security roles in "Microsoft Dataverse Security" on page 39. You can apply security to a particular BPF by enabling it only for a particular security role. For example, a salesperson might not be able to see the business process flow of a sales manager and vice versa. System Administrator and System Customizer security roles have access to all the business process flows by default.

Dataverse Classic Workflows

Classic workflows (also called Dataverse workflows) are used to perform step-by-step actions in the background without a user interface. App users use workflows to automate business processes that don't require any user interaction.

There are two types of classic workflows:

Background
    These workflows carry out tasks asynchronously and continue to operate in the background. This type of workflow is most frequently used for business scenarios

where immediate results are not anticipated, long-running operations, scheduled operations, and logic where you need to wait for some action to be finished.

A few examples of background workflows are as follows:

- Send birthday emails on the recipient's birth date.
- Send a reminder two days before an appointment date.
- Delete all completed tasks every Sunday.
- Create an approval process with varying levels, where level 1 approver needs to wait until level 2 approver has approved the request.

Real-time

These workflows perform the actions in real time, or synchronously. These workflows are usually used to perform actions where an outcome is expected immediately. They can roll back the transaction in case an error occurs while performing the operation in Dataverse. Additionally, they can perform operations both before and after the Dataverse transaction happens. This is the same as for plugins, which I will discuss in Chapter 7.

A few examples of real-time workflows are as follows:

- Update the case closure date on the case table, before updating the case status to completed in Dataverse.
- Throw an error if the user tries to disqualify the lead without entering a reason.
- Change the status of a record immediately when a toolbar button is clicked.

As of this writing, Microsoft is transferring all Dataverse classic workflow asynchronous features to Power Automate (flow) and transferring synchronous features to Dataverse Accelerator lowcode plug-ins (this will be covered in Chapter 9). Therefore, I would recommend adopting them instead of classic workflows to avoid having to later migrate.

Nevertheless, Microsoft has not made any official announcement about when the classic workflow will be decommissioned. And there are still some features that are not currently available in any other components. For example, DocuSign Integration with Dynamics 365 CE includes some DocuSign-specific custom workflows that can only be accessed through classic workflows.

Every Dynamics 365 user is entitled to use Power Automate, so there is no need to purchase an additional license. Please read Microsoft's official documentation to replace your classic workflows with Power Automate (*https://oreil.ly/geedY*).

Creating a workflow

To create a new workflow, you need to open your solution, click on +New from the toolbar, and then select Automation → Process → Workflow, as shown in Figure 6-23. This will open up the workflow designer.

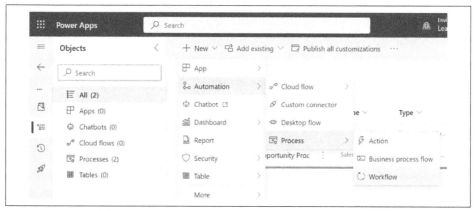

Figure 6-23. Workflow

Workflow designer

The workflow designer is used to configure and design the workflow. While creating a workflow you have certain areas to consider, as shown in Figure 6-24.

Figure 6-24. Workflow designer

Let's go over these areas in detail:

Basic properties of workflow (1)
> Set workflow name, owner, and notes. Click on the Administration and Notes tabs to find all these properties.

Workflow should run as (2)

Here you can decide whether to run the workflow as a background process, on demand, or as a child process. Enable the "Automatically delete completed workflow jobs (to save disk space)" option if you are concerned about space.

Workflow trigger and scope (3)

Here you can configure when the workflow will be triggered. Workflows can be triggered upon the following events:

- Record is created

- Record status changes

- Record is assigned

- Record fields change

- Record is deleted

The scope determines which records should be used to initiate the workflow. If scope is set to User, it triggers only on the records owned by you; if it is set to Business Unit, it triggers only on the records owned by users in your business unit; if it is set to Parent Child Business Units, it triggers only on the records owned by users belonging to your business unit and its child business units; if it is set to Organization, it triggers on all the records irrespective of the owner.

Workflow steps, conditions, and actions (4)

Here you can configure the steps necessary to execute the various operations step by step. Workflows can perform the following actions:

Check condition

You can add multiple conditions to determine under which condition the actions should be performed.

Create record

To create data in Dataverse.

Update record

To update data in Dataverse.

Assign record

To assign data to a user or team in Dataverse.

Send email

To send email to internal users or customers.

Start child workflow

To run another classic workflow that has been created as a child workflow.

Perform action

You can call the actions (which we'll discuss in the next section) directly from classic workflows.

Change status

To update the status of data in Dataverse.

Stop workflow

To stop or terminate the current workflow. When stopping a workflow, you can set a status of either Succeeded or Canceled and specify a status message. When real-time workflows are configured for an event, stopping a workflow with a status of Canceled will prevent the event action from completing.

Activate and convert workflow type (5)

From the toolbar you can save the workflow configuration and activate it. You can also change the workflow type from background to real time and vice-versa.

Process session (6)

Shows the workflow run history.

Start when (7)

As shown in Figure 6-25, when you are configuring a real-time workflow, there will be an option to choose when to perform operations in Dataverse, either before or after the actual transaction is performed.

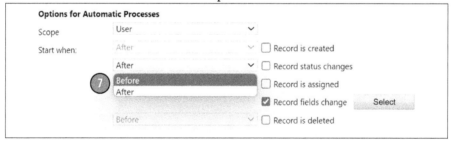

Figure 6-25. Real-time workflow pre- and post-operation events

When you create a workflow, there are a few important points to note:

- You can run one workflow inside another workflow as a child workflow.

- Workflows can be triggered on-demand (by clicking a toolbar button) or manually as well.

- If the out-of-the-box workflow steps are not sufficient to fulfill your business requirements, you can create a custom workflow using C# code (to be discussed in Chapter 7).

Finally, workflows can also be developed as process templates, allowing you to reuse them when creating new workflows rather than starting from scratch. As shown in Figure 6-26, I have created a classic workflow called Send Email and set Activate As to Process template so that I can reuse it in another workflow.

Figure 6-26. Creating a workflow from a template

Custom Actions

Custom Actions, also referred to as *Custom Process Actions*, are used to create custom messages (events or triggers) for Dataverse. Microsoft Dataverse has predefined actions such as create, update, delete, and retrieve. However, sometimes you might need a custom action to meet your business requirements and reuse it across the application. As shown in Figure 6-27, when you use any code components (plug-ins, JavaScript, etc.) or logic components (Power Automate, Power Fx, etc.) to execute actions from Power Apps, these components can call Custom Actions (reusable code or logic) to execute the desired actions or operations and return the results to the component and then back to Power Apps.

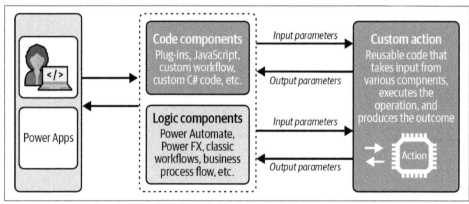

Figure 6-27. Custom Action architecture

For example, I want to create a Custom Action called Word to PDF Converter, that will take a Word file as input and return a PDF file as output. This action can be called from various other components including JavaScript, workflows, plug-ins, Power Automate, and Power Fx (discussed in Chapter 9) without writing the same business logic at the individual component level.

Custom Actions can be built either specifically for a table in Dataverse as a *bound action* or globally as an *unbound action*, irrespective of any tables.

Creating a Custom Action

To create a new Action, you need to open your solution, click on +New from the toolbar, and then select Automation → Process → Action, as shown in Figure 6-28.

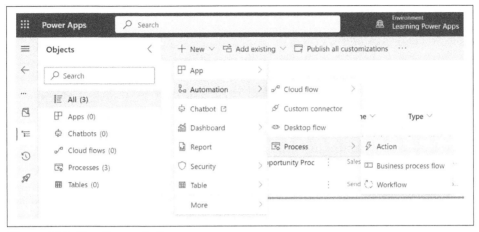

Figure 6-28. Creating an Action

Custom Action designer

Custom Actions use the workflow designer (discussed in an earlier section) to configure various properties. Therefore, all the properties of a Custom Action are the same as for a workflow, except those that follow (see Figure 6-29).

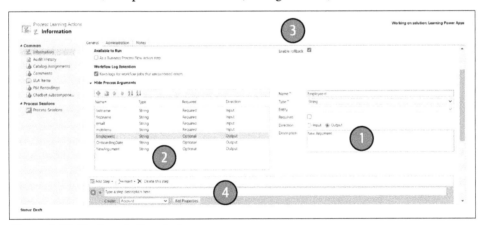

Figure 6-29. Custom Action designer

Let's go over these properties in more detail:

Input and output parameters (1)
> Here you can define multiple input and output parameters of various types (Boolean, string, decimal, datetime, etc.) that the action will use for processing.
>
> In 2021, Microsoft announced (*https://oreil.ly/WDH1_*) the advanced version of Custom Actions called Dataverse Custom API, which enables you to create your own APIs with input/output parameters and with some new advanced features. I will discuss this further in Chapter 7.

List of parameters (2)
> Here you can see a list of all input/output parameters.

Enable rollback (3)
> This setting ensures that the whole database transaction will be rolled back if anything goes wrong while executing the action.

Action to be performed (4)
> Here you can define the list of all predefined actions (conditional or nonconditional) that you want to perform when the Custom Action is called.

Calling Custom Actions

You can call Custom Actions from other Power Apps components, including workflows, JavaScript, Power Automate, Power Fx, and plug-ins. For example, as shown in Figure 6-30, I have added a step called Perform Action to a workflow to see the list of all available custom actions (out-of-the-box and your own) in my environment.

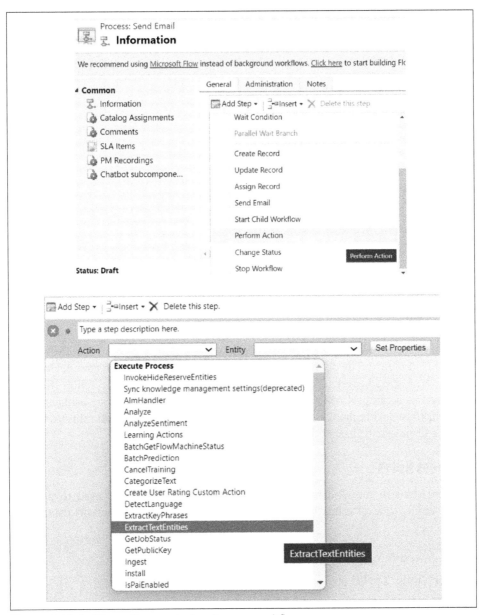

Figure 6-30. Calling a Custom Action from a workflow

Figure 6-31 shows an example of calling a Custom Action from Power Automate.

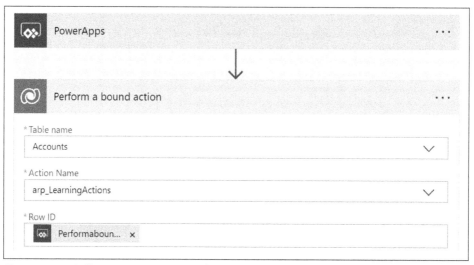

Figure 6-31. Calling a Custom Action from Power Automate

Model-driven apps use Xrm.WebApi.online.execute (*https://oreil.ly/vbO3q*) to run Custom Actions in client-side JavaScript. Note that Custom Actions are always synchronous in nature. The operation is executed as soon as they are triggered. However, there are no specific restrictions on the amount of overall time the action itself can take because it can perform multiple steps. Having said that, if you are using any custom workflow inside the Custom Action, then there is a limit of two minutes to execute the Dataverse transaction; otherwise, a timeout will occur.

Business Rules

Business rules in model-driven apps are server-side logic that is used to perform client-side form-level validations. You can perform the following actions using business rules:

- Show recommendations based on business intelligence
- Lock/unlock fields on the form
- Show error messages
- Set column values
- Set a default value for a field (an autopopulate value)
- Set business required (optional, required, recommended)
- Set the visibility of a field (hide/show)

Creating business rules

To create a new business rule for a table, open your solution, click New on the toolbar, and then select Automation → Process → Action (see Figure 6-32).

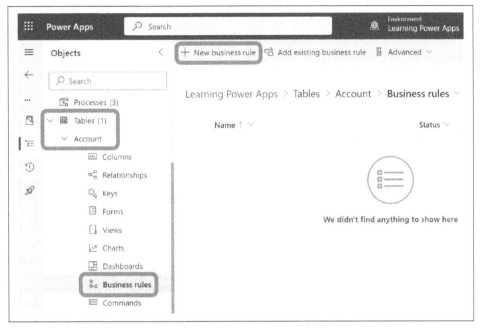

Figure 6-32. Creating business rules

Business rule designer

The business rule designer is used to create and configure the business rules details. A business rule has the following main components (see Figure 6-33):

Condition (1)

All business rules start with at least one condition and may have multiple conditions. Conditions are useful to perform the form-level validation conditionally. For instance, if a user chooses "email" as the customer's preferred mode of communication, then the Email Address column is required; otherwise, it is optional.

Action (2)

The action is the business logic that you want to perform on a particular column. Currently, business rules support seven different types of actions (as discussed earlier).

Scope (3)

Since business rules perform actions and validations at the form level, there must be an option to define the scope, which determines on which form the action will be performed. There are three scopes:

Table

Perform logic on all model-driven app forms and on the server side as well.

All forms

Perform logic on all model-driven app forms.

Specific form

Perform logic on a specific form.

Snapshot (4)

Choose Snapshot from the action bar to capture the whole business rule window. This is helpful, for instance, if you want to share and gather feedback from a team member regarding the business rule.

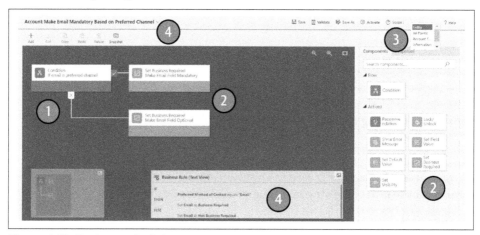

Figure 6-33. Business rule designer

When creating business rules, there are a few important points to consider:

- Business rules can display business recommendations and error messages in the user's preferred language.
- Users must have a minimum of read-level privileges on the Process table to use the business rule, as shown in Figure 6-34.

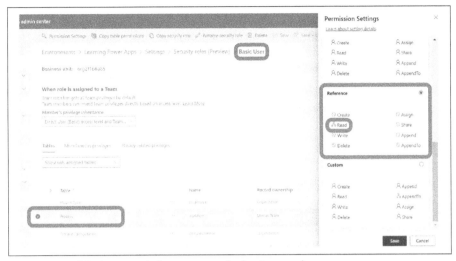

Figure 6-34. Minimum privileges to run the business rule

- Business rules can't perform actions on the following form components:
  - Editable subgrid
  - Subgrids
  - Tabs
  - Sections
  - Choices column (multiselect option)
- All the columns referenced in the business rules must be present on the form; otherwise, the rules will not work as expected.
- Business rules can unlock the columns on a read-only form.
- Business rules created for model-driven apps with the scope set to Table, work for canvas apps as well.
- If you set a business rule's scope to Table, it can also execute on the server side; then it can enforce the logic and data values that you enter into the Dataverse tables.
- Business rules cannot query Dataverse or interact with related tables to perform form validations. You should write JavaScript for advanced client-side validation.
- Business rules allow you to use a maximum of up to 10 IF-ELSE conditions.

- If you have a system script (written by the Microsoft product team), and your custom JavaScript and business rules are applied on the same column, then the system JavaScript will trigger first, your custom JavaScript will trigger second, and then the business rule will trigger.

- If you have multiple business rules activated on the same column, then they will run in the order they were activated.

Power Automate

Power Automate (it is still referred to as Cloud Flows or Flows in many places) is one of the Power Platform components that provides low-code, no-code capabilities to write server-side business logic for model-driven apps.

You have already learned about Power Automate in Chapter 2, so here I will only talk about Power Automate in the context of a model-driven app.

The ideal option for any server-side business logic in model-driven apps that doesn't need to be executed synchronously is Power Automate. The only options for synchronous business logic are real-time workflows, custom workflows, and plug-ins, which I will discuss in Chapter 7.

Power Automate is not a feature of model-driven apps, but it is a crucial component of them, and can be triggered from various places in the following ways:

Automatic

Runs automatically whenever an operation (create, update, delete, etc.) is performed in Dataverse.

Instant

Runs on-demand or manually as per the business needs. For example, you can trigger Power Automate instantly from either a business process flow step or the command bar.

Scheduled

Runs on a set schedule. Power Automate can execute logic every x seconds, minutes, hours, days, weeks, months, or any specific date at a specific time.

Creating a Power Automate flow

To create a new Power Automate flow to trigger on a particular table, you need to open your solution, click on +New from the toolbar, and then select Automation → Cloud flow, followed by either Automated, Instant, or Scheduled (see Figure 6-35).

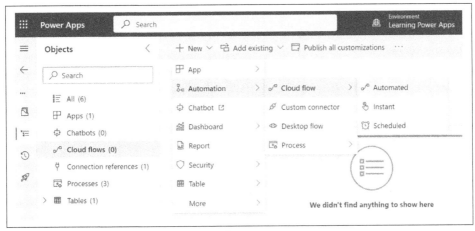

Figure 6-35. Creating a Power Automate flow

Power Automate designer

Power Automate provides a low-code, no-code UI designer tool that enables everyone to write the business logic by just choosing the appropriate data connector and adding it to the sequence of steps.

Power Automate designer consists of the following parts, as shown in Figure 6-36:

Trigger (1)
Determines when a Power Automate flow will initiate the execution. A flow can have only one trigger.

Actions (2)
Determines what sequential operations (either in Dataverse or an external data source) need to be performed.

Dynamic content and expressions (3)

You can set the dynamic content (the data in the table) from one stage to the next to perform the operation. When dynamic content needs to be transformed before being used in a subsequent step, Power Fx expressions can be written as well. As depicted in Figure 6-36, I want to create a task with Subject set to the contact's full name as soon as a new contact is created.

Flow checker (4)

Analyzes and checks the problems with your Power Automate flows. It also makes suggestions for potential causes of the problem and links to relevant community posts.

Figure 6-36. Power Automate designer

Testing a Power Automate flow

Before using your business logic, you might need to test it (see Figure 6-37). You can test the Power Automate flow manually or automatically using recently used triggers with the Test Flow tool. In case of error, the tool displays the possible cause, solutions, and related community articles as well.

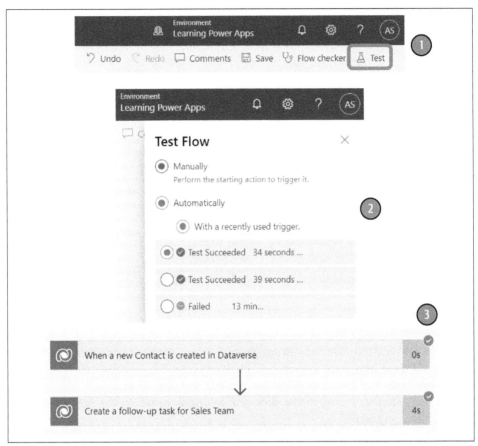

Figure 6-37. Testing a Power Automate flow

Follow these steps to test the flow:

1. Click the Test button on the toolbar.

2. Choose whether you want to test it manually (need to input test data manually) or automatically using recent triggers.

3. Power Automate will run and display the test results. In case of error, it displays the error details (as shown in Figure 6-38).

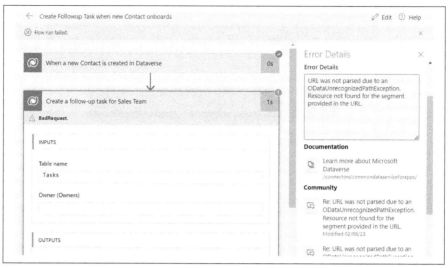

Figure 6-38. Power Automate error details with links to documentation and community articles

Power Automate run history

From the Power Automate run history page, you can check the last 28 days of history to track if Power Automate is running, failed, or succeeded, as shown in Figure 6-39. From this page, you can also check the Power Automate flow's owner, the different connection references used in the flow, the solutions in which the flow exists, and turn the flow on and off.

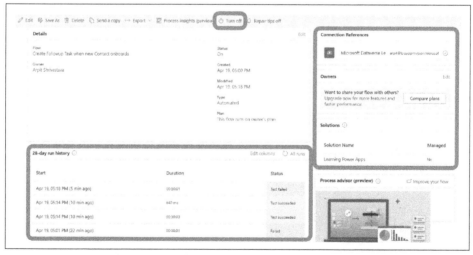

Figure 6-39. Power Automate run history page

For further information on Power Automate, see Chapter 2, where I covered its key concepts along with some real-world examples.

Visualization Components

In a model-driven app, the *visualization components* determine how the data will be visualized in the app in the form of charts and dashboards. To make business decisions and monitor an organization and its employees' performance, it's helpful to display data in graphical formats rather than having to read through millions of records in Dataverse.

The visualization components supported by model-driven apps are charts, dashboards, and embedded Power BI components.

Charts

A chart is a single graphic visualization of Dataverse data that can be added to a dashboard or displayed within a view or on a form. Model-driven apps currently support the following types of charts:

- Column
- Bar
- Area
- Line
- Pie
- Funnel
- Tag
- Doughnut

Creating a chart

To create a new chart, you need to open your solution, expand Tables, and then expand the table for which you want to create a new chart (for demonstration, I have expanded the Contacts table). Then, click on Charts from the left navigation panel; it will display all charts already created for the table. To create a new one, click on "New chart" from the toolbar, as shown in Figure 6-40.

The chart designer will open (shown in Figure 6-41), where you can create a new chart as per your business needs.

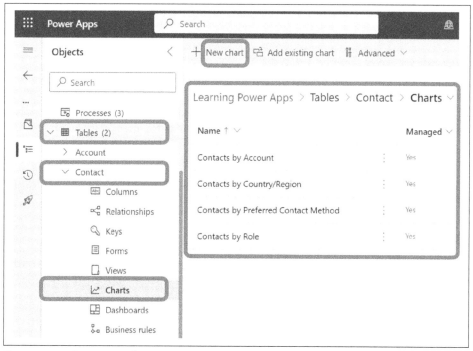

Figure 6-40. Creating a chart

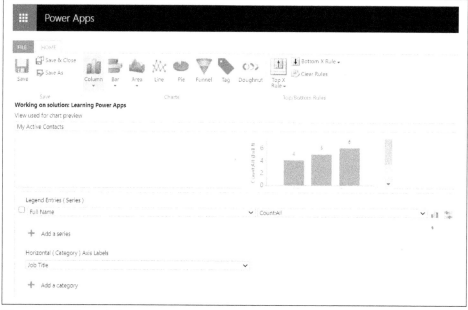

Figure 6-41. Chart designer

Defining colors

You can define the chart colors only for Choice, Yes/No, and Status Reason column types. For example, in Figure 6-42, Onboarding Status can be shown in green if it is approved, in yellow if it's in progress, or in red if it's rejected.

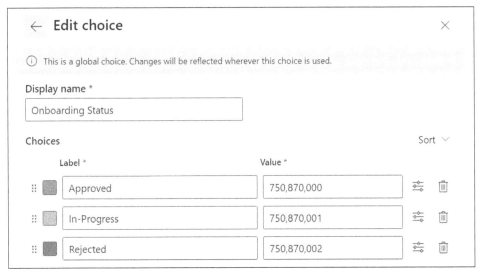

Figure 6-42. Changing the color in the Choice column type

Adding a chart to a form

You can show the graphical representation of table data on a form. For instance, on the Account form shown in Figure 6-43, I have used a "Contacts by Role" chart to display all contacts associated with a given account, grouped by their roles.

First, using the form designer, I selected the "Show chart only" option for the Contacts subgrid in the Account form.

When I launch the model-driven app and select any account data from the account view, the chart appears on the Account form, as shown in Figure 6-44.

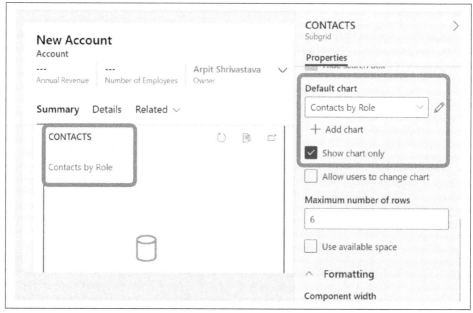

Figure 6-43. Enabling form designer to display a chart for a related record

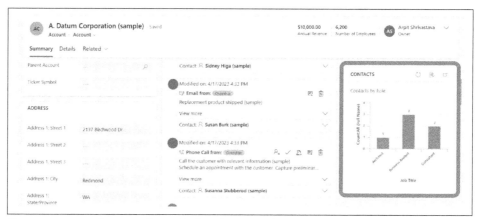

Figure 6-44. Displaying a chart of related contacts by role on the Account form

Adding a chart in the view

You can also add a chart to a table view to quickly visualize the data. As an example, I have created a chart named "Contacts by Role" on the Contacts table. To view that chart on the Contact view, first I need to launch the model-driven app, navigate to that table's view, and then click the Show Chart button on the toolbar, as shown in Figure 6-45.

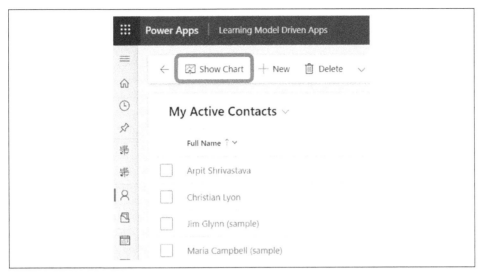

Figure 6-45. Show Chart option on the view toolbar

The chart will display the data present in that view, as shown in Figure 6-46. You can hide the chart as well by clicking the Hide Chart button on the toolbar.

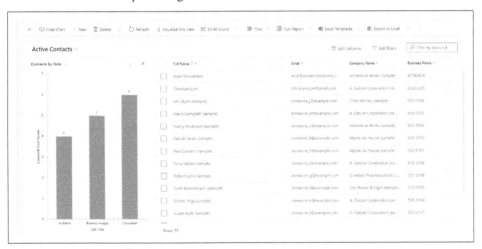

Figure 6-46. Chart within a view

Dashboards

It may not always be possible to visualize all of your business data by displaying just one chart. You may need to use a dashboard, a collection of charts with different filtering options. A dashboard can group numerous charts on a single page and display a holistic view of all the data. Dashboard layouts are based on the number of charts and controls that you want to display.

Types of dashboards

You can create two types of dashboards in the model-driven apps, *standard* and *interactive*:

Standard dashboards

Standard dashboards are the old way of creating dashboards, where you add one or more unrelated components such as charts, lists, web resources, and iframes. The number of charts and controls you want to display on the dashboard determines your dashboard layout options, as shown in Figure 6-47.

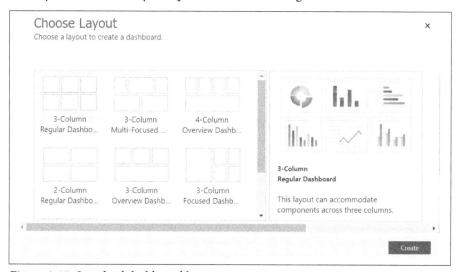

Figure 6-47. Standard dashboard layout

For example, in Figure 6-48, I have created a three-column standard dashboard, where I have added a list of records, charts, and an iframe to show my website. Note that the data selections that I've presented on the dashboard aren't related to each other, nor I can interact with the data.

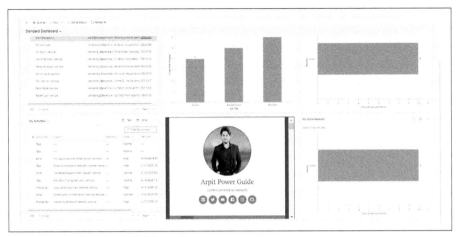

Figure 6-48. Standard dashboard

Interactive dashboards

Interactive dashboards are the modern way of creating real-time, interactive dashboards, where users can interact with the table data and charts. Interactive dashboards are further categorized based on streams. A *stream* is nothing but a view (list of data) that is linked to a particular table:

- A *single stream* is a table-specific dashboard where all the streams are based on the same table. The dashboard shown in Figure 6-49 is linked only to the Contacts table, and therefore all the charts and components are visualized based only on the Contacts table's data.

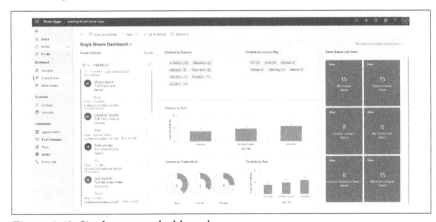

Figure 6-49. Single-stream dashboard

Figure 6-50 shows the layout options you have based on the number of charts and controls you want to display on the single-stream interactive dashboard.

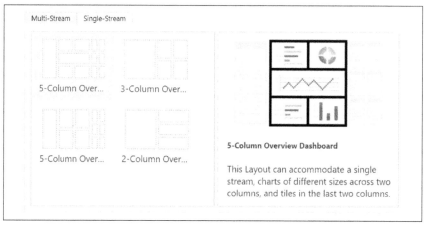

Figure 6-50. Single-stream dashboard layout options

- *Multi-stream* dashboards show data from various data streams in real time. There is no restriction on the number of streams you can set up on the dashboard. A stream's data can only be based on one table; however, each stream can be based on a different table.

The dashboard shown in Figure 6-51 is also linked only to the Contacts table and displays visualization based on that one table. However, it also has streams from other tables—Emails, Phone Calls, Appointments, Tasks— which are filtered based on the Contacts table.

Figure 6-51. Multi-stream dashboard

Figure 6-52 shows the layout options available based on the number of charts and controls you want to display on the multi-stream interactive dashboard.

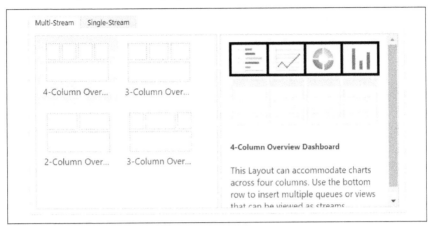

Figure 6-52. Multi-stream interactive dashboard layout options

Creating a dashboard

To create a new standard dashboard, you need to open your solution, click on +New from the command bar, and then select Dashboard, followed by the desired dashboard layout, as shown in Figure 6-53.

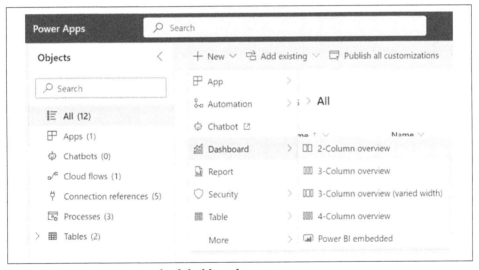

Figure 6-53. Creating a standard dashboard

To create a new interactive dashboard, you need to open your solution in the classic solution editor. To do this, open your solution from the solution list, click on the three dots (...) on the command bar, and click on "Switch to classic." You will then be taken to the classic solution editor screen, as shown in Figure 6-54.

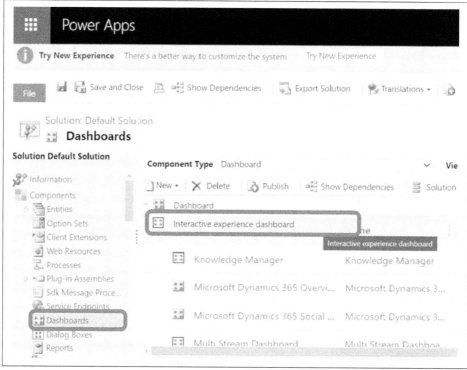

Figure 6-54. Creating an interactive dashboard

 As of this writing, interactive dashboards cannot be created from the modern solution UI designer, so you have to switch to the classic solution editor for the time being.

Dashboard Security

Based on the user type, dashboards are further categorized in two categories:

System dashboard

When you create any new dashboard (standard or interactive) from the solution (as discussed previously), it is always created as a system dashboard, which is globally available for all users using the model-driven app. System dashboards can only be created by a user who has either the System Administrator or System Customizer security role.

User (personal) dashboard

User dashboards are for personal use and are something that you can create for yourself. A user dashboard can't be accessed by other users in the organization unless you share it with them specifically. Any user can set their own dashboard as the default dashboard and override the system dashboard.

To create a personal dashboard, open your model-driven app and navigate to the page from the left navigation panel, where you are displaying all dashboards. Click on +New from the command bar to create your personal dashboard, as shown in Figure 6-55.

Figure 6-55. Creating your own dashboard

Embedded Power BI

As introduced in Chapter 2, Power BI is a Power Platform component that is a business intelligence tool that provides many low-code, no-code controls with various visualization options to create beautiful charts, reports, and dashboards. As discussed in an earlier section, you can create eight types of charts in model-driven apps and use them on dashboards as well. However, sometimes you need to show some advanced reporting features, like drill-down reports and a dashboard with more intuitive visualization controls (see Figure 6-56). In this situation, you can create the charts/reports/dashboards in Power BI and embed them in a model-driven app.

To create a new Power BI embedded dashboard in your model-driven app, you need to first create a report or dashboard in Power BI (*https://oreil.ly/uQ5Ap*), then you need to open your Dataverse solution, click on +New from the command bar, and select Dashboard → "Power BI embedded" to view all reports and dashboards created using Power BI (see Figure 6-57).

Creating a Power BI dashboard or report is beyond the scope of this book. But if you want to know more about it, you can navigate to "Create a Power BI dashboard from a report" (*https://oreil.ly/rDt29*).

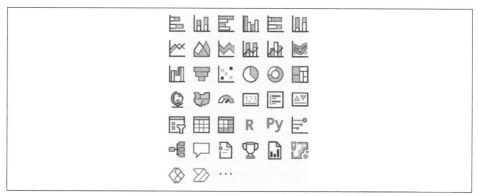

Figure 6-56. Power BI visuals

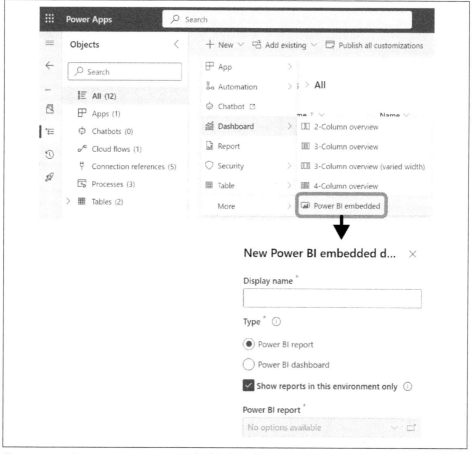

Figure 6-57. Creating a Power BI embedded dashboard

Sharing a Model-Driven App

Model-driven apps can be shared with both internal and external users. The only difference for external users is that they must be a guest user in Microsoft Entra ID. Then you can locate them in the same list as internal users and should have appropriate Power Apps license assigned.

Choose the user with whom you want to share the app, as shown in Figure 6-58, and then grant them the necessary Dataverse security roles. You can find more information about this in "Share a model-driven app" (*https://oreil.ly/EQ7UY*). Additionally, in a model-driven app, you can restrict access by assigning security roles directly to the app itself. This means that only users who have been assigned the specific security role associated with the app will be able to access it.

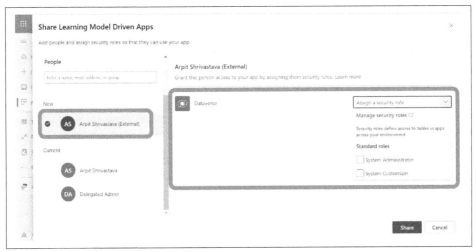

Figure 6-58. Sharing a model-driven app with an external user

Summary

In this chapter, you have learned what model-driven app components and features are from the citizen developer's perspective. Additionally, you learned the significance of using the various types of low-code, no-code model-driven app components: data components, UI components, logic components, and visualization components.

Sometimes, out-of-the-box components and features are enough to design your final product. But sometimes you need to customize the app and extend its capabilities by writing client-side (JavaScript) and server-side (C#) code, creating custom controls and components, integrating the application with external data sources, and extending the user interface to meet business requirements. I'll talk about the components that are used to extend the model-driven application capabilities in Chapter 7.

Extending Model-Driven App Features

Model-driven apps are primarily focused on business application development, with minimum custom development effort. In this chapter, I will discuss how you can extend the capabilities of a model-driven app.

Client-side development, also known as frontend development, involves business logic and code (JavaScript, Web API, etc.) that executes on a client's machine. This type of development focuses only on the front part of an application, whereas server-side development, also known as backend development, involves business logic and code that executes directly on the server (database).

The capabilities of a model-driven app can be expanded by using a variety of client-side and server-side components.

Code Components

In a model-driven app, the code components determine how to design custom components and write code when out-of-the-box components aren't enough to meet your business requirements or if you need to change their default behavior. These components are for professional developers to extend the capabilities of the app. Let's talk about each code component in more detail.

Web Resources and JavaScript

Web resources in model-driven apps are the container of all web-related resources or virtual files that are used to extend model-driven apps. Each web resource is stored as a record in Microsoft Dataverse and generates a unique relative URL that you can use to preview its outcome.

There are three categories of web resources based on the type of file you want to store:

Code
- JavaScript for writing business logic
- CSS to provide styles for pages
- Style sheet (XSL) to transform XML data to render a page that displays a table
- Web page (HTML) to design custom web pages

Images
> Used to store GIF, ICO, JPG, PNG, and SVG images that can also be used as icons at various places during UI design, such as on table forms, views, and dashboards.

Data
- Data (XML) to keep data in XML format to further use it in the code
- String (RESX) to keep the text/string in different languages

Web resources to store code

To create a new web resource, you need to open the solution, click on +New from the command bar, and then select More → Web resource, as shown in Figure 7-1.

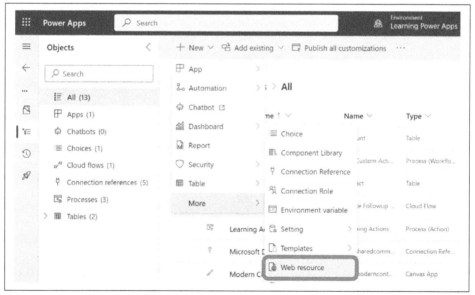

Figure 7-1. Creating a web resource

Once you click on Web resource, it will open a dialog box to provide web resource details. Here you need to provide your web resource name, its type, and, if necessary, upload the file, depending on your web resource type. For demonstration, I have created a web resource of "JavaScript" type and uploaded the script file, as shown in Figure 7-2.

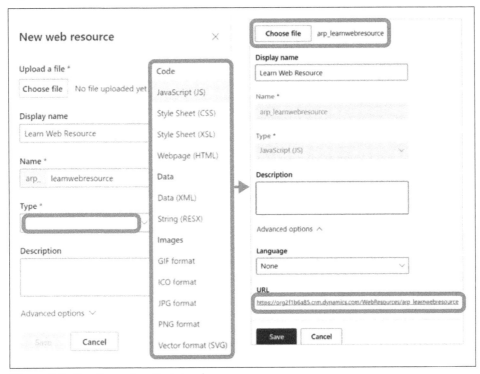

Figure 7-2. Creating a JavaScript web resource

The following are important points to know about web resources:

- Web resources don't support .aspx pages to execute server-side code.
- The maximum file upload size is 5 MB. But you can change that limit from the Power Platform admin center. Select your environment, select Settings, expand the Email section, scroll down to the Attachments heading, and change the file size in kilobytes.
- You can use a web resource to open an HTML page in a new window along with passing various parameters. The following is the method with required parameters you need to write in JavaScript to open the HTML web resource:

```
Xrm.Navigation.openWebResource(webResourceName,windowOptions,data);
```

where:

— `webResourceName` is the name of the HTML web resource that needs to be opened

— `windowOptions` sets the height and width of the window

— `data` is the data to be passed to the page in the form of data parameters

- You can reference one web resource within another web resource using its schema name (prefix_webresourcename) and can pass multiple parameters as well. Refer to "Sample: Pass multiple values to a web resource through the data parameter" (*https://oreil.ly/8mp21*) for more information.

- Sometimes editing files (especially JavaScript, HTML, XML, and XSL) in the default web resource editor is not user friendly. You can use WebResources Manager (*https://oreil.ly/8OFQv*), developed by community developers, instead.

- Web resources can be created in Dataverse programmatically as well.

Refer to the openWebResource documentation (*https://oreil.ly/_XWQB*) for more information.

Web resources to store images

You need to create image web resources to make images available for use in model-driven apps. These images can be in PNG, JPG, GIF, ICO, or SVG formats. The steps for creating image-type web resources are the same as for JavaScript-type web resources. The only change is that you need to upload the image file instead of the JavaScript file.

The following are uses of images in model-driven apps:

- Custom table icons

- Icons for custom ribbon controls and site map subareas

- Decorative graphics for forms and web page web resources

- Background images that are used by CSS web resources

- HTML pages that have images

Microsoft recommends using SVG over other image types. The advantage of SVG is scale, smaller in size, and if the fill color is removed the model-driven app can control the icon color to avoid contrast issues. With SVG, you can define one vector image and reuse it across the application rather than provide multiple sizes of images of PNG and JPG types.

You can learn more about image web resources from the Microsoft documentation (*https://oreil.ly/MXA_K*).

Web resources to store data

Web resources can also be created to store configuration data and settings that you can reuse in your code. You can create two types of data web resources, XML and RESX.

XML web resources. Sometimes while designing a solution or writing business logic, you need some collection of data or settings that will be static for the time being but may change in the future or in a different environment. For example, you might be calling an external API that has certain configurations such as API key, API endpoint URL, API domain, and API header details. Since these values may change in the future and wouldn't be the same across different environments, instead of using these details directly in the code, you can keep them in one place (often called a configuration) and refer to it from anywhere in your application.

To store such data, developers usually choose one of the following approaches:

- Use environment variables (this is the recommended approach, which I will discuss later in this chapter).

- Create a custom table in Dataverse to hold the data.

- Secure and unsecure configuration; this is only if you are using Dataverse plug-ins.

- Create an XML web resource:

```xml
<?xml version="1.0" encoding="utf-8" ?>
<SMSAPIConfiguration>
  <Url>http://smsgatewaytesturl.com</Url>
  <UserDomain>domain</UserDomain>
  <UserName>username</UserName>
  <UserPassword>Password</UserPassword>
  <APIKey>ApiKey</APIKey>
</SMSAPIConfiguration>
```

Although the recommended option is to use environment variables, it is up to the developer to choose which approach works best for their project requirements. Also, keep in mind that XML web resources are not an adequate solution for data that is often changed by multiple users. While one person is modifying an XML web resource, another user (or automated process) could modify it and that data would be lost when the first user saves their modifications.

RESX web resources. Use RESX (.NET resource file) web resources to handle localized strings in any user interface you create or to display error messages. Imagine you are creating a model-driven app where you need to enable various languages like German, Swedish, and Chinese and want to display errors, warnings, and other messages using code (plug-ins, JavaScript, etc.) in the same language as the logged-in user's preferred language. In this case, using the hard-coded string messages in your code for different languages is not a good choice; instead you can create a web resource of type RESX.

RESX web resources contain the keys and localized string values for a single language defined using the RESX XML format. When you create RESX web resources, you must explicitly set the language value and include the LCID for the appropriate language in the name of the web resource. For example, the *arp_/strings/ErrorMessages.1033.resx* file would contain resources for American English (LCID 1033):

```
<root>
    <data name="EmailDuplicateMsg">
      <value>Contact with duplicate email can not be created</value>
    <data>
    <data name="MobileNoDuplicateMsg">
      <value>Contact with duplicate mobile number can not be created</value>
    <data>
</root>
```

To extract the localized value, use the Xrm.Utility.getResourceString (*https:// oreil.ly/7ZWmz*) function. This function accepts two parameters: WebResourceName and keyValue.

For example:

```
Xrm.Utility.getResourceString("arp_/strings/ErrorMessages.1033.resx",
    "EmailDuplicateMsg");
```

will return the localized string value for the resource key EmailDuplicateMsg within the file *arp_/strings/ErrorMessages.1033.resx*.

Writing JavaScript

Client-side scripting using JavaScript is one of the ways to implement specific business logic for displaying data on a form in a model-driven app.

Writing JavaScript should not be your first choice to write client-side business logic. You should first check the other possible low-code, no-code options like using business rules or Power Fx. Microsoft is heavily investing in making Power Fx a standard language for writing business logic across Power Apps and other Power Platform components. Although it doesn't currently support everything that JavaScript does, there are plenty of options that you can use to avoid writing code for tasks that can be completed with a few lines of a Power Fx expression.

Some of the most common business requirements that need a JavaScript solution:

- Retrieve data from related tables (lookup columns) and perform client-side validation based on it.

- Hide and show sections and tabs conditionally on a form.

- Open a custom page on the click of a toolbar button and pass form context as parameters. (I will cover this in the next section.)
- Call an external API to update data on a form.
- Perform CRUD operations in Dataverse using a script. (You can also do this with a web API, which can only be triggered on the client side or when you open a specific record. I'll discuss this in the Dataverse Web API section.)
- Interact with other form controls like grids, quick forms, and quick views.
- Perform validation or write business logic on editable subgrid columns.

How to use JavaScript on model-driven app forms

You'll need to write JavaScript code when an event occurs on a model-driven app form or grid whenever a form or grid load is loaded, data is changed, or when it is saved. By associating the JavaScript code with an event, it will execute when the event occurs. There are events on which you can trigger your function (also called an *event handler*) to execute your code. These events are shown in Table 7-1. Further information can be found in the Microsoft documentation (*https://oreil.ly/XVOiX*).

As shown in Table 7-1, you can associate event handlers with some events using the UI. For events that are not available through the UI (addOnChange, addOnLoad, addOnSave, addPreSearch, etc.), you can use Client API methods to attach event handlers to the events using code. For more information, see the Microsoft documentation (*https://oreil.ly/LkQNw*).

Table 7-1. Events on various controls in model-driven apps

Component	Event	Event handler
Column	OnChange	UI
Control	OnOutputChange	Code
Form	OnLoad OnSave	UI
Form data	OnLoad	UI
Grid and subgrid	OnChange OnLoad OnRecordSelect OnSave	Code
IFrame control	OnReadyStateComplete	Code
Lookup control	OnLookupTagClick PreSearch	Code
Process	OnProcessStatusChange OnStageChange OnStageSelected	Code
Tab	TabStateChange	UI

You can read more about these events in the Microsoft documentation (*https://oreil.ly/133s6*).

 By default, the event handlers I just discussed aren't called when a form is in bulk edit mode. (*Bulk edit mode* allows you to select multiple records and apply changes to common fields all at once.) To enable an event handler in bulk edit mode, modify the Form XML by finding the relevant event element and creating/setting the `BehaviorInBulkEditForm` attribute to Enabled. Currently, this is only supported for `OnLoad` events. For more information on Form XML customization, see "When to edit the customizations file" (*https://oreil.ly/QBKLo*), "Customize forms" (*https://oreil.ly/CRsne*), and "Form XML schema" (*https://oreil.ly/YKC0t*) in the Microsoft documentation.

You can add JavaScript code to "respond" to these events so that it will run only when the particular event takes place on a specific control. JavaScript code can be added to the model-driven app form using web resources (of JavaScript type). Let's look at an example. I have created a JavaScript type web resource that will perform the following business logic and display an alert message when the Account form is loaded:

- Retrieve account's name and phone number from the account record
- Retrieve first name and last name from the parameters passed to the JavaScript function
- Display information in an alert message

The following steps are needed to have this run when the form is loaded.

Step 1: Create a web resource and open it in the classic editor. First, I need to create a web resource (described in an earlier section), then open it in the classic editor. To do so, open the solution from the solution list, expand the "Web resources" section in the left navigation panel, and select Code. This will display a list of all script type web resources in the right navigation panel. Click on the three dots next to the web resource that you want to edit, then select Edit → Edit in classic. This will open the web resource in the classic editor, as shown in Figure 7-3.

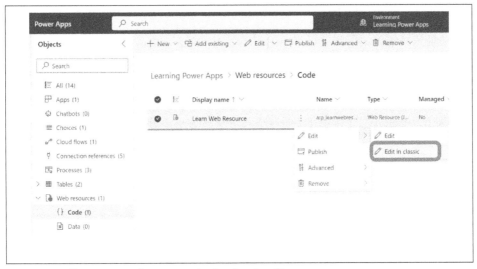

Figure 7-3. Opening a web resource in the classic editor

Step 2: Click on Text Editor to write JavaScript code. Next, you need to click the Text Editor button (shown in Figure 7-4) to open the JavaScript editor in Power Apps, where you can write the JavaScript code that will perform your business logic. Unfortunately, this editor is not very developer friendly. Instead, you may want to use Visual Studio Code (VS Code), GitHub, Notepad++, or the WebResources Manager (*https:// oreil.ly/Qp21q*) tool from XrmToolBox to write your code to avoid syntax- and formatting-related issues.

Figure 7-4. Web resource in classic editor

Example 7-1 shows the JavaScript code that I've written for this example. You can get it from the GitHub repo (*https://oreil.ly/pvoZI*) for this book.

Example 7-1. learnwebresource.js

```
function sayHelloOnFormLoad(executionContext,firstName,lastName) ❶
{
    var formContext = executionContext.getFormContext(); ❷
    var accountName = formContext.getAttribute("name").getValue(); ❸
    var accountPhone = formContext.getAttribute("telephone1").getValue(); ❹
    Xrm.Navigation.openAlertDialog({ text: "Hello! "+firstName+" "+lastName+".
      "+"Please call customer: "+" "+accountName+" on: "+accountPhone }); ❺
}
```

❶ Function name with parameters:

  - executionContext defines the event context in which your code executes.
  - The second and third parameters are passed from the form. They are usually used to pass the configuration-related data that you don't want to hardcode.

❷ Used to get the form context (current data available on the form) from the execution context. Form context is required to get the column data available on the form without querying Dataverse.

❸ Used to get the Account Name column data (logicalname: name) from the form context.

❹ Used to get the Phone column data (logicalname: telephone1) from the form context.

❺ Display the retrieved data in the alert message.

When you are finished writing the code in the text editor, click OK, and then Save and Publish to use the web resource on the Account form.

Step 3: Add this JavaScript on the load of the Account form using the web resource (library).
Next, you will need to add the web resource library named arp_learnwebresource to the form and call the JavaScript function on the load of the Account form. To do so, you will need to edit the form, click on Events from the right panel, expand the On Load section, and click on Event Handler. Then you need to select the web resource library, provide the function name, and select the checkboxes Enabled (to ensure that your function will execute when an event gets triggered) and "Pass execution context as first parameter" (to pass your form data to the JavaScript function so that you don't have to query Dataverse to read it). Additionally, I have provided the two parameters

"Arpit" and "Shrivastava" as the first and second parameters, which are required for my JavaScript function to call, as shown in Figure 7-5.

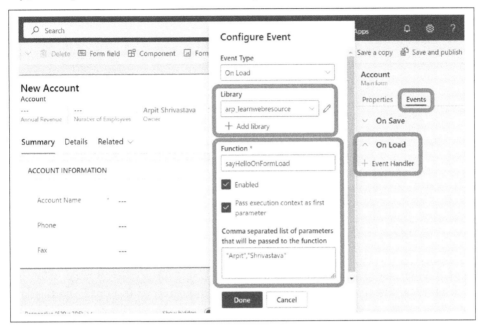

Figure 7-5. Adding JavaScript code on On Load event of the Account form

Step 4: Add dependencies column. All columns that are referenced in your JavaScript code *must be present on the form* for the JavaScript `formContext` object to retrieve them. When you are part of a large team, it may be possible that other developers may accidentally or purposefully remove the column from the form to meet their needs.

You can add the dependent columns to the Table Column Dependencies list to make sure they don't get removed from the form. Columns on this list are locked so that they can't be removed from the form unless they are also removed from the list of dependent columns.

To set the table column dependencies and event handler, open the form editor of the table, click on Events in the right navigation panel, expand the desired event, and set Table Column Dependencies and Handlers, as shown in Figure 7-6.

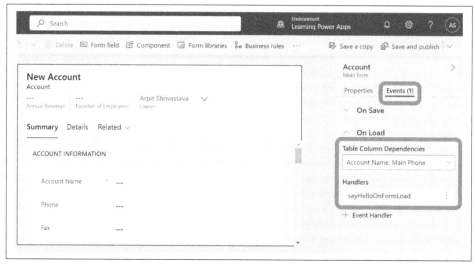

Figure 7-6. Adding code-dependent columns to the dependencies list

Step 5: Test the code by opening an Account record.   To test the JavaScript code, select an Account record from the Accounts view. The Account record will open and the data that was retrieved using JavaScript will display in the alert box, as shown in Figure 7-7.

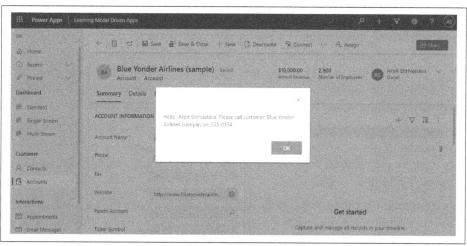

Figure 7-7. Alert box displays on load of the Account form

In the same way, you can add JavaScript using web resources on other events as well.

Client API object model for model-driven apps

The Client API object model describes how you can interact with or access the different objects (controls) present on the model-driven app form while writing JavaScript code to implement your business logic.

If you select the option "Pass execution context as first parameter" (see Step 3) when adding web resources to your form, any time an event (such as a form load or save, or a column value change) takes place on the form, executionContext keeps track of the information related to the event and the form context and passes it to your JavaScript code. To access the various controls available on the form, executionContext is the required parameter that must be sent to your JavaScript code. formContext can then access other controls on the form, including attributes, entities, quick forms, tabs, and values from the columns.

As depicted in Figure 7-8, the Client API object model for model-driven apps allows developers to write JavaScript mainly on two objects: data and UI. The *data object* provides properties and methods to work with the data on a form, including table data and data in the business process flow control. *UI objects* provide methods to retrieve information about the user interface, in addition to collections for several subcomponents of the form or grid. And the shaded boxes represent the collections, which provide access to data that represents an array.

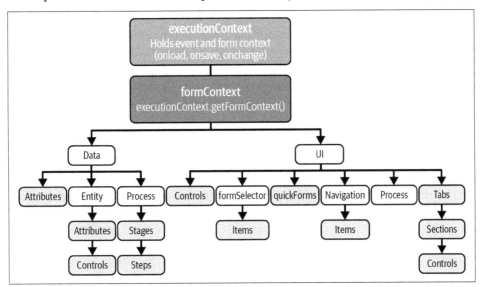

Figure 7-8. Client API object model

The following are important points about JavaScript:

- To avoid form loading performance issues, don't write too much JavaScript on the load of the form.

- Apart from running on a specific event, JavaScript can also be triggered manually or on-demand when a toolbar button is clicked. (We already discussed this earlier in the "Command Bar (Toolbar) Designer".)

- If you have multiple forms of the same table then, unlike business rules, web resources need to be added on each form individually.

- Web resources can also help make the code reusable. To avoid having to write the same code multiple times, you can write it once in a web resource and refer to it in many other web resources.

Web Services in Dataverse

Web services in Dataverse provide various services and APIs to interact with Dataverse data programmatically. When you perform any action (create, update, delete, read, etc.) from Power Apps, it calls a web service internally to perform the operation in Dataverse. Web services are of three types:

Global Discovery Service (GDS)
Used to discover the environment the user of your application can access. As we've discussed previously, you can have multiple environments in Power Apps. Each environment associates with Dataverse to store its data and metadata. GDS is used to retrieve the list of all environments for a particular tenant so that you can choose the environment in which you want to perform the operations in Dataverse. Refer to the Microsoft documentation (*https://oreil.ly/DyEx-*) to learn more about GDS and how to use it.

Organization service
Once you discover the environment and connect to it, the Organization service provides access to the data and metadata stored in Dataverse. All data operations, whether they are within Power Apps or outside Power Apps (external applications), go through the Organization service, which provides various classes and methods that you can use to perform CRUD operations in Dataverse. The Organization service was originally provided for those who wanted to interact with Dataverse data using ASP.NET, SDK assemblies, or C# code. It uses concepts of object-oriented programming (OOP) like inheritance, polymorphism, abstraction, interfaces, classes, objects, and methods to interact with Dataverse. Therefore, it is also used when you are writing plug-ins and custom workflow code using .NET Framework SDK assemblies.

Dataverse Web API

Also known as Web API, this is an extension of the Organization service that can be used by a wide variety of languages, platforms, and devices to interact with Dataverse. Dataverse Web API implements OData 4.0 (Open Data Protocol), which supports open standards to build and consume RESTful (representational state transfer) APIs. Since Dataverse Web API supports open standards, it doesn't require any assemblies or libraries to perform operations in Dataverse, unlike Organization services. Instead, you use HTTP requests for specific operations.

Dataverse Web API serves as an added layer above the Organization service, offering a RESTful programming experience. However, it's important to note that all data operations ultimately pass through the Organization service. The Web API doesn't use events (also called messages) like create, update, and delete as does the Organization service; instead, it uses GET, POST, PATCH, and DELETE HTTP methods. However, internally within the platform, create, update, delete, and retrieve events are invoked.

You cannot interact directly with data stored in Dataverse, as shown in Figure 7-9. Your Power Apps and Dataverse must communicate with one another via the Organization service, which serves as a mediator.

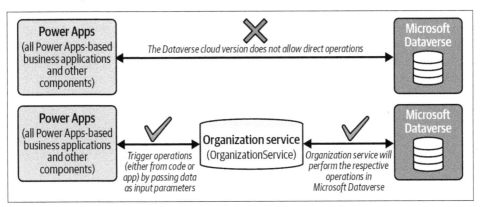

Figure 7-9. Communication between Power Apps and Microsoft Dataverse via Organization service

Dataverse Web API use cases

There are many business use cases where you need to call the Dataverse Web API to perform operations in Dataverse. A few of them are:

- Your client has an online application that has a page to manage the tickets (issues/concerns) raised by customers. This application can be implemented in C#, ASP.NET, Java, PHP, or Python. The client wants to store these tickets in Dataverse and perform all business logic, including sending email notifications, updating the status of the tickets, and elevating tickets to different levels, among other things. In this scenario, Dataverse Web API needs to be called by the developers of that online application portal to send and receive the data between that application and Dataverse.

- Your customer wants to use Microsoft Dataverse as a backend to store and execute business logic on their WordPress-based website. In this scenario, Dataverse Web API needs to be called by the WordPress developers to send and receive the data between the WordPress website and Dataverse.

- You are using the Dynamics 365 Sales app to handle the sales process of one retail company. The company has its own order management system that keeps track of customers' order details like order number, date, shipping status, and delivery date. Any changes made in the order details need to be immediately reflected in the Dynamics 365 Sales app, so that coworkers can share the updated details with the customer. In this scenario, Web API needs to be called by the developers of the order management system to update the order details in Dataverse.

How do I decide when to use the Organization service versus the Dataverse Web API?

It is not always required that you use Power Apps or a Microsoft-provided application or tool to interact with the data and metadata stored in Microsoft Dataverse. You may need to create your own custom applications, which could be web-based, console-based, or Windows-based, to perform operations in Dataverse. Sometimes, there is a scenario where developers of other platforms are using different programming languages and aren't familiar with Dataverse and Power Apps, but still need to be able to interact with Dataverse. Hence, there could be many business scenarios where you need to perform operations in Dataverse in different styles.

Figure 7-10 shows a decision tree that will help you determine when to use the Organization service versus the Dataverse Web API. (All of the "yes" branches refer to using the Organization service.)

As per the decision tree, if you get a new project or requirement to perform operations in Microsoft Dataverse, the first question you should ask yourself is which component you should use.

If you need to write the business logic by writing the code in ASP.NET using plug-ins or custom workflows (which I will discuss later in this chapter), then you will have to use the SDK assemblies provided by Microsoft. You can rest assured that there's no need for concern regarding the Dataverse Web API or any other services when performing operations in Dataverse. Microsoft internally employs the Organization service to interact with Dataverse. Your focus should solely be on utilizing its classes, objects, and methods to transmit your data to that service, as depicted in Figure 7-11.

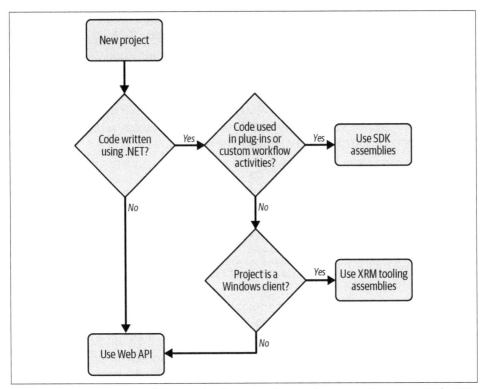

Figure 7-10. Decision tree for using the Organization service versus Dataverse Web API

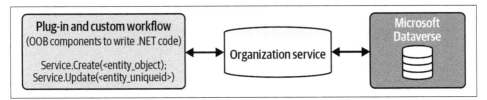

Figure 7-11. Plug-ins and custom workflows interact with Dataverse

While using plug-ins and custom workflows, you don't need to use Global Discovery Services (*https://oreil.ly/zjxwv*) in your code to find and connect to your Dataverse environment. It automatically happens at the time of plug-in registration. You need to connect the plug-in registration tool to the respective Dataverse environment to register the plug-ins and workflow assemblies.

If you need to write the business logic by writing the code in ASP.NET without using a plug-in or custom workflow, then how you will interact with Dataverse will depend on whether you are creating a Windows-based application (that needs to be installed on your machine to run; often called a desktop application) or non-Windows application (that runs in a browser; i.e., a web application). For a Windows-based application, you should use XRM tooling assemblies (*https://oreil.ly/OFqhX*) to connect and perform operations in Dataverse, as shown in Figure 7-12.

Since these applications are not registered via the Plug-in Registration tool, you need to first use GDS to find and connect your Dataverse environment, and then use the Organization service (same as for the plug-in and custom workflow) to perform the operation in Dataverse. The XRM tooling assemblies use the Organization service and Discovery Service SDK assembly APIs to easily implement authentication with fewer lines of code and through Windows PowerShell cmdlets.

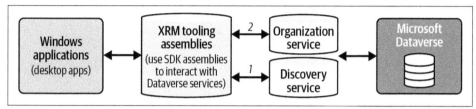

Figure 7-12. Windows application interacts with Dataverse

And, if you are creating a web-based or mobile-based application that uses a standard protocol like OAuth, then you should use the Dataverse Web API to connect and perform operations in Dataverse. It works the same as other RESTful APIs, where you call the Dataverse Web API along with passing some input parameters through your code. It will do the authorization from Microsoft Entra ID by verifying the caller's identity and then perform the operations using GET, POST, PATCH, etc. methods on Dataverse via the Organization service internally, as shown in Figure 7-13.

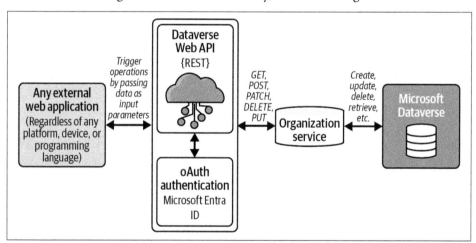

Figure 7-13. Web API interacts with Dataverse

Dataverse Web API structure and operations

You can use a wide variety of programming languages and libraries to connect with the data in Dataverse via the Web API, which offers a RESTful web service interface. As discussed in Chapter 3, you can find the Dataverse Web API details under the Developer resources settings, as shown in Figure 7-14.

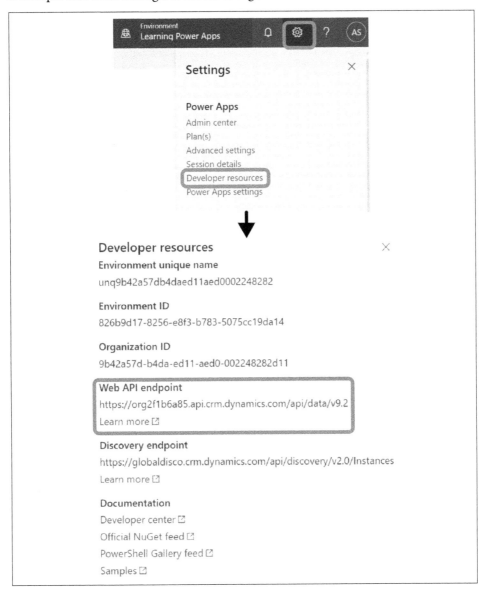

Figure 7-14. Developer resources and Dataverse Web API endpoint

The Dataverse Web API URL, or endpoint, would look something like the following:

```
https://org2f1b6a85.api.crm.dynamics.com/api/data/v9.2/contacts
```

This URL is made up of the following elements, which are defined in Table 7-2:

```
Protocol + Environment name + Region + Base URL + Web API path + Version +
                Resource
```

Table 7-2. Dataverse Web API URL elements

Element	Description
Protocol	https://
Environment name	Unique name of the environment, which you can get from the Power Platform admin center (*https://oreil.ly/iUqjx*).
Region	Region of the data center where your environment is created. Check the Microsoft documentation (*https://oreil.ly/Deycw*) for more details.
Base URL	dynamics.com
Web API path	The path to the Dataverse Web API is */api/data*.
Version	v[Major_version].[Minor_version][PatchVersion]. The current version is v9.2. Versions may change in the future based on updates to the Dataverse Web API.
Resource	The entity set name of the table or name of the function or action you want to perform. To get the set name of any table in Dataverse, you must first navigate to the Power Apps home page (*https://oreil.ly/WlAha*), click on Tables from the left navigation panel, and then select the specific table (I've chosen the Contacts table) from the list. Then select Advanced → Tools → Copy set name, as shown in Figure 7-15.

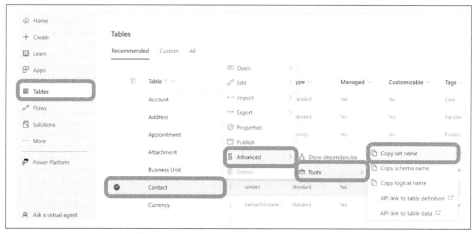

Figure 7-15. How to get the entity set name

You can check the response of the Dataverse Web API by accessing its URL in a browser, as shown in Figure 7-16.

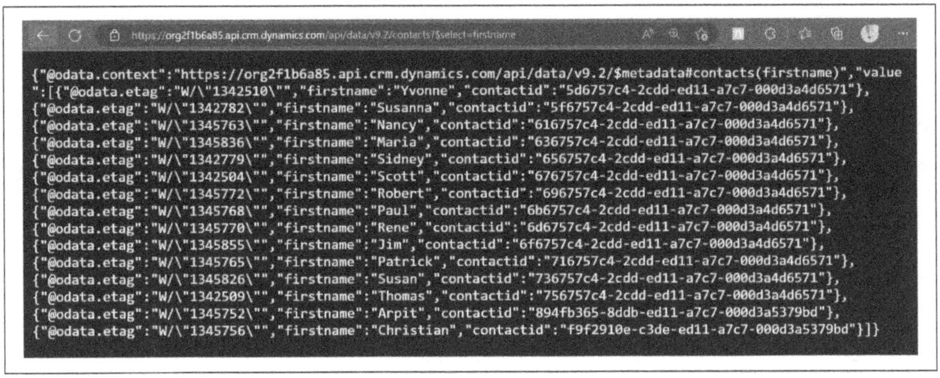

Figure 7-16. Dataverse Web API response

You can also apply a filter by adding the `$filter` query option to the URL. You can find detailed instructions in the Microsoft documentation (*https://oreil.ly/znm-L*).

For example, I've added a filter for my name to the following URL:

```
https://org2f1b6a85.api.crm.dynamics.com/api/data/v9.2/contacts?$select=firstname
            &$filter=firstname eq "Arpit"
```

Figure 7-17 shows the Dataverse Web API's response to this from the browser.

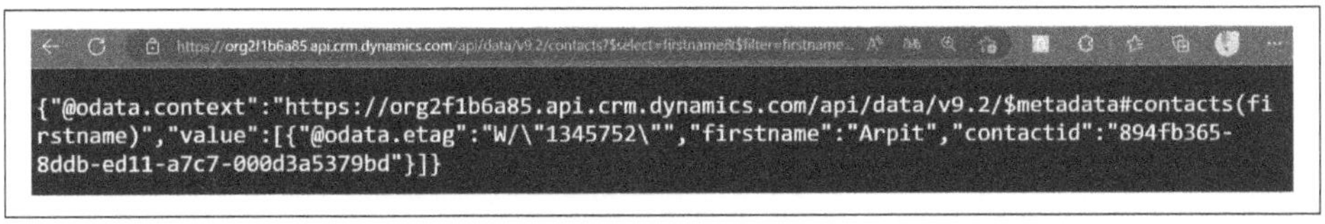

Figure 7-17. Dataverse Web API response with filter

Dataverse Web API methods.   Like other RESTful APIs, Dataverse Web API also uses HTTP methods to perform operations in Dataverse (see Table 7-3). These HTTP methods use actual messages or events internally to perform operations in Dataverse.

Table 7-3. Dataverse Web API HTTP methods

HTTP method	Purpose
GET	Retrieves data from Dataverse; calls the Retrieve event internally
POST	Creates the data or calling actions in Dataverse; calls the Update event internally
PATCH	Updates or upserts the data in Dataverse; calls the Update event internally
DELETE	Deletes the data from Dataverse; calls the Delete event internally
PUT	Used in limited situations to update table definitions (*https://oreil.ly/hvNGz*)

Dataverse Web API headers. Like other RESTful APIs, Dataverse Web API HTTP requests must have the header information shown in Table 7-4.

Table 7-4. Dataverse Web API header properties

Header property	Comments
Accept: application/ json	The Dataverse Web API only supports request and response in JSON format.
OData-MaxVersion: 4.0	This is the current version of Odata. It includes new capabilities and ensures that there is no ambiguity about the OData version that will be applied to your code in the future.
OData-Version: 4.0	Same as OData-MaxVersion.
If-None-Match: null	The Dataverse Web API caches the data in the browser to improve performance and get recent changes from Dataverse. Include the If-None-Match: null header in the request body to override browser caching of Dataverse Web API requests.

There could be some additional header properties based on requirements. See the Microsoft documentation (*https://oreil.ly/fw9Kz*) for more information.

Dataverse Web API operations. Using Dataverse Web API, you can do everything that the Organization service can do. Here is the list of all possible operations you can perform on Dataverse:

- Query data from Dataverse
- Retrieve and execute predefined queries
- Create data in Dataverse
- Retrieve data from Dataverse
- Update and delete data in Dataverse
- Associate and disassociate data in Dataverse
- Use Dataverse Web API functions
- Call Dataverse custom actions (which we discussed in an earlier section)
- Execute batch operations in Dataverse
- Impersonate another user to perform operations in Dataverse
- Perform conditional operations in Dataverse
- Manage duplicate detection during create and update operations

Dataverse Web API authentication

We discussed the several HTTP methods and headers that the Dataverse Web API uses to carry out various operations on Dataverse. But what about security, especially if a user connects to Dataverse using external or third-party applications?

Like other RESTful APIs, Dataverse Web API security also consists of authentication and authorization. Authentication is required to validate the identify of the user or process. Dataverse Web API uses Microsoft Entra ID to store and validate the user's identity. It supports many options to verify the identity of a user or process.

Authorization is the process or action of verifying whether an authenticated user has permission to access the resources that are being made available. Authorization of data is given at two levels: at the Microsoft Entra ID tenant level and at the Dataverse level associated with the Power Apps environment.

Dataverse Web API uses OAuth 2.0-based security to provide access to Dataverse data to any external applications. The OAuth authorization process uses an industry-standard protocol to provide authorization flows for web applications, Windows applications, mobile phones, etc. It also supports two-factor authentication (2FA) and client certificate-based authentication as well for server-to-server authentication scenarios.

Since the Web API supports OAuth 2.0 for authorization, all the external applications must support OAuth to access the Dataverse data via Dataverse Web API. However, if you are using model-driven apps, then you don't need to use OAuth 2.0, as the app is already tightly coupled with Microsoft Dataverse to access its data.

At a very high-level, OAuth-based authentication has three main personas:

Resource owner
> An external application or developer of external applications that wants to connect with Dataverse to access its data

Resource provider
> A Microsoft Entra ID that validates the user's identity and manages the authentication

Resource server
> The Dataverse environment that holds the data and metadata created through model-driven apps

Using OAuth authentication with Microsoft Dataverse. As of this writing, OAuth 2.0 provides Dataverse authorization at the Microsoft Entra ID tenant level. It cannot govern app-level security. Therefore, to manage security at the Dataverse or app level, you need to create an app user and assign appropriate roles to it from the Power Apps admin center.

To set up OAuth for Dataverse Web API, the Azure app needs to be registered in Microsoft Entra ID. The Microsoft Entra ID app establishes a trust relationship between your external app (or code from where you are calling the Web API) and the Microsoft Dataverse.

To register the app in Microsoft Entra ID, sign in to the Microsoft Entra admin center (*https://oreil.ly/7V_Ek*) as at least a Cloud Application Administrator (*https://oreil.ly/W-Bvd*). You will find Manage Microsoft Entra ID on the screen. Click on View to navigate to the Entra ID screen, then select "App registrations" from the left panel and click on "New registration." Enter a display name for your application and click Register. Once the registration process is complete, the Microsoft Entra admin center presents the Overview pane of the app registration. In this pane, you'll find the *Application (client) ID*, illustrated in Figure 7-18. This identifier, also known as the *client ID*, serves to uniquely distinguish your application within the Microsoft identity platform. You also need to know the *Directory (tenant) ID*, which will be required later to establish the connection with this app.

Figure 7-18. Microsoft Entra ID application client ID and tenant ID

You should now generate a secret key by selecting Certificates & secrets → Client secrets → New client secret, as shown in Figure 7-19. The lifetime of a client secret key is limited to two years (24 months) or less. You can specify a custom lifetime up to 24 months. Microsoft recommends that you set an expiration value of less than 12 months.

> Compared to certificate credentials, client secrets are seen as less secure. Developers may opt for client secrets during local app development due to their convenience. However, for applications running in production, it's advisable to employ certificate credentials (*https://oreil.ly/1Mapr*) for enhanced security measures.
>
> Client secrets are considered less secure than certificate credentials. Application developers sometimes use client secrets during local app development because of their ease of use. However, you should use certificate credentials (*https://oreil.ly/XR4qw*) for applications running in production.

Figure 7-19. Client secret key value

This Microsoft Entra ID app also needs delegated permissions on Microsoft Dataverse to give external apps access to Dataverse, as shown in Figure 7-20.

Figure 7-20. Adding delegated permission to use Microsoft Dataverse

Registering an app in Microsoft Entra ID and setting delegated API permission on Dataverse grants external app access to the Dynamics CRM tenant, but not to the environment or data from the associated Dataverse. To access Dataverse data from a particular Power Platform environment, you need to create an application (app) user (*https://oreil.ly/utMok*) (non-licensed user) in the desired Power Platform environment and assign it appropriate security roles based on the operation your external app is going to perform in Dataverse (as shown in Figure 7-21). App users act like a delegate user, which means this user will perform operations in Dataverse on behalf of the user who's using your application.

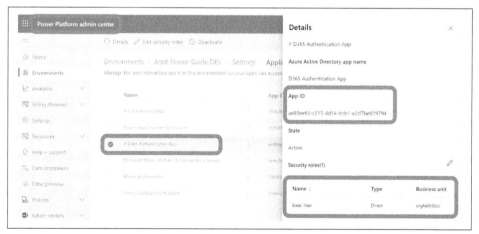

Figure 7-21. Creating an app user and assigned role in Dataverse

Once the aforementioned steps are done, you can now share the client ID, tenant ID, and secret key with the resource owner who is creating an external application and going to perform operations in Dataverse through a custom app.

Authenticating against Microsoft Dataverse by using OAuth. Once the Azure App registration is completed in Microsoft Entra ID and the app user is created in Dataverse, here's the high-level process to perform the Dataverse operations via the Web API (shown in Figure 7-22):

1. Resource owner makes requests to resource provider by sending the client ID, secret key, and tenant ID (provided by the resource provider).

2. Resource provider validates details; if they are valid, then resource provider issues a token (also referred to as an access token).

3. Resource owner uses the access token to connect with Dataverse and sends the data to the app user to perform the operation in Dataverse. For example, send first name and last name to create a contact in Dataverse.

4. Resource server is the Dataverse environment, where the app user will perform the operations in Dataverse on behalf of the external application.

5. Resource server gives the response back to resource owner; for example, a GUID or unique identifier for the contact data. (Creation of this was requested in step 3.)

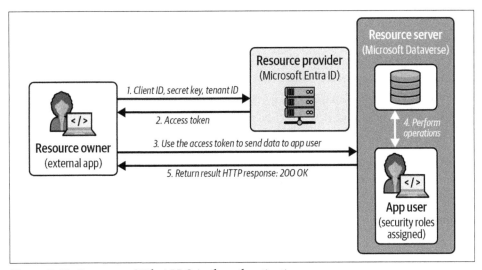

Figure 7-22. Dataverse Web API OAuth authentication process

You can refer to the article "Use OAuth Authentication with Microsoft Dataverse" (*https://oreil.ly/1E9Wx*) to find a step-by-step guide to register an app in Microsoft Entra ID and for information about the different types of app registration. Numerous client API tools like Insomnia (*https://oreil.ly/cfcxk*) and Postman (*https://oreil.ly/N9Jxc*) are available for authenticating to Microsoft Dataverse environments and facilitating the composition and sending of Dataverse Web API requests. These tools simplify the process of learning, testing, and executing ad hoc queries using the Dataverse Web API.

Calling Dataverse Web API using JavaScript

As discussed earlier, in model-driven apps, JavaScript is used to perform client-side business logic and validations. Along with that, there are numerous businesses use cases where it is required to perform operations in Dataverse, such as:

- Creating an HTML page in a model-driven app to add/update/delete data in Dataverse.
- Writing business logic based on its related table data. For example, update the case record priority to "High" if the associated customer type is "Premium."
- Applying custom filters on lookup based on related table data.

To use Dataverse Web API in JavaScript code, you can use the XRM.WebApi client API reference. XRM.WebApi provides various methods and properties to use Dataverse Web API to perform operations in Dataverse along with executing various functions and actions in model-driven apps.

There are two XRM.WebApi properties:

- The `online` property provides methods to create and manage records along with executing functions and actions in model-driven apps while connected to the model-driven app server (connected to the internet).
- The `offline` property provides methods to create and manage records in model-driven apps in mobile devices while working in offline mode (without an internet connection).

XRM.WebApi supports all methods that the Organization service supports:

- `createRecord`
- `deleteRecord`
- `retrieveRecord`
- `retrieveMultipleRecords`
- `updateRecord`
- `isAvailableOffline`
- `execute`
- `executeMultiple`

Creating a record in Dataverse using JavaScript. Let's create a record in Dataverse to learn how Web API is used in JavaScript to perform operations in Dataverse. Before doing that, first let's take a look at its syntax to know what parameters or properties it requires to create the data in Dataverse. Some parameters are required and some are optional. Figure 7-23 shows the API syntax.

Figure 7-23. Dataverse Web API syntax

The parameters are as follows:

(1) `entityLogicalName` *(required)*
Logical name of the table (in lowercase).

(2) `data` *(required)*
Collection of data (table column values) wrapped in a JSON object.

(3) `successCallback` *(optional)*
A function that is called when a record is created in Dataverse. It requires these two properties:

`entityType` *(String type)*
The logical table name of the new record

`id` *(String type)*
The GUID of the new record

(4) `errorCallback` *(optional)*
A function that is called when the Dataverse operation fails. You will get the following information in case of failure:

`errorCode` *(Number type)*
The error code (e.g., 404, 500)

`message` *(String type)*
An error message describing the issue

When the Dataverse operation is successful, it returns a Promise object with the values provided earlier in the `successCallback` parameter's description.

Creating a record in Dataverse using Dataverse Web API. Now let's create a record in Dataverse using the Dataverse Web API in JavaScript. Example 7-2 shows how to use the Dataverse Web API to add a new record to the Account table. Here I used the createRecord method to push sample values into the name, description, and revenue columns for demonstration purposes.

Example 7-2. Creating a record in Dataverse using JavaScript (Dataverse Web API)

```
function createAccountUsingWebAPI()
{
// define the data to create new account
var data =
    {
        "name": "Arpit Power Guide",
        "description": "This is the sample account",
        "revenue": 5000000,
    }
// create account record
Xrm.WebApi.createRecord("account", data).then(
    function success(result) {
        console.log("Account is created in Dataverse with ID: " + result.id);
        // perform operations on record creation
    },
    function (error) {
        console.log(error.message);
        // handle error conditions
    }
);
}
```

You can download the code from this book's GitHub repo (*https://oreil.ly/pvoZI*). In a similar way, you can perform various other operations in Dataverse. You can find more examples and syntax for other operations in the Microsoft documentation for Xrm.WebApi (*https://oreil.ly/7rdBm*).

Plug-ins

Plug-ins in model-driven apps are the custom event handlers written in C# code using .NET Framework assemblies. They always execute and perform business logic when an event triggers in Dataverse either from Power Apps or via external applications. Plug-ins are the only component after the real-time workflow (discussed earlier) that can execute business logic synchronously.

Years ago, the options for creating server-side business logic or components to extend the business process were extremely restricted. As a result, when server-side logic had to be written, plug-ins became the go-to option. Since the release of numerous low-code, no-code development components like Power Automate, Power Fx, classic workflows, calculated fields, rollup fields, and custom actions, we no longer need to use plug-ins unless they are the only option left to write the business logic.

Here are a few use cases where using a plug-in is the only choice:

- Calling an Azure function when an event occurs in Dataverse to push the data to the external system in real time.

- Restricting users to create duplicate data and throw customized error messages. Nowadays, you can also accomplish this using low-code plug-ins, as explained in Chapter 9. However, since it's still in preview, you'll need to write plug-in code to make it work.

- Calling Azure Service Bus when an event occurs in Dataverse to push the data to the external system in real time.

- Writing real-time business logic by impersonating a user.

- Calling external APIs to fetch data and update it in Dataverse in real time.

- Designing a component such as a payment system where payment needs to be done in real time and the customer needs to be updated immediately.

Plug-in event execution pipeline

When an event (create, update, delete, etc.) occurs either from Power Apps or an external application, internally it goes through the event execution pipeline before the actual operation happens in Dataverse, as shown in Figure 7-24. In this event execution pipeline, there are four stages: two stages exist before the Dataverse operation (PreValidation and PreOperation), one is itself a Dataverse operation (MainOperation), and one stage exists after the Dataverse operation (PostOperation).

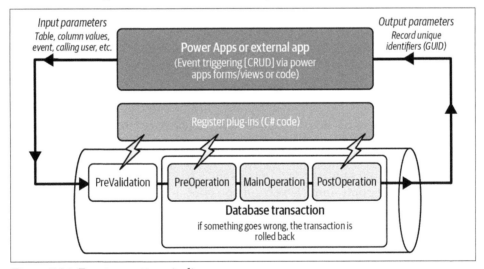

Figure 7-24. Event execution pipeline

A plug-in is the only component that lets you write your business logic on all three stages (PreValidation, PreOperation, and PostOperation). Real-time workflows allow you to write the logic only on PreOperation and PostOperation, while other components like Power Automate, business rules, and classic (background) workflows can perform the business logic only on PostOperation.

Dataverse operations and transactions differ slightly from one another because one database transaction may involve a number of database operations like create, assign, update, delete, associate, and retrieve. Since the plug-in executes the code within the database transaction, it can roll back the whole transaction if a problem occurs while performing operations in Dataverse. For example, if you registered a plug-in on creation of contact, this creates a task, assigns the tasks to the sales teams, and then sends an email to the customer. You are performing three different operations in Dataverse: create task, assign task, and send an email. Imagine if the plug-in fails while sending an email; the preceding two operations will be rolled back.

Let's discuss each stage of the event execution pipeline in more detail:

PreValidation

This stage validates some predefined security checks configured by Microsoft, such as whether the calling user has appropriate permissions to execute the logic in Dataverse. Since this stage is to validate the permissions before performing the operation in Dataverse, it executes the logic outside the transaction. You can register the plug-in on this stage if you want to validate something before executing your business logic in Dataverse. For example, I want to associate the contact with an account only if its onboarding status is Completed. If not, then I want to create a task, assign it to the HR team to take further action, and throw an error on the screen. Since this stage executes the business logic outside the database transaction, it won't roll back the operation of creating a task and assigning it to the HR team in case of error.

PreOperation

This stage allows developers to modify the input parameters (column values) sent from the application (inside or outside) to execute in Dataverse. For example, say you created a new contact by providing only first name and last name in the contact form, so ideally the contact should be created in Dataverse with first name and last name only. However, if you want to copy the first name and last name to the full name column before the contact is created in Dataverse, then you need to register the plug-in on the PreOperation stage.

MainOperation (CoreOperation)

This stage performs the main operations in Dataverse. This stage is internal because at this time the main database operation is being performed. Hence, you cannot use a plug-in on this stage.

PostOperation

This stage allows you to either modify the column values once the operation is executed in Dataverse or read the output value to use it in further operations. For example, I need to create a new contact on when a new Account is created, with the last name the same as the Account name. In addition, I need to update that newly created contact in the Primary Contact column of the Account table. In this scenario, after the creation of the Account, I must wait for the contact to be created in Dataverse, because I need its unique identifier (GUID) to update it in the primary contact field of the Account form. The GUID of any record can be found once it is created in Dataverse. In this scenario, the plug-in needs to register on the PostOperation stage when the Account is created.

Writing a plug-in

The following are the steps to start writing your first plug-in code. You need Visual Studio (*https://oreil.ly/fPEOV*) 2019 or 2022, Power Platform Tools for Visual Studio (*https://oreil.ly/geiwJ*), .NET Framework 4.6.2, and the Power Apps environment (trial or licensed). Once you have those, you can use any of the following methods to write the plug-in code in Visual Studio:

Power PlatformTools for VisualStudio

Check this quickstart article (*https://oreil.ly/7WjUO*) to learn how to write the plug-in using Power Platform tools. With this approach, you don't need to use any additional tools such as a Plug-in Registration tool for registering your plug-in, configuring plug-in steps, adding plug-in images, or deploying it.

Power Platform CLI

If you like working in Visual Studio Code (a light version of Visual Studio), you might want to use the CLI (command-line interface) commands (*https://oreil.ly/mhZch*) provided by Power Platform CLI, which you can run in a terminal window to create the plug-in.

Manually write plug-in code

You can manually write the plug-in code using your favorite editor or IDE. In this approach, you will have to use a Plug-in Registration tool to register the plug-in and its steps.

It's your choice which option you prefer to use to write and register the plug-in. I recommend using Power Platform Tools for Visual Studio, as it is a modern way and uses the latest development tools provided by Microsoft. However, in this section, I will show you how to manually write and register the plug-in code so you can see how it all works.

Plug-in code skeleton

Example 7-3 shows a typical plug-in code skeleton. Start with this, and then write your own business logic as per your business requirements. You can get this code from the book's GitHub repo (*https://oreil.ly/pvoZI*).

Example 7-3. Plug-in code skeleton

```
using System;
using System.ServiceModel;
using Microsoft.Xrm.Sdk;
namespace PowerGuide_Plugin_Solution.NotifyPlugin
{
    public class NotifyContactCreate: PluginBase
    {
        public NotifyContactCreate(string unsecure, string secure) :
          base(typeof(NotifyContactCreate))
        {
            // TODO: Implement your custom configuration handling.
        }
        protected override void ExecutePluginCode(LocalPluginContext localContext)
        {
            if (localContext == null)
            {
                throw new InvalidPluginExecutionException(nameof(localContext));
            }
            ITracingService tracingService = localContext.TracingService;
            try
            {
                IPluginExecutionContext context =
                  (IPluginExecutionContext)localContext.PluginExecutionContext;
                IOrganizationService service = localContext.OrganizationService;
                // TODO: Implement your custom Plug-in business logic.
            }
            catch (Exception ex)
            {
                tracingService?.Trace("An error occurred executing Plugin
                  PowerGuide_Plugin_Solution.NotifyPlugin.NotifyContactCreate :
                    {0}", ex.ToString());
                throw new InvalidPluginExecutionException("An error occurred
                  executing Plugin
                    PowerGuide_Plugin_Solution.NotifyPlugin.NotifyContactCreate
                    .", ex);
            }
        }
    }
}
```

This plug-in code has the following components:

SDK assemblies

Defining SDK assemblies will provide the required classes and methods to inter-act with the Organization service. You can get the latest SDK assembly from NuGet (*https://oreil.ly/lqb0_*). For that you need to right-click on your plug-in project (BasicPlugin in Figure 7-25) and select Manage NuGet Packages from the context menu, and then browse for `Microsoft.CrmSdk.CoreAssemblies` and install the latest version.

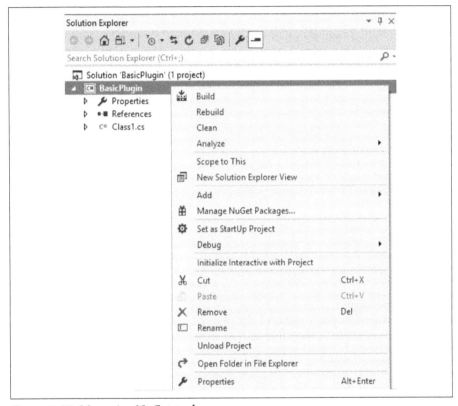

Figure 7-25. Managing NuGet packages

Plug-in interface

Each plug-in class must implement the `IPlugin` interface that has the definition of the `Execute` method.

Plug-in constructor

Optionally, while registering a plug-in, you can specify configuration data to be passed to the plug-in at runtime. This data is given as string data to the parame-terized constructor parameters to your plug-in class. These parameters are referred to as *unsecure* and *secure* configurations. Unsecure parameters are used for nonsensitive configuration data, while secure parameters are used for sensitive configuration data. Secure configuration data is stored in a separate table in Dataverse that only the system admin has privileges to read. For example, as depicted in Figure 7-26, I have passed API details as secure configuration and email reminder duration in unsecure configuration.

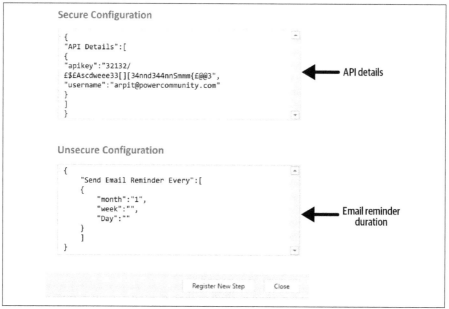

Figure 7-26. Secure and unsecure configurations in the Plug-in Registration tool

Execute method

This is the main entry point of the plug-in code, where you write your business logic that needs to be executed in Dataverse.

Plug-in execution context

Execution context will have contextual data passed to the plug-in code. It contains the table name on which the plug-in is registered, the event name that invoked the plug-in, and the data that is being passed while triggering the event (either from Power Apps or an external app). For example, if I create a contact by entering the first name and last name on the contact form and click Save, then you can get the Contacts table, the `Create` event, and the first name and last name column's values from the plug-in context. Similarly, if you create a contact using C# code, then the context data is also passed to the plug-in.

In Example 7-4, you are passing `contactEntityObj` as context parameter (contains first name and last name), while invoking the `Create` event in Dataverse.

Example 7-4. C# code to create data in Dataverse

```
// Define entity(Table) object where you need to create the data.
Entity contactEntityObj = new Entity("contact");
// provide first name
contactEntityObj["firstname"] = "Arpit";
// provide last name
contactEntityObj["lastname"] = "Shrivastava";
// create contact in Dataverse using organization service
Guid ContactId = service.Create(contactEntityObj);
```

Plug-in services

The following services have to be used in any plug-in to execute your code:

- The Organization service is used to perform operations in Dataverse, as discussed earlier.

- The Tracing service is used to trace logs and store them in the `PluginTrace Log` table. It is helpful if you need to investigate and troubleshoot the plug-in code line by line and understand what occurred when the code ran.

Your business logic

Then, finally, there's a place in your plug-in code where you can write your own business logic to perform CRUD operations in Dataverse.

Registering and deploying your plug-in

Once your plug-in code is written and ready to be used, you must do the following:

1. Build the plug-in code. As with other .NET projects, you need to build your plug-in class or solution to generate its assemblies or DLLs (dynamic-link libraries), which will later be required to register it to a particular event.

2. Sign the assembly. Before an assembly can be registered, it must be signed. Sn.exe (Strong Name tool) (*https://oreil.ly/XlAjm*) or the Visual Studio Signing tab on the project can be used for this.

3. Register the plug-in. The Plug-in Registration tool (PRT) is used to register the plug-in and its steps. You can download the PRT from NuGet (*https://oreil.ly/ CSKto*) and follow the instructions in the documentation (*https://oreil.ly/PEUfw*). (Optionally, if you have XrmToolBox (*https://oreil.ly/S2XWv*) already installed, you can access the PRT within that application.) Once you download and install the PRT, you can establish the connection with a Power Apps environment and register your plug-in. Follow the step-by-step guide (*https://oreil.ly/Ce2sz*) to learn how to do this.

You can now start testing your plug-in by triggering the event on which it is registered. In case of any issues, you can troubleshoot it and debug the plug-in code (*https://oreil.ly/o0w7N*) as well. You can also check the plug-in trace logs under the Plug-In Trace Log table (*https://oreil.ly/yWSnE*).

Important points to know about using plug-ins in Power Apps

The following are important things to consider when using plug-ins in Power Apps:

- Avoid writing too many synchronous plug-ins; it may impact application performance.

- Avoid using long-running processes or code in a synchronous plug-in because it won't let users do anything on the app until it finishes executing all operations in Dataverse.

- Plug-in has a timeout limit of two minutes irrespective of its types.

- You can have multiple plug-in steps on the same event. In this scenario, you should define the execution order so that they execute the operation in a specific order rather than at the same time.

- Plug-ins also have pre- and post-images that provide the column value before and after the Dataverse operation, respectively. See my article (*https://oreil.ly/BoMMl*) for details.

- Like workflows, plug-ins can be both synchronous and asynchronous. And plug-ins can do everything that workflows can do, but the inverse is not true.

- There are two special types of plug-ins called WebHook (*https://oreil.ly/XR6Ah*) and service endpoint (*https://oreil.ly/7DrE9*), which are used to directly send the Dataverse data to Azure Functions and Azure Service Bus (see Figure 7-27). I will talk more about this in "Integration Components" on page 277.

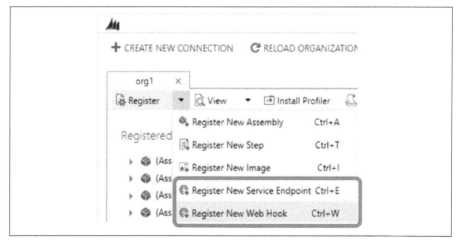

Figure 7-27. Plug-in for Azure integration

- When registering a plug-in on the update event of any table, make sure you are defining the filtering attributes (*https://oreil.ly/E2_Mr*) in the Plug-In Registration tool to avoid triggering the update plug-in on all attributes of that table. In Figure 7-28, the plug-in will only trigger when there are updates made on either the first name, last name, email, or mobile phone column in the Contacts table.

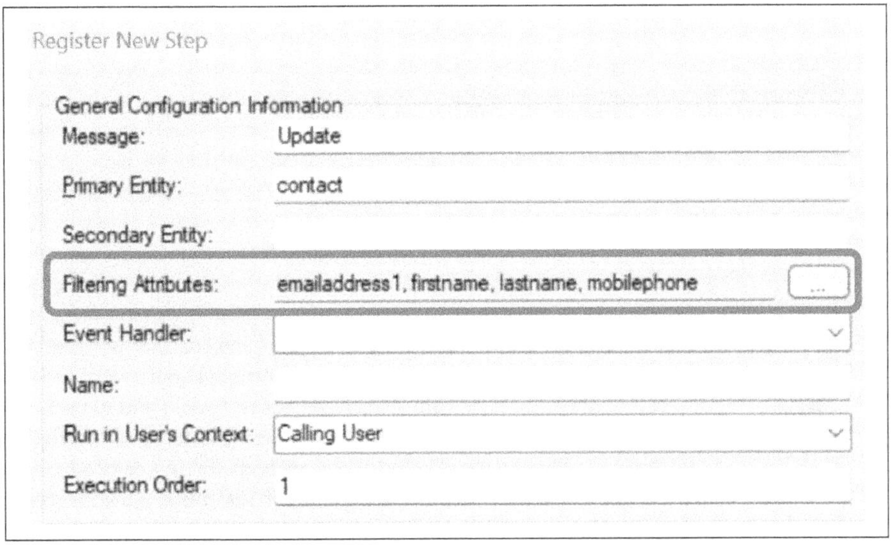

Register New Step

General Configuration Information

Message:	Update
Primary Entity:	contact
Secondary Entity:	
Filtering Attributes:	emailaddress1, firstname, lastname, mobilephone
Event Handler:	
Name:	
Run in User's Context:	Calling User
Execution Order:	1

Figure 7-28. Filtering attributes in a plug-in

- Plug-ins can be used to specify business logic for creating custom APIs or Custom Actions. Custom APIs, discussed later in this chapter, are used to create your own APIs for custom business events in Dataverse.

- Plug-ins are solution-aware components, which means you can deploy them to target a Power Apps environment by exporting and importing the solution file. Plug-in components are made up of three subcomponents, as shown in Figure 7-29:

  — Plug-in assemblies are the main plug-in project code assembly/DLL.

  — Plug-in steps are all steps (events) on which the plug-in is registered.

  — Plug-in packages hold any external assemblies or resource files (*.resx*) used in the plug-in code (e.g., *Newtonsoft.Json.dll*). See the Microsoft documentation (*https://oreil.ly/YqFd9*) to learn more about how to build and package plug-in code.

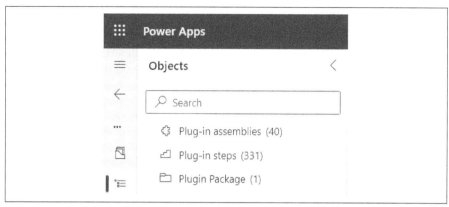

Figure 7-29. Plug-in solution components

In late 2023, Microsoft announced low-code plug-ins that use the Power Fx expression language to provide business logic to your apps and connect directly with Dataverse business data and external data via Power Platform connectors. Low-code plug-ins also allow you to easily create rich workflows without writing any code. They can be considered as a replacement for real-time workflows in the near future. I'll discuss more about this in Chapter 9.

Custom Workflow Activities

You learned about the capabilities of classic workflows (background and real-time) and their various events. However, sometimes you don't find the functionality you require using the default process activities. In this case, you can add *custom workflow activities* (also referred to as *custom activities, custom workflow assemblies,* or *workflow extensions*) so that they're available in the editor used to compose workflow, dialog, and action processes.

For example, in a classic workflow there is no way to query (retrieve) data stored in Dataverse. To do that, you might need to create a custom workflow activity.

The advantages of creating a custom workflow activity include:

- You can reuse it and call it within multiple background and real-time workflows.
- You don't need to write the whole business logic in code. You can combine it with default steps or actions of workflows, as shown in Figure 7-30.

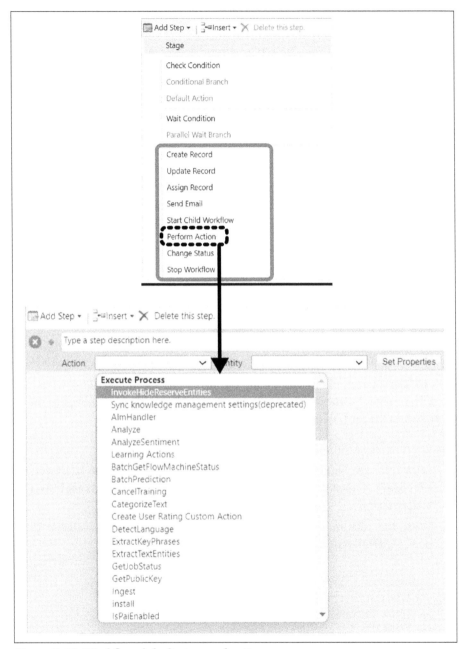

Figure 7-30. Workflow default steps and actions

Since the introduction of various low-code, no-code tools and components, custom workflows are very rarely used in model-driven apps to write business logic. Background workflows will soon be replaced with Power Automate, so it's best to avoid using custom workflows. If there is any need to use custom workflows within real-time workflows, you can use the following high-level steps to create and use them within model-driven apps' out-of-the-box workflows.

Writing custom workflow code is mostly the same as writing plug-in code except for the following:

SDK assemblies

Workflows use the `Microsoft.Xrm.Sdk` and `Microsoft.Xrm.Sdk.Workflow` SDK assemblies, while plug-ins use only `Microsoft.Xrm.Sdk`.

Class to be implemented

Workflows inherit the `CodeActivity` class, while plug-ins inherit the `IPlugin` interface.

Input/output parameters

Unlike plug-ins, which use input parameters to read input data sent to the event execution pipeline and output parameters to read value returns from Dataverse, workflows can pass input parameters from previous workflow steps to subsequent steps.

Let's look at an example that takes any number as an input parameter from a classic workflow, writes business logic to increment it by 100, and sends it back to the classic workflow in the form of an output parameter:

1. Create a Visual Studio Class Library project.

2. Select Manage NuGet Packages in the project and install the latest versions of `Microsoft.CrmSdk.Workflow` and `Microsoft.CrmSdk.CoreAssemblies` (*https:// oreil.ly/0p86X*).

3. Write the custom workflow code shown in Example 7-5 (available from the book's GitHub repo (*https://oreil.ly/pvoZI*)).

Example 7-5. SampleCustomWorkflowAssemblyCode.cs

```
using Microsoft.Xrm.Sdk;
using Microsoft.Xrm.Sdk.Messages;
using Microsoft.Xrm.Sdk.Query;
using Microsoft.Xrm.Sdk.Workflow;
using System;
using System.Activities;
namespace PowerApps.Samples
{
    public sealed class IncreamentBy100 : CodeActivity
```

```
{
    //Define the Input and Output Parameters
    [RequiredArgument
    [Input("input")]
    public InArgument<integer> WFInput { get; set; }
    [Output("output")]
    public OutArgument<integer> WFOutput { get; set; }
    protected override void Execute(CodeActivityContext
        executionContext)
    {
        IWorkflowContext context =
          executionContext.GetExtension<IWorkflowContext>();
        //Create an Organization Service
        IOrganizationServiceFactory serviceFactory =
          executionContext.GetExtension<IOrganizationServiceFactory>();
        IOrganizationService service =
          serviceFactory.CreateOrganizationService(context.
            InitiatingUserId);
        //write your custom business logic here
        Int input = WFInput.Get(context);
        WFOutput.Set(context, WFInput + 100);
    }
  }
}
```

4. Here is the description of the code written in the custom workflow activity:

   a. Inherit the `CodeActivity` class and add the `Execute` method to write the business logic.

   b. Define input and output parameters.

   c. Define the workflow context to get the execution context information. (Same as a plug-in.)

   d. Define the Organization service to perform operations on Dataverse. (Same as a plug-in.)

   e. Add the business logic to increment the number (received from the input parameter) by 100, and then set the output value to the output parameter.

5. Sign and build the assembly (same steps that you used for a plug-in).

6. Register your assembly (same as a plug-in). Custom workflows don't require any steps to register, because they will be triggered inside the classic workflows.

7. Once registered, you will find your custom workflow activity within your classic workflow, as shown in Figure 7-31.

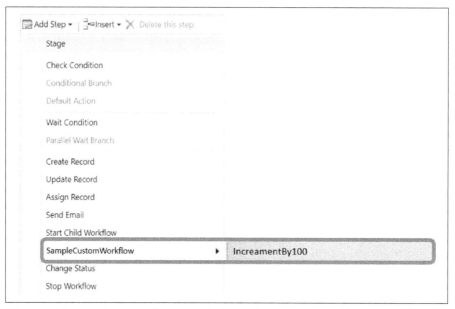

Figure 7-31. A custom workflow activity is available as a step within a workflow

8. Add your activity to a solution to deploy it to the target environments.

You can find some more examples (*https://oreil.ly/8AVB2*) and a step-by-step guide to creating custom workflow activities in the documentation (*https://oreil.ly/kV-jX*). Additionally, you should also check out Dynamics 365 Workflow Tools (*https://oreil.ly/yAotr*), which is a community solution that expands Dataverse classic workflow features with lots of new possibilities. This helps you to build very advanced no-code solutions in Dynamics 365 CE applications. This tool is nothing but a Dataverse solution that contains a workflow activity and the activities to be used in workflows, so importing this solution will not affect any existing form, entity, view, or navigation item.

Custom API

A custom API is an advanced version of a Custom Action (discussed in Chapter 6) that extends the capabilities of Custom Actions along with some advanced features. You can find the major differences between Custom Actions and custom APIs in the Microsoft Dataverse Developer Guide (*https://oreil.ly/DBoY1*).

Custom API in Power Apps provides two capabilities:

- You can create your own APIs and consolidate with one or more operations that can be called by you or other developers using various components like canvas app, Power Automate, JavaScript, workflows, and plug-ins.

- You can create your own trigger events so that you can register the plug-ins and workflows on that event.

As depicted in Figure 7-32, you can call a custom API that accepts input from various components, such as workflows, plug-ins, and JavaScript, and then call the plug-in to perform the desired business logic for the Dataverse operations. Post completion of the Dataverse operation, the response is returned to the calling components.

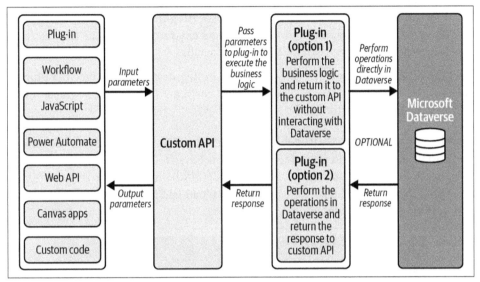

Figure 7-32. Custom API

Custom API allows you to combine multiple messages (events) into a single message. For example, in a call center support application, you may want to combine create, assign, and update messages into one escalate message.

Creating a custom API

You can create a custom API in four ways:

Plug-in Registration tool
This is an easy-to-use GUI tool that I have already discussed that can create plug-ins and custom workflows. You can use this tool to create the custom APIs as well. See the tutorial from Microsoft (*https://oreil.ly/WwAim*) for more details.

Power Apps
Custom API has a separate table in Dataverse. You can provide the details in the custom API form to create it. Each Custom API requires a new entry in the custom API table. See the tutorial from Microsoft (*https://oreil.ly/pEHag*) for more details.

With code

Custom API is also a table (*https://oreil.ly/2I0hN*) in Dataverse that stores the details about the API and its parameters. So, if you have a need to create a custom API programmatically, you can create it using either the Organization service or Dataverse Web API. See the tutorial from Microsoft (*https://oreil.ly/ogBqd*) for more details.

With solution files

You can also create the custom APIs by exporting the solution from the source environment and importing it into the target environment. See the tutorial from Microsoft (*https://oreil.ly/sd2US*) for more details.

Let's create a new custom API using the Plug-in Registration tool. Since the Plug-in Registration tool uses a designer to create the custom API, this will be the simplest way to configure the custom API.

Downloading and installing the Plug-in Registration tool.　First, you need to download and install the Plug-in Registration tool, if you haven't already. Follow the instructions from Microsoft's tutorial (*https://oreil.ly/1U4R0*). As shown in Figure 7-33, I have used the command `pac tool prt` to download and install the Plug-in Registration tool on my local machine.

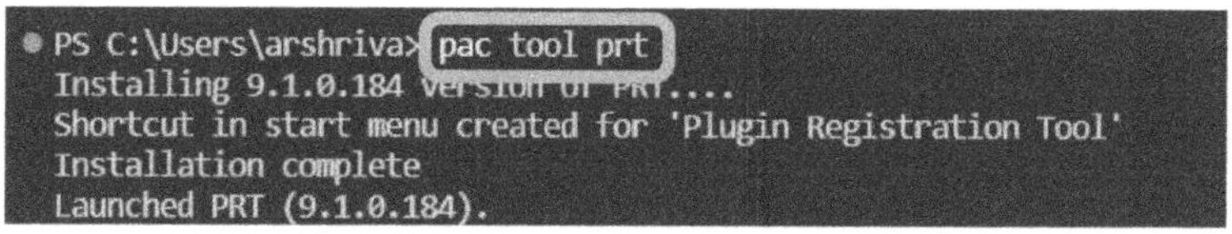

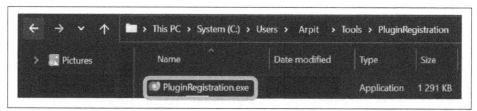

Figure 7-33. Downloading and installing the Plug-in Registration tool

Connecting to the Power Apps environment.　Navigate to the folder where you have downloaded the Plug-in Registration tool and double-click on PluginRegistration.exe to launch it, as shown in Figure 7-34.

Figure 7-34. Launching the Plug-in Registration tool

Enter your credentials to log in to your Power Platform environment, as shown in Figure 7-35.

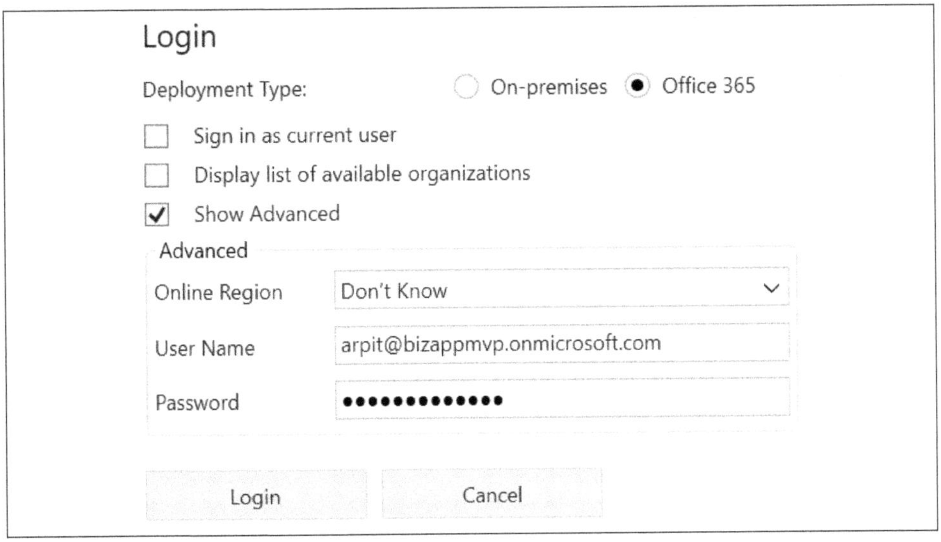

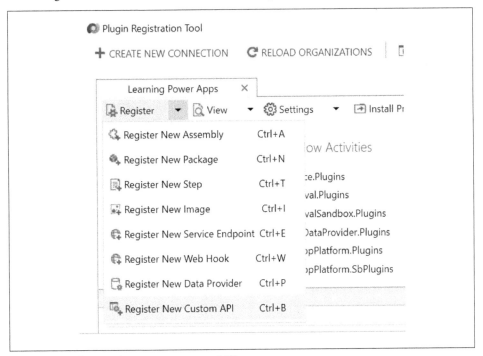

Figure 7-35. Logging in to the environment

Creating a new custom API. Once you're logged in to the Power Platform environment, select Register New Custom API, as shown in Figure 7-36.

Figure 7-36. Registering a new custom API

Provide details about your custom API such as its name, the solution where you want it to be created, and the binding type. Then, click on Add Request Parameter and Add Response Parameter to configure input and output parameters, respectively, for your custom API. Once the parameters are configured, click on Register to register your custom API, as shown in Figure 7-37.

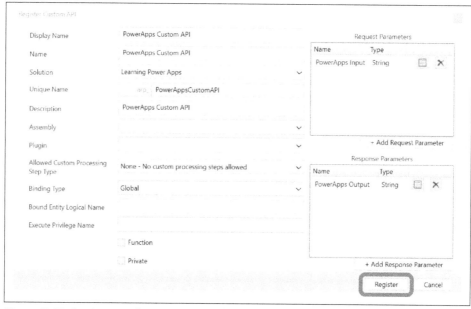

Figure 7-37. Registering the custom API

Writing a plug-in for your custom API.   So far, you've created the custom API, along with the input and output parameters that it will require. But the business logic it will use to perform operations on Dataverse still needs to be specified. You must always develop plug-in code to write business logic for a custom API. This plug-in code is identical to what we covered in "Plug-ins" on page 236, with the exception that no Plug-in Registration tool is required to register the plug-in.

> Custom API and custom virtual tables are the only two components in Power Apps that directly perform the business logic in MainOperation.

I have written some sample plug-in code that doesn't perform any operations in Data-verse; it simply reads the custom API input parameter and appends it after the static string "Your Input parameter is:". So, if you call a custom API by passing the input parameter "Arpit," then the output parameter of the custom API would be "Your Input parameter is: Arpit."

As shown in Figure 7-38, I have registered the plug-in using the Plug-in Registration tool. (The steps are the same as I described earlier in this chapter.)

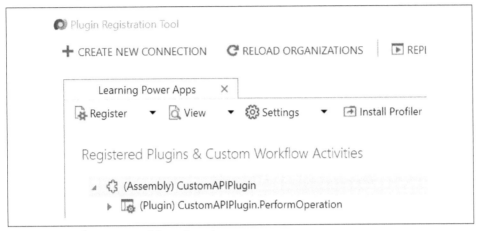

Figure 7-38. Plug-in assembly registration

Example plug-in code can be downloaded from the book's GitHub repository (*https:// oreil.ly/pvoZI*).

Linking your plug-in code with the custom API. You have created the custom API and plug-in code separately, and there is no link between them yet. You need to link them so that whenever you call the custom API, it triggers the plug-in to execute the business logic. To do that, you need to open the Plug-in Registration tool, click on "Display by Message" under the View tab, find your custom API, and double-click to open it. Then you'll need to provide Assembly and Plug-in details in the pop-up window (as depicted in Figure 7-39).

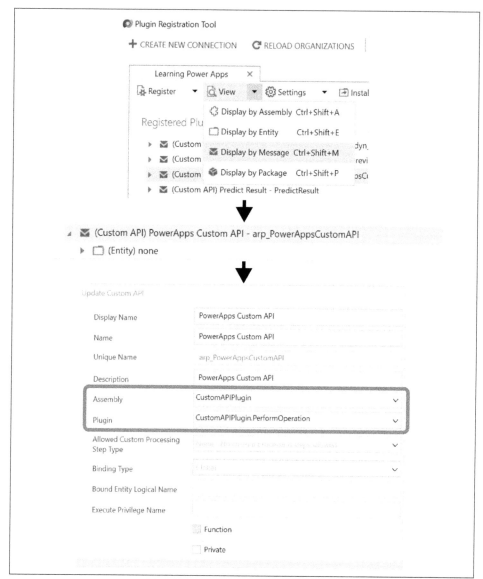

Figure 7-39. Linking a custom API with plug-in code

Invoking or testing your custom API. One of the major advantages of using custom APIs is their reusability across Power Apps components. You can write and keep your reusable code in a custom API and then invoke it by passing the required input parameters, either from classic workflows, plug-ins, Power Automate flows, JavaScript code, Dataverse Web API, canvas apps, or your custom code based on your business requirements.

For testing your custom API, you can use the Postman tool (*https://oreil.ly/Ccgan*). Once you set up Postman in your environment (*https://oreil.ly/8CU-v*), it should look like Figure 7-40. Environment setup lets you connect with the Power Apps environment where you want to perform your business logic. You need to provide all the details as per your environment. This is a one-time activity and not only helpful to test the custom APIs, but also the Dataverse Web APIs as well.

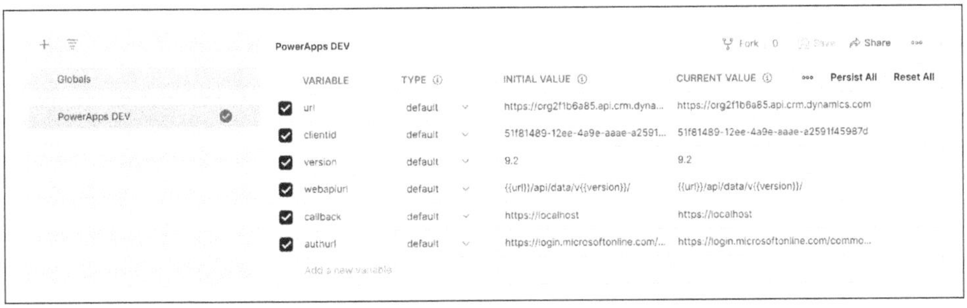

Figure 7-40. Postman Power Apps environment setup

Once the environment setup is done in Postman, it's time to call the custom API using the environment details. To call the custom API, you need to pass the required input parameters that you configured when using the Plug-in Registration tool. Like the Dataverse Web API, a custom API is also a RESTful API; hence, it uses JSON for data transmission. So you need to provide your input parameters in JSON format (as shown in Figure 7-41).

Figure 7-41. Calling a custom API by passing input parameters in JSON format

Then, you need to set the Content-Type header value to "application/json," as shown in Figure 7-42.

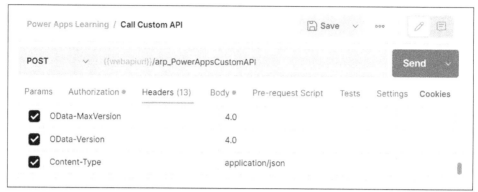

Figure 7-42. Defining Content-Type in header

Once you click the Send button, it will invoke the plug-in code linked with the custom API (as we did earlier in the Plug-in Registration tool). The plug-in will read the input parameter (Arpit) and will return the result in the form of the output parameter.

The custom API will give the response shown in Figure 7-43.

Figure 7-43. Custom API response

Important points to know about custom APIs

The following are important things to remember when using custom APIs:

- You can set the Binding Type for a custom API to associate the operation with a specific table, as shown in Figure 7-44:
  - Global indicates the operation performed by the custom API doesn't apply to a specific table.
  - Entity indicates the operation performed by the custom API applies to a specific table.
  - EntityCollection indicates the operation performed by the custom API applies or returns a collection of a specific table.

Figure 7-44. Custom API binding

- You can define a custom API as a function by enabling the property during custom API creation. This allows you to call the custom API by passing its input parameters in a URL instead of in the body in JSON format, as you can do with Dataverse Web API. And if you are calling it in Postman or any other component, you need to use the HTTP GET method.
- By default, all custom APIs you create are public, which means any other developers in your team can discover and use them. However, if you do not want to allow other developers to use your custom API, you can mark it as private by enabling the property during custom API creation.
- A custom API allows you to define the privileges that you must have in Dataverse to use it. Developers will get an "insufficient privilege" message if they try to run the API without having the correct privilege defined in the Execute Privilege Name property.
- Explore the Dataverse Custom API Manager (*https://oreil.ly/O8N3j*), an XRMToolBox-based community tool that provides a 360-degree view of Dataverse custom APIs along with providing CRUD operations on custom APIs, request parameters (inputs), and response properties (outputs).

Custom Pages

Custom pages (also referred to as Pages) are a relatively new enhancement that enable model-driven apps to have the capabilities of canvas apps. Model-driven apps have many features that can meet your business requirements; however, you still may sometimes need to create your own page within a model-driven app for the following purposes:

- Create a modal pop-up screen or dialog box and open it in either the left panel, right panel, or center of the screen.
- Create a custom landing page for your model-driven apps.
- Display external system data in model-driven apps without storing it in Dataverse.
- Create your own page with some advanced fluent UI and React-based controls.
- Replicate the out-of-the-box pages of model-driven apps by adding a few more controls to them. For example, currently model-driven app view pages can only display one view at a time, with the rest of the views listed in the view drop-down list. If you want to display multiple views on that page, you can replace it with a custom page with the same UI and controls as the out-of-the-box view page.

Previously, when we had to design a custom page or modal pop-up in model-driven apps, we needed to rely on HTML- and JavaScript-based web resources, which are not responsive and don't follow the same UI guidelines and standards as model-driven apps. Microsoft then announced the convergence of canvas apps with model-driven apps, but this only allows embedding of the canvas apps on the model-driven app form. You can't use it in other places as you can with custom pages.

Custom pages are the recommended component to design custom pages in model-driven apps; they use the same UI designer tool (Power Apps Studio) as canvas apps. Hence, you don't need to write code to design the custom pages. Instead, you can use various built-in drag-and-drop controls to design the page and write Excel-like formulas and expressions for your business logic.

Example of custom pages in model-driven apps

Custom pages can be shown either on the main screen (home page) or on forms.

On the main screen, custom pages can be displayed as a landing page, a dialog box in the center of the screen, or as a right navigation panel, as seen in Figure 7-45.

You can also show custom pages on forms in the center, left panel, or right panel.

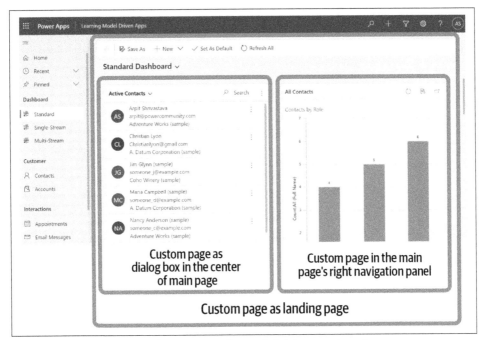

Figure 7-45. Custom page placement on the model-driven app's main screen

Creating a custom page

Custom pages can be created either within the model-driven app designer or directly from the solution. To create the custom page within the solution, open your solution from the solution list, click on +New, and select App → Page, as shown in Figure 7-46.

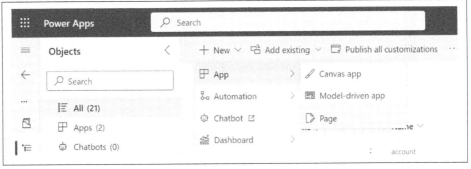

Figure 7-46. Creating a custom page from a solution

To create a custom page within a model-driven app, open your solution, click on the three dots (...) next to your app, and click on Edit to open the app in the app designer.

Then click on +New from the left navigation panel to create a new custom page, as shown in Figure 7-47.

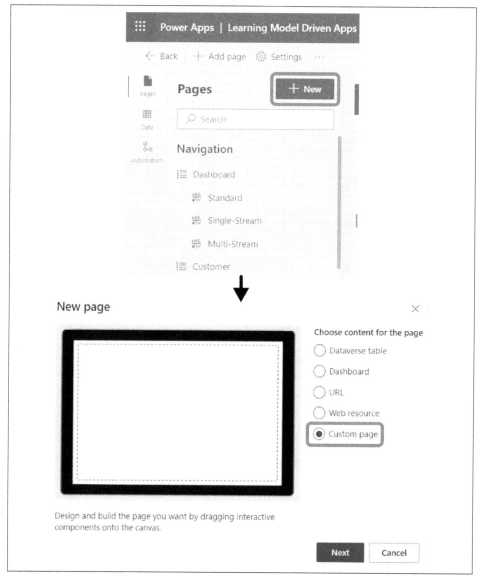

Figure 7-47. Creating a custom page from the model-driven app designer

Once you create the custom page, it takes you to the Power Apps Studio. This is the same designer that we use to design the canvas app.

For demonstration, I added a label control from the command bar and wrote a welcome message, as shown in Figure 7-48. Once your design is complete, save the custom page and publish it using the buttons in the top right corner.

Figure 7-48. Sample custom page with one label control

Once page publish is done, publish your model-driven app as well and run your app to see your custom page on the app's home screen, as shown in Figure 7-49.

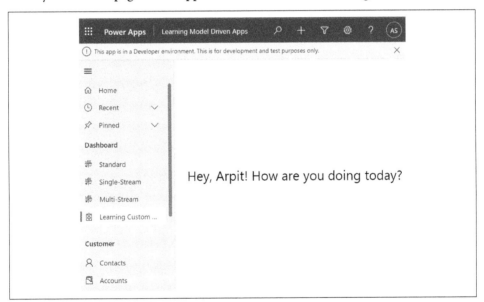

Figure 7-49. Custom page output after running the model-driven app

Opening a custom page using JavaScript

Sometimes you may need to open the custom pages using JavaScript code in the following scenarios:

- Passing contextual information like record ID, logged-in user's role, and logged-in user's language. from a model-driven app to your custom page to write some advanced business logic using a Power Fx expression
- Opening the custom page from a toolbar button

You have to use the JavaScript `Xrm.Navigation.navigateTo` (*https://oreil.ly/-IDPU*) method to open your custom page. It has two main parameters:

`pageInput`
> Input about the page to navigate to. The `pageInput` parameters depend on which page you are using to open the custom page and pass the parameters. You can have different types of pages (view page, form page, dashboard page, etc.) from which you may want to pass information to the custom pages. Each type of page has a different set of parameters. You can see all possible page type options and their parameters in the documentation (*https://oreil.ly/jqcO_*).

`navigationOptions`
> Here you can define the following properties:
>
> `target`
> > Set this to 1 to open the page inline or 2 to open the page in a dialog.
>
> `width`
> > Specify the width of the page in either "%" or "px."
>
> `height`
> > Specify the height of the page in either "%" or "px."
>
> `position`
> > Set this to 1 to open the page in the center or 2 to open the page in a side panel.
>
> `title`
> > Specify the title of the page.

Examples that show sample JavaScript code to open custom pages on a model-driven app's main page and to open a custom page on a form to pass record IDs as a contextual parameter can be downloaded from my GitHub repo (*https://oreil.ly/pvoZI*).

To read the `recordId` parameter in the custom page, you need to write a Power Fx expression on the app's `StartScreen` property of the custom page, as shown in the following code and in Figure 7-50:

```
Set(
    RecordItem,
    If(
  IsBlank(Param("recordId")),
  First(Contacts),
  LookUp(
Contacts,
Contact=GUID(Param("recordId"))
        )
  )
      )
```

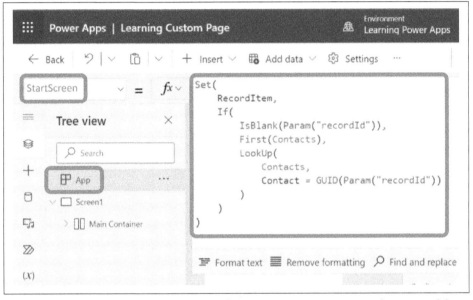

Figure 7-50. Power Fx expression to read the recordId parameter sent from a model-driven app form

The Power Apps Component Framework (PCF Controls)

Power Apps Component Framework empowers professional developers to create code components to enhance the user experience of Power Apps. You can create PCF controls for the data shown on model-driven app forms, views, dashboards, and canvas app screens.

One of the major limitations of earlier versions of CRM products was the lack of a UI extension and ways to customize the UI controls. PCF controls overcome this challenge and allow you to create your own control using JavaScript, TypeScript, React, CSS, and HTML outside Power Apps. Once it is ready to use, you can import it into the Power Apps environment.

A few examples of some out-of-the-box components are:

- Replace a numeric column value with a slider control.
- Replace a Boolean column value with a toggle control.
- Replace a multiline text column with a rich text editor control.
- Replace a multiline text column with a pen control.
- Replace a normal grid with an editable grid.
- Replace a choice column with an option set control.

Figure 7-51 shows a model-driven app form without adding PCF controls.

Figure 7-51. Model-driven app without using custom controls

Figure 7-52 shows a model-driven app form after adding custom controls.

Figure 7-52. Model-driven app with out-of-the-box custom controls (components)

You can see from the image how to change the data visualization of column values using custom controls. However, what if you want to create your own control that is not available in the default custom control list? For example, you might want a control to:

- Display credit/debit card details in interactive cards.
- Display country names with their flags.
- Display a flag next to a phone field according to the calling code.
- Validate a credit card number.
- Autopopulate an address.
- Display an address on Bing or Google Maps.

You can find thousands of ideas to create such controls in the PCF Gallery (*https://pcf.gallery*), created by community members, Microsoft MVPs, and PCF control experts.

There are several advantages to using PCF controls, such as:

- Unlike HTML web resources, code components are rendered as part of the same context and loaded simultaneously with other components in Power Apps, providing the user a seamless experience.
- Code components can be reused multiple times in model-driven apps and canvas apps across multiple tables and forms.

- You can create code components using HTML + TypeScript + CSS + React and can package them into a ZIP file to move across multiple environments.

- Code components can be created by developers as an ISV (independent service vendor) solution and published to AppSource (*https://oreil.ly/yGaAL*) as well, so that developers from other organizations can use them.

- They provide seamless server access using Dataverse Web API.

- They provide contextual data and metadata.

- They enable professional developers who have good knowledge of TypeScript, React, Node JS, PowerShell, etc., to create components independent from the Power Apps environment.

- Premium code components link to external services or data directly through the user's web client rather than through connectors. When these elements are incorporated into an app, the component is deemed premium, and Power Apps licenses are necessary for end users to use it.

- When code components that don't communicate with outside services or data are used in Power Apps that use only standard features, then end users must have, at a minimum, a Microsoft 365 license.

As it is such a broad topic, understanding what PCF components are and how they can be used is sufficient from the standpoint of studying Power Apps. Nevertheless, you can get step-by-step instructions on how to create and build a code component from the Microsoft documentation (*https://oreil.ly/gDIOH*).

Environment Variables

I've discussed many code components that allow you to write code to customize Power Apps and extend its capabilities. Sometimes, while writing business logic either in low-code, no-code components like Power Automate or in pro-code components like plug-ins, JavaScript, and custom APIs, you might need to keep some configuration details that can either change in the future or vary across environments, like data source connections, API keys, usernames, passwords, and external API URLs.

For plug-ins, we already have secure and unsecure configurations to do this (as we discussed earlier). However, for other components like Power Automate, canvas apps, and custom APIs, we didn't have any way to manage these configuration values, except creating a custom table to hold them.

Environment variables (see Figure 7-53) allow developers to store configuration values in the form of key-value pairs, which then serve as input to various data components like Power Automate, Power Apps, and plug-ins. Environment variables are recommended for storing configurations that may need to be modified in the future or that can change when you move the components to different environments.

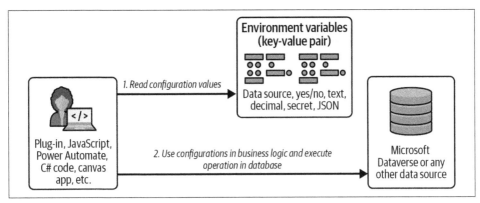

Figure 7-53. Environment variable usage

Types of environment variables

You need to specify the data type when creating an environment variable. I have explained each of the available data types with real-life examples from my personal experience in Table 7-5. You are free to use them in accordance with your personal preferences and in line with your business use cases.

Table 7-5. Environment variable usage and examples

Data type	Description	Example
Data source	Used to store the connections to external data sources. As of this writing, only SharePoint, Dataverse, and SAP ERP connections are supported.	You can have various data source connections (typically, connection URLs and credentials that might change in the future) in your environment; for example, Microsoft Dataverse, SharePoint, and SAP ERP. These connections are often made with different user accounts or service principles for development, UAT, and production environments. Instead of directly using these connections in Power Apps or Power Automate, you can keep them in environment variables and reuse them across environments. Keeping them in an environment variable is also beneficial in case you need to change the user account for a connection. Rather than change it for each component, you can change it in the environment variable and it will automatically be reflected everywhere that variable is referenced.
JSON	Used to store data objects or array type information.	You may need to store multiple values in the configuration, such as table data, custom API details, or a configuration specific to your own business logic. Let's say in Power Automate you need to send emails from a particular queue or mailbox that is different in the development, testing, and production environments. You can group mailbox or queue details together and distinguish them by adding an environment tag to a single JSON-type environment variable rather than having three separate environment variables. Similarly, if you need to set up the Teams approval functionality and you have various approvers' or teams' channel IDs throughout the environment, you can also maintain multiple values in JSON format.

Data type	Description	Example
Secret	Used to store sensitive information (username, password, API keys, secret keys, client ID, or other sensitive data) based on your requirements. Values are stored in Azure Key Vault (*https://oreil.ly/ouUf7*). See the Microsoft documentation (*https://oreil.ly/zR6_n*) for more information.	You may need to store credentials, Azure app secret values, and other confidential details in encrypted format in Dataverse and then refer to them in your code or code components. These values could be different for different environments; hence, holding them in environment variables of type Secret is the best way to use them.
Text	Used to store plain text configuration values.	Text environment variables are useful when you need to, for example, send an email or SMS reminder x days before an event. Here x can be changed by the client anytime in the future, so it's better to store it in an environment variable than to hardcode it.
Boolean	Used to store Boolean (yes/no) configuration values.	You may want to store a Boolean value that enables/disables some of the features you provide in Power Apps or determines whether to perform business logic. For example, you are creating an event management app and have an environment variable named "Allow Registration." Based on its value, you can enable/disable the event registration option in your app without changing anything in the app code.
Decimal number	Used to store decimal configuration values.	You can also keep decimal values in an environment variable; for example, say you are designing an app for retail customers, who provide discounts on the products they sell. This discount may be a whole number or decimal, and it may change in the future. To avoid hardcoding these values in your code or data component, you can keep them in an environment variable and then refer to it in various components.

Creating environment variables

To create a new environment variable, open your solution from the solution list, click on +New from the command bar, and then select More → Environment variable, as depicted in Figure 7-54.

To create a new environment variable, enter information such as the display name, data type, default value, and current value.

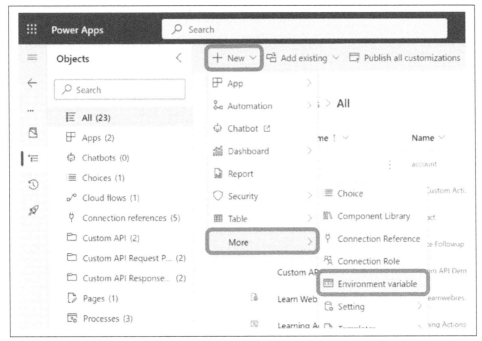

Figure 7-54. Creating an environment variable

Here are some important things to remember before setting the default and current values for environment variables:

- When a current value is present, it's used, even if a default value is also present. The default value is only used if there's no current value provided.

- Set a default value if you want to have the same value across different environments.

- Set a current value if you want to have different values in different environments. So always remove this value from your solution in the source environment if you don't want this value used in the target environment.

As shown in Figure 7-55, I have created an environment variable called Allow Event Registration, with the schema name arp_AllowEventRegistration.

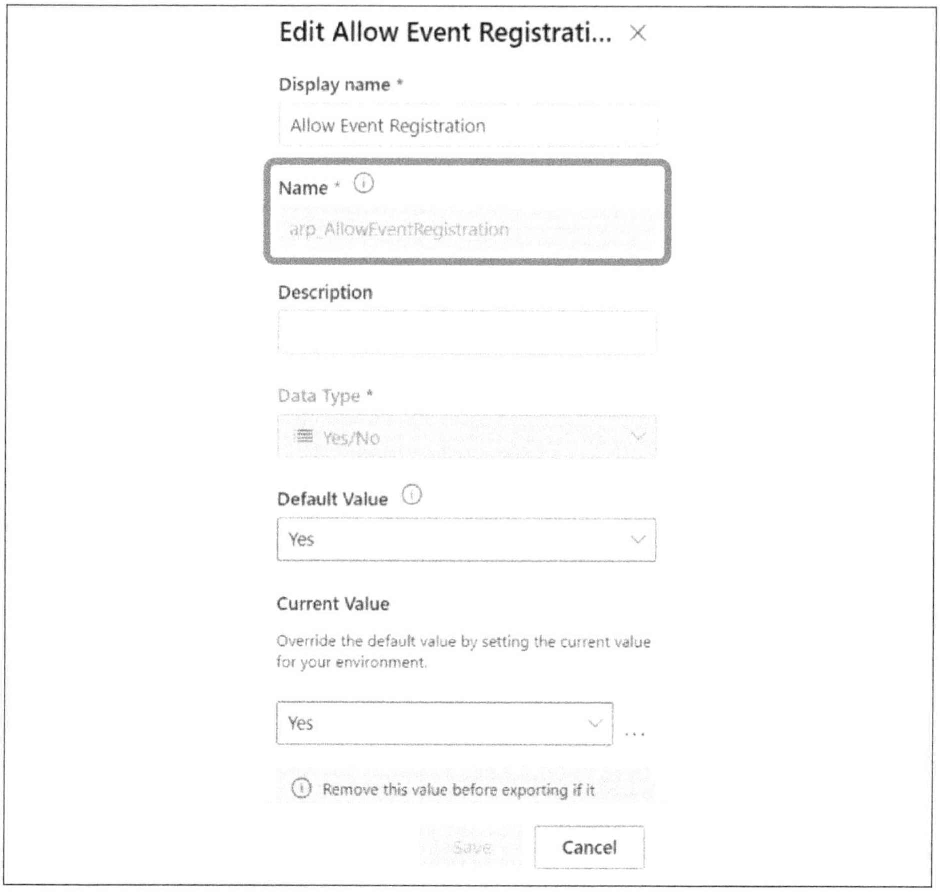

Figure 7-55. Boolean environment variable

Now, wherever you need the value of this environment value, you can retrieve it through its schema name: arp_AllowEventRegistration.

Using environment variables

Once the environment variable is created, you can read its value from either low-code, no-code or pro-code components within the Power Platform environment. I have used Power Automate and a custom page to demonstrate.

Environment variables in Power Automate.   I have set up a manual trigger Power Automate flow that will only send an event registration email if the environment variable arp_AllowEventRegistration has the value "true." As shown in Figure 7-56, all environment variables that are present in a specific environment can be found in Power Automate within the expression box.

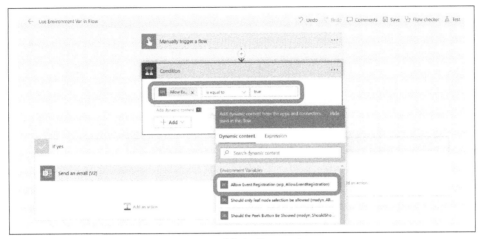

Figure 7-56. Using an environment variable in Power Automate

Environment variables in custom pages.   I have created a custom page and added it to my model-driven app's main page. As shown in Figure 7-57, it displays a greeting message and the option to register for an event. Now I want to manage the visibility of the event registration button based on an environment variable. If the value is Yes, the button should be visible; otherwise, it should not be visible.

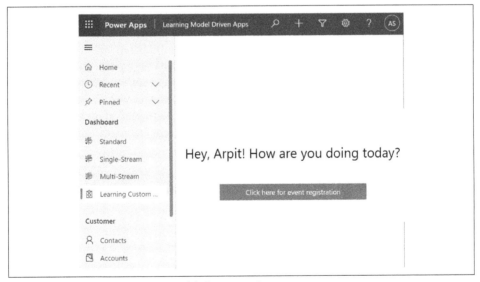

Figure 7-57. Custom page on model-driven app's main page

Open your solution, click on the three dots (...) next to your model-driven app, and then click on Edit to open the app in app designer. Open Power Apps Studio, click on the Datasource icon in the left panel, and click on "Add data" to display all Dataverse tables available in the environment. Select the Environment Variable Definitions and Environment Variable Values tables to add to the app as data sources, as shown in Figure 7-58.

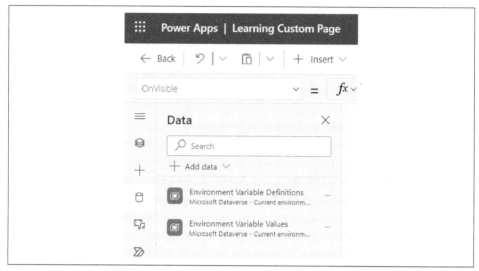

Figure 7-58. Add Environment Variables tables as data source to custom page designer

Write the following Power Fx expression on the App's `OnStart` property of the page. I'll talk about Power Fx in detail in Chapter 9, but to use an environment variable custom page or canvas app you would need to add the Power Fx expression in Example 7-6. This expression queries the Environment Variable Values table in Dataverse and retrieves the configuration value with the schema name (created previously), as shown in Figure 7-59.

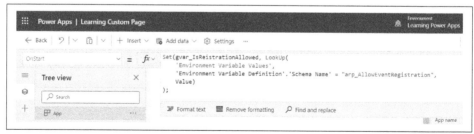

Figure 7-59. Power Fx expression to read the value from environment variable on app's `OnStart` *property*

Example 7-6. Power Fx expression to read the value from an environment variable based on app's `OnStart` property

```
Set(gvar_IsRegistrationAllowed, Lookup(
'Environment Variable Values',
'Environment Variable Definitions'.'Schema Name' = arpit_AllowEventRegistration",
Value)
);
```

Finally, write the Power Fx expression given in Example 7-7 on the `OnVisible` property of the button control, as shown in Figure 7-60. This expression says, if the value retrieved from the environment variable is "yes" then set the button visible property to true; else, set it to false.

Example 7-7. Power Fx expression to check the value of the global variable `IsRegistrationAllowed`

```
If(gvar_IsRegistrationAllowed="yes",true,false)
```

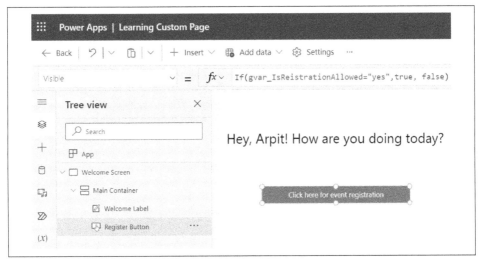

Figure 7-60. Managing the visibility of a button control based on environment variable value

After making the changes to the custom page, save it, publish it, and publish the model-driven app.

Now change your environment variable value to "Yes" and run the app. You will see the greeting message along with the button, as shown in Figure 7-61.

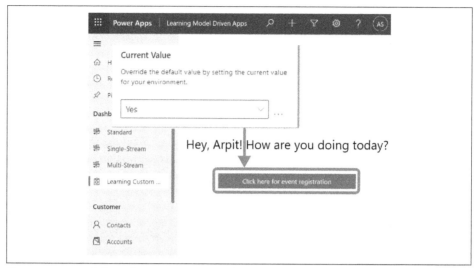

Figure 7-61. Visibility of event registration button when environment variable's value is Yes

And, if you change your environment variable value to "No" and run or refresh the app, you'll see the greeting message without a registration button, as shown in Figure 7-62.

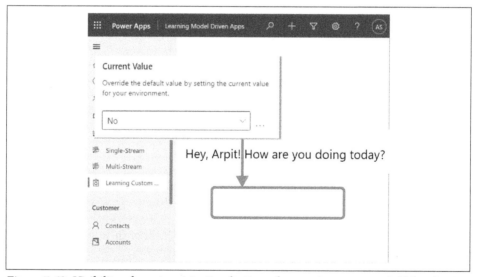

Figure 7-62. Visibility of event registration button when environment variable's value is No

Now, you can manage the visibility of the event registration button using an environment variable rather than making any changes in the code or Power Fx expression.

Environment variables in canvas apps.   As we discussed earlier, the designer for custom pages is the same as for canvas apps. Therefore, canvas apps use environment variables just like custom pages.

Environment variables in other code components.   Environment variables can also be read from JavaScript (using Dataverse Web API), C# code, plug-ins, and other code components by simply querying the Environment Variable Definitions table.

Integration Components

While designing a business application, we often need to integrate it with some other internal or external application to provide a consolidated view of the data. Let's say I am designing a model-driven app to provide highly detailed information about a customer (customer 360-degree view), where some information about the customer, such as profile details, sales details, marketing, and service-related details, is stored in Dataverse, while the customer's finance, accounting, and invoicing details are stored in some external system. In this situation, you can integrate your Dataverse with that external system, either via the prebuilt connectors provided by Microsoft or by creating your own custom connector.

The components and approaches of integrating two applications or systems depend on the nature of that integration. The most common types of integrations are:

Real-time integration or trigger-based integration
> Immediately brings the data from the external systems to process it further in Dataverse. An example is a payment gateway integration, where you need the immediate response of the bank transaction.

Non-real-time integration or asynchronous integration
> Used when the data is not immediately required in Dataverse. For example, as soon as customer information is updated in an external system, it should be updated in the CRM system as well, so that the next time coworkers open the application, they have updated details about the customer.

Scheduled or batch-based integration
> Migrates data to Dataverse in scheduled batches, such as hourly, weekly, or monthly.

One-time integration or data migration
> Migrates all data from an external system to Dataverse in one go. This type of integration is used, for example, when a customer wants to completely shut down

a legacy application and replace it with Power Platform/Dynamics 365, so all data must be migrated to Dataverse.

Virtual integration

The external system's data is not stored in Dataverse, but is still accessible to users via mechanisms like virtual tables and custom pages.

There are different types of data components available based on the integration requirements. A few of these components are as follows:

- Power Automate (flows)
- Connectors (Standard, Premium, or custom)
- Azure Logic Apps
- Plug-ins (C# code)
- WebHooks (a special type of plug-in for API integration)
- Service endpoints (a special type of plug-in for API integration)
- Custom API
- Azure Functions
- Azure API Management
- Power Query or Data Integrator (*https://oreil.ly/14bR_*)

Figure 7-63 depicts how various Power Platform low-code, no-code components can communicate with external data sources (whether run by Microsoft or not) via built-in connectors like Gmail, Azure DevOps, and Microsoft Teams and store the data in Dataverse to be used by applications.

You now know the many integration strategies that Dataverse offers as well as the components that may be utilized to construct the business logic necessary to make this integration happen. Nevertheless, have you considered if two distinct systems—possibly developed on various platforms and using various programming languages—can connect with each other? The answer is yes, with APIs.

Dataverse integration is not always unidirectional; sometimes it is required to be used bidirectionally as well. Dataverse Web API enables developers of external systems to communicate with Dataverse data.

Before the Dataverse Web API, we used OData (which was REST-based and used JSON for communication) and SOAP (which used XML for communication) within Dynamics 365 CE to perform CRUD operations in Dataverse. External organizations could only use these services via .NET-based applications, not other programming languages. So there was a need for an API that could be used across a wide variety of programming languages, platforms, and devices. Hence, Microsoft introduced a new

REST-based API called Dataverse Web API, which supports CORS (cross-origin resource sharing). This means that you can call it from any platform and any language to establish communication with Microsoft Dataverse.

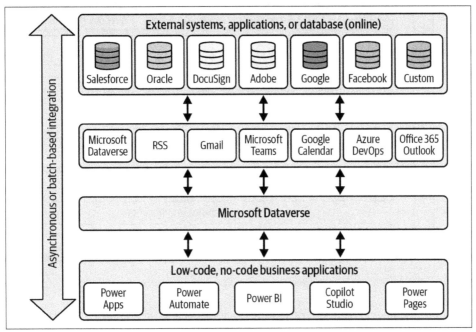

Figure 7-63. Microsoft Dataverse integration via Power Platform out-of-the-box connectors

Dataverse Web API alone is not always enough to allow an external system to complete a transaction in Dataverse. Before executing transactions to Dataverse, you might need to add some additional business logic or transform the data coming from an external system. In this case, you may need to develop your own unique API (using C#, Power Automate, Azure Functions, Logic Apps, or Azure APIM), which would act as a wrapper around the Dataverse Web API and execute your own business logic on the data you receive from the external system before calling the D365 API internally to perform the transaction in Dataverse.

Figure 7-64 shows how to use an external API to establish communication between Power Platform-based low-code, no-code components and external data sources (whether run by Microsoft or not). There are several ways to call custom APIs to bring data into Dataverse. You can call them directly in your JavaScript or C# code, or you can build a custom connector from the API definition and call it in either Power Automate or canvas apps. They can also be called directly from Power Automate and Logic Apps using the "HTTP trigger" action, or they can be called via Azure APIM to add an extra security layer and write additional data transformation logic.

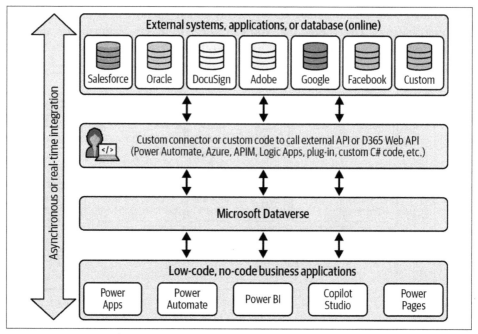

Figure 7-64. Microsoft Dataverse integration via custom connector or code

Not every business requirement requires that external data should be kept in Dataverse. There are various scenarios when you might not want to migrate or replicate data from external sources:

Security
> When data is highly sensitive and your client does not want to migrate it to another database (such as Dataverse) and only wants to perform operations on the original database.

Storage cost
> There is a lot of data stored in external data sources and it does not need to be replicated in Dataverse. This will result in lower Dataverse storage costs.

App performance
> It is not always necessary to migrate a large amount of data to Dataverse if it is not required for CRM purposes. Your app's performance would improve if there is less data to load.

Data duplication
> Your client does not want to keep a duplicate copy of the data in Dataverse and prefers to perform CRUD operations directly on their primary database from Dataverse to avoid data syncing or mismatching issues.

For these kinds of scenarios, Dataverse provides integration via *virtual tables*, as shown in Figure 7-65. Virtual tables, also commonly referred to as *virtual entities*, make it possible to integrate data from external systems into Microsoft Dataverse tables without duplicating data and frequently without writing custom code.

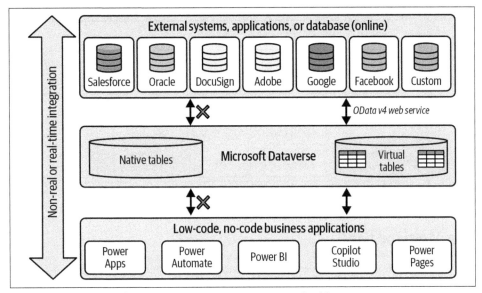

Figure 7-65. Microsoft Dataverse integration via virtual tables

In some integration scenarios, the data in the external system doesn't need to be stored in Dataverse, even if it's not sensitive. Your business apps, such as Power Apps, Power Pages, and custom pages, may require that you pull in data on the fly without storing it in Dataverse. In this situation, developers can display the data by directly calling the client's provided APIs either via Power Automate, custom connectors, or custom code, as shown in Figure 7-66.

For example, imagine that you don't store the customer's order information in Dataverse because your client has an order management system for doing so. Now, CRM users should be able to retrieve a specific order status from the order management system in CRM if a customer contacts them to inquire about the status of an order. In this situation, you can directly call the order API your client has provided and fetch the status of the order without having to save the order information in CRM.

The integration of Dataverse data may also be necessary with various internal Microsoft applications, including Excel, Word, Outlook, SharePoint, Exchange Server, Teams, and OneDrive for Business, among others. Microsoft offers built-in, seamless integration with these applications, removing the need for any bespoke business logic or programming.

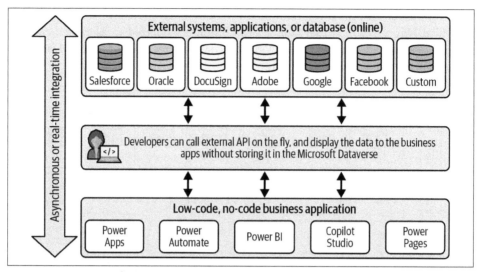

Figure 7-66. Microsoft Dataverse integration via external APIs

The Monitor Tool

You've learned a variety of ways to extend your model-driven app's capabilities. However, sometimes customizing the application results in errors and bugs that require troubleshooting, debugging, and fixing. Since model-driven apps can be customized from both the client and the server side, you may need to troubleshoot errors on either side. Server-side components can be debugged in their own ways. As I mentioned in the plug-in section, the plug-in profiler can be used to debug both custom and plug-in workflows.

To troubleshoot client-side issues, such as issues loading form controls, JavaScript errors, working with events (load, save, etc.), or saving data in Dataverse, Microsoft offers the built-in Monitor tool that can assist app developers. By providing a log of activities in the app as it runs, it offers a detailed look at how an app functions. In addition to form events (discussed next), the Monitor tool supports monitoring and debugging for the following:

- Network or connectivity
- Page navigation
- Command (toolbar buttons) executions

Let's have a look at how the Monitor tool helps you troubleshoot form-related issues. There are numerous instances where the Monitor tool can assist developers in understanding why a form behaves in a particular manner. Business rules, JavaScript, form events, or client APIs that admins and makers have established are the root of many form-related problems. If an issue arises, the Monitor tool can help determine whether it is a result of customization or an out-of-the-box design flaw. To run the Monitor tool for model-driven apps, you must have the System Administrator or System Customizer security role.

You can open the Monitor tool to troubleshoot model-driven apps in two ways:

- Log in to the Power Apps home page (*https://oreil.ly/WlAha*), choose your environment, select Apps from the left navigation panel, and then select Monitor from the command bar. Optionally, you can choose the app from the list, click the three dots (...) next to the app name, and select Monitor, as shown in Figure 7-67, to connect your app to the Monitor session.

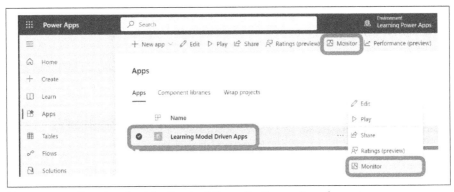

Figure 7-67. Opening the Monitor tool from the Power Apps home page

- Play your model-driven app. Then add "&monitor=true" to the end of the URL in your web browser and refresh the page. Select the Monitor icon on the command bar, as shown in Figure 7-68, to connect your app to the Monitor session.

Figure 7-68. Opening the Monitor tool after running the app

Once you open the Monitor tool and run your app within it, it opens the app and begins monitoring. You can perform various actions and interact with various controls like opening a form, changing data, and saving it. Every action is recorded in the Monitor tool, as shown in Figure 7-69. You can filter your session as well by various categories and operations.

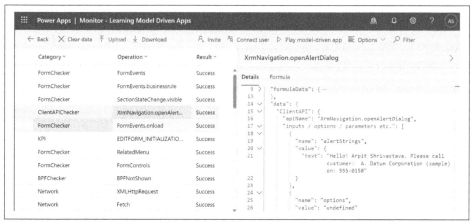

Figure 7-69. Monitoring session

As of this writing, the Monitor tool supports the form events shown in Table 7-6.

Table 7-6. Monitor tool form events

Form event	Use
FormEvents.onsave	When performing a save operation
XrmNavigation	When performing various navigations in the app
FormEvents.onload	When a form loads
FormControls	Interacts with various app controls
TabStateChange.visible	Hide/show a tab or switch tabs on the form
RelatedMenu	Navigate to a related tab on the form to view related table data
ControlStateChange.disabled	When a control gets disabled on the form
ControlStateChange.visible	Hide/show a control on the form
SectionStateChange.visible	When a control gets disabled
UnsupportedClientApi	When an unsupported client API is called

The Monitor tool can also be used to troubleshoot errors and issues in canvas apps, which I will discuss in Chapter 8.

Development Tools

The Microsoft Dataverse community has created many useful tools. Many of the most popular tools are distributed via the XrmToolBox (*https://oreil.ly/uUGj3*), a Windows application that connects to Dataverse, providing tools to ease customization, configuration, and operational tasks. It includes more than 30 plug-ins to make administration, customization, and configuration tasks easier and less time consuming. Some of these plug-ins are listed in Table 7-7.

Table 7-7. Useful development tools

Tool	Use
Dataverse REST Builder (*https://oreil.ly/lxVDy*)	Generate JavaScript code for use with Dataverse Web API.
Easy Translator (*https://oreil.ly/aQoeS*)	Export and import translations with contextual information.
Export to Excel (*https://oreil.ly/ATBKU*)	Export records from a selected view (fetch XML) to Excel.
FetchXML Builder (*https://oreil.ly/e07BR*)	Create queries for Microsoft Dataverse, Dynamics 365, and Power Platform; explore data and get code.
Iconator (*https://oreil.ly/7vmpL*)	Manage custom table icons in a single screen.
Ribbon Workbench (*https://oreil.ly/OQ8DJ*)	Edit the ribbon or command bar from inside XrmToolbox.
View Designer (*https://oreil.ly/kf8fT*)	Design views and alter queries using FetchXML Builder.
View Layout Replicator (*https://oreil.ly/TkSNS*)	Apply the same layout to multiple views of the same table in a single operation.
WebResources Manager (*https://oreil.ly/gurte*)	Manage your web resources.

> The Microsoft support team does not provide any support for community-created tools. If you have any concerns or issues with any of these community tools, contact the tool's publisher.

Summary

In this chapter, you have learned about various client-side and server-side code components that enable developers to write code to customize model-driven apps when prebuilt components might not be ideal for an app's needs. Along with creating reusable custom APIs, you also explored various ways to connect model-driven apps with external applications.

In the next chapter, you'll learn about the canvas app's built-in features, controls, and components to get started with canvas app development.

CHAPTER 8

Canvas App Controls and Features

In the last two chapters, you learned about model-driven app features that come standard as well as various extensibility options to design business applications. Model-driven apps are the best fit to design process-driven, data-model-driven apps, but they are not advised for designing mobile applications that require highly customizable user interfaces, or where you need to store data in a location other than Dataverse.

In this case, you'll want to design a canvas app. In this chapter, you'll learn about a variety of canvas app out-of-the-box features along with various extensibility options to meet complex business requirements.

It's important to know that the canvas app can also use Dataverse as its primary data source to store the business data. If you do so, then all the Dataverse features that run the business logic on the server side like plug-ins, custom APIs, workflows, business rules, and security roles will also be applicable for your canvas app. However, canvas apps don't support model-driven, app-specific UI components, such as business process flows, dashboards, custom pages, charts, site maps, forms, command bars, editable subgrids, and so on.

Figure 8-1 shows that a canvas app can be designed using only its many built-in features and controls, but if the built-in features do not meet your requirements, then you can create custom controls using PCF components.

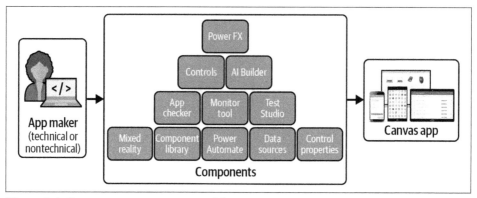

Figure 8-1. Canvas app components and features

As discussed in Chapter 3, you can create a canvas app from scratch, from data, from a page design, or from an app template. You can also create apps using Microsoft Copilot by describing the app requirements in natural language. In this chapter, I'll talk about how to make your first canvas app from scratch and use the variety of features and controls that set it apart from model-driven apps for designing business applications.

Power Apps Studio

To create a new canvas app from scratch, you first need to navigate to the Power Apps home page (*https://oreil.ly/WlAha*), select the environment where you want to create your canvas app, click on Solutions from the left navigation panel, open your solution, and click on +New on the toolbar. Then select App → Canvas app, provide your App name, choose a format (either Tablet or Phone), and click Create. This will open the app in Power Apps Studio.

As we discussed in Chapter 3, Power Apps Studio offers a UI experience similar to PowerPoint, and building an app feels like creating a slide deck.

Controls and Properties

Canvas app controls and properties determine the appearance and behavior of the application. Controls in canvas apps (e.g., text input, label, button) are very similar to other Microsoft applications like PowerPoint and Word. Some controls are free to use, while others are premium and require a license (indicated by a diamond icon next to the control). Each control has its own properties that you can change from the right panel. For example, if you add a text input control, you can click on it to change its properties, such as height, width, background color, border color, font family, and font size, from the right panel, as you learned in Chapter 3.

Canvas app controls can be divided into a number of categories (as shown in Figure 8-2), which we'll discuss next.

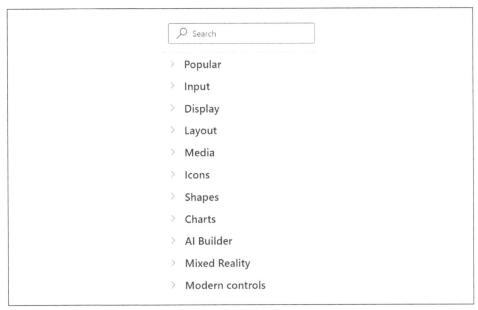

Figure 8-2. Canvas app controls

Input Controls

Input controls are used to get information from users. The user is expected to interact with the control while using the app. This input can then be used to create or update data in a data source. There are various types of input controls available that you can use, as shown in Table 8-1.

Table 8-1. Canvas app input controls

Input control	Purpose
Button	Performs an action upon clicking or tapping
Text input	Allows users to type text, numbers, and other input
Pen input	Allows users to draw sketches and signatures and also allows them to erase and highlight areas of image
Drop-down	Allows users to select one option from a list of predefined choices
Combo box	Allows users to make selections from given choices. It also supports search and multiple-choice selections.
Date picker	Helps users to select a specific date and time in the correct format
List box	Allows users to select one or multiple items from a list
Check box	Allows users to select or clear to set its value to true or false
Radio	Displays multiple options, of which users can select only one
Toggle	Allows users to turn something on or off

Input control	Purpose
Slider	Allows users to specify a value by dragging the handle
Rating	Allows users to provide a rating between 1 and a maximum number that you specify
Timer	Behaves like a stopwatch; executes business logic when a certain amount of time has passed
Edit form	Allows users to directly create a form with the columns linked to the data source and update the data in that data source (Dataverse, SharePoint, Excel, etc.). To show the Edit form, you need to provide the table name of the data source in the Data Source property.
Display form	Allows users to display all fields of a record from the data source
Rich text editor	Allows users to enter and format (e.g., bold, italic, change font size) input inside a WYSIWYG editing area

All input controls are designed to take user input in a specified format. Figure 8-3 shows an Insert form with various input controls to gather the user's input and insert the data in Dataverse.

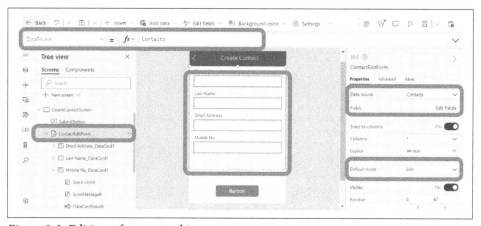

Figure 8-3. Editing a form control in a canvas app

There are two more form controls—Edit form and Display form—which are collections of multiple input controls, allowing you to directly affect an existing record within your data source. For example, in Figure 8-4, I have used the LookUp function on the Item property of the DisplayForm control, to retrieve the specific contact record from Dataverse.

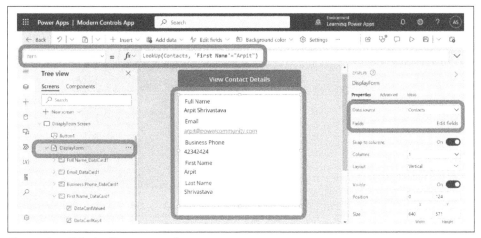

Figure 8-4. DisplayForm control

Display Controls

Display controls are used to display the content in the app. Unlike input controls, display controls are meant only to be viewed—not interacted with—by the app user. There are two display controls:

Text label
> Displays the text, number, or any other data that appears exactly the way you type it

HTML text
> Allows app makers to write HTML tags (*https://oreil.ly/Het1A*) and display rich text content

For example, you could use a text label control to display some static text like the title "Registration Form," in Figure 8-5.

Figure 8-5. Text label control

Figure 8-6 shows how an HTML text control is used to display an image on the app screen.

Figure 8-6. HTML text control

Layout Controls

Layout controls include gallery and container controls. *Galleries* are used to display a list of other controls and data similar to what you have on your mobile device, while *containers* are used to group logically related controls to create hierarchies.

Galleries show images and text about several related items. They can be used to display data vertically or horizontally on the canvas app screen. For example, you can use galleries to show information about products, lists of customers, employee directories, or upcoming events. Galleries enable you to display any data source's table data directly in the canvas app screen. You can display filtered data by using a Dataverse table view instead of writing filter expressions.

Containers are used to hold a set of controls like labels, text inputs, combo box, galleries, buttons, and so on. Containers can be either horizontal or vertical based on how you want to align your controls on the screen. Whatever controls you add inside the container remain inside the container; therefore, they are used to design responsive apps as well.

 In the vertical gallery, horizontal gallery, and flexible height gallery controls, you have a predefined or a default layout applied to the canvas app, unlike the corresponding blank Gallery control.

The layout controls are listed in Table 8-2.

Table 8-2. Canvas app layout controls

Layout control	Purpose
Vertical gallery	Displays data vertically on the app screen
Horizontal gallery	Displays data horizontally on the app screen
Flexible height gallery	Displays data on the app screen such that the row height is automatically adjusted based on content
Blank vertical gallery	Displays a blank vertical gallery on the app screen so that you can add and organize controls vertically according to your needs for displaying data
Blank horizontal gallery	Displays a blank horizontal gallery on the app screen so that you can add and organize controls horizontally according to your needs for displaying data
Blank flexible height gallery	Displays a blank gallery on the app screen with flexible height to display data
Data table	Displays data in tabular format (currently available only in preview)
Horizontal container	Arranges the position of the child components horizontally, so that you don't have to set X, Y for individual components inside the container. Used to design responsive canvas apps.
Vertical container	Arranges the position of the child components vertically, so that you don't have to set X, Y for individual components inside the container. Used to design responsive canvas apps.

Figure 8-7 shows a vertical gallery displaying the Active Contacts of Dataverse. I used the expression "Filter(Contacts, 'Active Contacts')" on the Items property of the Gallery control.

Figure 8-7. Gallery controls

Figure 8-8 shows an example of a vertical and a horizontal container. In the vertical container, controls are automatically arranged vertically on top of each other, whereas in the horizontal container, controls are automatically arranged next to one another.

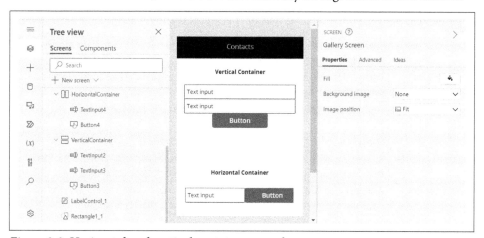

Figure 8-8. Horizontal and vertical container controls

Media Controls

You can add media, such as images and interactive objects, to your canvas app. Table 8-3 shows the media controls you can add to your app.

Table 8-3. Canvas app media controls

Media control	Purpose
Image	Displays an image on the screen. You can add images from your local machine or data sources.
3-D object	Adds interactive 3-D content from a variety of sources. You can find more details about 3-D content in the Microsoft documentation (*https://oreil.ly/5cORE*).
Camera	Takes pictures using the camera on the device
Measuring camera	Takes pictures using the camera on the device and calculates area, volume, and distance in the real world
Barcode reader	Scans a barcode or QR code displayed on any item or product
Video	Plays an audio file, video file, or YouTube video
Microsoft Stream	Displays a video player to play a Microsoft Stream video (*https://oreil.ly/-eCWZ*)
Audio	Plays an audio track from a video file, a recording made with a Microphone control, or a sound clip from a file
Microphone	Allows you to record sound from the microphone on the device
Add picture	Allows you to take a photo, or loads images from the local device. This control is a grouped control that includes two controls: Add picture and Image. The "Add picture" button prompts the user to upload an image. The Image control shows either an uploaded image or a placeholder.
Import	Allows users to import data to canvas apps from the local machine
Export	Allows users to export data from canvas app to the local machine
PDF viewer	Displays the content of a PDF file (currently experimental)
Map	Adds an interactive map to your canvas apps. Markers should be plotted from a data source that contains addresses or latitude and longitude pairs.

For demonstration, shown in Figure 8-9, I used Image and Video controls to show a picture and a YouTube video.

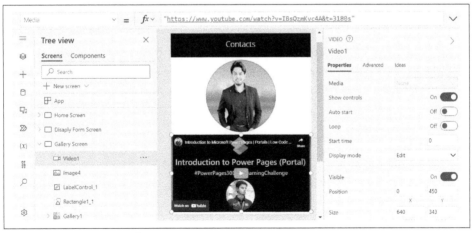

Figure 8-9. Media controls

Icons and Shape Controls

Because mobile apps have limited screen space, using icons and shape controls will help you condense the app without degrading the user experience. For example, you could use a back arrow icon to direct the reader back to the previous screen, a check-mark icon to submit a form, and so on. You can write expressions on the `OnSelect` property of the icon to perform various actions in the app.

In Figure 8-10, you can see some of the icons and shapes. When you build an app, you'll find more in the list. Microsoft may add more icons and shapes in the future.

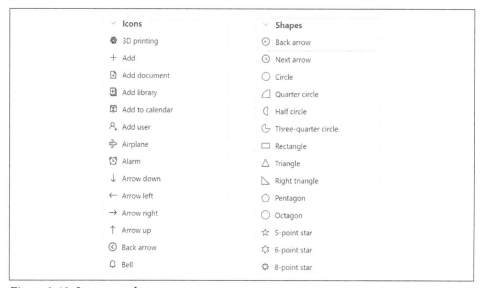

Figure 8-10. Icon controls

Here is an example of how a canvas app uses an icon. For demonstration in Figure 8-11, I've added a back arrow and the Power Fx expression `Back();` to allow users to go back to the previous screen.

Figure 8-11. Using icons on the app screen

Chart Controls

Charts are used in canvas apps to graphically represent data. Canvas apps' built-in chart controls can show charts with limited visuals. For advanced and complex reporting, you can design your report in Power BI and embed it in a canvas app as a tile. Canvas apps support four types of built-in chart capabilities to visualize data, as shown in Table 8-4.

Table 8-4. Canvas app chart controls

Chart control	Purpose
Column chart	Shows data with x- and y-axes
Line chart	Shows data with x- and y-axes
Pie chart	Shows relative values in comparison to each other
Power BI tile	Shows a Power BI tile within the canvas app

Figure 8-12 shows a line chart and a pie chart to represent data in graphical format.

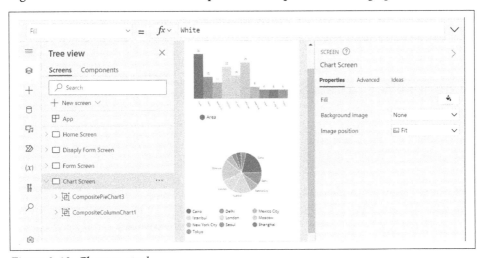

Figure 8-12. Chart control

AI Builder Controls

Canvas app provides various built-in AI Builder capabilities that I'll discuss in Chapter 11. In general, they scan and extract information from business cards, receipts, and forms. More generalized capabilities include object detection and text recognition.

All the AI capabilities in Figure 8-13 are premium (indicated by the diamond icon next to their names), so you need to have a separate license to use them. Check the AI

Builder calculator (*https://oreil.ly/TX17T*) for pricing info. As of this writing, some of them are still in preview and are not available for production use yet.

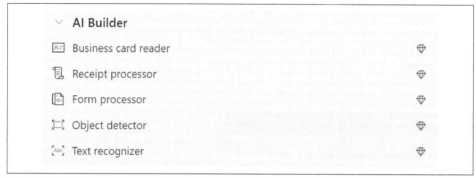

Figure 8-13. AI Builder premium features

Mixed Reality Controls

Canvas apps can include mixed reality (MR) controls for 3-D interaction with the real world, including those shown in Table 8-5.

Table 8-5. Canvas app mixed reality controls

Mixed reality control	Purpose
View in MR	Views and interacts with 3-D content using 3-D objects
View shape in MR	Overlays 3-D content and 2-D images on the camera feed
Measure in MR	Measurement tools for volume, area, and distance
Markup in MR	Paints 3-D lines and arrows to mark locations and areas

You can see some examples of mixed reality in Power Apps in the article "Create an App with 3D and Mixed Reality Controls (*https://oreil.ly/TX17T*)" and in the "Introducing Mixed Reality in Power Apps" (*https://oreil.ly/j16Na*) video.

Modern Controls

Modern controls is a new feature for canvas apps that allows app makers to add fluent UI-based controls that are the same as those used in model-driven apps. Modern controls in canvas apps are based on the Microsoft Fluent Design System. Modern controls are visually appealing, highly functional, and simple to use since they are developed with accessibility, usability, and performance in mind.

To enable modern controls in your canvas app, open your canvas app in Power Apps Studio, click on the three dots (...) from the toolbar, and select Settings. This will open the settings screen of the canvas app. Here you need to select "Upcoming features" from the left panel, search for "modern control," and toggle its value to On, as shown in Figure 8-14.

The setting to enable modern controls will eventually move to the General section, instead of Upcoming features.

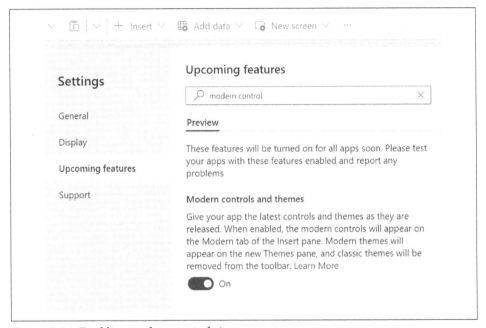

Figure 8-14. Enabling modern controls in your canvas app

As of this writing, modern controls are in preview and cannot be used in production. However, in the future, modern controls will replace the input controls that I discussed in "Input Controls" on page 289. Figure 8-15 shows the modern controls that are in preview as of this writing.

	Modern controls
🖼	Badge
ᴄᴛʀˡ	Button
☑	Checkbox
📅	Date picker
⊱≡	Dropdown
ⓘ	Info button
⊖	Link
➡	Progress Bar
◉	Radio group
◠	Spinner
▣	Tab list
🗐	Text
Ⓣ	Text input

Figure 8-15. Modern controls

Figure 8-16 shows how the two forms appear when designed using the classic and modern controls.

Figure 8-16. Difference between classic and modern controls

Components

You may want to develop an app that has multiple screens. To give a cohesive user experience, those screens should look similar to each other. To do that in canvas apps, you can create *components* that can be reused throughout your app. Components are reusable building blocks that enable canvas app makers to create reusable features and controls. You can even reuse components across multiple apps.

There are numerous scenarios where it may be necessary to use the same controls and features across different screens. To illustrate, I've chosen the header and footer of an app, which commonly have a lot of icons and controls that are the same on multiple screens.

Imagine you have a canvas app that has more than 50 screens, and you want the header and footer to appear on each screen. Instead of copying and pasting the same icons and controls used to design the header and footer onto each screen, it would be easier to construct certain features or controls as reusable components to be used throughout the application.

Figure 8-17 shows creating a header and footer as reusable components for your canvas app and using them in various screens across the app.

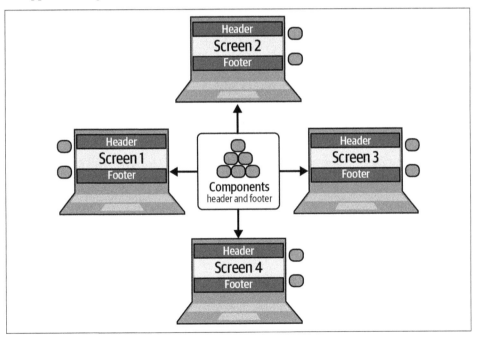

Figure 8-17. Component in a canvas app

Creating Components

Let's say that I've created a home screen with a header and footer, as shown in Figure 8-18.

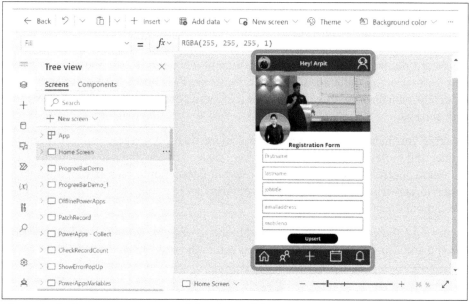

Figure 8-18. Canvas app screen with header and footer

The header contains a profile image and customer support icon, while the footer contains home, contacts, add new, calendar, and bell icons. Now, I would like to create more screens in the app and reuse the same header and footer without re-creating all the controls on other screens.

Instead of creating a header and footer only for the home screen, I will create them as part of a component so that I can reuse them on other screens.

To create a new component in Power Apps Studio, you need to first navigate to the Components tab and click on "New component," as shown in Figure 8-19.

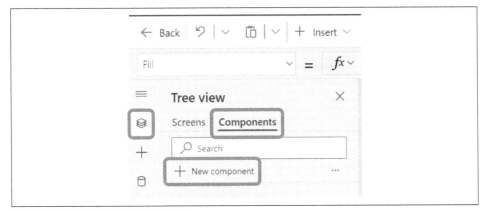

Figure 8-19. Creating a new component

Design the header and footer components using some icons and images (as shown in Figure 8-20).

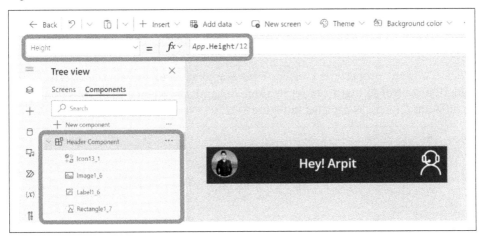

Figure 8-20. Creating a header component

You can create custom properties for your components, which will set control properties dynamically, so that you can change the value as needed. For example, if you want to set the header title dynamically for different screens, create a custom property for your component of type Text and set its value dynamically when adding it to multiple screens.

As depicted in Figure 8-21, I have selected my custom component (Header Component) from the left panel and created a custom input property with the name "HeaderTitle."

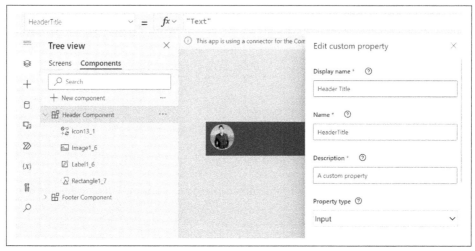

Figure 8-21. Creating a custom property for header title

Once the input property is created, I have applied it to the Text property of the Label1_6 control so that I can set its value dynamically when adding my component to different screens, as depicted in Figure 8-22.

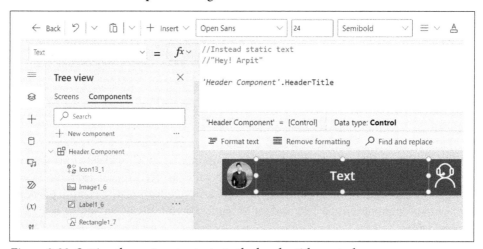

Figure 8-22. Setting the custom property to the header title control

Figure 8-23 shows setting the height of my component based on the app screen's height, so that the component fits or adjusts automatically according to screen size.

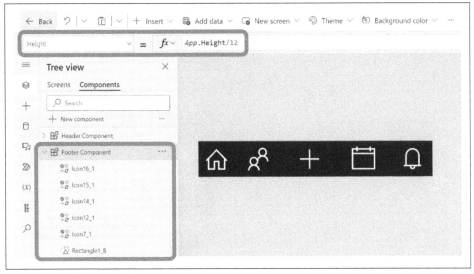

Figure 8-23. Creating a footer component

Using Components on Canvas App Screens

Once the components are created, navigate to the Screens tab, click on the plus (+) icon in the left panel, expand the Custom section, and add the header and footer components to the screen, as shown in Figure 8-24.

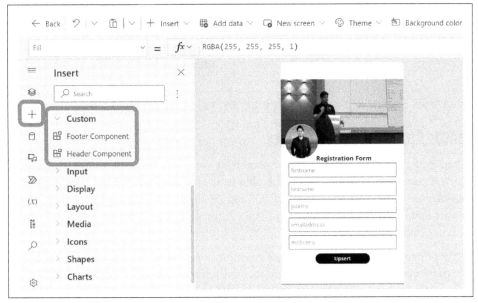

Figure 8-24. Adding a component to the canvas app screen

Once the components are added to the app's screen, you can adjust the alignment by dragging and dropping the header component to the top and the footer component to the bottom, as shown in Figure 8-25.

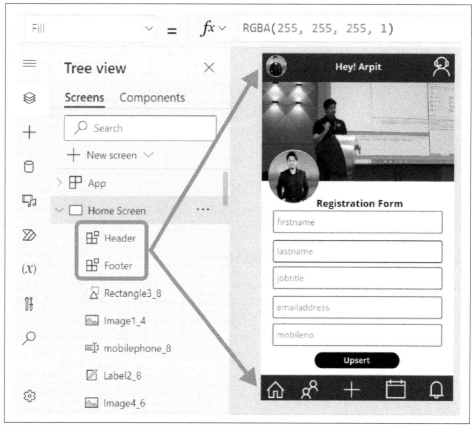

Figure 8-25. Using and aligning components in the canvas app screen

Canvas App Component Library

When you create a canvas app component, it can only be used within the app in which it was made. If you want to be able to use the component in other apps, you should create them as a *component library*. As Figure 8-26 shows, you can create Header and Footer as reusable components in the component library and use them in different canvas apps.

A component library is a collection of multiple components and is created outside of any particular app; then, app makers manually import these components into individual canvas apps. Component libraries cannot be modified within a consuming canvas app.

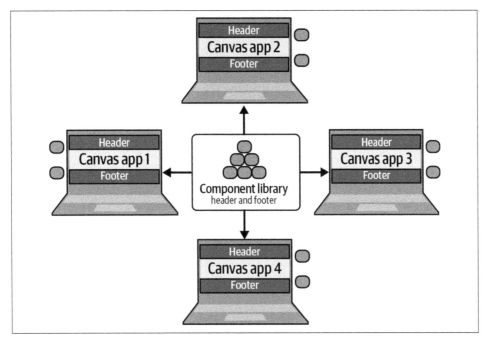

Figure 8-26. Component library in canvas apps

Component libraries allow you to create properties for your controls, the same as out-of-the-box control properties. For example, you can create a background-color property for the header and footer component, so that app makers can customize its background-color to their needs.

Note that you can't delete a component library unless you first delete it from all of the canvas apps that use it. You can use the "solution dependencies" feature (we'll discuss more about this in Chapter 10) of the solution to view which canvas apps are dependent on a particular component library.

On that point, component libraries are solution aware; hence, you need to include them in the solution container to move them across different environments.

> Component libraries are a canvas app feature; you can't use them in model-driven apps.

Creating a New Component Library

To create a new component library, you first need to navigate to Solutions from the Power Apps home page (*https://oreil.ly/lbi5Z*), select New from the toolbar, and then select More → Component Library. Now add two new components, Header and Footer, and add the desired controls (or use the same ones described earlier in the component creation section).

The component library allows you to create custom properties for the controls you are adding to the screen to let app makers adjust them as needed. As depicted in Figure 8-27, I have created a Header component along with two custom properties: HeaderTitle and HeaderIconColor.

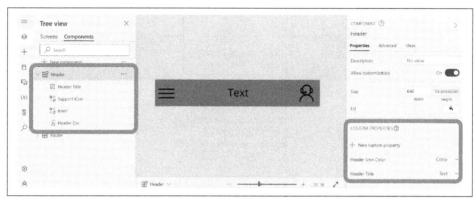

Figure 8-27. Header component with custom properties

Similar to the Header component, I have also created a Footer component, which has one custom property named FooterIconColor, as depicted in Figure 8-28.

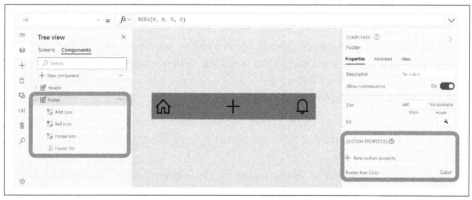

Figure 8-28. Footer component with custom properties

Now apply the custom properties you've created to the corresponding out-of-the-box properties of the controls you've added to the components. As shown in Figure 8-29, for instance, I've applied the HeaderTitle custom property to the Label control's Text property.

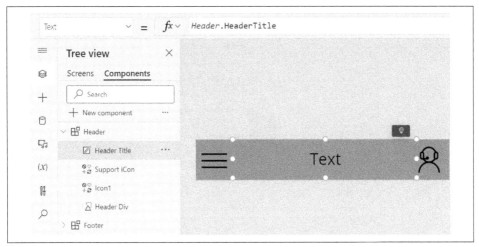

Figure 8-29. Set the custom property to the Text label's Text property

I also applied the HeaderIconColor custom property to the Color property of the icons that are available on the component, as shown in Figure 8-30. As a result, depending on their business requirements, app makers will be able to apply the value to these custom properties dynamically.

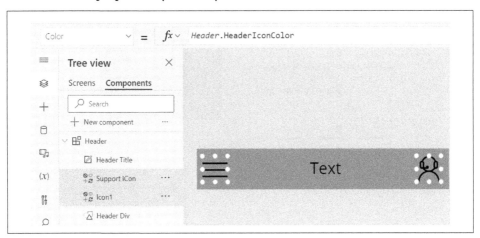

Figure 8-30. Set the custom property to the icon's Color property

Once a component is created, save the component library and publish it in order to use it in canvas apps. Your newly created component library will be listed under the Component Libraries section in the solution.

Now open your canvas app where you want to use the components you just created. Click on the plus (+) icon in the left panel, then click on "Get more components." You'll find all the components listed here. Choose the components from the list and click the Import button, as shown in Figure 8-31. This will add the selected components to your canvas app.

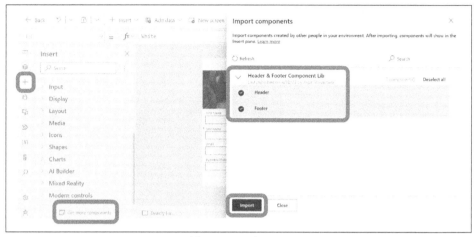

Figure 8-31. Importing component libraries to the canvas app

After importing the components to your canvas app, you can find the selected components under the "Library components" section, as shown in Figure 8-32.

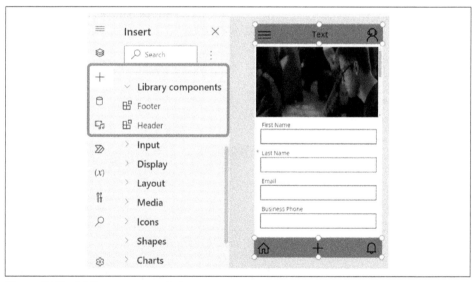

Figure 8-32. Adding components to your canvas app screen

Now you can add these components and personalize their properties on any screen in your canvas app. I added the Header and Footer components to my canvas app screen and set the Header Title property to "Registration Form" and the Header Icon Color property to Yellow, as shown in Figure 8-33.

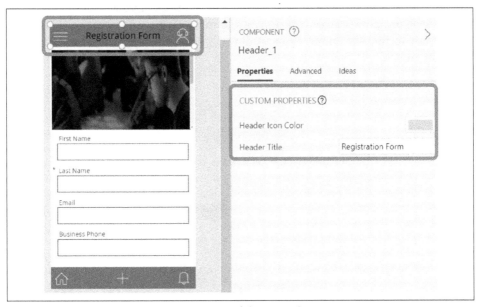

Figure 8-33. Setting the custom properties of the controls

If I make any changes to the component library, it should automatically notify app makers about the updates. For example, as shown in Figure 8-34, I have added two more icons (customer and calendar) to the Footer component, and then saved and published the component library.

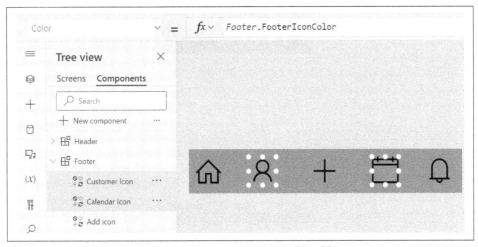

Figure 8-34. Making changes in the Footer component by adding two more icons

After making the changes in the component library, if I reopen/reload the canvas app where the component library is being referred, I'll see a notice about the updates. I can click the Review and then the Update buttons, the changes will automatically be reflected in my canvas app, as shown in Figure 8-35. If you reject the changes or choose not to update, Power Apps Studio will keep notifying you each time you reload or launch.

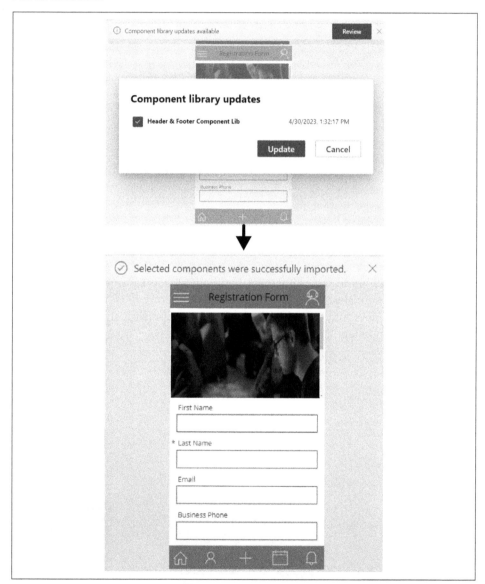

Figure 8-35. Review and update the components library in the canvas app

App Checker

Just like other application development platforms, canvas apps also require validating the issues in the app or the formula expressions written on the controls. App checker is a tool inside the canvas app that automatically tracks down the errors and lets app makers know about the possible root cause so they can solve them.

App checker finds the following types of issues:

Formula errors
  Lists all the errors in the formula expressions used in the app.

Runtime errors
  Lists all the errors that occur while performing operations in the data source.

Rules errors
  Canvas apps support only business rules with a scope of "entity" (i.e., they run on the server side), so App checker also lists all the errors that occur while running business rules in Dataverse.

Accessibility errors
  Lists all the errors related to the accessibility of the app and helps you find solutions for creating an accessible canvas app.

Performance errors
  Lists all errors that may impact the app performance, such as long-running formula expressions or queries.

To run App checker in your canvas app, just open the app and click on the stethoscope icon on the toolbar, as shown in Figure 8-36. App checker categorizes the errors to help you investigate and solve the issue related to a particular control or expression. For example, if I expand Formulas, it will display errors on the Submit button used on the Registration Form screen. If I expand Performance, it shows the Media controls that may impact the app performance.

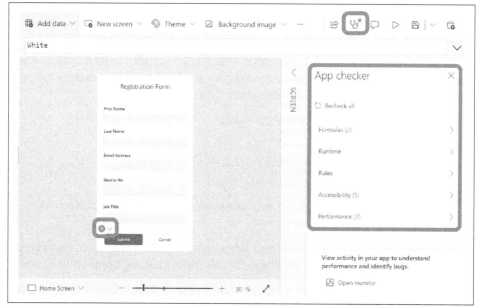

Figure 8-36. Running App checker in a canvas app

The error message (shown in Figure 8-37) tells me that an operator is expected in the formula because I have omitted the semicolon to terminate the Patch function expression.

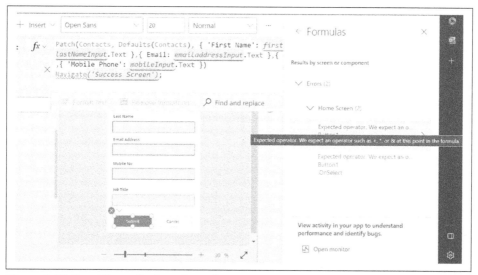

Figure 8-37. Providing a fix for a formula error

Similarly, to fix the performance issues, it suggests that I need to remove an unused media file (*Picture1.jpg*) from the app, as shown in Figure 8-38.

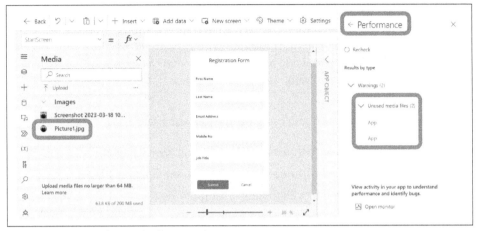

Figure 8-38. Providing a fix for a performance warning

App checker is the best way to check the compile-time errors in your app so that you can fix them before publishing your app. For advanced monitoring and troubleshooting, canvas app also provides a built-in monitoring tool, which we'll discuss next.

Monitor Tool

The Monitor tool helps you monitor how your app is performing and functioning. You can also use the debugging feature to help you diagnose and troubleshoot issues in the app. You can access the Monitor tool by choosing it from the Power Apps home page or by clicking the Monitor option in the command bar. You can also access it from within the canvas app by selecting Advanced tools → Open Monitor in the left navigation panel.

When using Monitor, you can find issues and queries like the following:

- A high number of network calls
- Data retrieved from the same data source
- The response data size
- The duration of a request
- Errors

You can create more robust apps with the aid of the Monitor tool by diagnosing and resolving issues more quickly. It offers a comprehensive look at your app by logging all the significant activities that take place when it is in use. Additionally, Monitor gives you a better understanding of how the events and formulas in your app operate so you can enhance performance and spot any errors or issues.

Having a deeper grasp of what your app does and how it does it is essential for troubleshooting issues. Sometimes it's challenging to pinpoint a problem based just on an examination of the app's formulas or even runtime errors. You can diagnose issues and find errors more quickly by keeping an eye on the events as they happen in your app and by understanding the sequence of actions and how your app is operating.

Monitoring for canvas apps doesn't support the following scenarios:

- Canvas apps embedded within a model-driven app (see Chapter 7)
- Canvas apps embedded within Microsoft Teams (see Chapter 12)
- Canvas apps connected to a SharePoint custom form

To run the Monitor tool for canvas apps, you must have the Environment Admin or Environment Maker security role.

The Monitor tool also helps with debugging canvas apps. For debugging, you need to turn on an additional setting. Click on the three dots (...) from the Power Apps Studio command bar, select General, and then turn on the toggle in the "Debug published app" dialog box, as shown in Figure 8-39. This generates a debug file to provide detailed error information for further investigation.

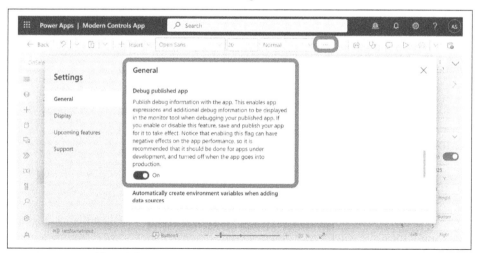

Figure 8-39. Enabling debugging

The "Debug published app" setting enables app expressions and additional debug information to be displayed in the Monitor tool when debugging your published app. If you enable or disable this feature, you have to save and publish your app for it to take effect. Notice that enabling this flag can have negative effects on the app performance, so it is recommended that it should be done for apps under development and turned off when the app goes into production.

How to Monitor a Canvas App

In this section, I will demonstrate how the Monitor tool helps keep track of how various app functions are running, including which controls are handling which events, how long the actions take to complete, and what data sources are being used. In Figure 8-40, I've created a contact form in the canvas app, and when the Submit button is clicked, I'm using the `Patch` function to insert the data into the Dataverse Contacts table. In Chapter 9, I'll discuss more about the `Patch` function and the Power Fx expression in Figure 8-40. For the time being, you just need to know that this expression inserts the values from the various controls available on the screen into the Contacts table in Dataverse.

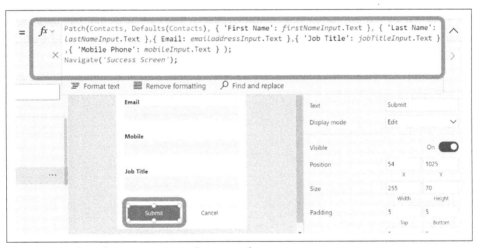

Figure 8-40. Sample canvas app with contact form

Then, you have the following two options to open the Monitor tool:

Within Power Apps Studio, as shown in Figure 8-41, you can open the Monitor tool by clicking on the Advanced tools icon from the left navigation panel and selecting "Open monitor."

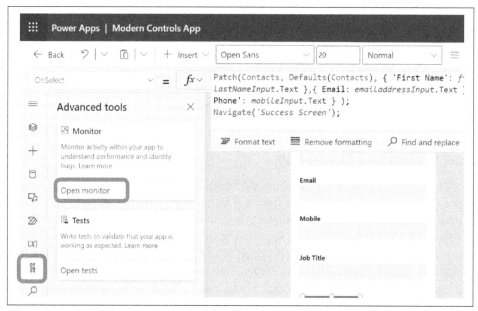

Figure 8-41. Opening the Monitor tool from a canvas app

From the Power Apps home page (*https://oreil.ly/WlAha*), select your canvas app from the app list and then click the Monitor button on the toolbar, as shown in Figure 8-42.

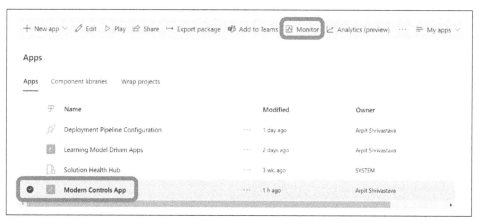

Figure 8-42. Opening the Monitor tool from the Apps home page

Figure 8-43 shows how a sample Monitor dashboard for a canvas app looks. For every event shown in the Monitor, you can review a variety of properties. Depending on the type of event, some of these attributes could be empty. Since there are no errors/issues in the app, all operations are successful.

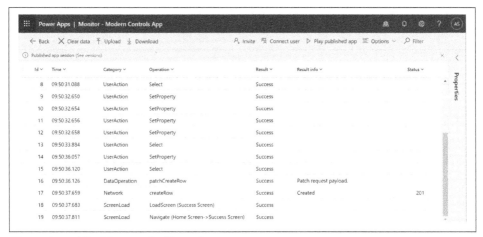

Figure 8-43. The Monitor dashboard

To showcase how the Monitor tool trace log can be used to debug, I have intentionally put the wrong expression in the Patch function (as shown in Figure 8-44).

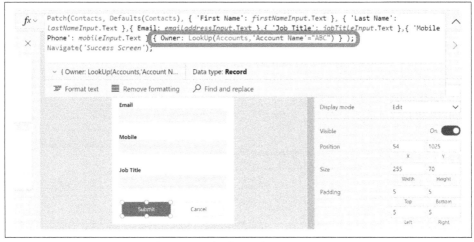

Figure 8-44. Canvas app with issue in the formula

Now, after saving and publishing the app, if I open the Monitor tool, it shows an error on the dashboard, as shown in Figure 8-45.

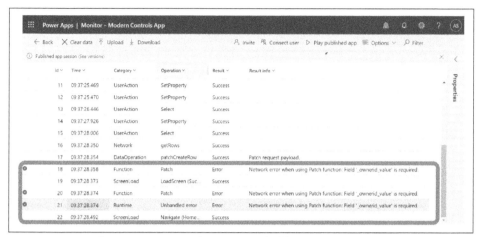

Figure 8-45. Displaying an error in the Monitor dashboard

Figure 8-46 shows how to select a specific row from the trace log, analyze the formula running behind it, and determine the root cause of the problem or error. You can download the trace log (in JSON format) locally to share with other developers or send to Microsoft to investigate offline.

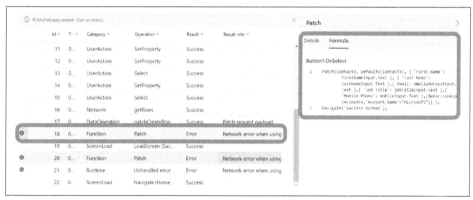

Figure 8-46. Checking the formula causing the error

Collaborative Troubleshooting Using the Monitor Tool

While troubleshooting and monitoring any issues, you often need to:

- Invite other developers/experts/support technicians from your team or organization to help investigate the issues.

- Connect live users to run the app and watch the sequence of events/steps they are performing while interacting with the app.

Inviting users

To troubleshoot and investigate app issues, you can share a real-time Monitor session with others, such as support staff or professional developers, without needing to share your screen. They can see the exact same app events in their own browser when you ask them to join a session, without having to open the app or re-create the particular scenario you're debugging. To find the issue, you and the other participants may separately explore, observe, and check the app events without interfering with one another or switching control back and forth.

Figure 8-47 depicts how you can select the Invite option from the Monitor tool screen and invite other app makers to join the Monitor session.

Figure 8-47. Inviting other app makers by sending them an email invite

Figure 8-48 depicts how two app makers can view the same Monitor dashboard to investigate the issue together.

Figure 8-48. Inviting an app maker to help investigate an issue

Connecting users

You can use the "Connect user" option to enable an app user to launch a published canvas app in a live environment and connect through a monitoring session. You can then watch the user go through a sequence of events/steps while interacting with the app. By watching their actions, you may be able to troubleshoot the issue at hand.

Figure 8-49 depicts how you can select the "Connect user" option from the Monitor tool screen and start a session with an end user to view their session data.

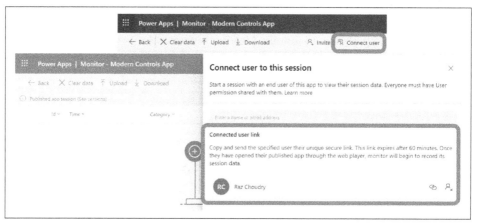

Figure 8-49. Sending a secure link to an app user to connect

Figure 8-50 demonstrates how an app maker connects with an app user, who then plays (runs) the app. The trace log displays on the Monitor dashboard, which the app maker can view to investigate the issue.

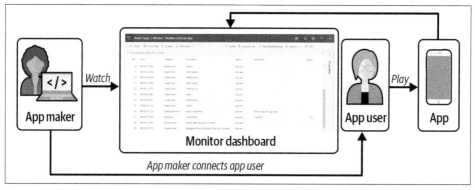

Figure 8-50. App maker connects with an app user to troubleshoot an issue

Test Studio

You can use the Test Studio tool to perform end-to-end testing for your canvas apps. It can spot problems or faults at an early stage of the release process, giving developers the chance to address them and improve the app before going live with modifications. Using this tool will help you maintain app quality by consistently verifying that your app performs as expected after the deployment of new modifications or updates.

Using Test Studio

You must be either owner or co-owner of an app to use Test Studio within the app.

As shown in Figure 8-51, to open Test Studio, open your canvas app and select the "Advanced tools" icon from the left panel and click on "Open tests."

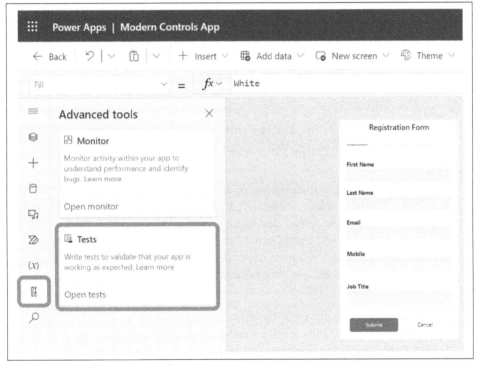

Figure 8-51. Opening Test Studio

Once Test Studio is launched, it has the main components shown in Figure 8-52.

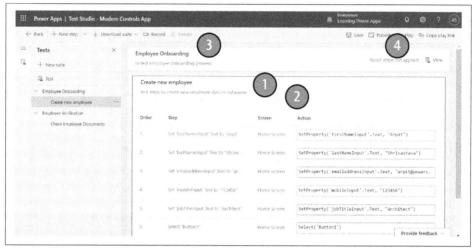

Figure 8-52. Test Studio components

Let's look at each component in more detail:

Test suite (1)

The particular process in your app that you want to test. For example, I have designed an Onboarding app that handles the employee onboarding process.

Test case (2)

The feature (a series of instructions or actions) of that process that you want to test. For example, employee onboarding processes can have various features like create new employees, upload documents, conduct background checks, or share the company handbook. Each feature can have multiple actions. For example, to create a new employee, you need to provide the employee's first name, last name, email, mobile phone, etc. and then click the Create/Submit button.

Record (3)

You can either manually write the formulas/expressions to test a particular feature or you can record the steps by directly opening the canvas app within Test Studio. Figure 8-53 demonstrates that when you click Record, it starts recording your test results by performing the set of actions in the sequence described in the test case and displays the results as pass or fail in the left panel.

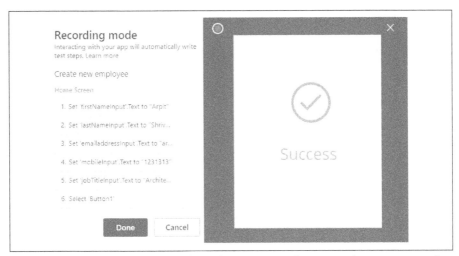

Figure 8-53. Click on Record, perform the actions, and generate the test cases in the left panel

Save and publish (4)

Once the test cases are generated, you can save and publish your test cases, as shown in Figure 8-54.

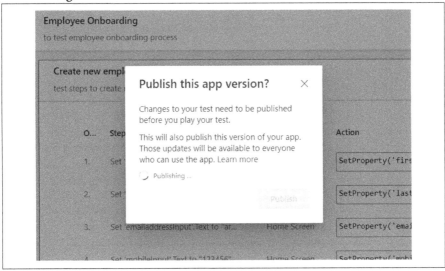

Figure 8-54. Publishing the test cases

You can run the test cases by clicking on the Play button from the toolbar, as shown in Figure 8-55. This is helpful when you add new features to the app and want to do a quick sanity check to ensure that nothing is broken in the existing functionality.

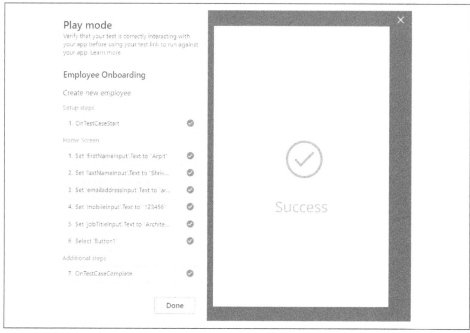

Figure 8-55. Test case result after running the test cases

Test Suite Events

Sometimes you might need to set up, process, and send the results of your tests to other data sources or to Dataverse. To perform your own business logic (written in Power Fx expressions) on test case start or test case completion, test suites provide three types of events:

OnTestCaseStart

Executes your business logic before the test cases begin executing. For example, you might need to always begin your test case execution from the login screen, set up test data or initialize variables or collections for your app, or notify app makers before the test case starts executing.

OnTestCaseComplete

Executes your business logic after the test cases complete execution. For example, you might need to send an email to a customer once test cases are executed, send a test case report to the app makers, or store the test cases execution log in Dataverse or another data source.

`OnTestSuiteComplete`
Executes your business logic after the whole test suite execution is completed.

`OnTestCaseComplete` and `OnTestSuiteComplete` events are very helpful if you're using Azure DevOps-based deployment because based on the test results, you can decide whether to proceed with the app deployment or not.

Important Points to Know About Test Studio

The following are important things to remember when using Test Studio:

- The results of test case executions are stored in TestCaseResult and TestSuiteResult tables in Dataverse.
- Test Studio is not recommended to test all types of functionalities of canvas apps. Manual testing should also be performed after test automation for features that have a high impact on your business.
- While a single, large test case can be used to test every feature of your app, it is recommended that you break it up into multiple test cases instead of writing one large test case.
- Don't keep multiaction test expressions in a single step. Breaking it into multiple steps will help you debug the issue more quickly.
- Carefully choose which features need to be evaluated manually versus which can be tested with Test Studio while keeping the following Test Studio restrictions in mind:
  - It can't test canvas app components and component libraries.
  - It can't test code components (PCF controls) included in canvas apps.
  - It can't test nested galleries and media controls.
  - It doesn't support Select and Set property functions.
  - It's not the best choice for high business impact functionalities.
  - It's not the best choice for features that require multiple data sets.

Canvas App Versioning

If your canvas app gets corrupted or if something was accidentally deleted, you can get everything back by restoring the features from an earlier version. Canvas apps maintain the versions every time you publish the app. You can restore the previous version (created within the last six months) that was saved to the cloud from your Power Apps account.

To view the previous canvas app version and restore option, you need to navigate to the Power Apps home page, choose your canvas app, click on the three dots either next to the app name or from the toolbar, and select Details, as shown in Figure 8-56.

Figure 8-56. Going to canvas app details

To view the app versions, click the Version tab, as shown in Figure 8-57. The word "Live" in the Published column denotes your current app version.

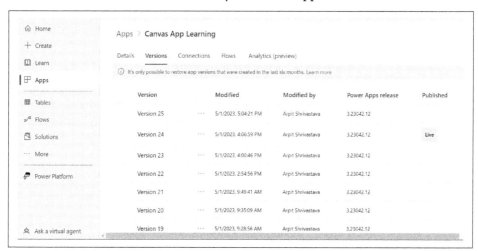

Figure 8-57. Canvas app versions of last six months

Choose the version that you want to restore and click on Restore from the toolbar, as shown in Figure 8-58. Once you restore a previous version, it shows up as Live.

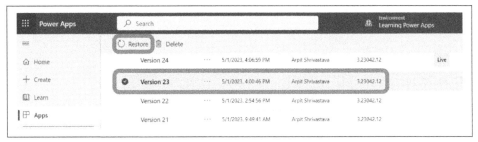

Figure 8-58. Restoring a previous version

Canvas App Analytics

If you have the Environment Admin security role, you often need to review the analytics of your canvas app to check its overall health, such as app performance, app usage, and errors. Canvas apps provide a built-in, Power BI-based analytics tool that enables users with the security roles Environment Admin, Power Platform Admin, Dynamics 365 Admin, or Global Admin to view reports in Power Apps analytics.

These analytics are only applicable for canvas apps—not for model-driven apps.

To view the analytics, navigate to the Power Apps home page, choose your canvas app, and click on Analytics in the toolbar, as shown in Figure 8-59.

Figure 8-59. Viewing canvas app analytics

You can view the reports based on the app's usage, performance, and location. By default, it retains data for the last 30 days. The data refresh cycle is about every three hours (see Figure 8-60).

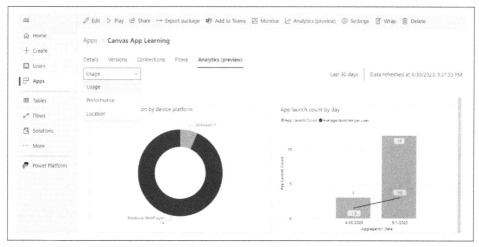

Figure 8-60. Canvas app analytics based on usage, performance, and location

Canvas App Sharing

Once you develop the canvas app that addresses a business need, you can now share it with others in your organization for the following purposes:

- To run the app and start using its features
- To modify the app's controls/features and reshare it with others
- To make it possible for other app makers to work with you on development and add comments if needed

A canvas app needs to be shared with all users who want to use/edit it. You can share the canvas app with:

- Individual users
- A Microsoft Entra ID security group
- Everyone in the organization

Sharing Canvas Apps with Internal Users

To share the canvas app, navigate to the Power Apps home page, choose your app, and click on Share from the toolbar, as shown in Figure 8-61.

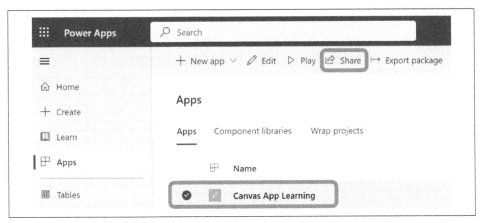

Figure 8-61. Sharing a canvas app

The Share Canvas App window displays the options shown in Figure 8-62.

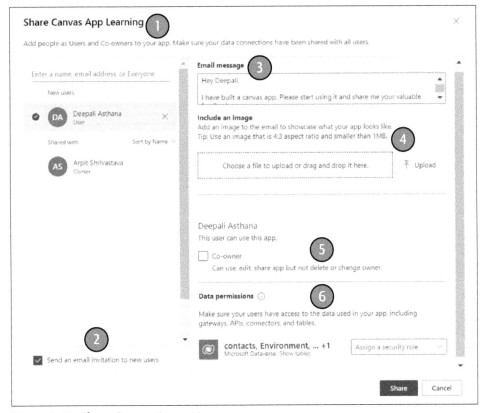

Figure 8-62. Share Canvas App options

Let's look at these options in more detail:

Add people as Users and Co-owners to your app (1)

Here you can either provide a list of all internal users (people within your organization) by providing their name or email address, or you can specify a Microsoft Entra ID security group, or you can type "everyone" to share the app with everyone in the organization, as shown in Figure 8-63. The same step can be used to share a canvas app with external users (people outside your organization), but first they must register in Microsoft Entra ID as guests. I'll talk about them in a later section.

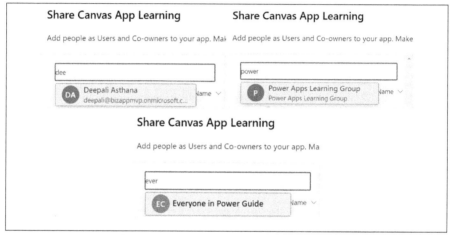

Figure 8-63. Various sharing options

Send an email invitation to new users (optional) (2)

Enabling this option sends a notification email to all invitees.

Email message (optional) (3)

If you choose to send an email to new users, type the message that you want to send here.

Include an image (optional) (4)

If you choose to send an email to new users, you can provide the image of your app to let your invitees know about your app.

Co-owner (5)

Enable this option to allow invitees to use, edit, and re-share the app. (But they can't delete it or change its ownership.)

Data permissions (6)

Make sure the invitees have access to the data used in your app, including gateways, APIs, connectors, and tables. For example, if you are using the Dataverse connector in your app and using the Contacts table to create the data, then invitees must have Read and Create access on the Contacts table in Dataverse.

Sharing Canvas Apps with External Users

Sometimes you want to invite external contractors, business partners, and other external people to use your company's canvas apps temporarily by sharing the app with them as guest users in Microsoft Entra ID:

1. Create a guest user account in the Microsoft Entra ID tenant by navigating to the Azure Portal (*https://oreil.ly/Zge-J*), clicking on View Microsoft Entra ID, selecting "All users" from the left panel, and then selecting "New user" → "Invite external user," as shown in Figure 8-64.

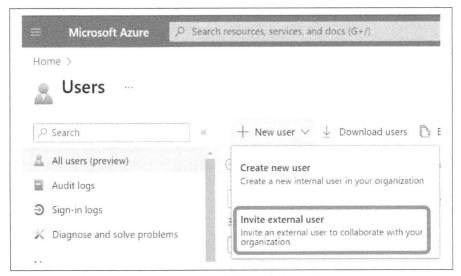

Figure 8-64. Creating a guest account in Microsoft Entra ID

2. Provide the guest user's details like email and display name, as shown in Figure 8-65.

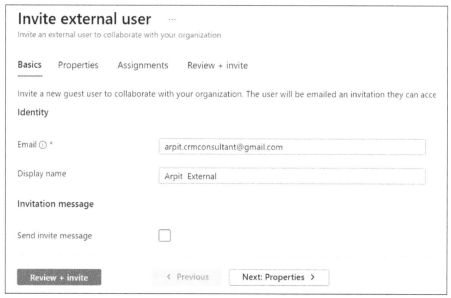

Figure 8-65. Entering an email address and sending the invitation

3. Assign a Power Apps per app or per user license to the guest user, as shown in Figure 8-66. Otherwise users will get the error "You do not have a valid Power Apps plan. To access Power Apps you must have a Power Apps plan assigned to you by your organization or the organization in which you're a guest."

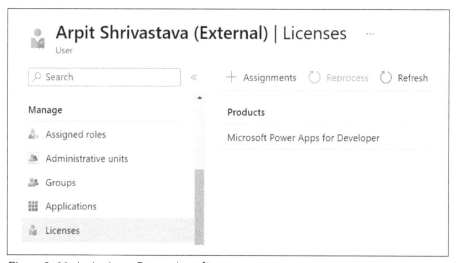

Figure 8-66. Assigning a Power Apps license

4. Once a guest user has been created and invited to use the application, go to the Power Apps home page, choose the canvas app, and click Share from the toolbar to share the canvas app with the guest user by entering their email address.

5. A guest user will receive the invitation (shown in Figure 8-67) and can start using the app via the app URL. Guest users can't log in to the Power Apps environment with this URL.

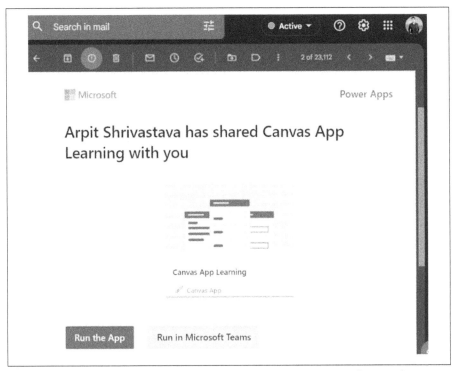

Figure 8-67. External users will receive an invitation announcing the app sharing

Canvas App Comments

If you write code or collaborate with others in text documents, you are probably familiar with annotating code or text with comments. You can add comments to your canvas app as well. Comments help you, and others, to make notes when evaluating the app, offer suggestions, or even note more details on the app's implementation. Comments in your canvas app will appear in a panel on the right side of your screen.

Make sure to share the app with other makers so they can access your app and add comments.

You can add the comments in your canvas app at the following places:

Tree view

You can add the comments in the left panel, which displays all controls added to the app, as shown in Figure 8-68.

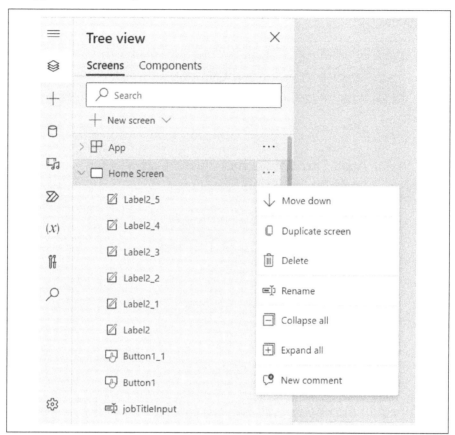

Figure 8-68. Adding comments to the Tree view controls

Design screen

You can add the comments in the middle panel, which displays the preview of the app, as shown in Figure 8-69.

Figure 8-69. Adding comments to the Design screen controls

App level

You can add the comments for your app by clicking on the comment icon from the toolbar, as shown in Figure 8-70.

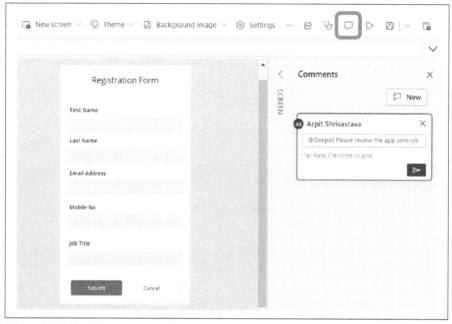

Figure 8-70. Adding comments for the app

Once you add a comment, a comment icon displays next to the control in the app. You can also mention/tag other app makers' names (e.g., @deepali) while writing the comment, and they will receive an email that invites them to review and reply to your comment (see Figure 8-71).

Figure 8-71. Adding comments in the tree view, main screen, and app

Comments are frequently queries, feedback, or suggestions that provide important context for your app. However, they are not necessarily live conversations. To better keep track of the active comments, you can resolve a comment or reopen a resolved comment thread by clicking on the three dots (...) on the top right corner of the comment box and selecting "Resolve thread."

Canvas App Coauthoring

The fact that only one app maker could work on a canvas app at a time had been one of the canvas app's main drawbacks. For example, if Deepali (app maker1) tries to launch an app that Arpit (app maker2) is currently editing, Deepali receives the message "This app is locked for editing by Arpit. Contact the user or wait for them to close it," as shown in Figure 8-72.

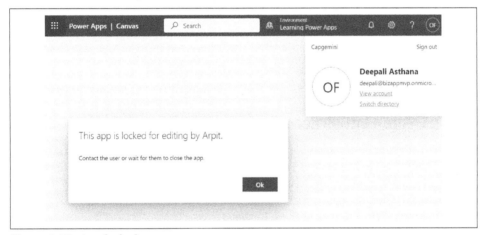

Figure 8-72. App locked message

This gets difficult when you have to create large apps with many screens to design. How can you get the job done faster if you cannot ask someone to work alongside you? To overcome this challenge, Microsoft has rolled out a new feature called *coauthoring* of canvas app, which enables multiple app makers to work simultaneously on the same app.

Figure 8-73 demonstrates how several app makers can collaborate on app development by storing the app in a Git repository. For example, when Arpit (app maker) wants to make changes to the canvas app, he will first *pull* the most recent app changes from the Git repo, which will sync the newest changes from the repo to Power Apps Studio. Arpit makes adjustments to the app and, when he's done, *pushes* the changes to the Git repo, making them available to the other app maker (Deepali). If Deepali makes updates to the same app, she follows the same steps as Arpit.

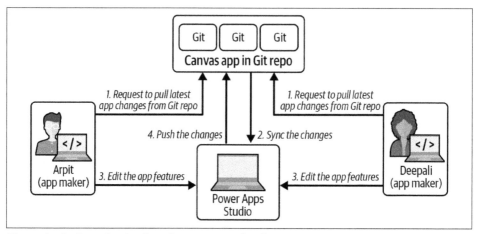

Figure 8-73. Coauthoring based canvas app development

By following this process, all app creators will have the most recent app changes in the Power Apps Studio before making any changes to the app locally.

To enable coauthoring in a canvas app, you need to perform the following five steps.

Step 1: Create a GitHub Repository

To use coauthoring in a canvas app, it needs to have a GitHub repository. If it has one already, skip to Step 2. If it doesn't have a GitHub repo yet, you must create one following the instructions in the GitHub documentation (*https://oreil.ly/pBvLn*). After setting up the GitHub repository, make a note of the branch name, directory name, and repository URL; you'll need these in step 3.

 Any Git provider can be used with Power Apps Studio—Git (*https://git-scm.com*), GitHub (*https://github.com*), or Azure DevOps (*https://oreil.ly/qOmbe*).

Step 2: Create a Personal Access Token

Next, you need to create a personal access token (PAT) in GitHub to enable the canvas app to connect with the repository. To generate a PAT, access your GitHub repository, click on your profile icon (right top corner), and select Settings. Then select Developer Settings (from the left panel), expand "Personal access tokens," and select Tokens (classic) → Generate new token (classic). In the Note field provide a token name, and then specify the expiration time and scope (shown in Figure 8-74). Click "Generate token" to copy the token to the clipboard; this is important because it disappears once you leave the page. If you need help with these instructions, see the GitHub documentation (*https://oreil.ly/N8bxV*).

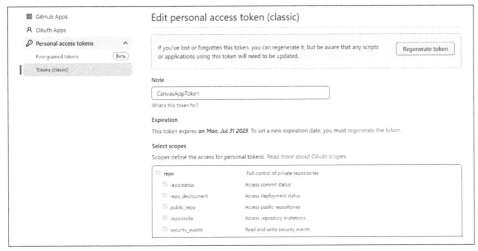

Figure 8-74. Generating a personal access token (PAT) in a GitHub repo

Step 3: Enable Git Version Control

Now, you need to enable the Git version control setting in the canvas app and connect it with the app's Git repository. Open your canvas app, then, in Power Apps Studio, select Settings from the toolbar, click on "Upcoming features" in the Settings dialog, select Experimental, scroll to locate the "Show the Git version control" setting and toggle it on, as shown in Figure 8-75.

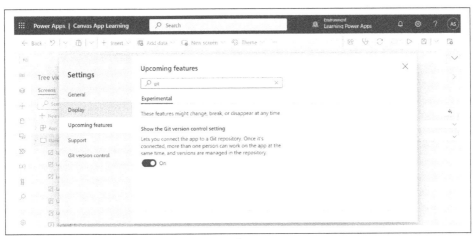

Figure 8-75. Enabling the Git version control setting in your canvas app

Once you enable it, you will see a new tab appear in the left panel named "Git version control." Click on it and connect your Git repo with the canvas app. Enter your Git repository URL, branch name, and directory name, and click the Apply button, as shown in Figure 8-76.

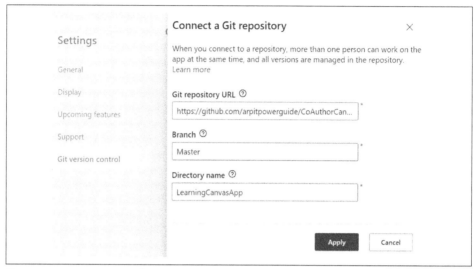

Figure 8-76. Connecting the Git repository

Provide your Git repository username and the PAT generated in the previous step (in the Password field), as shown in Figure 8-77, and then click the "Sign in" button.

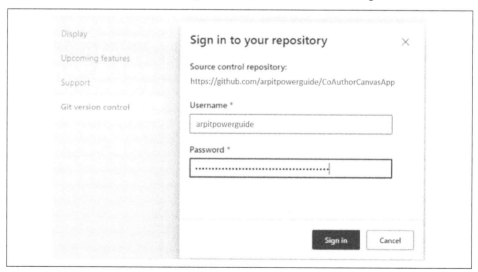

Figure 8-77. Entering username and PAT

Step 4: Create Branch and Directory in the Git Repository

Once you sign in, you'll be asked to create a branch and directory (folder) in the repository, if it doesn't exist already. Once you've done this, your Git repo will be connected to your canvas app, as shown in Figure 8-78.

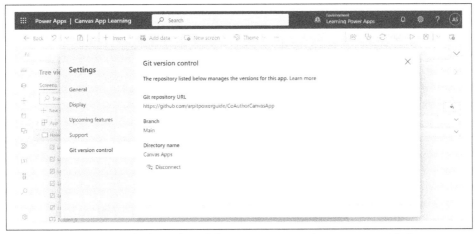

Figure 8-78. Providing the branch and directory name and connecting with the repo

Step 5: Make Changes to the Canvas App

Now multiple app makers can work on the same canvas app simultaneously. They can get the latest app changes from the Git repo by clicking on the sync icon (as shown in Figure 8-79) before they start making changes to the app.

When you make changes to the app in Power Apps Studio and then click Save and Publish, your app's modifications are automatically published to the Git repository, as illustrated in Figure 8-80.

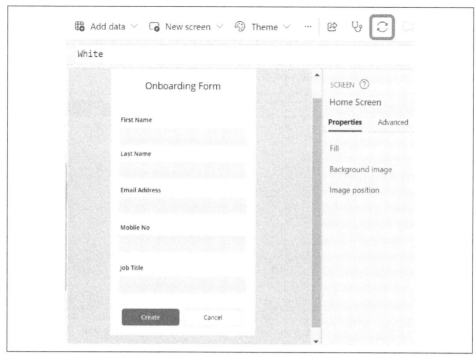

Figure 8-79. Syncing the latest app changes from Git repo in your app

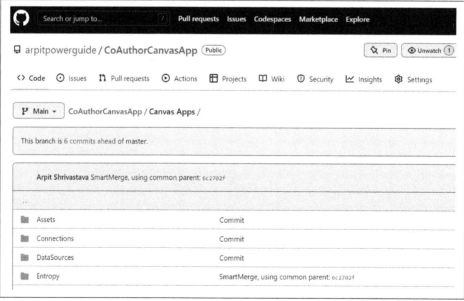

Figure 8-80. Canvas app files in the Git repo

Canvas App Accessibility

Canvas apps are often used for mobile and tablet devices. These apps rely heavily on visual, audio, and tactile interaction. However, you can make your app more accessible to people of different abilities by following some design guidelines.

Apps are more usable for all users when they are designed with some design principles and simplicity in mind. The following are some of the ways you can design your app to be accessible:

- Layout and color
  - Make sure the text is large enough and that all parts are easily visible. The written and visual content must all be simple to read and comprehend.
  - Be sure to designate the input fields on the screen. What a screen reader will announce is determined by the `AccessibleLabel` attribute.
  - If changing the colors, make sure the contrast ratio between the text and the background is at least 4.5:1.
  - Make sure the layout follows a logical flow when read from top to bottom and left to right.
  - Make your app is responsive so that people with low vision may zoom in and use it without having to scroll back and forth.
- Keyboard
  - Only set TabIndex to 0 or less.
  - Set TabIndex to 0 for Label, Picture, Icon, and Shape controls if they are designed to be interactive. TabIndex should be set to –1 if not.
  - Verify that the Simplified tab index app configuration is active.
- Screen readers
  - Verify that the `AccessibleLabel` attribute is set on each input control.
  - Set an appropriate description for the image's `AccessibleLabel` property.
  - Make sure the `AccessibleLabel` is empty or not set if an image isn't being used as a button or link.
  - When an image or an icon is used as a button, set TabIndex to 0 and `AccessibleLabel` to the link's description.
- Control type and structure
  - On each screen of the app, use at least one heading. You can make a heading by changing a Label's Role attribute.
  - For interactive text, a Button should be used instead of a Label.

— Use containers to group related items.

— Be mindful of invalid design patterns (*https://oreil.ly/9p14T*).

- Multimedia

— Make sure that every video has captions and that every audio recording has a transcript that the user can access. The `ClosedCaptionsUrl` attribute of the video control facilitates the use of closed captions in WebVTT format.

— The Timer control does not announce button text when the screen reader is enabled; instead, it announces how much time has elapsed. Even when the timer is partially hidden, announcements cannot be disabled.

- Signature control

— You must allow a different mode of signature input if your signature field makes use of the PenInput control.

— It is advisable to provide a TextInput control for users to enter their names.

— Make sure to place the signing instructions in the `AccessibleLabel` property and to position the control to the right of or directly beneath the Pen input.

In addition to these guidelines, there are further recommendations about the logical ordering of controls on screens, the definition of meaningful names for controls and screens, the logical grouping of controls, the sequence of keyboard navigation, etc. It is impossible to go through every rule in the book. It is recommended that you read all guidelines in the Microsoft documentation (*https://oreil.ly/uUiYP*).

Setting the AccessibleLabel Property

Let's look at an example of one way to make your canvas app more accessible, the `AccessibleLabel` property. I have set the `AccessibleLabel` property for different types of controls on the app's screen.

Figure 8-81 shows how to set the `AccessibleLabel` property for a text input control.

Figure 8-82 shows how to set the `AccessibleLabel` property for a toggle control.

Figure 8-81. Setting the AccessibleLabel *property for a text input control*

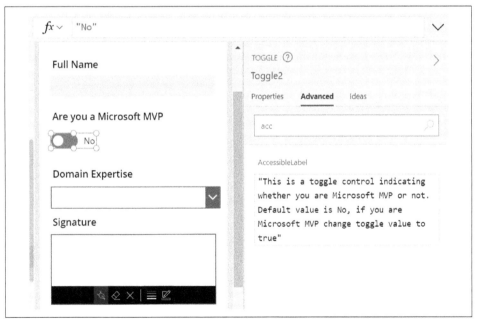

Figure 8-82. Setting the AccessibleLabel *property for a toggle control*

Figure 8-83 shows how to set the `AccessibleLabel` property for a combo box control.

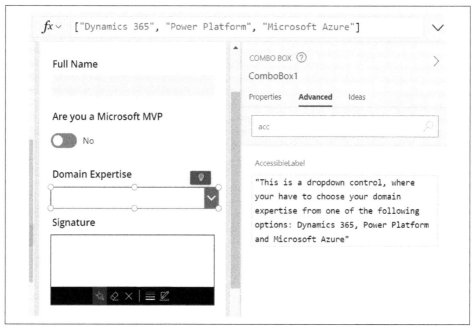

Figure 8-83. Setting the `AccessibleLabel` property for a combo box control

Figure 8-84 shows how to set the `AccessibleLabel` property for a pen input control.

Figure 8-84. Setting the `AccessibleLabel` property for a pen input control

Checking Accessibility Issues

From App checker (discussed earlier in this chapter), you can view all accessibility-related issues in your canvas app, and it will guide you to the appropriate control to address each one. In Figure 8-85, you can see that I haven't set the `AccessibleLabel` property for the email address, mobile number, and job title input controls.

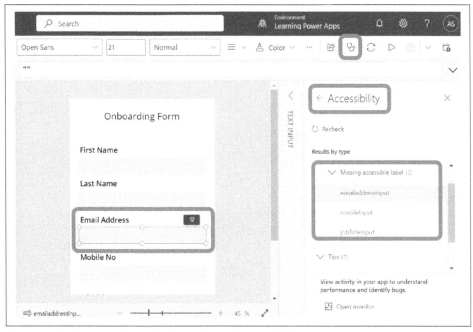

Figure 8-85. Running App checker to find all accessibility issues in your app

Summary

This chapter provided a thorough overview of all the features and components of canvas apps. To get the app development process started, it is crucial to understand these features. Keep in mind that if Microsoft Dataverse is used to store the data, the majority of model-driven apps and canvas apps use the same components. But if you need to store data somewhere other than Dataverse and need to heavily customize the app, canvas apps should be your only choice.

After reading this chapter, you must be wondering: Why don't we have a common programming language that I can use to create business logic across the Power Platform? Yes, Microsoft has introduced Power Fx, an Excel-like, formula-based expression language that enables developers and citizen developers to write both client- and server-side code. I will go into more depth regarding Power Fx in the next chapter.

CHAPTER 9

Power Fx: A Low-Code Language

In the previous chapters, you have learned about various techniques and components to design Power Apps-based business applications. You always start with no-code components to build your application. If that doesn't fit your requirements, then you can move to pro-code components for writing JavaScript and C# code to extend the built-in capabilities of the applications. Sometimes, writing code is one of the major pain points for organizations because it makes them dependent on professional developers and technical folks for app development, which means it can take a lot of time to design the end-to-end business solution.

With the growing demand for low-code, no-code application development platforms, so that anyone in an organization can design an application and write business logic without having prior knowledge of any programming language, Microsoft introduced a new low-code programming language called Microsoft Power Fx, as shown in Figure 9-1.

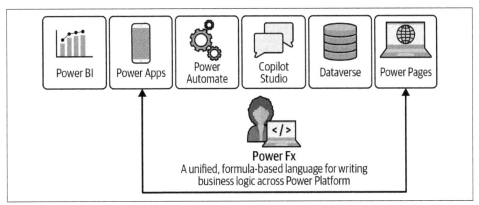

Figure 9-1. Microsoft Power Fx, a unified, formula-based language for Power Platform

The "Fx" in Power Fx refers to a formula-based language plus Excel-based expressions. Power Fx was first introduced for use in Power Apps canvas apps to write expressions, but it has now been extended throughout the Power Platform. In this chapter, I'll discuss how Power Fx can be used by all levels of app creators across the Power Platform, discuss its architecture, and then go through how Power Fx is used in each Power Platform product.

What Is Power Fx?

Microsoft has many low-code, no-code tools to design business solutions. However, professional developers still have to write code to customize the application. And, no matter what, no business applications can be developed without customizing the existing features and writing code. Low-code, no-code components can only help you expedite app development, but coding is still required. So how can non-technical folks also write the code without knowing any programming languages?

The answer lies with Microsoft Excel.

Today, hundreds of millions of business users (*https://oreil.ly/5IjeZ*) create worksheets with Excel every day. What if you could take advantage of their existing Excel knowledge and concepts that they already know? This inspired Microsoft to create a new low-code and Excel-based formula language called Power Fx. It uses the same formulas, functions, and expressions for data manipulation, data transformation, and complex calculations as Excel, and thus feels familiar to those who are already well-versed in using Excel.

In Figure 9-2, I have shown an example of the `Concatenate` function in Power Fx, which is inspired by the `CONCAT` function in Excel. The major advantage of using Power Fx over Excel and other business logic components in Power Platform is that it is always live and changes are reflected immediately. There is no compile or run mode; whenever a formula changes, it immediately recalculates the value. Any errors are also shown immediately.

You can see how Power Fx would seem familiar to someone who is familiar to Excel, even if they didn't know any programming languages. It's used throughout the Power Platform to create custom pages within model-driven apps, Power Automate, Microsoft Copilot Studio, and Microsoft Dataverse.

Power Fx is a strongly typed programming language, which means that each type of data (such as integers, string, or decimals) is predefined. This allows for the early detection of errors at compile time. Later in this chapter, I will describe this with a real-world example.

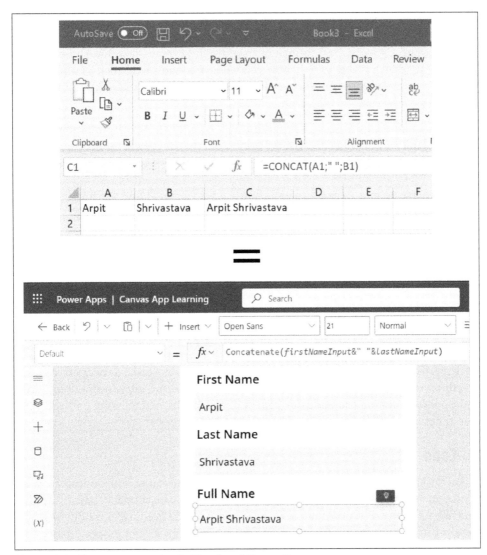

Figure 9-2. Concatenate string in Excel and Power Fx

Power Fx is a *declarative programming language* focuses on declaring the results of the code or formula rather than how the results should be carried out. For example, when you order a sandwich from a restaurant, you only need to specify which sandwich from the menu you want. You don't need to specify what exactly goes into the sandwich. This is how Excel works.

Power Fx is an *imperative programming language,* on the other hand, focuses on steps that describe how code or formulas will be executed. This is how languages such as JavaScript and C# work. To continue our sandwich example, it would be like having to tell the sandwich maker exactly how you want your sandwich, such as what type of bread you want, if you want the bread toasted, if it should be vegan, what toppings and sauces you want on it, and so on.

Power Fx supports both types of programming techniques to perform business logic. It has declarative functions like visible, color, concatenate, patch, and collect that can be used directly to produce results without describing how they will be executed. In addition, there are imperative functions, such as buttons/controls clicks, where you can specify the actions to be taken and choose what you want to do on a click.

Finally, Power Fx is open source and can be contributed to on GitHub (*https://oreil.ly/ aW9kU*) by members of the community. Microsoft has embraced the open source movement and has introduced open source languages such as C#, TypeScript, and JavaScript. With Power Fx, the company has brought the same open source approach to the low-code world.

Power Fx Is for Everyone

Anybody can write Power Fx expressions to write business logic, regardless of technical expertise. It provides a number of functions that no-code developers can use exactly as is, functions that low-code developers can use and alter to suit their needs, and opportunities for pro-code developers to expand its functionality and add their own functions. Let's discuss each of them in more detail.

No-Code

If you do not want to use any code (because you are unfamiliar with code, for convenience, or for any other reason), you can use many built-in, property-based formulas and functions that Power Fx offers in your app without needing to modify them or have any prior knowledge of Excel or Power Fx. There are several property-based formulas that can be understood on their own:

Concatenate
    To concatenate two string values

Sum
    To add two numbers

Notify
    To notify/show message (error/warning/information) to app users

Visible
    To hide/show app controls

Color
> To change the color of controls in the app

Fill
> To fill the background color of the app controls

FontSize, FontWeight, Font
> To change the font's size, weight, and typeface

A canvas app's screen has a number of built-in properties for each control, which you can use to modify that control's characteristics and properties (see Figure 9-3).

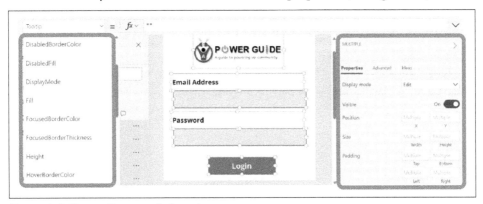

Figure 9-3. Power Fx no-code functions

Low-Code

If you are open to using some code, Power Fx provides concise, yet effective, formulas for explaining business logic. With plenty of expressiveness and control for complex requirements, most logic can be condensed into a single line. Before Power Fx, you had to write JavaScript code to write the logic; PowerFx makes the task a little easier.

Power Fx provides various low-code, user-friendly functions that can be used to create more complex business logic, particularly when conducting data operations such as create, read, and update in data sources. For example, a few of those functions are:

Lookup
> To look up or retrieve a single record from a data source

Filter
> To retrieve a collection of data from a data source

Search
> To search for data in the data source based on conditions

`Patch`

To upsert (update or insert) data in a data source

`Navigate`

To navigate from one screen to another

`Back`

To navigate back to the previous screen

`Collect`

To store data temporarily in a local database in a canvas app

In Figure 9-4, I have demonstrated how to use the `Patch` function on click (`OnSelect` property) of the Register button to insert data into the Contacts table in Dataverse. The `Patch` function is used to perform upsert (both update and insert) operations in a database; however, you are free to choose how to use it, when to trigger it, which database to connect to, and what data to provide it.

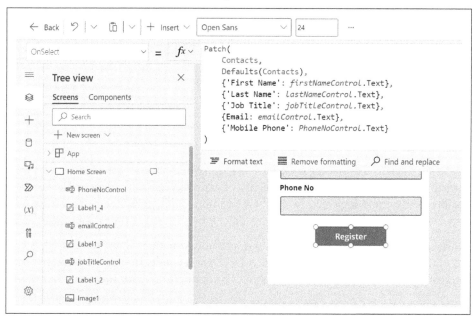

Figure 9-4. Power Fx low-code functions

 Power Fx *formulas* are the collection of functions, operators, and values that defines a particular action or behavior within the app, whereas Power Fx *functions* refer to predefined operations or actions that perform a specific task and are called within formulas.

You can find the complete Power Apps formula reference in the Microsoft documentation (*https://oreil.ly/XCjIU*).

Pro-Code

Sometimes, low-code developers create things that need to be taken over by professional developers to maintain and enhance. Professional developers want to use tools like Visual Studio, Visual Studio Code, or other code editors to be more productive and enable Power Fx to be put in source control like GitHub or Azure DevOps to work collaboratively with other developers.

Power Fx formulas can be stored in YAML (*https://oreil.ly/Setm1*) source files, so that they are easy to edit with Visual Studio or other code editors, and so that you can push/pull your code directly to GitHub or Azure DevOps. You can find more information about YAML files from the official YAML website (*https://oreil.ly/PgPTu*).

In Chapter 8, I demonstrated how to integrate GitHub with canvas apps to enable collaborative development and coauthoring. Here, I'll show the relationship between a canvas app and a YAML file. The canvas app can be exported as a package file (*.msapp*), which can then be extracted to access the underlying components. This extraction process often results in YAML files, a text format that represents the structure and configuration of the app components. For now, in Figure 9-5, I have edited Power Fx code in a YAML file from the canvas app in GitHub as an example.

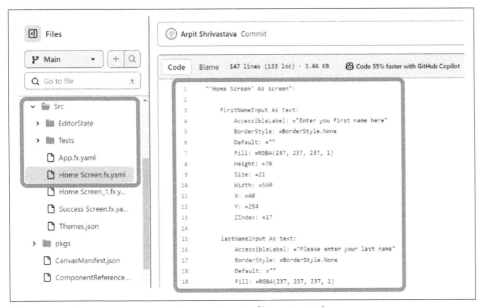

Figure 9-5. Editing Power Fx code in a YAML file in GitHub

In the following example, I have downloaded the canvas app LearningCanvasApp to my local machine as an *.msapp* package file. Then I used the Power Platform CLI unpack command to unpack (*https://oreil.ly/wx0pp*) the *.msapp* file into the *Extract* folder on my machine:

```
C:\Users\Arpit> pac canvas unpack --msapp LearningCanvasApp.msapp --sources
C:\Users\Arpit\Extract
```

Now I can edit the files in VS Code, as shown in Figure 9-6. If you expand the *Src* folder in VS Code, you'll see *.yaml* files that you can directly edit. When you're done editing, pack the canvas app (*https://oreil.ly/wPu7E*) back to the *.msapp* file. Now, the updated canvas app can be opened in Power Apps Studio by selecting File → Open → Browse and choosing your canvas app *.msapp* file from your local machine.

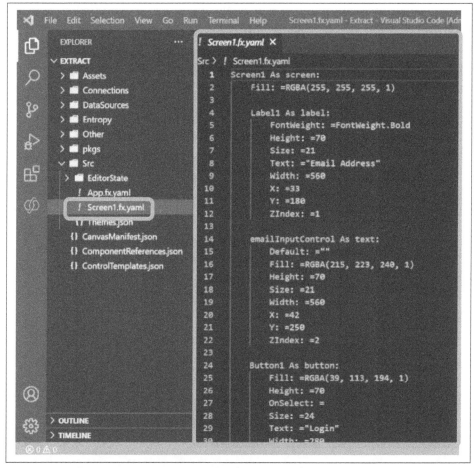

Figure 9-6. Editing canvas app Power Fx code in VS Code

As an open source language, Power Fx enables professional developers to develop their own C#-based applications and create their own functions by consuming two NuGet packages: Microsoft.PowerFx.Core (*https://oreil.ly/BFzXi*) and Microsoft.PowerFx.Interpreter (*https://oreil.ly/PSYJu*). Microsoft provides a sample C# application (*https://oreil.ly/8aMTb*) that can help you learn how NuGet packages are used and how to create custom Power Fx functions within C# code.

Power Fx Architecture

Although Power Fx empowers app makers to write business logic using Excel-based formulas, in the background many programming languages (including JavaScript, C#, TypeScript, Angular, React, SQL query, and Monaco Editor) are used to provide its end-to-end architecture. The following are the five components of Power Fx architecture, also shown in Figure 9-7.

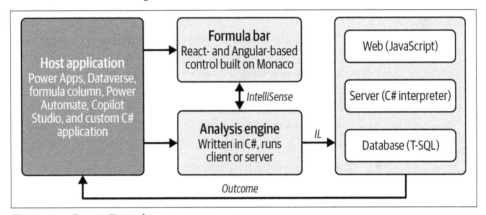

Figure 9-7. Power Fx architecture

Host application

This is the application where you use the Power Fx formula bar to write formulas or expressions. For example, Power Apps, Power Automate, and Microsoft Copilot Studio are host applications. Power Fx is open source, which means you can create your own host application based on C# and create your own formulas and expressions.

Formula bar

The formula bar is an integral part of the Power Fx experience, providing suggestions and immediate warning/error feedback while you are writing a formula, as shown in Figure 9-8. It is a client-side, Angular-based control built on open source Monaco (*https://oreil.ly/J0ClM*) to provide features like identifying typing mistakes, offering completion suggestions, and providing function tool tips to help you write formulas.

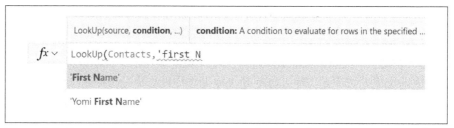

Figure 9-8. Formula bar displaying typing mistakes, completion suggestions, and function tool tips

Analysis engine

An analysis engine in the background provides IntelliSense support in the formula bar. When you enter or edit text in the formula bar, it calls the analysis engine to do the IntelliSense and return the results back to the formula bar.

Intermediate language (IL)

The analysis engine converts the language used on the frontend to *intermediate language* (also called *machine language*) so that the compiler backend can understand it. For example, when you write Power Fx expressions in Power Apps, it uses a JavaScript code generator in the background. When you write Power Fx expressions in the Dataverse Formula column, it uses SQL code generators in the background. And you can create your own Power Fx expression in C# as well.

Compiler

The compiler accepts the intermediate language from the analysis engine, processes it, and produces the desired outcome. It then sends it to the host application, which displays the result to the user.

Power Fx in Power Apps

You can write two types of Power Fx expressions in Power Apps:

Transactional (low-code)

Often used to perform operations on data sources; for example, patch, lookup, filter, search, and user.

Non-transactional (no-code)

Often used to manage the properties of Power Apps canvas app controls; for example, manage visibility of the controls, change color of the control, change screen sizes, set font size, or to perform field validation, calculation, etc., that doesn't require database interactions.

Let's discuss how Power Fx is used in canvas and model-driven apps.

Power Fx in Canvas Apps

To write Power Fx expressions in canvas apps, you need to choose your environment from the Power Apps home page, select Apps from the left navigation, choose your canvas app from the list, and then click Edit from the command bar. You'll see a formula bar in Power Apps Studio, as shown in Figure 9-9.

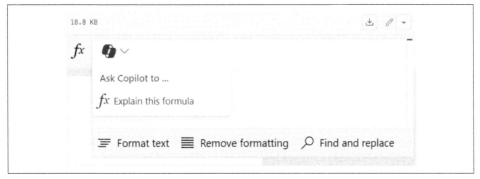

Figure 9-9. Canvas app formula bar with Copilot control

Nowadays you can use Microsoft Copilot in Power Apps canvas app to create and modify Power Fx formulas quickly. You can use Copilot in the formula bar to help explain Power Fx formulas in natural language, or create Power Fx formulas from natural language. As of now, this feature is in preview or experimental stages and comes with some known limitations. Learn more from the Microsoft documentation (*https://oreil.ly/urcoV*).

 You have two options for selecting various properties of the canvas app's controls, as shown in Figure 9-10. You can use the property picker located to the left of the Power Fx formula bar, or you can access and modify properties through the Properties pane positioned on the right side of the screen. However, updating properties via the Power Fx bar is more convenient because IntelliSense offers helpful feedback as you input and adjust formulas, so that's what I use here.

You can write two types of Power Fx expressions here:

Expressions to change properties of controls
As shown in Figure 9-10, I am changing the font-size property of the text label (Email Address) control by setting its value to 21 using a Power Fx expression. You can also change its other properties (text, alignment, weight, style, etc.) in the right navigation panel in a similar way.

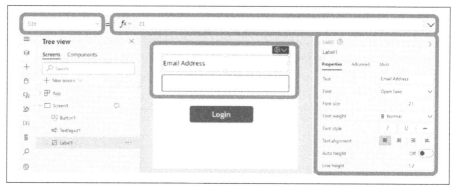

Figure 9-10. Power Fx expression to change a control's properties

Expressions that directly interact with data sources

We often call these Power Fx expressions *functions*. Each canvas app function that interacts with data sources is made up of three elements:

Input parameters (optional)

Some canvas app functions require input parameters to execute their business logic, whereas others don't require any parameters to execute the logic.

Function body (logic)

The business logic that a particular function is going to perform. This could be at the app level, screen level, or data source level.

Output parameters

Some canvas app functions return parameters after they execute. This could be a single value or a collection.

In Figure 9-11, I am using the `LookUp` function on the `OnSelect` property of the Login button control. This will retrieve a contact from the Dataverse Contacts table, based on the text entered by the user in the email input control (`emailInputControl`).

Figure 9-11. Power Fx expression to read data from a data source

---

The LookUp function accepts the following input parameters:

Table (required)
> This is the table to search.

Condition (required)
> The condition by which each record of the table is evaluated. The function returns the first record if the condition returns multiple results.

ReductionFormula (optional)
> This formula is evaluated over the record that was found and then reduces the record to a single value. You can reference columns within the table. If you don't use this parameter, the function returns the full record from the table.

Once you pass input parameters, the LookUp function executes a retrieve query or operation on the relevant data source to retrieve the pertinent data based on the condition and return one row from the data source. (Unlike the Filter and Search functions, which retrieve a collection of data.)

In short, if you need to write an expression in a canvas app to accomplish your goals—whether you're playing around with control properties, working with data sources, performing calculations, or calling Power Automate—use Power Fx.

Power Fx in Model-Driven Apps

Although model-driven apps cater to professional developers, they have some low-code, no-code features, such as business rules and business process flows. However, developers still need to use code to write complex business logic. With the introduction of Power Fx in model-driven apps, now even citizen developers can write complex business logic with ease.

Here are some of the components where you can write Power Fx expressions in model-driven apps.

Power Fx in the command bar

Microsoft has transformed the model-driven app's command bar from being developer-friendly to being citizen developer-friendly. Previously, you had to use the Ribbon Workbench tool (*https://oreil.ly/F1vsH*) created by Microsoft MVP Scott Durow, which was more suitable for people with technical backgrounds. Microsoft has now released a new command bar designer that enables you to manage commands using Power Fx.

To create or edit a command, you first need to edit your app in app designer (as described in Chapter 6). Then, select Pages from the left navigation panel, click on the three dots (…) next to the table whose commands you want to edit, and select Edit command bar → Edit in new tab, as shown in Figure 9-12.

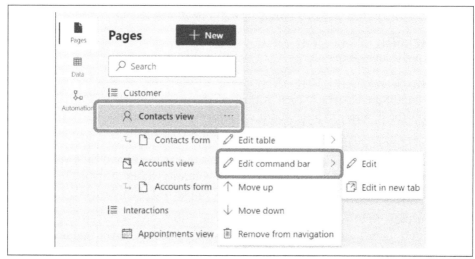

Figure 9-12. Open command bar of Dataverse table

You'll then see a dialog to choose the command bar you want to edit: Main grid, Main form, Subgrid view, or Associated view.

Once you open the table command bar, you can either add a new command to the command bar by selecting New from the top left corner, or you can edit an existing command by choosing any of those from the middle pane, as shown in Figure 9-13.

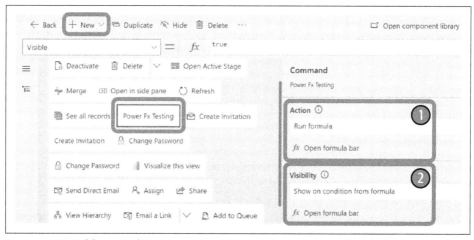

Figure 9-13. Adding or editing a command in the command bar designer

Power Fx is a recent addition to model-driven apps as of this writing; as a result, not all Power Fx functions that are supported in canvas apps are supported in model-driven apps. The following functions were not supported by command in model-driven apps as of early 2024:

- Back()
- Clear()
- Collect()
- Disable()
- Enable()
- Exit()
- InvokeControl()
- Language()
- LoadData()
- Param()
- ReadNFC()

- RequestHide()
- ResetForm()
- Revert()
- SaveData()
- ScanBarcode()
- Set()
- SubmitForm()
- UpdateContext()
- User()
- ViewForm()

You can find more information about the model-driven app commands and supported Power Fx formulas in the Microsoft documentation (*https://oreil.ly/-DHgy*).

In the command bar designer, you can write Power Fx expressions for the following two purposes:

Perform an action when the user clicks on the command
You can write a Power Fx expression for the OnSelect property of the command that executes when the command is selected within the model-driven app. As shown in Figure 9-14, I am updating the First Name of the contact by writing a Power Fx expression on the OnSelect property of the Power Fx Testing command, where the contact record is either the currently open record or the user has selected a record from the contact view.

Figure 9-14. Power Fx expression on OnSelect property to perform an operation on click of command

Set command visibility based on conditions

Here you can write a Power Fx expression on the `Visible` property of a command, which defines the logic for hiding or showing the command when running the app. As shown in Figure 9-15, I am displaying the Power Fx Testing command only if the selected contact record's annual income is more than 50,000, where `Self.Selected.Item` is either the currently open contact record or the record the user has selected from the contact view.

Figure 9-15. Power Fx expression on `Visible` property to set visibility of command

Power Fx in custom pages

Custom pages are the convergence of model-driven app and canvas app, as you learned in Chapter 7. They are used to create full pages, dialogs, or side panes with the flexibility of Power Apps Studio. Custom pages are not fully low-code, no-code components, because you need JavaScript code to launch them within a model-driven app; then you can write the business logic with Power Fx expressions in Power Apps Studio.

I covered custom pages in detail in Chapter 7, so here let's concentrate on how to write Power Fx expressions. As shown in Figure 9-16, I've created a Publish News command bar button on the Main grid of the Contacts table and called a JavaScript function `openCustomPage`, which was created within the `arp_learnwebresource` web resource of type Script.

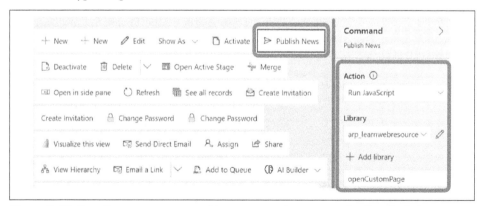

Figure 9-16. Creating a new command to open a custom page using JavaScript

Then you need to write the following script in the web resource (`arp_learnweb resource`), shown in Figure 9-17, to launch the custom page. You can find more about opening a custom page using Client API in a model-driven app in the Microsoft documentation (*https://oreil.ly/MTmRj*):

```
// This code will open the custom page as a dialog in the center of
// model-driven app
function openCustomPage()
{
var pageInput = {
    pageType: "custom",
    name: "arp_publishnewspage",
};
var navigationOptions = {
    target: 2,
    position: 1,
    height: {value: 50, unit:"%"},
    width: {value: 50, unit:"%"},
    title: "Publish News"
};
Xrm.Navigation.navigateTo(pageInput, navigationOptions)
    .then(
function () {
        // Write your logic that will be executed when the dialog closes
    }
    ).catch(
        function (error) {
            // Handle error
        }
    );
}
```

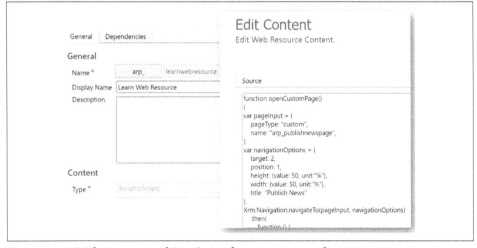

Figure 9-17. Web resource and JavaScript function to open the custom page

Finally, you need to write the following Power Fx expression for the Send button to create a new row in the News table in Dataverse (see Figure 9-18):

```
Patch(
    News,
    Defaults(News),
    {Subject: subjectTextbox.Value},
    {Message: messageTextbox.Value}
)
```

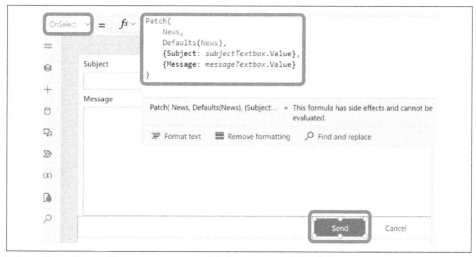

Figure 9-18. Power Fx expression to publish news on click of the Send button in Publish News page

Once all the aforementioned steps are done, add your custom page to your model-driven app, and then save and publish to see your changes, as shown in Figure 9-19.

Figure 9-19. Launching a custom page on click of Publish News command button

Power Fx in formula type columns

Formula is a new type of column in Dataverse that empowers citizen developers to directly write Power Fx expressions in a column to calculate a value. Since the calculations are done at the Dataverse level, results can be seen and used in all components connected to Dataverse, including model-driven apps, canvas apps, Power Automate, Power BI, and Dataverse Web API.

Although you can use calculated and rollup fields for calculating a column's values, they have only limited functions (ADDDAYS, ADDHOURS, ADDMONTHS, ADD-WEEKS, ADDYEARS, CONCAT, etc.). (You can find the complete list in the Microsoft documentation (*https://oreil.ly/VzN_8*).) Formula columns were introduced to extend the capabilities and overcome the limitations of calculated and rollup columns.

To create a formula column, perform the following steps:

1. Log in to the Power Apps home page (*https://oreil.ly/WlAha*), choose your environment, and click on Solutions in the left panel.

2. Expand Tables and choose your table (I have used the Account table). Select Columns, click "New column" in the command bar, and create a new column of data type Formula, as shown in Figure 9-20. My formula column is called "Mask Account No" and will mask the last four digits of the Account No column.

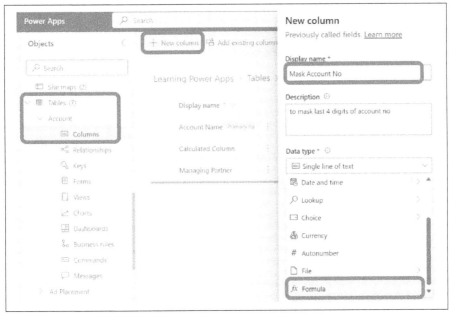

Figure 9-20. Creating a formula type column

3. To mask the last four digits of the Account No field, I've written a Power Fx expression in the Mask Account No column, as shown in Figure 9-21. This expression will read the first six digits of the account number from the Account Number column and concatenate it with "****" to mask the last four digits.

Figure 9-21. Power Fx expression to mask the last four digits of the account number

4. Finally, save the column and publish the table to reflect the changes, as shown in Figure 9-22.

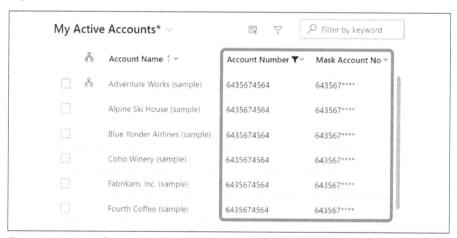

Figure 9-22. Run the model-driven app to see the masked values in the Mask Account No column

As of early 2024, formula columns support only READ operations and do all calculations on-the-fly directly on a SQL database using a SQL SELECT query. Therefore, results are always real time. In the future, Microsoft has plans to introduce other modes of operation where values can be calculated and stored in Dataverse.

Additionally, in the future, the formula column will have features of both calculated and rollup fields. As of this writing, Microsoft (*https://oreil.ly/Tk4mV*) doesn't plan for this functionality to replace existing calculated columns and rollups. More details can be found in the Microsoft documentation (*https://oreil.ly/PHgr3*) for formula columns.

Power Fx in low-code plug-ins

Low-code plug-ins are one of the major enhancements in model-driven apps. They empower citizen developers to write trigger-based, server-side logic using Power Fx expressions. You have already learned about Dataverse plug-in code in Chapter 7, where you had to write .NET code and use various NuGet packages and SDK assemblies to write server-side logic. Once created, you had to manually register the plug-in on a particular event (create, update, delete, etc.).

Those plug-ins were made only for professional developers to extend the platform's capabilities. However, with the introduction of low-code plug-ins, you can write server-side logic using Excel-based Power Fx formulas without the need for manual registration.

There are various other advantages to using low-code plug-ins:

Integrated with other components
Low-code plug-ins stored in Dataverse can be seamlessly integrated into Power Apps and Power Automate. Additionally, various Power Platform connectors can also be used in low-code plug-ins to easily integrate data with external data sources such as SQL Server, SharePoint, Salesforce, Microsoft 365, Outlook, Bing Maps, and OneDrive for Business. You can also use custom connectors from within a low-code plug-in in a Power Fx formula.

No coding knowledge required
With the help of low-code plug-ins, creators can quickly build complex workflows with minimal or no coding knowledge, leading to a more streamlined and effective data architecture.

Increased security
Low-code plug-ins run server-side logic directly on the server, which helps prevent unauthorized access to sensitive data or processes.

Improved performance
Logic is written in Power Fx with minimal code, which makes execution faster. In addition, because execution is on the server side, the amount of data transferred between client and server is reduced, resulting in faster processing times.

Easier maintenance and upgrades
There is no need to use NuGet packages, DLLs, or additional tools such as plug-in registration tools. Therefore, there is no need to upgrade DLLs, packages, tool versions, etc. Additionally, business logic is directly written on the server and

changes can be made in one place, rather than using Visual Studio on individual developer machines to maintain the code.

Reusable logic and manual triggers

Unlike pro-code plug-ins, low-code plug-ins can be triggered instantly or on-demand from the command bar, canvas apps, or using Dataverse Web API. This means you can write reusable business logic using low-code plug-ins and trigger it from various places.

To create a low-code plug-in, you must have either the System Administrator or System Customizer security role in the Power Platform environment where you want to create the plug-in. Follow these steps:

1. Install Dataverse Accelerator (*https://oreil.ly/xzZ5U*) (developed by the Microsoft Power Customer Advisory Team) in your environment. To install it, you need to navigate to the Power Platform admin center (*https://oreil.ly/xSoTj*), select Environments from the left panel, open your environment, click on Resources from the toolbar, and select Dynamics 365 Apps.

2. Click on "Install app" in the toolbar and search for "Dataverse Accelerator" (as shown in Figure 9-23). Click Next and then click the Install button. Wait for a few minutes until installation is done.

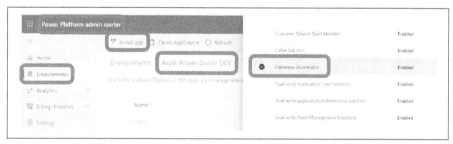

Figure 9-23. Installing Dataverse Accelerator in the Power Platform environment

3. Once installation is done, you will find the Dataverse Accelerator app in your app list, as shown in Figure 9-24.

Figure 9-24. Dataverse Accelerator app

4. Select the Dataverse Accelerator app and click Play from the toolbar to launch the app. You'll land on the home page of the app, where you'll have two options to create a low-code plug-in, Instant and Automated. Instant plug-ins are used to write reusable business logic and can be invoked manually or on-demand from Power Apps, flows, and the Dataverse API. Automated plug-ins will invoke automatically after a designated table event happens in Dataverse.

5. Let's create a low-code automated plug-in that displays an error when a duplicate contact with the same email address is created in the Contacts table. You need to provide the details in Table 9-1, as shown in Figure 9-25.

Table 9-1. Creating a duplicate email address error

Display name	A human-readable name for the plug-in, which can't be changed once it's created. I named mine "Duplicate Detection based on Email."
Table	The table on which you want to register this plug-in. In our example, it will be the Contacts table.
Run this plug-in when the row is	The event (Created, Updated, or Deleted) on which you want this plug-in to be invoked. In our example, I have chosen Created.

Expression	The Power Fx expression that contains your business logic. For example, the following expression determines whether any contacts with the same email that the user provided while creating the contact already exist. If it is not blank or duplicate contacts exist, then an error displays; otherwise, not:
	
	 `If(!IsBlank(LookUp([@Contacts],Email=ThisRecord.Email)),`
	 `Error("You have existing contacts with the same Email Address") )`
	
	 Where `IsBlank` is the function that checks whether the expression returns a blank value or not. `LookUp` is the function that retrieves the contact based on condition from Dataverse. `ThisRecord` is the current contact record or the contact record that you are creating in Dataverse, and `ThisRecord.Email` is the email address you entered in the contact form while creating the record. `Error` is the message that will be thrown when a contact is found with the same email address. This error is also called a business process error.

When should this run	This is where you want to register your plug-in in the event execution pipeline. Choose Pre-operation if you want to execute your logic just before the main operation is performed in Dataverse, or Post-operation if you want to execute your logic right after the main operation has been performed in Dataverse. (The event execution pipeline was covered in Chapter 7.) In our example, I am running the plug-in Pre-operation.
Solution	Choose the solution where you want to create your low-code plug-in. I have selected the Learning Power Apps solution.

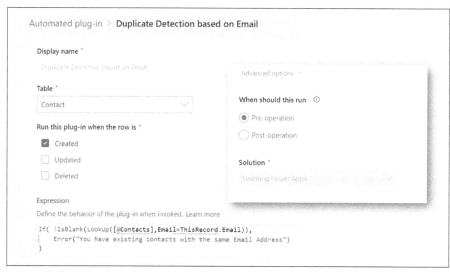

Figure 9-25. Creating an automated low-code plug-in to check duplicate contacts with the same email address

Now, let's test the low-code plug-in by creating a new contact with a duplicate email address. You should see the error shown in Figure 9-26.

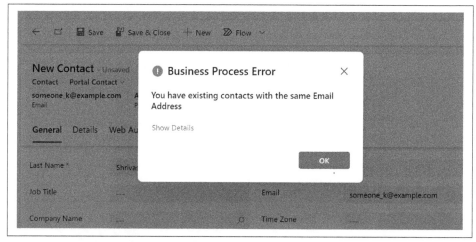

Figure 9-26. Business process error displays when a duplicate email is entered

Automated low-code plug-ins must always use a Dataverse table as a trigger, as opposed to instant low-code plug-ins, which can either be global or table-specific. If they are global, they are not dependent on any table. For instance, if you need a current weather update based upon your current location (*https://oreil.ly/_A0g5*), you can develop an instant plug-in of type global and link to the MSN Weather connector to obtain the desired outcome without depending on any Dataverse tables.

 As mentioned earlier, the low-code plug-in was in preview and had restricted functionality at the time the book was being written. You can find more information about its current limitations in the Microsoft documentation (*https://oreil.ly/Kwk02*).

Power Fx in Power Automate

You often need Power Automate with Power Apps to perform complex business logic, automate business processes, and handle complex integrations with external data sources.

When creating a Power Automate flow, it's simple to get started by adding a trigger, actions, and data passing between them using dynamic content. But the majority of the time, you need to carry out more complex operations. You might need to retrieve, convert, and compare values or perform a calculation or data transformation to get the desired results. You can use Power Fx expressions to do these tasks.

To write an expression in Power Automate, select a field to open the "Dynamic content" menu and select Expression (see Figure 9-27). You can type your expressions in the formula box by combining one or more functions. I have used the following Power Fx expression to add values provided in Variable1 and Variable2 steps:

```
add(variables('Variable1'),variables('Variable2'))
```

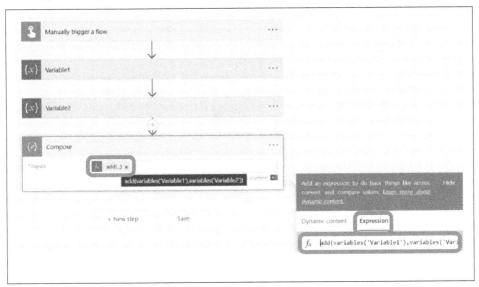

Figure 9-27. Writing a Power Fx expression in Power Automate

Power Automate provides Power Fx functions, which are primarily used for calculations and data transformation, but does not provide functions like User(), Patch(), and Collect(), that we were using in Power Apps to interact with data sources.

You can find a complete list of Power Fx functions used in Power Automate in the Microsoft documentation (*https://oreil.ly/D00Oz*).

Power Fx in Copilot Studio

You often need to integrate Copilot Studio with Power Apps to embed chatbot capabilities in business applications. Copilot Studio also supports Power Fx for various purposes:

- Write complex business logic that allows bots to manipulate data.
- Transform data being passed between nodes. For example, you might need to set user input in a variable and transform it using an expression. In Figure 9-28, I added the Question node "Please enter your full name," and in the subsequent node I used a Power Fx expression to concatenate the entered full name with the word "Hey!"

Figure 9-28. A Power Fx expression in Microsoft Copilot Studio

- Use variables. Power Fx formulas support the use of variables. To read the appropriate variable value, you must use the variable's scope. For instance, I have created a Global variable called fullName to save the full name entered by the user; hence, I am using Global.fullName in the Power Fx expression to get its value:

- For system variables, use System.

- For global variables, use Global.

- For topic variables, use Topic.

Considering that Power Apps is the main emphasis of this book, I won't go into excessive detail about how Power Fx is used in Microsoft Copilot Studio. If you'd like to understand more about it, see the Microsoft documentation (*https://oreil.ly/O8EZ9*).

Power Fx in Power BI

When I say Power Fx is a unified language for writing business logic across the Microsoft Power Platform, you might be wondering if there are any implications with existing M (*https://oreil.ly/KC8bu*) and DAX (*https://oreil.ly/ya9vh*) languages that are already supported by Power BI. The answer is no.

Power Fx is complementary and has no impact on these languages; thus, they can all coexist peacefully. While Power Fx concentrates on reading and writing smaller chunks of relational data, M and DAX concentrate on reading, structuring, merging, and summing up vast amounts of data.

Power Fx in Power Pages

In June 2024, Microsoft announced the addition of Power Fx support for Power Pages. This feature offers Power Pages creators and developers a low-code language for:

- Authoring dynamic content within Power Pages websites

- Easily creating dynamic webpages through the Power Pages design studio, enabling the design of custom user experiences aligned with business goals

- Using the new fx command for Text, Image, Button, and Iframe components to write Excel-like formulas and expressions

- Securely reading data from Dataverse tables by adhering to Table Permissions, and leveraging site user context to provide a data-enriched, personalized experience on the site

Summary

In this chapter, you learned about Power Fx, a strongly typed, declarative, imperative, and open source programming language for the Power Platform that can be used by app developers of all levels. Although it is called a unified programming language for the Power Platform, only canvas apps, Power Automate, and Microsoft Copilot Studio support it fully as of this writing. Some of the components (Dataverse formula column, low-code plug-ins, model-driven app command bar, and custom pages) have only a limited feature set.

You also learned how Power Fx formulas' architecture works and how an Angular-based client-side control, which is built on Monaco framework, offers IntelliSense support for formula creation. Microsoft has made the C# implementation of Power Fx (*https://oreil.ly/zQ2_b*) accessible and plans to eventually offer open source support for SQL and JavaScript in Power Fx.

You have now learned everything about creating and customizing model-driven and canvas apps. In the next chapter, you will learn how to use a solution to stitch these components into a single ZIP file and move it to different Power Platform environments to make your Power Apps available for testers and end users for feedback.

CHAPTER 10

Power Apps Deployment

Once you finish developing your Power Apps-based application, you need to transport that app and its related components to other environments, either for testing or live usage. Microsoft uses the Solution table in Dataverse to consolidate your components in one place. Once your solution is ready, you can deploy the changes to the target environments using a variety of deployment options.

In Chapter 6, you learned about creating a solution prior to embarking on the creation of components for designing a business application in Dataverse. This chapter delves further into additional features of the solution, exploring how it is used for deployment.

Power Apps Solutions

A *solution* is a container that holds all the components (as shown in Figure 10-1) that you use to customize your application, except for the data. The components held in the solution are collectively called *solution components*. You can have multiple solutions in your environment based upon your business needs. Some organizations prefer to have a common solution to keep all types of components, whereas some prefer to keep different solutions for different types of customization. For example, they might have one solution for plug-ins, one for app configurations (forms, views, columns, dashboards, etc.), one for security-related components, and so on. There is no rule of thumb as to how many solutions you can have in an environment. However, you should avoid creating a very large solution because there is a size limit of 32 MB.

Along with keeping track of your app customization components, solutions are also used to package all of your components in a ZIP file to move them from one environment to another.

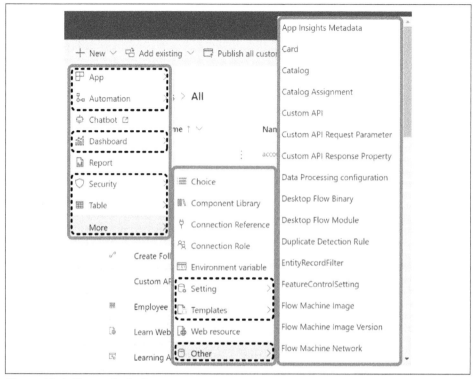

Figure 10-1. Types of solution components

Solutions hold not only the components related to Power Apps, but also all other components like Power Automate flows, Power Pages sites, connectors, and any other components that are used to customize your application.

Types of Solutions

There are different types of solutions. The two main ones you will use are *unmanaged* and *managed*. However, there are two more solutions that you find when you create a new Power Apps environment: the Common Data Service Default Solution and the Default Solution.

Common Data Service Default Solution

Once you create a trial or licensed Power Apps environment, a Common Data Service Default Solution is created by default to hold the components for that environment's customizations. You should use this solution only to test out or learn Power Apps features. For real projects, it is advised that you create your own unmanaged solution and create your components there.

Default Solution

The default solution contains all components in a particular environment that are created by default when the environment is created or that are created by the app makers or developers. It is often used to find the components in the environment.

Now let's discuss the main solutions that you need to use in real projects.

Unmanaged Solution

Unmanaged solutions are used in the development environment while you are making changes to your application. Components in this type of solution indicate that your app is still under development. Only unmanaged solutions can be packaged and exported in a ZIP file, either as an unmanaged or managed solution, to deploy to other environments. Deleting the unmanaged solution only deletes that specific solution record from Dataverse; the components of the solution remain in the environment.

An unmanaged solution could be compared to a building that is under construction and not yet ready for use, as shown in Figure 10-2.

Managed Solution

Once your development is done and you are ready to distribute your Power Apps to the end user, you can export your unmanaged solution as a managed solution and deploy it to the target environments. Managed solutions are considered to be fully developed and ready to use. Components within a managed solution cannot be modified except for changing a few properties (called managed properties, which I will discuss later in this section). Once you delete or uninstall the managed solution from a particular environment, it deletes completely from that environment along with all the components it holds. A managed solution is like installing an app on your phone from the Google Play Store or App Store: you can't change that app's features or controls except for a few settings that are specific to your device. Once you delete or uninstall that app, it gets removed completely from your phone.

 You should always use managed solutions in nondevelopment environments for better solution management and deploying a bug-free application.

A managed solution could be compared to a building whose construction is completed and ready for possession, as shown in Figure 10-2.

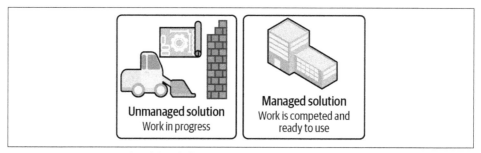

Figure 10-2. An example of the difference between unmanaged and managed solutions

Setting Your Preferred Solution

All solution components are by default saved in the Common Data Services Default Solution, unless they are already in the context of an unmanaged solution. This is usually not an effective model because there is no component separation across app makers, and the Common Data Services Default Solution can't be exported for import into other environments.

Setting a *preferred solution* allows you to specify which solution will support each maker's edits done anywhere in Power Apps, as well as enabling users to view and update which solution they're using. Once a preferred solution is specified, components created in that solution are automatically included in it, giving you control over the solution components. The preferred solution can be exported and imported into other environments.

To set your preferred solution, navigate to the Power Apps home page (*https://oreil.ly/ WlAha*) and select Solutions from the left navigation panel. If Solutions doesn't display in the left panel, select More and then select Solutions. Then select the unmanaged solution that you want to make your preferred solution. Select "Set preferred solution" on the command bar, as shown in Figure 10-3.

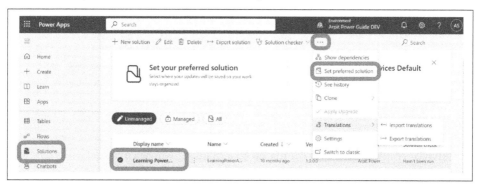

Figure 10-3. Setting your preferred solution

As of this writing, this feature is in preview and currently doesn't work with cards, dataflows, AI Builder, chatbots, connections, gateways, custom connectors, and canvas apps created from an image or a Figma (*https://www.figma.com*) design.

When a component is already part of an existing unmanaged solution, it will still be added to the preferred solution. And, components created in the classic solution explorer won't go into the preferred solution.

Managed Properties in Managed Solutions

Managed solutions are ready-to-use solutions that are created to share with end users. However, your organization may want to customize some of the managed solution components to fit its business needs; for example, change the display name of the component, or create new forms or views.

Managed properties are created to guard against changes being made to your solution's components that could harm it. Using this feature, you can control which of your managed solution components can be customized. The critical solution components that provide the core functionality of your solution cannot be modified.

Properties are managed separately for each component. To control the managed properties, open your solution and then select All from the left navigation panel to view all components in the solution. Select the table (or other solution component; I selected the Account table), click on the three dots in the command bar, select Advanced, and then select "Managed properties," as shown in Figure 10-4.

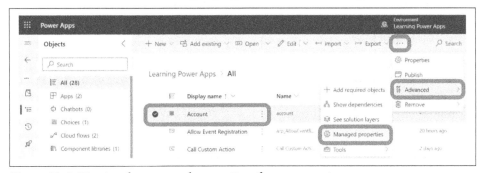

Figure 10-4. Viewing the managed properties of a component

The Managed Properties dialog lists the properties that can be managed for the selected component (summarized in Table 10-1 for tables and columns). First toggle on "Allow customizations," then select the other customization options that you want to allow. This toggle is the main setting that controls whether to permit modifications for a particular custom table in the target environment. If you switch the toggle off, the listed characteristics will be disabled and non-customizable in the target environment.

Table 10-1. Managed properties

Component	Managed property	Allowed to change?
Table	Display name	Yes
	Change additional properties	Yes
	Create new forms	Yes
	Create new views	Yes
	Create new charts	Yes
	Create new columns	No
	Change hierarchical relationship	Yes
	Enable/disable change tracking	Yes
	Can enable sync to external search index	Yes
Column	Change display name	Yes
	Change requirement level	Yes
	Change additional properties	Yes

Solution Export and Import

Exporting and importing solutions is a process whereby you migrate your Power Apps configurations and customizations from one environment to another. Exporting and importing solutions for deployment can be done either manually or automatically using Power Platform pipelines, Power Platform CLI, or Azure DevOps-based Power Platform Build Tools. I will discuss them in a later section.

Solution Export

When exporting a solution, you export your app customizations (in a ZIP file) from one environment so that they can be imported into another environment. You should also export your customizations periodically, either to a local machine or cloud repository (Azure DevOps, GitHub, etc.), so that you have a backup in case anything goes wrong.

If you plan to import the solution into another development environment or source control, you should export it as unmanaged. If you plan to import the solution into a UAT or production environment, you should always export it as managed. You can't export the default solution or a managed solution. (That is, if you export a solution as managed, and them import it into another environment, you can't export it from the target environment because it is now a managed solution.)

Exporting a solution exports only the app's customizations—not any of the data available in that environment. This means that data, like business units, teams, queues, or any master data (that will remain the same across environments) like country, state, city, or any project-specific data is not exported. You should refrain from re-creating this data manually in the target environment because this will generate a new identifier (GUID) for it, and if you have referenced the data in your code or any other components, it will break your code. Hence, you should either use the Excel export/import feature (*https://oreil.ly/bnwR-*) or the Configuration Migration tool (*https://oreil.ly/VX2ae*) to migrate data across the environments.

> You can run the solution checker (*https://oreil.ly/FqNNY*) to validate your solution components while exporting the solution.

Solution Import

You can import either managed or unmanaged solutions into an environment. The user importing a solution should have the System Administrator security role to avoid issues while creating and updating components. Optionally, you could have the System Customizer role, because it has create privileges on most components that are commonly imported; however, it doesn't have create privileges on the Plug-In Assembly table, which the System Administrator role does.

When you import a managed solution, all components are brought into the environment in published state, which means you don't need to publish your solution after deployment. However, if you import an unmanaged solution, the imported changes are in draft state, so you must publish them to make them active.

When you import managed solutions to your environment, you need to choose one of the following solution actions: upgrade, stage for upgrade, or update.

Upgrade
Upgrades your solution to the latest version. Any component not present in the newest solution will be deleted from the target environment. Figure 10-5 shows how the solution upgrade process works.

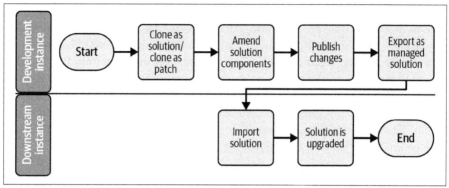

Figure 10-5. Solution upgrade process

Stage for upgrade

Upgrades your solution to the higher version, but defers the deletion of the previous version and any related patches until you apply an upgrade later. Figure 10-6 shows how the stage for upgrade process works.

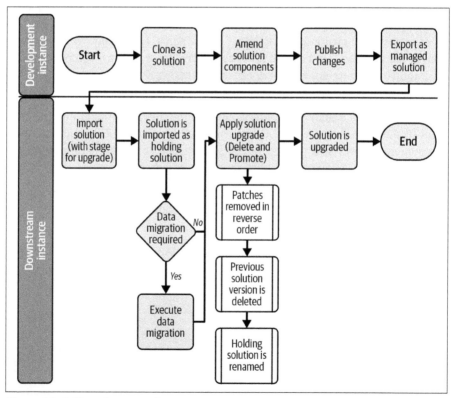

Figure 10-6. Stage for upgrade process

Update

Update solution replaces your older solution with a new version. Components that aren't in the newer solution won't be deleted and will remain in the system. Be aware that the source and destination environment may differ if components were deleted in the source environment.

Let's look at an example to help understand these three options. Imagine I have a solution in my development environment that has two tables: Table A and Table B. I export the solution (1.0.0.1) as managed and import it into the production environment. Now the production environment will also have this solution with Table A and Table B. Then I delete Table B from the development environment and again export the solution (1.0.0.2) as managed, choosing Upgrade to import the solution into production. It will delete Table B from the production environment as well.

Now I delete Table A and add a new Table C in the development environment and export the solution (1.0.0.3) as managed. This time, I chose Update while importing it into production. It will create Table C but will not delete Table A from the production environment.

This means that in both Upgrade and Update your original solution and its version get changed in the target environment. The only difference is whether components are deleted. Upgrade allows add, update, and deletion of the components, whereas Update only allows add and update.

So I just mentioned that Upgrade allows you to delete components from the target environment that were originally deleted from the source environment. However, in practice, deleting a component can be challenging since it may be dependent on other components and connected to customer data as well. As a result, you cannot simply delete any component from the production environment without taking care of existing data or components. For example, if you delete Table B and create a new Table C as replacement in the development environment and then deploy the solution to production using Upgrade, the data of Table B will be deleted from production.

So, how can you deal with such a situation and avoid data loss?

To deal with such deletion scenarios, you should use the "Stage for upgrade" option when importing your solution into the target environment. This will create a "holding" solution, named solutionName_upgrade, in the target environment, which contains your updated solution components, while keeping your original solution intact in the target environment.

You can now migrate data from Table B (available in the original solution) to Table C (available in the newly created upgraded solution). After you have completed your data migration process, you can choose your original solution and select Apply Upgrade from the toolbar (as shown in Figure 10-7) to override it with the holding solution. This will update the original solution version to 1.0.0.5 from 1.0.0.4 and delete the original solution from the target environment.

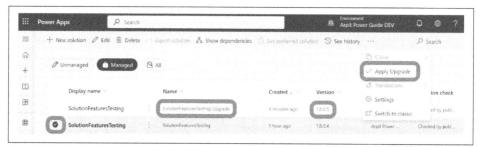

Figure 10-7. Applying the solution upgrade in the target environment

Solution Segmentation

Solution segmentation gives you tighter control over what customization you distribute through your solution. With solution segmentation, you export a solution in patches, with only selected components (relationships, charts, fields, forms, views, etc.) rather than entire tables with all assets. This is illustrated in Figure 10-8. First, I deployed the entire solution (version 1.0.0.0) to the production environment. After using the application for a while, the end users encounter some bugs. To fix them, instead of deploying the entire solution again, I will create a patch solution from the main solution, and then deploy that specific update or fix to production. As you can see in Figure 10-8, I have prepared three patch solutions to deploy three small updates to production. You can create more patches based on project-specific needs.

Now, if I need to add any major functionality to the app, then I will clone the solution, which will merge all patch solutions to the main solution with an updated solution version by incrementing the major or minor release number.

Let's discuss more about the solution segmentation features, clone a patch and clone solution.

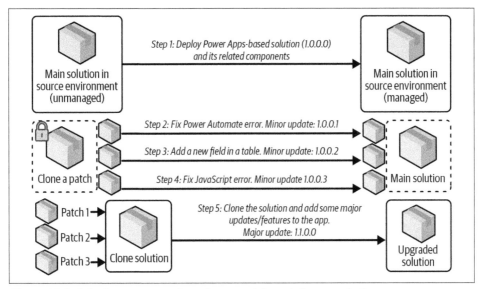

Figure 10-8. Solution segmentation: clone a patch and clone a solution

Cloning a Patch

A patch represents a minor, incremental update of your parent (base or main) solution. A patch can add or update components and assets in the parent solution when installed on the target environment, but it can't delete any components or assets from the parent. A patch can have only one parent solution, but a parent solution can have multiple patches. And, a patch can be created only for unmanaged solutions.

After you have created the first patch for a parent solution, the parent solution becomes locked, and you can't make any changes in this solution or export it. However, if you delete all of its child patches, the parent solution becomes unlocked.

You can only change the build and release numbers of the solution's version when creating a patch, as shown in Figure 10-9.

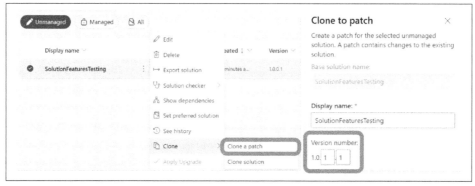

Figure 10-9. Cloning a patch

Cloning a Solution

In solution cloning, all child patches are rolled up into the base solution with a new version. You have the ability to add, edit, or delete components and assets within the cloned solution. Once installed in the target environment as a managed solution, the cloned solution serves as a substitute for the base solution. Typically, a cloned solution is used to deliver significant updates to the previous solution.

When cloning, you can change only the major and minor numbers of the solution version. The build and release numbers get reset to zero (see Figure 10-10).

Figure 10-10. Cloning a solution

Solution Versioning

Solution versioning is one of the key features that keeps track of the functionality included in a given solution release. A solution version in Dataverse has the format major.minor.build.revision (for example, 1.0.0.0). A base solution default format starts from 1.0.0.0. How to increment it in subsequent deployments depends on the type of update or solution release. If you are creating a patch solution to add or update a small change (such as a bug fix) in your application, then you are allowed to update only the build and revision numbers. If you are creating a clone of the base solution, where you are either adding a new feature or making a major update to the application, then you can update only the major and minor numbers.

Let's look at an example. Let's say I have a base solution in my development environment with the version 3.1.5.7. I need to make a small update to fix a bug in my application in production, so I create a patch of my base solution in the development environment with the version 3.1.5.8. And, if I have to make a slightly more significant update, then I again create a patch solution, but with version 3.1.6.0. This means every time I create a patch solution to add or update a small change in the application, I can either change the build or the revision number, but not the minor and major version from the UI.

Now, I have to deploy some major updates or add some new features to my application. In this case, I will clone my base solution by rolling up all patch solutions and creating a new version, 3.2.0.0. As discussed previously, I can increment only the major and minor version numbers, not the build and revision. Additionally, a cloned solution version must have a version number greater than or equal to the version of the base solution. So if the base solution version is 3.1.5.7, then the clone solution version can be either 3.2.0.0 or 3.1.5.7.

Solution Layering

Solution layering refers to the practice of organizing solution components into logical layers or tiers within a solution. Each layer typically represents a specific aspect or functionality of the solution. This approach allows for better organization, management, and control over the customization and configuration of the solution (see Figure 10-11). Every environment has default, out-of-the-box features when it's first set up. On top of that, you deploy the managed solution components, and then modify some settings and properties (unmanaged) based on your business requirements.

Hence, the app and its components included in the managed solution that you deploy to production are the culmination of the default solution, managed solution, and unmanaged solution. Any Dataverse solution includes the following layers:

- Any Power Apps solution starts with a default solution that doesn't have any customization or custom components. It defines the default behavior of the application.

- Then you start customizing the application by creating custom components or modifying the default solution components in the development environment. After testing you export it as a managed solution and deploy it to the production environment.

- Now the managed solution is installed on top of the default solution in the production environment. With time, you can keep on installing or importing multiple managed solutions in production as your app changes. That means managed solutions can be layered on top of other managed solutions.

- You can then customize the managed solution components and change their properties in a controlled manner defined in managed properties. These types of customizations done directly in the managed solution are called *unmanaged customization*.

Hence, the final application behavior in the production environment has the solution layering shown in Figure 10-11.

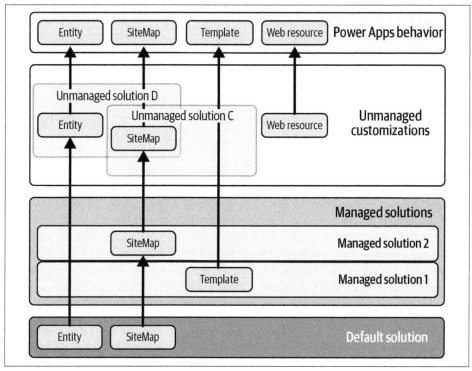

Figure 10-11. Solution layering

Solution Dependency

Every Dataverse solution, as we already discussed, is composed of a variety of components—tables, apps, web resources, etc. While some of the components are independent, some depend on other components that might or might not be present in the solution. Therefore, whenever an add, remove, or delete operation is performed on a solution component, its dependencies on other environment components are checked automatically. The dependency information is used to protect the system's integrity and stop actions that might result in an inconsistent state.

The following behaviors are enforced as a result of solution dependency tracking:

- You cannot delete any component from the solution if another component in the same Power Platform environment or the same solution is dependent on it.
- When a solution is exported, the user is warned if any necessary components are missing, which might prevent the solution from working properly when imported into the target environment.
- Import of the solution fails if all the required and dependent components are not included in the solution and don't exist in the target environment.
- You often need to install an external solution or add-on, such as DocuSign or Adobe Reader, to your development environment to enable features that are not already present in your app. These external programs are either available in AppSource (*https://oreil.ly/w6omI*) or are provided by ISVs (*https://oreil.ly/C7Atx*). These external solutions install components in your environment that have dependencies on your own solution components. Therefore, prior to deploying your own solution from the source environment, that external solution or add-on must be manually installed in the target environment.

You can check the dependencies of any solution component by choosing the particular component from the components list, clicking on the three dots next to the component name, and selecting Advanced → Show dependencies. This will display all the dependent components of that particular component.

Solution Deployment

Once development of your Power Apps-based app is completed, you are ready to move your app components to the target environments (testing, production, etc.). You can deploy your app manually or automatically.

Manual Deployment

You can manually export the solution (as unmanaged or managed) and import it to the target environments. To export the solution, you need to open the development environment, choose the solution from the solution list, and click "Export solution" from the toolbar. This will export it as a ZIP file on your local machine.

To import it to the target environment, open the environment, navigate to the solutions, select your solution, and click "Import solution" from the toolbar (see Figure 10-12).

The manual deployment approach is for both technical and citizen developers.

Figure 10-12. Manually deploying a solution

Automatic Deployment

You can automatically deploy the solution from one environment to another using Power Platform Build Tools, the Power Platform CLI, or Power Platform pipelines.

Power Platform Build Tools

First, you can use Azure DevOps Pipelines to move your solution from one environment to another. Microsoft provides Power Platform Build Tools (*https://oreil.ly/ Dx7au*) in Azure DevOps to automate build and deployment tasks in Power Apps environments. These tasks include logging in to the Power Apps source environment, running solution checker, exporting the solution, logging in to the Power Apps target environment, making a backup before deployment, importing the solution, and publishing customizations, as shown in Figure 10-13. This tool also enables you to unpack the solution ZIP file, break it into component-wise folders, and store the components in the respective repository using unpack/pack build tasks. You can find the complete list of build and deployment tasks in the Microsoft documentation (*https://oreil.ly/9LmIk*).

Setting up a CICD pipeline using Power Platform Build Tools is ideal for both DevOps engineers and citizen developers. Once it is set up, anyone in the team can use it for deployment.

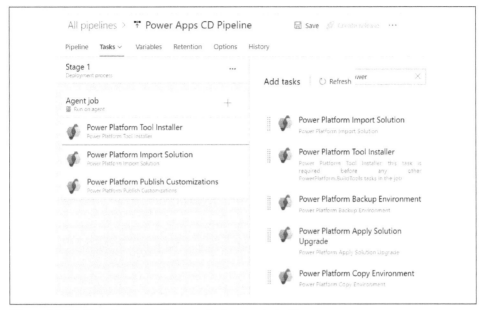

Figure 10-13. Creating a continuous deployment pipeline

Power Platform CLI

Another option is to use Power Platform CLI. Sometimes, it's not enough to manage all your deployment activities through Power Platform Build Tools because you need to write your own logic to perform operations on the components. Microsoft provides Power Platform CLI (*https://oreil.ly/7JdtF*), which empowers professional developers and ISVs to interact with the Power Apps environment resources and components and deploy them by running the commands either in PowerShell or Visual Studio/Visual Studio Code Terminal. You can find all the commands and their usage in the Microsoft documentation (*https://oreil.ly/T1HCn*).

You can find all solution-related CLI commands in the Microsoft documentation (*https://oreil.ly/5RKcv*).

Power Platform pipelines

The last option for automatic deployment is to use Power Platform deployment pipelines. The previously discussed deployment options are quite effective, but they are not user-friendly for citizen developers and frequently depend on a DevOps team to spearhead implementation and manage the process. Pipelines aim to close this gap in a way that is considerably easier, quicker, and more reasonably priced to set up and operate.

The following are requirements to work with pipelines in Power Platform:

- All environments used in pipelines must have a Microsoft Dataverse database.
- All target environments used in a pipeline must be enabled as managed environments.
- To install the pipelines application, you must have the Power Platform Administrator or Dataverse System Administrator role.
- To create or set up the deployment pipeline, you must have the Deployment Pipeline Administrator security role and share the pipeline with anyone who has only read access to allow them to run the pipeline.
- To deploy the solution you must have the Deployment Pipeline User security role in the target environment.

Once all prerequisites are met, you should perform the following actions to deploy the solution using the pipeline:

1. Install the Power Platform pipelines solution in your source environment: navigate to the Power Platform admin center, click on Environments in the left navigation panel, open your environment, and then click on "Install app" from the toolbar. Select Power Platform Pipelines, click the Next button, and click Install, as shown in Figure 10-14.

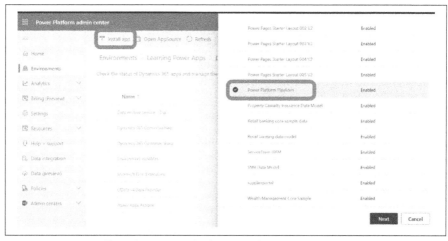

Figure 10-14. Installing the Power Platform pipelines solution

2. As soon as the solution installation is complete, you will notice a new model-driven app listed under the Apps section with the name Deployment Pipeline Configuration, as shown in Figure 10-15.

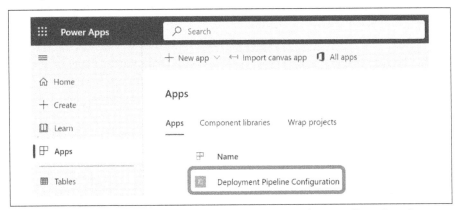

Figure 10-15. Deployment Pipeline Configuration app after installing the solution

3. Launch the Deployment Pipeline Configuration app and navigate to the Environments section in the left pane. Click on the New button and input the required details such as name, environment type, and environment ID to generate environment records in Dataverse. Afterward, refresh the form and ensure that the Validation Status column indicates Success. Repeat these steps for each environment involved in the pipeline until environment records are created for all (see Figure 10-16).

Figure 10-16. Opening the Pipeline app and the created source and target environments

4. Navigate to the Pipelines section on the left navigation panel and click on +New to initiate the creation of a new deployment pipeline. Input the pipeline name and description as required. In the Linked Development Environments grid, select Add Existing Development Environment and associate one or more development environments. A pipeline requires at least one development environment and one stage before it can be executed (see Figure 10-17).

5. In the Deployment Stages grid, click on New Deployment Stage to include the staging or target environments. Repeat this step for each stage you wish to incorporate into the pipeline. At least one stage is mandatory, and you can add up to seven stages (see Figure 10-17).

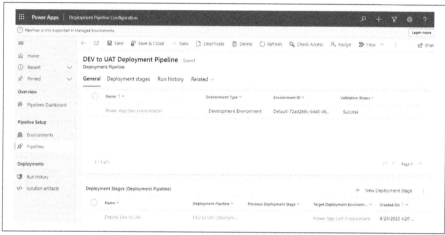

Figure 10-17. Creating a pipeline and linking the environments

6. Open your solution and click on the rocket icon in the left panel, as shown in Figure 10-18, to navigate to the pipeline deployment page.

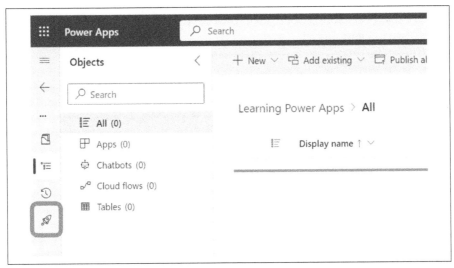

Figure 10-18. Opening the solution in the source environment

7. Click "Deploy here" to navigate to the pipeline final review step, as shown in Figure 10-19.

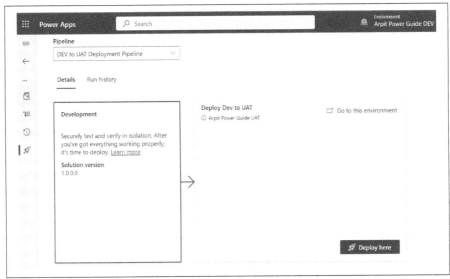

Figure 10-19. Running the pipeline

8. Provide a solution version and click Deploy after reviewing the changes, as shown in Figure 10-20.

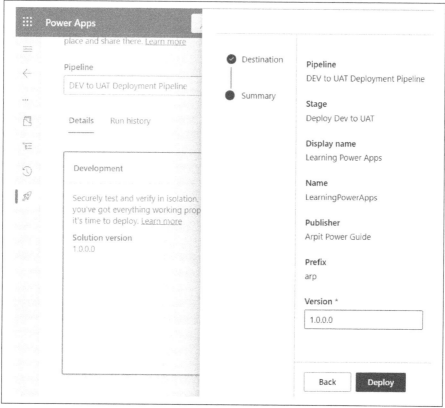

Figure 10-20. Providing a solution version, reviewing the details, and deploying the solution

Refer to "Set up pipelines in Power Apps" (*https://oreil.ly/B-DIq*) to learn more about the deployment pipeline feature and its use.

Post Deployment

After you deploy your solution to the target environment, the role of the end users comes into play where they start using the app features in real time. While using the application, users may face some issues or bugs in the application and have some questions or feedback regarding the application. So after deployment, the application will be subject to ongoing maintenance and improvement to manage and monitor the performance of the released application. While planning and prioritizing new updates, the support and development team also fixes any remaining bugs at this stage.

Summary

In this chapter, you have learned about Power Apps solutions and various deployment options to deploy your Power Apps applications and their components. Proper planning, following best practices, and choosing the right deployment option can help you ensure that the solutions you're building will go more smoothly. After reading this chapter you should also read more detailed information about solutions from the official Microsoft documentation:

- Solution Lifecycle Management (*https://oreil.ly/CjImP*)
- Strategies to organize solutions (*https://oreil.ly/pKlAV*)
- Plan your deployment (*https://oreil.ly/4fvcW*)
- Plan for solution development (*https://oreil.ly/c7TdN*)

In the next chapter, I'll talk about one of the most demanding and popular topics, Microsoft Copilot in Power Apps, where we'll learn about modernizing app development and increasing the productivity of everyone in the organization.

CHAPTER 11

Microsoft Copilot in Power Apps

Artificial intelligence (AI) is a technology used to develop software and business applications that mimic human intelligence. AI is made up of many algorithms that learn from patterns, analyze and process data, and then produce outcomes based upon it. This process is called machine learning, which is a subfield of AI.

Even if you're not aware of it, you probably deal with AI daily. AI is already widely used in many facets of our lives, from smartphones to chatbots. Have you ever noticed, when you reply to someone on chat either on LinkedIn or Microsoft Teams or another social media platform, the system automatically suggests possible responses, such as "Thank you!" or "Sounds interesting," based on the chat conversation you are having with the recipients? This means AI is working behind the scenes.

In early 2023, Microsoft announced its partnership with OpenAI (*https://oreil.ly/ EdPrk*), with an investment of several years and billions of dollars, in order to accelerate the development of AI and ensure that its advantages are widely available to all.

Evolution of Artificial Intelligence in Power Platform

Microsoft Power Platform has been on a journey to empower all developers with an AI-powered development experience since 2019, as shown in Figure 11-1.

In 2019, Microsoft boosted its investment in AI. The first effort to integrate AI capabilities into Power Platform was AI Builder, which businesses could use to add intelligent features, such as a business card reader, sentiment analysis, and form processors. In 2021, Microsoft added natural language support to Power Fx in Power Apps canvas apps and DAX in Power BI. These two formula-based languages, which are similar to Microsoft Excel, now supported natural language to write business logic. Even users without any prior programming experience could build calculating code and complex business logic by describing what they wanted to do in their own language.

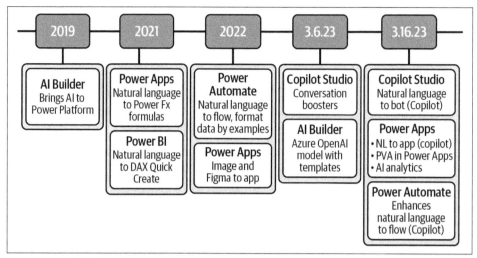

Figure 11-1. Microsoft Power Platform AI evolution

By 2022, AI had advanced to the point where it was possible to develop Power Automate flows in natural language as well by only stating the trigger and the subsequent actions you needed to do. Moreover, Power Apps began integrating with Figma, allowing you to turn your hand-drawn designs or diagrams into usable apps. In March 2023, Microsoft announced (*https://oreil.ly/F85fc*) Copilot, a next-generation AI-based product in Power Platform, which was a further step toward the no-code capabilities in the Power Platform and transforming low-code development. Soon you will begin to see Copilot-based AI capabilities across Power Platform components in Power Apps, Power Automate, Copilot Studio, Power BI, and Power Pages. I will discuss Copilot in the next section.

 As of early 2024, Copilot is available for preview in the US, Sweden, Australia, and the UK. You can keep track of its general availability (GA) in the Dynamics 365 and Microsoft Power Platform release planner (*https://oreil.ly/4koDw*).

Introduction to Microsoft Copilot

Microsoft Copilot is a ChatGPT-like, AI-powered digital assistant that is built on top of GPT (Generative Pre-trained Transformer) AI models and aims to provide personalized assistance to users for a range of tasks and activities. Using Copilot, app makers can leverage natural language to describe the app's requirements to suit their needs. Now, everyone can build an app, and professional developers can also save more time, focusing on more complex code, components, and integrations.

Copilot not only connects with Microsoft Bing to provide responses from the public data available on the internet, but also uses Azure OpenAI Service (REST services based on Azure OpenAI) and Microsoft Graph to provide responses in the context of your business and customer that are specific to your organization. For instance, I can ask Copilot to assist me in composing an email to a customer to gather more details regarding the issue they are facing. And Copilot will first gather the information relevant to that particular customer from Dataverse and other Microsoft 365 applications like email from Outlook, documents from SharePoint and OneDrive, and chat conversations from Microsoft Teams. It will then create the relevant contextual answer to provide the response in the Copilot prompt, as displayed in Figure 11-2.

Figure 11-2. How Copilot generates a contextual response

Power Platform has introduced Copilot in Power Apps, Power Automate, Power BI, and Power Pages to further democratize development and empower more individuals to use natural language to create innovative solutions. Now, all you have to do is visualize your solution, explain it in your natural language, and Copilot will build it for you using a low-code experience that is both intelligent and intuitive. For both citizen and professional developers, Copilot will expedite app development.

One way to understand Copilot is to compare it with ChatGPT. ChatGPT and Microsoft Copilot are both AI-based digital assistants (chatbot-based applications) that were developed with the intent of helping you accomplish tasks and activities faster and more efficiently. While they seem similar, there are significant differences between the two.

ChatGPT (*https://oreil.ly/t4EMx*) is a natural language processing-based chatbot application developed by OpenAI (*https://openai.com*), an American AI and research company. The GPT in ChatGPT stands for "Generative Pre-trained Transformer," which is an AI model that has been trained on vast amounts of data available on the internet, including books, articles, websites, and social media. ChatGPT is also available as an API, which can be integrated with various other applications like Microsoft Power Platform, Dynamics 365, and Microsoft Azure.

ChatGPT provides a prompt where you can ask questions in natural language. Then it uses various machine learning algorithms and natural language processing AI models to mimic human conversation, understand the question and its context, and generate the appropriate responses in an engaging and conversational way. The more details you provide in your prompt, the more precise answers ChatGPT can offer.

Soon after the launch of ChatGPT, Microsoft extended its partnership with OpenAI (*https://oreil.ly/XNK4n*) and called this collaboration Azure OpenAI, which encompasses a range of products, services, and APIs provided by both Microsoft Azure and OpenAI to bring OpenAI capabilities to Microsoft's own SaaS-based products and applications hosted on Azure. These include Microsoft 365 applications (Word, Excel, Outlook, Teams, PowerPoint, OneDrive, SharePoint, etc.), Dynamics 365 applications, and Power Platform components along with other Microsoft products like Microsoft Windows and its applications (Paint, Snipping Tool, Photos, Clipchamp, Notepad, etc.), LinkedIn, Bing Search, Bing Chat, and Microsoft Edge.

Does that mean OpenAI and Microsoft's Azure OpenAI are the same? Partially. Both are derived from the same OpenAI technology and built on the same foundational structure. However, it's important to understand that Azure OpenAI is specific to Microsoft products and applications hosted on Microsoft Azure and offers enterprise-level security for your organizational and customer data in a secure, compliant, and privacy-preserving way. Azure OpenAI secures the data in accordance with Microsoft's data privacy policy (*https://oreil.ly/aBThc*).

Unlike OpenAI, where AI models have been trained on vast amounts of data that is publicly available on the internet, Azure OpenAI-based AI models are not only trained on public data available on the internet, but also on data specific to a particular organization and its customers. This means your organization's data always remains within Microsoft Azure and is accessible only by authorized users within your organization, unless you explicitly consent to other access or use. Also, Azure OpenAI doesn't use data from other customers or organizations to train the AI model; it always provides responses and generates answers in the context of your business: your documents, emails, calendar, chats, meetings, and other business data.

 Consider Microsoft Copilot to be like a copilot of an airplane. A copilot is responsible for helping the captain (the primary pilot) of a plane with navigation, flight operations, and general operating assistance. Microsoft Copilot puts you in the pilot's seat and helps you create and manage apps. Copilot will only offer you AI-powered assistance in accordance with what it has learned from public data and the data within your organization. It's an app maker or end user's responsibility to make the final decision and determine whether the response is relevant or needs further refinement.

Architecture of Copilot

Now that you know the fundamentals of Copilot, you need to understand how its architecture works in the context of Power Apps, Power Platform, and Dynamics 365 CE.

Microsoft Copilot architecture has three major components (shown in the boxes in Figure 11-3):

Business applications
> This is an app UI where you see the Copilot prompt. This can be any Microsoft product or application, such as Power Platform, Dynamics 365, or Power Apps-based business applications. This is also applicable for other Microsoft products and applications such as Word, Excel, PowerPoint, Edge, Paint, and Teams.

Data
> This is the data source where your organization and customer data is stored. Data can be stored in Dataverse, Azure, or other Microsoft 365 applications like Outlook, Teams, OneDrive, and SharePoint.

> Data gets pulled from these various data sources to your own application with Microsoft Graph. Microsoft Graph serves as a gateway to data and insights within Microsoft 365, offering a unified programmability framework for accessing vast

amounts of data across Microsoft 365, Windows, and Enterprise Mobility + Security.

It provides a REST API called Microsoft Graph API (*https://oreil.ly/QWtDa*) that provides a single endpoint to perform operations on data stored in various Microsoft data sources. Microsoft Graph plays a crucial role in Copilot architecture to fetch the contextual data from various Microsoft sources that you consent to and grant permissions.

Large language model (LLM)
LLMs are natural language processing-based AI models (GPT-1, GPT-2, GPT-3, etc.) that have been pretrained on vast amounts of data and generate answers in human natural languages. They internally use machine learning, deep learning, and transformer algorithms to learn, analyze, and process data, and then generate the outcome in natural language. Data retrieved from various Microsoft cloud services can be in different formats (images, documents, texts, etc.). LLM plays a crucial role in converting that data to human-understandable format.

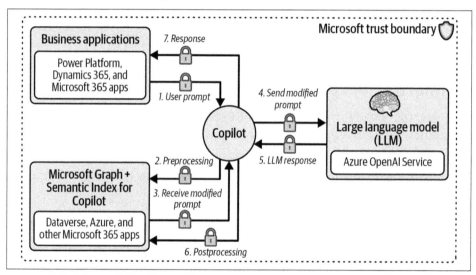

Figure 11-3. Microsoft Copilot architecture

Let's discuss how these three components work together to provide answers to users:

User prompt (1)
When you launch any Power Apps application (Dynamics 365 Sales, Customer Service, etc.) you see the Copilot-based AI digital assistant in your application. Here, you enter your input or questions that will be sent to Copilot. (This is also the case when you use other Microsoft products or applications where the Copilot feature is available like Word, Excel, and PowerPoint.)

Preprocessing (2)

Copilot preprocesses the input sent from Power Apps through an approach called *grounding*. Grounding is a process where Copilot retrieves the user's input and, based on that input, collects data from various Microsoft sources like Dataverse, Azure, and Microsoft 365 applications. You must be wondering how Copilot brings the data from various Microsoft sources related to your specific tasks. Here, two important components, Microsoft Graph and semantic index for Copilot, play crucial roles:

- Microsoft Graph contains data regarding the connections between users, activities, and your organization's data. It uses the Microsoft Graph API to bring more contextual data from customer emails, chats, documents, and meetings, as shown in Figure 11-4.

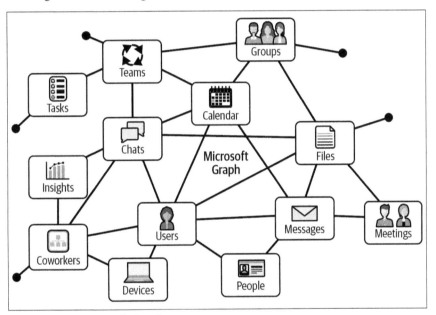

Figure 11-4. Microsoft Graph

- Semantic index for Copilot sits on top of Microsoft Graph to interpret and understand the meaning of user input or queries and display more precise results. Unlike keyword-based search, which searches information based on a particular keyword, semantic index-based searching goes beyond keywords and focuses on the meaning of a query, its synonyms, other related concepts, and even ambiguous terms behind each query to produce personalized, relevant, and multilingual responses.

For example, if a user asks Copilot "How rich is the Microsoft CEO?" it will understand the meaning of your query and automatically break it down into two parts: "how rich" and "Microsoft CEO." Then it will search for "net worth," "Microsoft CEO," "current CEO of Microsoft," "who is the founder of Microsoft," and "Microsoft CEO net worth," and will provide you more precise and accurate results, as shown in Figure 11-5. This is how the Google and Bing search engines also search for information.

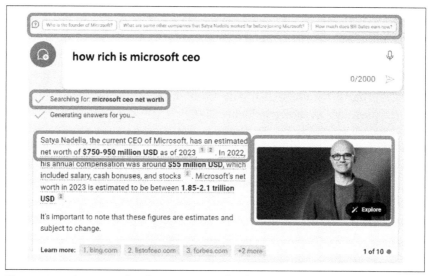

Figure 11-5. An example of a semantic index-based search

Microsoft Copilot also uses Bing Search to find public data on the internet. It enables developers to expand the Copilot capabilities by creating plug-ins (distinct from Dataverse plug-in code) that connect with APIs from various software and services. This allows Copilot to access real-time information, utilize company data, and perform advanced calculations. Presently, there are over 50 plug-ins available from partners such as Atlassian, Adobe, Service-Now, Thomson Reuters, Moveworks, and Mural, with thousands more expected from businesses and other entities in the coming months.

Receive modified prompt (3)

Once Copilot collects the data from various Microsoft sources, it processes the data to make it more specific and relevant to your task, so that you can get more precise answers. This is called *retrieval-augmented generation*. This information is always retrieved from the specific Microsoft 365, Dynamics 365, or Power Platform tenant belonging to the customer, not from tenants or organizations of other customers.

Send modified prompt (4)

The information retrieved by Copilot during retrieval-augmented generation can be structured (text, or any readable format) or unstructured (files, images, documents, etc.). Copilot modifies the prompt (the user's input) by combining the information sent by the user and the information collected from various Microsoft sources, and then sends it to the LLM to get a response in natural language.

LLM response (5)

LLM takes the input data from Copilot, analyzes it using pretrained algorithms, processes it, produces the outcome in natural language, and sends it back to Copilot.

Postprocessing (6)

Copilot takes the response from the LLM and fine-tunes it further with postprocessing, including additional grounding calls to Microsoft Graph, responsible AI checks, and security, compliance, and privacy reviews. So, in this step, Copilot ensures that data that needs to be sent to the user is secure and compliant.

Response (7)

Finally, Copilot returns a relevant and contextual response to the user along with any commands that the user can use to complete the task.

Copilot iteratively follows this process to produce results that are relevant to your business, accurate, and secure. Whatever data communication happens between Copilot, business applications, Microsoft sources, and LLM is encrypted via HTTPS and takes place within the Microsoft trust boundary.

Let's look at an example. Say you are a customer service agent working in the Dynamics 365 Customer Service app. One of your existing customers raises an issue regarding a product that is not functioning. You might need:

- Information about the specific product that the customer is complaining about
- The customer's existing conversation or issues history to better investigate the issue and resolution
- The customer's product warranty information
- Assistance in writing an email to provide more information about the issue or have a call to discuss it further

Here, you can use Copilot to assist you instead of handling everything manually. You launch Copilot within your application, and Copilot automatically collects the data from knowledge articles stored in Dataverse and several other Microsoft sources that pertain to the particular customer and issue. This information might include whether the customer has previously emailed or spoken with another agent about the problem, opened a support ticket, and whether any other customers have previously reported the same problem. Then, Copilot will use LLM to transform the response into natural language, and turn on security so that you, as the service agent, only have access to the data that you are allowed to view.

It's important to understand that Copilot always generates answers based on pre-trained AI models. That's why it's not guaranteed that the outcome will always be 100% factual. Copilot isn't a search engine; it might not look up the latest information available on the internet, and it might not have the most recent data available. Therefore, it always leaves you in the driver's seat. You should check and modify the data that Copilot gives you because it may contain errors or inaccurate answers in its responses.

I will discuss how a user interacts with Copilot in Power Apps in the next section.

Prerequisites for the AI Features in Power Apps

So, you now have a thorough understanding of Microsoft Copilot and its architecture. Let's discuss how Microsoft brings the power of Copilot in Power Apps to empower both application makers and end users to build and interact with business applications. Using Copilot, you can create an app just by describing what you need through multiple steps of conversation.

But before getting started with Microsoft Copilot in Power Apps, there are few prerequisites that you need to consider:

- As of this writing, Copilot is available in the US, Sweden, Australia, and the UK. It will gradually be rolled out to other regions as well. You can keep track of its general availability in your region from Dynamics 365 and the Microsoft Power Platform release planner (*https://oreil.ly/Xb3Oj*).

- You must have a Microsoft Dataverse database in your environment.

- If you want to use AI models or controls leveraging AI models in your environments, you'll need to enable AI Builder features as well (see Figure 11-6):

  — Navigate to the Power Platform admin center (*https://oreil.ly/HuBNp*).

  — Click on Environments in the left panel, select your environment, and go to Settings → Product → Features.

  — On the feature settings page, under AI Builder, enable AI Builder preview models.

  — You can also enable/disable Copilot features for your environments by turning on/off the Copilot setting.

Figure 11-6. Enabling/disabling Copilot and AI Builder features in your environment

- To enable/disable Copilot features in Power Apps for your tenant, click on Settings from the left panel and go to Tenant settings. Then select "Copilot (preview)," set the toggle to Off, and click Save, as shown in Figure 11-7.

Note that turning off Copilot for your tenant will only disable Copilot for app makers. It won't disable Copilot control for canvas apps (*https://oreil.ly/SFTZa*) or Copilot for model-driven apps (*https://oreil.ly/w-l7R*). I will discuss them in later sections.

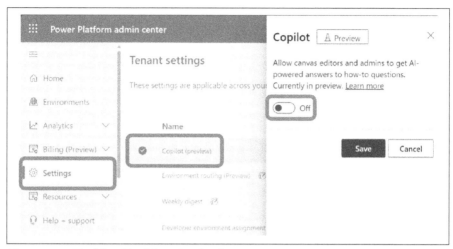

Figure 11-7. Enabling/disabling Copilot for your tenant

Copilot in Model-Driven Apps

Copilot for model-driven apps in Power Apps is a feature that allows app users to gain insight about the data in their apps through natural language conversation. Copilot helps app users increase their productivity by providing AI-powered insights and intuitive app navigation.

Microsoft Copilot features in model-driven apps depend on what type of model-driven app you are using:

Custom model-driven app
Copilot shows answers to app users from the configured table in the Dataverse connected to your model-driven app. For example, as shown in Figure 11-8, you can ask Copilot about any data available in your Contacts table, such as "What is Arpit Shrivastava's job role and email address?"

It also helps app users to navigate to a specific page in the app. For example, as shown in Figure 11-9, I can ask Copilot, "Take me to the appointment booking page" or "how to book a new appointment."

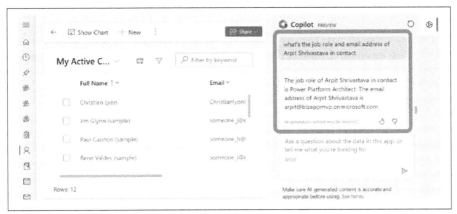

Figure 11-8. Asking Copilot to get contact details in a model-driven app

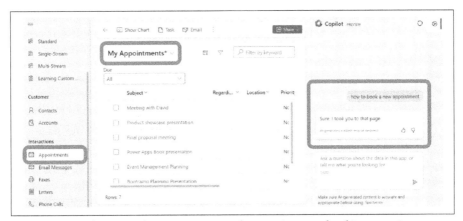

Figure 11-9. Asking Copilot to navigate to the appointment booking page in a model-driven app

Dynamics 365 CE apps

Microsoft has provided Copilot features in these apps based on app-specific features. For example, in a Sales app, Copilot helps to:

- Elevate your customer engagements with AI-recommended content.

- Show emails you haven't replied to.

- View and copy email summaries.

- Get an AI-generated account summary.

- Leverage manager dashboards to coach sellers.

- Stay up to date with the latest news about your customers.

You can find more information in "Copilot in Dynamics 365 Sales overview" (*https://oreil.ly/WL9fl*). Similarly, in the Customer Service app, Copilot helps to:

- Write email messages based on customer past conversations and issues.
- Find information on the internet to answer queries from customers.
- Search knowledge base articles based on customer queries.
- Suggest accurate and better responses while you're chatting with customers.
- Summarize chat conversations.

You can find more information in "Use Copilot to solve customer issues" (*https://oreil.ly/N55rk*).

As of the writing of this book in early 2024, Copilot is available with limited features and in preview in most regions (*https://oreil.ly/HGPxt*). But you can keep an eye on all its upcoming features for each Dynamics 365 CE App from the Dynamics 365 and Microsoft Power Platform release planner (*https://oreil.ly/_NPm3*).

Copilot in Canvas Apps

With the Copilot feature in canvas apps, you can create apps by communicating your requirements and get in-app guidance using natural language (Figure 11-10).

A Copilot-based AI assistant is available on the Power Apps home page (*https://oreil.ly/WlAha*). You can tell the AI assistant what sort of data you want to gather, track, or display, and the assistant will build responsive canvas apps along with a Dataverse table with the required columns and populate sample data.

Figure 11-10. Microsoft Copilot assistant on the Power Apps home page

Design a Canvas App Using Copilot

To help you get started, let's build an interview app for managers to provide and share applicants' interview feedback.

Step 1: Create an app with the help of Copilot

Sign in to Power Apps (*https://oreil.ly/WlAha*) and type "Interview feedback app," as shown in Figure 11-11, and press Enter.

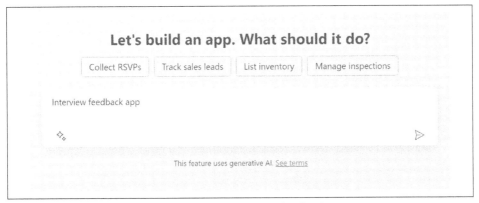

Figure 11-11. Asking Copilot to create an interview feedback app

Step 2: Review the table and columns for your app

Based on your description, Copilot will generate a Dataverse table with columns specific to the app's requirements, as shown in Figure 11-12.

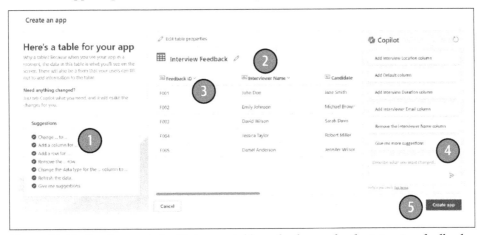

Figure 11-12. Copilot created a Dataverse table and columns for the interview feedback app

Let's review each area in more detail:

Suggestions (1)

Here you will see suggested actions to make necessary modifications in your table and its columns. For example, you can tell Copilot, "Give me suggestions," and it will show suggestions like "Add interview duration columns" and "Add interview location column." You can also add/remove and change the label of the columns with the help of Copilot. As shown in Figure 11-13, I have asked Copilot to create an interview mode column.

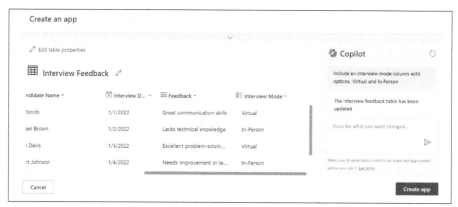

Figure 11-13. Asking Copilot to add an Interview Mode column in the Interview Feedback table

View table properties (2)

Here you can view the table name and its other properties.

View column properties (3)

Here you can view the column name and its other properties.

Microsoft Copilot assistant (4)

Here you can ask Copilot to make changes in your table, column, and data.

Create app button (5)

This will create an app based on the table and columns you finalize. Otherwise, you can click Cancel to start the app creation process over.

Editing Your App with Copilot

Once you create a Dataverse table and app using Copilot as described in the previous section, you can also use Copilot to build and continue editing your app within Power Apps Studio. You can change the appearance of your app by telling Copilot what changes you want to make, such as adding a new screen, configuring navigation, customizing a particular control, or bulk editing.

As shown in Figure 11-14, I asked Copilot to "add an email screen," so that I could send an email to HR after the interview to share the applicant's feedback.

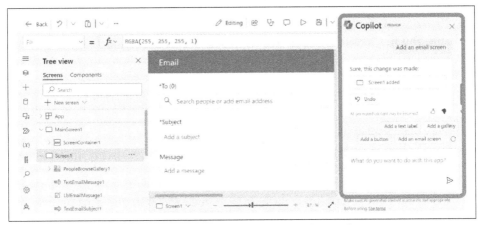

Figure 11-14. Using Copilot assistant in Power Apps Studio to edit a canvas app

As of this writing, Copilot supports only the following commands:

- Add a new screen from screen templates or layouts (blank, split, sidebar, header and footer).
- Modify the properties of various controls. The supported controls are Screen, Horizontal and Vertical containers, Gallery, Edit form, Button, Text Input, and Text Label.

Add a Chatbot Control to a Canvas App

Imagine you are interviewing a candidate; you may need assistance regarding:

- The points to be considered while capturing feedback
- The process to verify the applicant's identity in case of a virtual interview
- Any specific predefined questions that need to be asked
- Getting contact details of the HR team or recruitment team
- Other questions related to the interview process or company policies

You can add a Copilot Studio-based Chatbot control to your canvas app to help app users with a variety of requests, including simple answers to common questions.

Prerequisites to adding a Chatbot control in a canvas app

To add a Chatbot control to your canvas app, you need to:

- Create a Copilot Studio-based chatbot in the same environment as your canvas app. You may create any type of bot, such as an AI bot or a new generative AI-enhanced Copilot Studio bot. You can read the instructions in the Microsoft documentation (*https://oreil.ly/WY7VR*).

- Publish the copilot. Unpublished bots are grayed out in canvas apps.

Creating a chatbot using Copilot Studio

Let's use Copilot Studio to build a chatbot called "Interview Assistant" that will help app users with the interview feedback process:

1. Go to the Power Apps home page (*https://oreil.ly/WlAha*) and click on Solution in the left panel. From there, open your solution and select New → Chatbot, as shown in Figure 11-15.

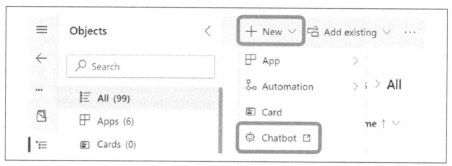

Figure 11-15. Creating a chatbot from within a solution

2. Provide a chatbot name, language, and the URL of any external public website that you want to use as a source of information to help the chatbot answer questions, as shown in Figure 11-16.

   You can click on "Edit advanced options" to change the chatbot icon, solution, and schema name.

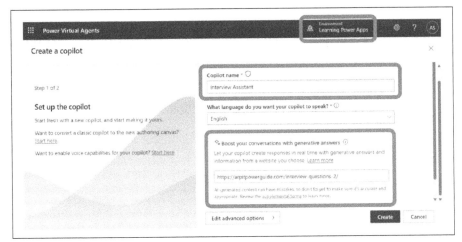

Figure 11-16. Providing chatbot details

3. When you're done, click Create to create the chatbot, as shown in Figure 11-17.

Figure 11-17. Providing chatbot details

 Microsoft's ongoing updates to its product branding and enhancements can result in varying names for the same product or component in different locations. This applies to Power Virtual Agent, now known as Copilot Studio, and Chatbot, which has been rebranded as Copilot. However, remnants of the old names may persist, so it's essential to remain aware of both the old and new terminologies to avoid confusion.

4. You can now either create new topics or edit existing topics to configure the chatbot and make it more relevant to your app. I have added a Microsoft Learn URL in the generative AI section to get answers from external websites, as shown in Figure 11-18.

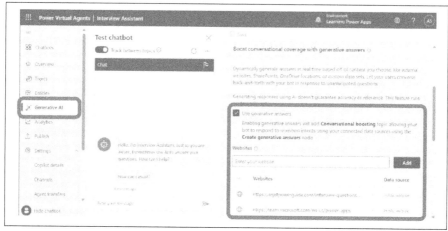

Figure 11-18. Configuring the chatbot for your app and adding external websites to get answers

5. Once you configure your chatbot to fit your app needs, save it and click the Publish button to embed it in your canvas app, as shown in Figure 11-19.

Figure 11-19. Publishing the chatbot

Adding the chatbot to your canvas app

Finally, it's time to add your Chatbot control to your canvas app. To do this, navigate to the Power Apps home page (*https://oreil.ly/WlAha*), open your canvas app, select Insert from the left panel, select "Chatbot (preview)" to add the control to your screen, and then select the chatbot that you just created, as shown in Figure 11-20.

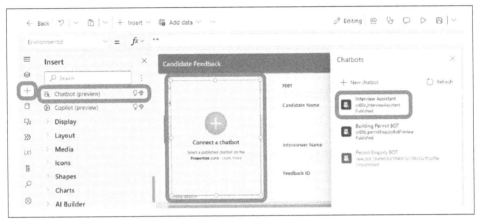

Figure 11-20. Adding the chatbot to a canvas app

Adding a Copilot Control to a Canvas App

App makers can add a Copilot control to any canvas app and choose what data the app can respond to queries about. For instance, a Copilot control can be used by managers to see what previous interviewers have said about a candidate before providing their own comments via the Interview Feedback app.

Now let's add a Copilot control to a canvas app.

Step 1: Enable Copilot for your environment

In "Prerequisites for the AI Features in Power Apps" on page 412, I discussed how to enable Copilot for your environment. Please refer to that section for further details.

Step 2: Enable the Copilot component for a canvas app

To enable the Copilot component for your canvas app, open your canvas app, click on Settings from the command bar, select "Upcoming features," and set the toggle for Copilot component to On, as shown in Figure 11-21.

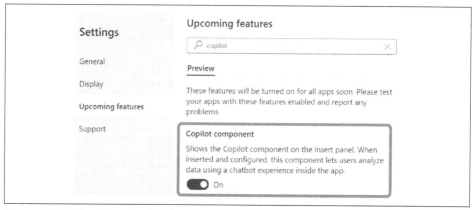

Figure 11-21. Enabling the Copilot component in a canvas app

Step 3: Add a Copilot control to your canvas app

To add a Copilot control to your canvas app screen, select the plus icon (+) from the left navigation panel, expand Input, and select "Copilot (preview)," as shown in Figure 11-22.

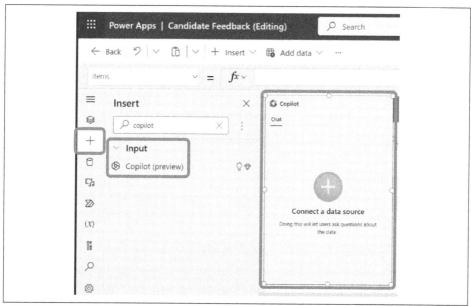

Figure 11-22. Adding a Copilot control to the canvas app screen

Once the control is added to the screen, select a data source from the pane. Copilot can offer data insights only on a single Dataverse table. As shown in Figure 11-23, I have selected the Candidate Feedback table.

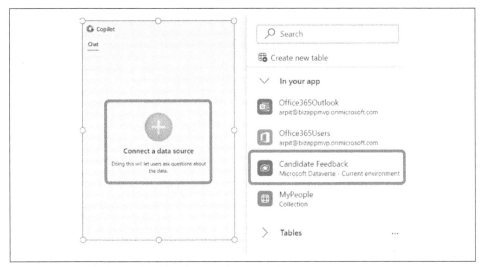

Figure 11-23. Choosing data for the Copilot control

In the right panel, you can change the properties of the Copilot control, as shown in Figure 11-24. For example, you can select the specific fields and/or views in the Dataverse table that the Copilot control will query to answer questions.

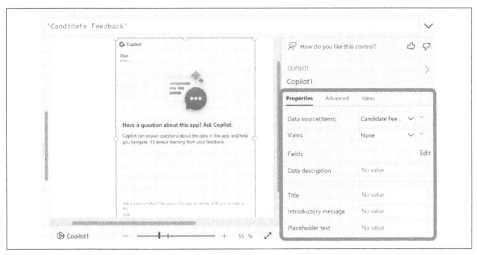

Figure 11-24. Changing properties of the Copilot control

Step 4: Test the Copilot control

Finally, launch the application and ask questions of the Copilot control about the data in the Dataverse table that it has been trained on. For example, as you can see in Figure 11-25, I asked Copilot about James Anderson's feedback, and it responded with the correct result.

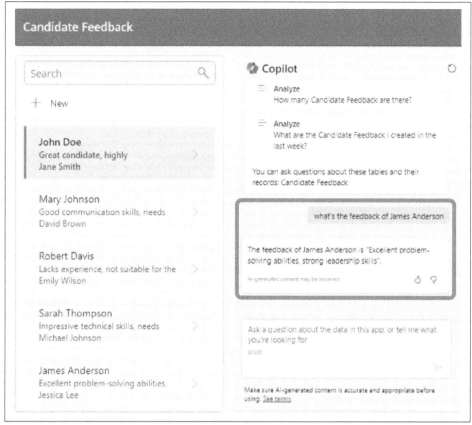

Figure 11-25. Testing Copilot: running the app and asking about the candidate's feedback

AI Builder (Hub) in Canvas Apps

AI Builder, also called AI Hub, is a key feature of the Microsoft Power Platform that enhances organizational effectiveness and efficiency by automating processes and forecasting results. Using AI Builder, you can easily add AI to your Power Apps applications and Power Automate flows that link to your business data housed in the underlying data platform (Dataverse) or in a variety of cloud data sources, including SharePoint, OneDrive, and Microsoft Azure.

AI Builder Capabilities

The following are all of the AI capabilities powered by AI Builder that you could potentially use in your Power Apps applications and Power Automate flows.

AI models

AI Builder provides a variety of built-in AI models (shown in Figure 11-26) tailored to specific business requirements. I have categorized them by requirements:

- Documents
  - — Extract information from invoices, receipts, identity documents (such as passports), and business cards
- Texts
  - — Detect positive, negative, or neutral sentiment in text data
  - — Classify customer feedback into predefined categories
  - — Extract key elements from text and classify them into predefined categories
  - — Extract the most relevant words and phrases from text
  - — Detect the predominant language of a text document
- Structured data
  - — Predict future outcomes from historical data
- Images
  - — Extract all the text in photos and PDF documents (OCR)
  - — Detect custom objects in images

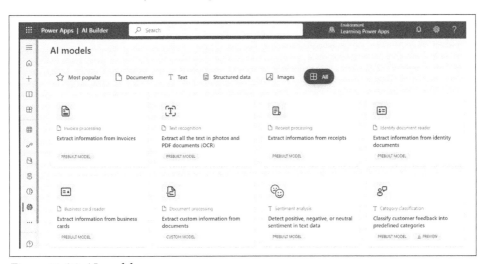

Figure 11-26. AI models

AI prompts

An AI prompt is a kind of task or goal you give to the LLM. You can also use input variables to provide dynamic context data at runtime. For example, you can create an AI prompt to create a to-do list for your team members based on meeting notes with customers. You can pass meeting notes to the AI prompt, and it will automatically generate the to-do list as an outcome.

Sentiment analysis is one type of AI prompt (as shown in Figure 11-27) that can be used to automatically analyze customer feelings based on their feedback and make decisions without human intervention.

Similarly, you can use AI prompts for the following purposes:

- Classify text
- Summarize text
- Respond to a complaint
- Extract information from text
- Create custom AI prompts to fit your business needs

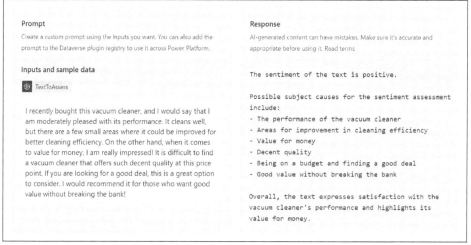

Figure 11-27. A sentiment analysis AI prompt

Document automation

Document automation is an AI capability that helps you extract information from documents received from customers and perform business logic. You can also import document information to other data sources of your choice like SharePoint, OneDrive, or any ERP application. Power Automate plays a key role in document automation; it uses AI Builder and offers a comprehensive solution for processing documents at scale, including pipeline monitoring, process orchestration, human validation, AI-powered data extraction, and more. Then, you can review these documents in Power Apps, perform further business logic, and make business decisions based on that.

Figure 11-28 depicts the document automation process using Power Automate, AI Builder, and Power Apps.

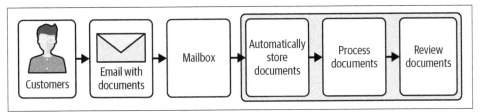

Figure 11-28. Document automation using Power Automate, AI Builder, and Power Apps

How AI Models Work

The AI model is the foundation for enabling AI features in Power Apps. It consists of numerous built-in algorithms operating in the background to generate results in a format that can be understood by humans. Think of it like a newborn baby that knows nothing at the time of birth, but is later taught a lot of things through letters, pictures, symbols, and other aids. The baby learns from this and responds to questions based on what they have learned. Here, the baby brain is similar to an AI model that generates an outcome based on its training and learning.

Since AI models are always being trained and learning from the data we provide as well as the data that is available on the internet, the results they generate may or may not be 100% correct and may contain inaccurate information about specific people, places, or facts.

AI model architecture works in the following manner (see Figure 11-29):

1. Take a user's input. First you need to provide some sample data to train the AI model. For example, if you want an AI model to extract a name from an ID document, then first you need to provide it sample documents like passports, driving licenses, and national ID cards to train where it should find the person's name and ID number on a particular document.

2. Analyze the data. The AI model learns from that sample data. Some AI models can also learn from the data available on the internet and a variety of other data sources.

3. Process the data. Once the AI model is trained, it starts analyzing your data based on its training and learning.

4. Make decisions and predictions. The model processes the outcome in human-readable format or natural language.

5. Provide relevant output. Finally, the model produces an outcome and sends it to the application.

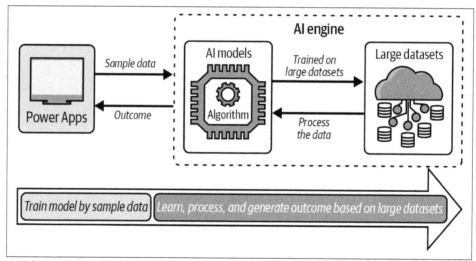

Figure 11-29. How an AI model works

You can use AI Builder to build unique AI models that are tailored to your company's requirements, or you can pick from a variety of prebuilt models. The AI derived from these models can then be applied to your Power Apps applications and Power Automate flows.

Using AI Builder to Create an App

In this section, I'll take you through a real-world example of using AI Builder to create an app. In 2021, after COVID shutdowns, when businesses started resuming office operations, my client needed an app to generate office passes. These passes needed to be issued only if an employee had the required number of COVID vaccinations. If done by hand, checking each employee's vaccination certificates and issuing passes would be time-consuming. As a solution for my client, I created an app using AI Builder, as shown in Figure 11-30.

AI Builder is like a robot that behaves like a human based on the training provided to it. First, it needs to be trained based on the set of sample data we provide, then it learns from that data, processes it, and produces the outcome based on that knowledge.

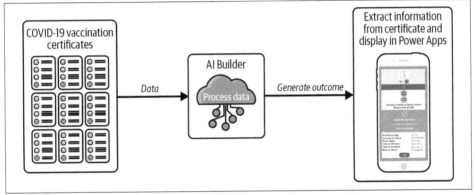

Figure 11-30. How AI Builder processes vaccine certificates and produces an outcome to a canvas app

For example, to extract the information from COVID vaccination certificates, you need to train the AI model on:

- What the COVID vaccination certificate structure looks like
- What information it might contain

To do that, you need to upload a few sample vaccination certificates. Based on that training, the model will learn and process that information and produce the outcome to be used in either Power Apps or Power Automate.

I have created an AI model of type document processor and named it COVID Vaccination Processor to be used in the canvas app. This AI model will take COVID vaccination certificates as input, process them, and extract the beneficiary name and age, the vaccine name, the number of doses, and other information (see Figure 11-31).

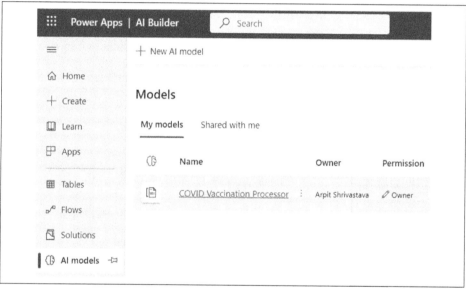

Figure 11-31. Creating a new AI model

I uploaded some collections (at least five) of COVID certificates to train the model, as shown in Figure 11-32.

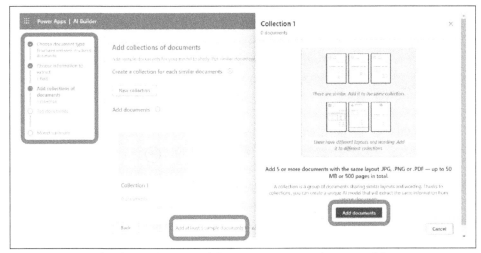

Figure 11-32. Uploading collections of documents to train the AI model

Then, I used the AI model in the canvas app to process the vaccination certificates, as shown in Figure 11-33.

Figure 11-33. Using the AI model in a canvas app to process the certificates

The AI model will extract the information from the certificate and display it on the screen, as shown in Figure 11-34.

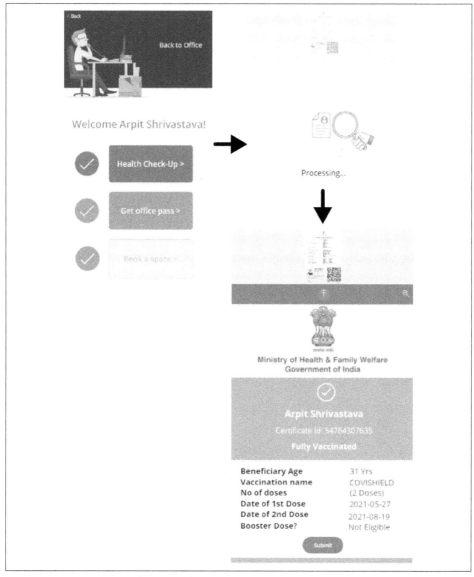

Figure 11-34. Outcome of AI model on canvas app screen

AI Model Accuracy

You can also check the accuracy of your AI model to identify what your model is struggling to extract. Model evaluations include recommendations for raising the score. For example, as shown in Figure 11-35, the accuracy scores for Number of Doses, Date of 2nd Dose, and Booster Dose are lower compared to the rest of the information present in the certificate. To improve the AI model accuracy score:

- Verify that each document has the field, table, or checkbox correctly tagged.
- Provide more sample training documents with fields, tables, and checkboxes.
- Verify that the documents within the collection all have the same formatting.

Figure 11-35. Accuracy of the AI model

Turn Images and Sketches into a Canvas App

Making an app usually starts with the planning and design phase to decide how it should look. Creating an app from scratch can take a while, even if you're using a design from paper, a whiteboard, or screen captures from a legacy software application. The *Image to app* feature makes it simpler for developers, no matter their experience level, to kickstart the app-making process. It lets you create an app from a picture of how you want it to look and connect it to data through a few easy steps in a guided interface (see Figure 11-36).

When you want to convert images to a working app, I recommend the following:

- Use clearly legible forms with a light background color.
- Don't use forms with colored backgrounds or underlined input boxes.
- Use only simple, one-page—not multipage—forms.
- Use images no larger than 4MB.
- Use hand-drawn images that are neat.

Figure 11-36. Converting an image into an app

To create an app from an image:

1. Go to the Power Apps home page (*https://oreil.ly/WlAha*), select Create from the left navigation panel, and then select Image, as shown in Figure 11-37.

Figure 11-37. Option to create app from image

2. Read the recommendation given on the screen and select Next to upload your image along with the app details and its format.

3. Click Next and then draw boxes, or tags, around things that should appear in the app. Then assign a component to each tag. If something doesn't have a tag, draw a box around it, as shown in Figure 11-38.

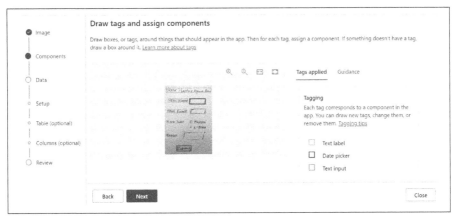

Figure 11-38. Draw tags and assign components screen

4. Set up the data that will connect your app with Dataverse. You can choose either "Connect to a Dataverse table" or "Skip this for now" if you want to do this step later, as shown in Figure 11-39.

Figure 11-39. Setting up your data for the app

5. If you want to connect your app with a Dataverse table, you can either create a new table or choose an existing table from the list, as shown in Figure 11-40.

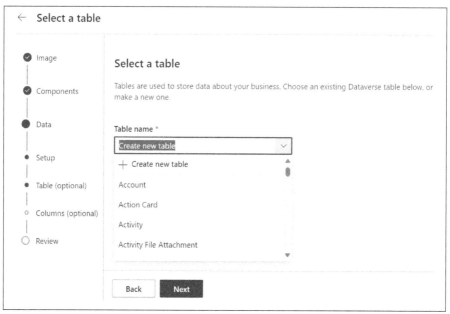

Figure 11-40. Selecting a table

6. In the next screen, you will see the app has automatically created the table and columns in Dataverse based on the uploaded image, as shown in Figure 11-41.

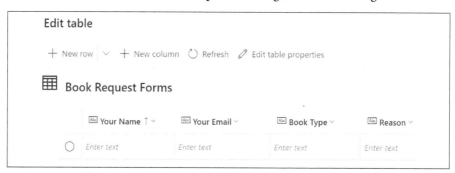

Figure 11-41. The generated table and its columns

7. Review the table and columns; if it's satisfactory click Next to start creating the app. It will take a few moments for the creation process, and then the finished app will display, as shown in Figure 11-42.

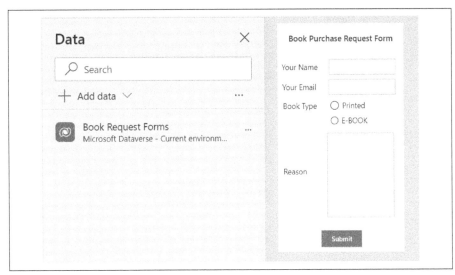

Figure 11-42. The generated app

As with all AI tools, it may make some mistakes in understanding your image, especially if the image is not clear. You can find more information on the image requirements and current limits of this feature from the Microsoft documentation (*https://oreil.ly/_MSrY*) before using it in real projects.

Additionally, canvas apps offer seamless integration with Figma (*https://www.figma.com*), a collaborative-design platform for creating software. Previously, it could be difficult and time-consuming for developers to reproduce the UX that designers had created in a design tool. However, with Express design (*https://oreil.ly/aIK5A*), designers can create designs using the Power Apps Figma UI Kit (*https://oreil.ly/IkIm-*), and developers can quickly turn that design into a functional app, removing the need for multiple feedback loops. The "Figma to app" feature bridges the gap between designers and developers to deliver an optimal experience for end users, saving a significant amount of time and giving developers more control over the end-to-end build experience.

To create an app using Figma, go to the Power Apps home page, select Create → Figma, and then provide your app and Figma details to start creating the app, as shown in Figure 11-43. The remaining procedures are the same as those we previously used for the Image to app process.

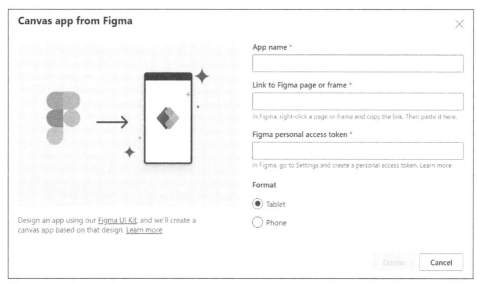

Canvas app from Figma ✕

App name *

Link to Figma page or frame *

In Figma, right-click a page or frame and copy the link. Then paste it here.

Figma personal access token *

In Figma, go to Settings and create a personal access token. Learn more

Format

(•) Tablet

( ) Phone

Design an app using our Figma UI Kit, and we'll create a canvas app based on that design. Learn more

Create   Cancel

Figure 11-43. Creating an app using Figma

Copilot Studio

From the earlier discussion, you might be curious to know: Can I create my own copilot or customize the default Copilot controls? The answer is yes.

At Microsoft Ignite 2023, Microsoft announced Copilot Studio (*https://oreil.ly/ 9PkOL*), which is essentially a rebranded Power Virtual Agent with generative AI capabilities. It is a low-code tool to customize Microsoft Copilot for Microsoft 365 and empowers citizen and professional developers to create their own standalone copilots.

Power Virtual Agent, announced in 2019, was used to design powerful chatbots using a guided, no-code graphical interface. However, more recently there has been a tremendous shift in the conversational AI and chatbot market, especially after the launch of ChatGPT. Generative AI and LLMs changed chatbots in many ways. Now chatbots can generate context-aware and personalized answers that match the tone, style, and intent of the user. Generative AI also allows chatbots to learn from data and feedback, improving their performance over time and adapting to changing user needs and preferences.

With this advancement, Microsoft combined the power of generative AI and LLM capabilities with Power Virtual Agent and designed a new low-code comprehensive conversation AI solution called Copilot Studio.

As of this writing, Copilot Studio can only customize the Copilot control for Microsoft 365 applications, not for Dynamics 365 apps and Power Platform components. Furthermore, you can create custom copilots only for canvas apps (as described earlier) and Power Pages along with some other channels like Teams, Facebook, external websites, Skype, and Telegram.

In early 2024, Microsoft announced Microsoft Copilot for Service (*https://oreil.ly/UUlLo*) with the aim of enriching customer interactions and boosting agent efficiency through integration with existing contact center and CRM solutions. This feature can be implemented in Microsoft 365 applications like Outlook and Teams, providing immediate access to up-to-date responses from diverse content sources, including external knowledge bases such as Salesforce, ServiceNow, and Zendesk.

Copilot Licenses

Microsoft Copilot licenses depend on which type of Microsoft product or applications you are using:

Microsoft 365
> To use Copilot with applications such as Word, Excel, PowerPoint, Teams, and Outlook, see Microsoft 365 Copilot licensing (*https://oreil.ly/8Ek_W*).

Dynamics 365
> To use Copilot with applications such as Dynamics 365 Sales and Dynamics 365 Customer Service, see Dynamics 365 Copilot licensing (*https://oreil.ly/0V6Py*). As of this writing, Copilot capabilities are only available in Dynamics 365 Sales, Customer Service, Field Service, Customer Insight, and Finance apps; however, in the future it might be available in other Dynamics 365 applications as well.

Power Platform
> For Power Platform components such as Power Apps, Power Automate, Power BI, and Power Pages, Copilot features are enabled by default and *cannot be turned off*. To disable them, a tenant admin must contact Microsoft support (*https://oreil.ly/9zHTb*).

Copilot features in preview are also enabled by default, but can be disabled by an administrator, as discussed earlier in this chapter. As of this writing, there is no additional cost to use Copilot features in Power Platform; it is included with your current Power Platform licensing plan.

As of this writing, you need to pay $200 for 25,000 messages/month to customize Microsoft Copilot for Microsoft 365 or create your own copilots. Check the Microsoft

Copilot Studio pricing page (*https://oreil.ly/FNKR7*) for the latest pricing information.

Summary

In this chapter, you learned how Microsoft Copilot offers a range of features that benefit both app makers and app users, enhancing productivity and user experience. It not only lets app makers create apps faster than before, but also boosts the productivity success rate compared with those who don't use Copilot. You also learned how the Microsoft Copilot-based digital assistant overall architecture works and interacts with other Microsoft products and applications to generate relevant answers for app users in natural language. It accesses only your organization's data and doesn't have access to data outside of your organization. Using Copilot you can bring Microsoft 365, Dynamics 365, Power Platform, and Microsoft Azure together and make technology more accessible through the most universal interface—natural language.

This chapter also explained that Microsoft has provided some built-in AI models for the most common business scenarios; this enables your business to use AI to automate complex business processes without having knowledge of data science or coding skills. Additionally, professional developers can create custom AI models and prompts to extend its capabilities.

If you have any questions or concerns about how Copilot guarantees the security of your organization's data, and how it learns from your organization's data to generate relevant outcomes inside Microsoft's trust boundary, I would highly recommend that you check out the "FAQ for Copilot data security and privacy for Dynamics 365 and Power Platform" (*https://oreil.ly/Rlzna*).

In the next chapter, you'll learn how Power Apps can be used with Microsoft Teams to further boost business users' productivity.

CHAPTER 12

Power Apps with Microsoft Teams

As of 2023, there were more than 300 million monthly active users who use Microsoft Teams to create, collaborate, and connect.[1] With so many employees working remotely and meeting and collaborating via Microsoft Teams, there is a lot of interest in developing low-code and no-code applications that can make remote work easier and more effective.

Microsoft Dataverse for Teams brings the power of Microsoft Dataverse and Power Platform to Microsoft Teams. It is a built-in low-code data platform for Teams that enables you to build custom apps, flows, and chatbots in Teams by using Power Apps, Power Automate, and Copilot Studio. It also offers relational data storage, rich data types, enterprise-grade governance, and one-click solution deployment.

The following are a few real-life business use cases:

- Create an app to connect and share with people in your organization with similar interests and skills.
- Create an app for employees for company announcements and communications.
- Create an idea app for employees to share ideas and suggestions.
- Create a helpdesk app for organization employees to enter a ticket for issue reporting.
- Create an appraisal app for organization employees to manage the end-to-end appraisal process.
- Create an app to keep track of project activities, initiatives, and progress.

---

1 Microsoft Fiscal Year 2023 Third Quarter Earnings report (*https://oreil.ly/gcxbp*).

You can download sample app templates for use in Teams from Microsoft's Official GitHub page (*https://oreil.ly/hbIBg*). On Microsoft's Customer Stories page (*https://oreil.ly/t9rOl*), you can also read case studies of some giant customers like Domino's, Coca-Cola, NHS, ING Bank, and others, that use Dataverse with Teams.

In this chapter, you will learn the following:

- How Dataverse for Teams differs from Dataverse
- How to use Power Apps in Teams to create custom apps that are built using the enhanced performance and scalability of Dataverse for Teams

Dataverse for Teams can also be used for the following, which you can explore in the Microsoft documentation:

- How to automate repetitive tasks (*https://oreil.ly/g01h-*) with Power Automate in Teams
- How to respond to employee needs by building chatbots (*https://oreil.ly/jWoF0*) with Microsoft Copilot Studio from within Teams
- How to present powerful and interactive charts and data (*https://oreil.ly/_zmWZ*) with Power BI in Teams

Dataverse for Teams Versus Dataverse

You can see the comparison between Dataverse for Teams and Dataverse at the component levels in Figure 12-1.

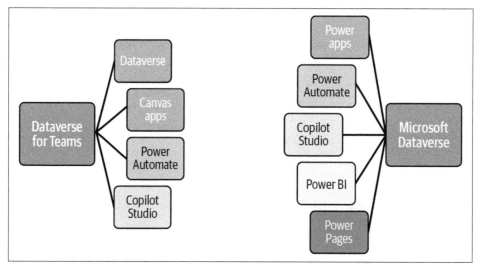

Figure 12-1. Dataverse for Teams versus Microsoft Dataverse

Microsoft Dataverse for Teams enables you to create canvas apps, Power Automate flows, and Copilot Studio chatbots within Microsoft Teams. It also includes Dataverse in Power Platform to store the data and design components. But wait a minute—you can also create all these components *outside* of Microsoft Teams as well. Then, how would you decide when you should create these components within Teams and when you should create them outside of Teams?

It all depends on your business scenario and your organization's needs. The following are the major factors that will help you decide which one to use. To remain in the context of this book, I will primarily focus on Power Apps within Teams instead of other components.

Purpose

If you want to create a productivity app either for yourself or a few of your colleagues or project team members to use within your organization for day-to-day activities, then creating a Power Apps application within Teams is the best choice. For example, let's say that I am a project manager for a support team, and I manage team members in different time zones across the globe. I am currently using Excel to keep track of each team member's availability, task assignments, and working hours to ensure that each team member has proper work assigned and no team member sits idle despite being in a different time zone to prevent breaches of service level agreements (SLAs) on support tickets.

To boost my team's productivity, instead of manually keeping track of everything in Excel, I can make a Power Apps canvas app in Microsoft Teams and share it with my team members. With this app, everyone can update their tasks, working hours, and support ticket status. I can also use Power Automate with my app to write automation logic for sending weekly reports, approvals, and notifications; and I can use Copilot Studio to create a chatbot to query the data stored in Dataverse within Teams.

But, Power Apps must be created outside of Teams if you want to create a business-critical app that will handle a key business scenarios and integrate with external data sources, which may require custom development and the assistance of professional developers, in addition to low-code citizen developers.

Persona

Power Apps within Teams is a great option for businesspeople who do not have technical knowledge and spend most of their time in Microsoft Teams handling clients and managing their project team members. If your app has complex features, and custom development is required, then create the app outside Teams.

Licensing

Licensing plays a crucial role in deciding whether to use Power Apps within Teams or outside. You don't need any additional licenses if you are already using Microsoft 365 subscriptions with Microsoft Power Platform and Microsoft Teams capabilities, excluding plans for EDU A1 and SUB SKUs (Education Faculty and Student licensing plans). You can find more information about this in Teams for Education (*https://oreil.ly/SLo8p*) and Education SKU reference (*https://oreil.ly/lJR9h*).

If your goal is simply to create a basic app or chatbot and integrate it with Power Automate for your employees in Teams, then you do not need to buy a license for Power Apps or Copilot Studio. In these situations, Dataverse for Teams is the ideal option. You can use Dataverse for Teams and Power Apps if your organization has any of the following Microsoft 365 licenses:

- Office 365 E1
- Office 365 E3
- Office 365 E5
- Office 365 F3
- M365 Business Basic
- M365 Business Standard
- M365 Business Premium

- Microsoft 365 F3
- Microsoft 365 E3
- Microsoft 365 E5
- Office 365 A3
- Office 365 A5
- Microsoft 365 A3
- Microsoft 365 A5

Licensing and pricing of Microsoft products are subject to change at any time, so always refer to the official Power Platform Licensing Guide (automatic download) (*https://oreil.ly/FX9Uj*) to get the latest pricing information.

If you have any of the aforementioned licenses, you are only allowed to create and embed canvas apps, Power Automate cloud and desktop flows, Microsoft Copilot Studio, and Dataverse for Teams within Microsoft Teams with limited functionality. These licenses do not allow you to embed Power BI reports and model-driven apps. For this, you must have the appropriate premium licenses listed in the Power Platform Licensing Guide. However, in this chapter, I will demonstrate how to embed Power BI reports and model-driven apps as well.

Storage

Both Dataverse and Dataverse for Teams store data in the Power Platform environment linked to them. Dataverse for Teams creates an environment in Teams for every team where you can create data, apps, chatbots, and flows. These environments support disaster recovery, backups, and point-in-time restores. Dataverse for Teams measures capacity using relational, image, and file data. A team's 2 GB capacity can typically store up to 1 million rows of data. Additionally, Dataverse for Teams is limited to one environment per team and a maximum of 10,000 teams.

Dataverse, on the other hand, offers an infinite number of environments and unlimited data storage, along with features like copy or reset environments. It also offers more granular security and governance controls, which include role-based access as well as compliance features. So, if you require a database capacity of more than 2 GB or 1 million rows, then Dataverse is the best choice.

See Table 12-1 for the storage comparison between Dataverse for Teams and Dataverse.

Table 12-1. Storage comparison between Dataverse for Teams and Dataverse

Environment lifecycle	Dataverse for Teams	Dataverse
Environments	1 per Team	Unlimited
Maximum size	1 million rows or 2 GB	Unlimited
Upgrade to Dataverse	Yes	N/A

Complexity

Dataverse for Teams is not the ideal option for developing apps that require professional developers to create complex features and custom components using code. For creating such applications, Dataverse is a better option because it has a variety of built-in capabilities and components such as Dataverse global search, granular-level security roles, plug-ins, WebHooks, and various premium connectors that Dataverse for Teams does not offer.

Dataverse for Teams is the best solution for building basic apps with built-in, drag-and-drop controls and automation logic intended to reduce time and effort by automating manual and repetitive tasks.

Table 12-2 shows a feature comparison between Dataverse and Dataverse for Teams, which will help you determine where to develop your app.

Table 12-2. Feature comparison between Dataverse for Teams and Dataverse

Feature	Dataverse for Teams	Dataverse
Basic data types	Yes	Yes
Advanced data types (customer, multiple transaction currencies)	No	Yes
Advanced and Dataverse search	No	Yes
Mobile offline	No	Yes
Relational storage	Yes	Yes
Auditing or activity logging	No	Yes

Feature	Dataverse for Teams	Dataverse
File and image support	Yes	Yes
Data visualization	Yes	Yes
Paginated reports (SSRS)	No	Yes
Azure API Management	Yes	Yes
Dataverse plug-ins	No	Yes
Power Apps component framework (PCF controls)	No	Yes
Admin security roles	Only System Administrator and System Customizer	System Administrator, System Customizer, and other prebuilt service admin roles
User security roles	Teams Owners, Members, and Guests	Provides more security features along with custom roles
Business units	One	Unlimited
Column-level security, hierarchical security, record sharing	No	Yes
Integration with Power Automate	Yes	Yes
WebHooks, Data Export service, Azure Synapse Link, Event Hubs, service bus, server-side sync, SQL Server Management Studio	No	Yes
Managed Data Lake	No	Yes
App sharing	Cannot be shared outside the Team it is built for	Can be shared with the entire organization, and with external audiences by adding them as guest users in Microsoft Entra ID
Premium connectors	No	Yes

Getting Started with Creating Apps in Teams

To demonstrate how to create an app within Teams, let's use a real-world scenario.

Let's say that, as a project lead in my organization, I oversee 10–15 team members who work from different countries. To prevent work interruptions, I have to share my team members' leave plans every three months with my client. Currently, I have to ask each of them to send me their leave plans for the next three months in advance, either by email or Teams, or sometimes by shared Excel files. Once I have reviewed and approved the leave, I have to share the final plan with my client via email or Teams. There are a lot of manual steps required and challenges maintaining the leave details in spreadsheets along with keeping track of leave requests and balances.

As a solution, I want to develop an app for my team called Leave Planner, where every team member can see their leave balance, type of leave, and upcoming company holidays based on their location. They can also use the app to request leave, and, as manager, I can view all of the leave requests, approve or reject them, and then send them straight to my client. I would like to do all of these things within Teams without having to open any other applications.

Prerequisites

Before creating an app in Teams, you need to:

- Have an appropriate Teams license that includes Dataverse for Teams
- Identify the team or create a new team in Microsoft Teams where you want to create Power Apps

I have created a new team named "Arpit Power Guide," which has automatically created a Dataverse for Teams environment in Power Platform with the same name and an environment type of "Microsoft Teams," as shown in Figure 12-2. This environment will store all the components created for the Arpit Power Guide Team.

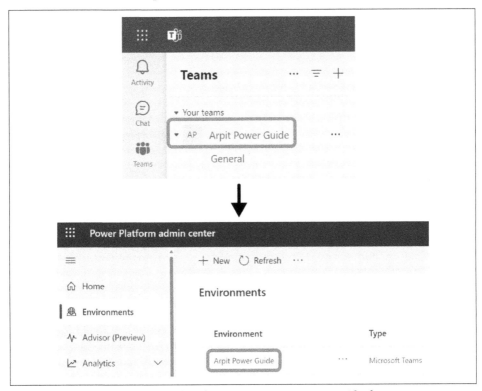

Figure 12-2. New Teams channel and its environment in Power Platform

Installing Power Apps in Microsoft Teams

Power Apps is available as a personal app for Teams, meaning that it has a personal scope; that is, the Power Apps functions are available only to the user accessing them—not to other members of the team. Here's how you add it to Teams (see Figure 12-3):

1. Open Microsoft Teams and select Apps from the left navigation bar.

2. Click on "Manage your apps" and search for Power Apps.

3. Select Add. This adds Power Apps to Teams and displays the Power Apps icon in the left navigation bar. You can pin it by right-clicking on the icon in the navigation bar and selecting Pin.

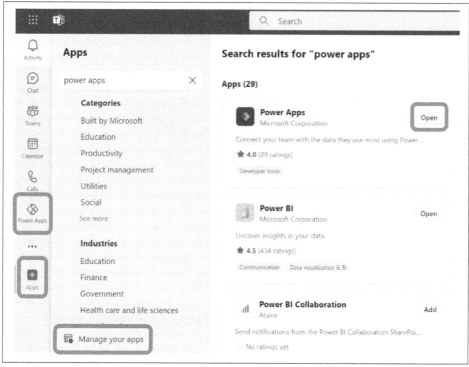

Figure 12-3. Installing Power Apps in Teams

In the left panel of Figure 12-3, you can see there are additional ready-made apps available that you can filter by industries and categories and add to Teams. Some of the apps may be free, whereas others may require a license.

Once Power Apps is installed, click on Power Apps from the left navigation bar, click on Build, choose your team, and click "See all." It will show all the components that you can create within Teams, as shown in Figure 12-4.

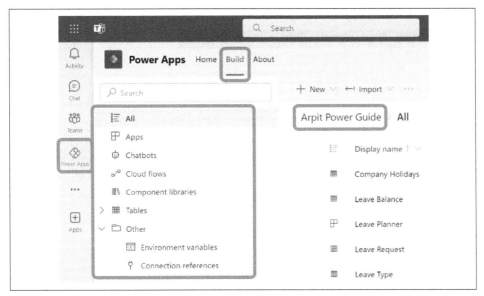

Figure 12-4. Power Apps for Teams components

You can create the components shown in Table 12-3 within Teams.

Table 12-3. Power Apps components

Component	Purpose
Apps	Create Power Apps within Teams
Chatbots	Create Copilot Studio-based chatbots within Teams
Flows	Automate processes, write complex business logic, send communications that are integrated with apps and chatbots
Component libraries	Create reusable components for your Power Apps that you can also use in other apps within the same team
Tables	Create Dataverse tables to store app data
Environment variables	Hold configuration data
Connection references	Hold connection details of data sources or connectors used in apps or flows

Setting Up Dataverse for Teams

To create our app in Teams, we first need to create a data model (table, column, relationships, etc.) in Dataverse to store the leave request details along with other leave-related information. Table 12-4 shows the tables I have created in Dataverse for Teams, as shown in Figure 12-5.

Table 12-4. Tables created in Dataverse for Teams

Table	Purpose
Company Holidays	Store company holidays based on country
Leave Balance	Store the available leave balance for a particular employee
Leave Request	Store leave request details
Leave Type	Store leave type: sick, vacation, parental, etc.

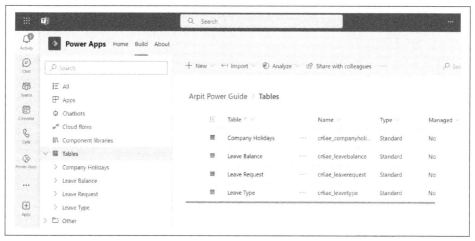

Figure 12-5. Setting up tables in Dataverse for Teams

Creating and Customizing Power Apps in Teams

Let's create a new app, design its UI, and connect it with Dataverse. I won't go into too much detail about designing the app, as I have discussed such details in earlier chapters. All you have to know is that I plan to have three main screens in my app: Login, Home, and Create Request.

The Login screen has options to "Login as an employee" and "Login as a manager," as shown in Figure 12-6.

Figure 12-6. Login screen

The Home screen is the landing screen where employees will see the options described in Table 12-5

Table 12-5. Options available on the Home screen

Option	Purpose
Create Request	Create a new leave request; takes you to the Create Request screen
My Leave Requests	View all leave requests, with an option to filter the list based on status (Pending, Approved, Declined)
My Leave Balance	View remaining leave
Company Holidays	View a list of holidays
About	View information on holidays and leave policies
Log out	Exit the app and return to the login screen

The manager will see similar options along with additional options to approve or decline a leave request. Here are the high-level steps to use the app as an employee and manager:

1. Log in as an employee or manager.

2. After logging in, you'll see the Home screen, where all leave-related information will be available along with a Create Request option (see Figure 12-7).

Figure 12-7. Home screen for employees

3. If you're an employee, you'll click Create Request to create a new leave request, which will display the Create Request screen shown in Figure 12-8.

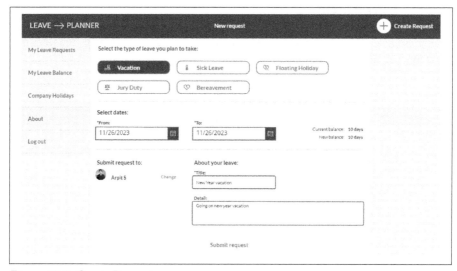

Figure 12-8. Create Request screen

4. If you're a manager, you'll log in and be able to approve or decline leave requests, as shown in Figure 12-9.

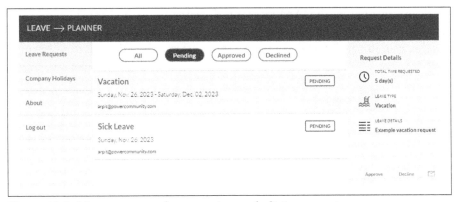

Figure 12-9. Manager screen for approving or declining requests

Publishing Power Apps to Teams

After you have developed an app, you will want to distribute it to your team. To do this, you need to publish the app to Teams, which will make it available for your team to use. To publish the app to Teams, click Save and then click the Publish to Teams icon on the command bar, as shown in Figure 12-10.

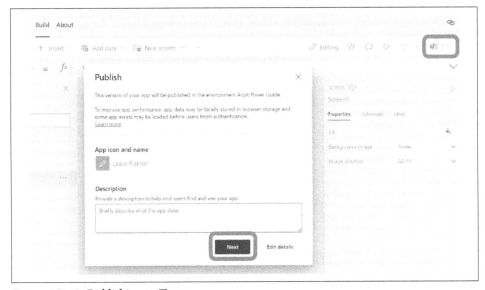

Figure 12-10. Publishing to Teams

Click the plus (+) on the "Add to channel" dialog for each channel where you want the app to appear as a tab, as shown in Figure 12-11. You can only publish to channels for the team in which you generated the app. After adding the app to a channel, click Save & Close.

Figure 12-11. Adding the app to your team's channel

You can now open your app by clicking the tab that appears in the channel that you selected, as shown in Figure 12-12.

Figure 12-12. Viewing the app in Teams

Sharing Your App with Others in Your Organization

Your published app can only be accessed by your team members, but sometimes you may want to share it with colleagues outside of your team. To do that, verify you are the owner of the team where you published the app. Then, click on the Power Apps icon in the left navigation bar, open the Build tab, and click the "Share with colleagues" button, as shown in Figure 12-13.

Figure 12-13. Sharing the app with others in your organization

In the dialog pop-up to share with colleagues, enter the Microsoft 365 group or Microsoft Entra ID security group name. Toggle the "Colleague can use" switch for your app and click Save, as shown in Figure 12-14.

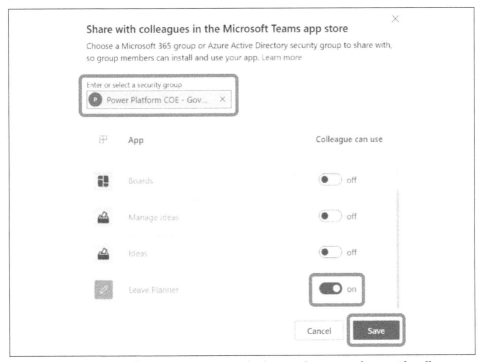

Figure 12-14. Entering the security group and selecting the app to share with colleagues outside your team

After a few moments, a success message will appear letting you know that the selected group or team can now install and use the app in Teams. The app will then show up on the "Built by your colleagues" tab when users choose Apps in Teams.

Installing Canvas App Template Apps to Teams

In the previous section, you learned how to create Power Apps in Microsoft Teams. In this section, you'll learn how to use Microsoft's built-in app templates, which can be used as is or customized to meet your specific business needs. You can find the app templates on the Home tab under Power Apps, as shown in Figure 12-15.

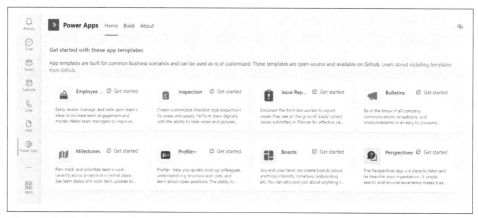

Figure 12-15. App templates

These templates are stored on GitHub (*https://oreil.ly/6py9B*) and can be downloaded for free. Clicking on any app template in that section will take you to the GitHub link for that template. Each template uses different Microsoft 365 services, but typically they are made up of apps, flows, and tables. Depending on what is required, the installation process may vary slightly, but each app will have documentation and an installation guide.

Embedding a Model-Driven App in Teams

Microsoft Teams is typically used by business users and colleagues to communicate with customers, whereas model-driven apps are used for tasks connected to CRM. However, there are situations when these applications need to be used simultaneously, and users find it challenging to switch between multiple applications.

For example, consider sales team members who frequently need to use Teams to interact with various customers. They need to access the files and documents specific to customers stored in Teams and use it for audio and video calls, screen sharing, and chatting. At the same time, the sales team members need to perform CRM-related tasks, such as creating leads, converting them to opportunities, and tracking order status. In this case, integrating a model-driven app within Microsoft Teams is the best option to complete all communication and CRM-related tasks in one place.

Back in 2019, Microsoft introduced the "Add to Teams" feature in the Power Apps maker portal, enabling you to seamlessly integrate your Power Apps (model-driven app or canvas app) into Microsoft Teams. Since its introduction, many users have embraced this feature, incorporating their personal productivity apps into Teams. In 2021, Microsoft enhanced this experience to simplify the process of adding your existing Power Apps to Microsoft Teams even further. Hence, you see two different options to add your apps to Teams.

There are two ways to add model-driven apps to Microsoft Teams.

Option 1: Embed a Model-Driven App as a Tab App in Teams

To embed a model-driven app as a tab app in Teams, open the Teams application, click on the Teams icon in the left navigation bar, then open the team's channel (we're using the General channel), and click on the + icon to add a new tab, as shown in Figure 12-16.

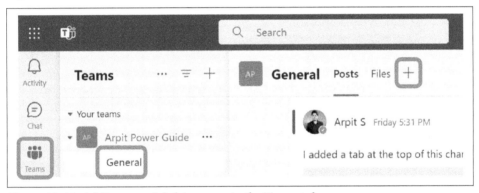

Figure 12-16. Adding a model-driven app in the Teams tab

In the "Add a new app" dialog box, select Power Apps, as shown in Figure 12-17.

Figure 12-17. Adding Power Apps

Select "Model-driven apps" in the drop-down list and then select the model-driven app that you would like to pin, as shown in Figure 12-18. I have added an Asset Checkout app for demonstration.

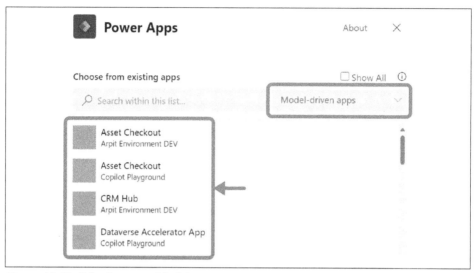

Figure 12-18. Selecting a model-driven app

The app is now available to use in the team's channel, as shown in Figure 12-19.

Figure 12-19. Model-driven app available in team's channel

Option 2: Embed a Model-Driven App as a Personal App in Teams

To embed a model-driven app as a personal app in Teams, first open the Teams application. Then, in your browser, navigate to the Power Apps home page (*https://oreil.ly/WlAha*), choose the Power Platform environment where you have created the model-driven app, click on Apps from the left navigation panel, select your model-driven app from the list, and select Share from the command bar, as shown in Figure 12-20.

You will have two options: Add to Teams and Download app. The steps from here on are the same as for adding a canvas app. Select "Add to Teams" to incorporate the app as a personal app or opt for "Add to a team" or "Add to a chat" to add the app as a tab within an existing channel or conversation.

Figure 12-20. Adding a model-driven app to Teams

It's important to know, regardless of the Power Platform environment, you can add any Power Apps created within Teams.

Features Currently Unavailable

Embedding model-driven apps in Microsoft Teams is a great way to boost user productivity. However, you should be aware that embedded model-driven apps in Teams do not support all of the functionality that model-driven apps created in Dataverse offer.

As of this writing, these model-driven app features are not supported in Teams:

- Running model-driven apps on the Microsoft Teams mobile app
- Model-driven apps that have embedded canvas apps
- Custom pages

Embedding a Canvas App in Teams

In the previous sections, you learned how to create Power Apps and all its related components within Teams, but imagine you have already developed an app outside Teams and want to show it within Teams. For example, I have an app named Power Apps Training that I have created using a Power Apps template in a Power Platform environment. Now, I want to add the same app to Teams, as shown in Figure 12-21.

Figure 12-21. Adding a Power Platform environment app to Teams

After you select Share, followed by "Add to Teams," you'll see two choices: "Add to Teams" and "Download app."

 Back in 2019, Microsoft introduced the Add to Teams feature in the Power Apps maker portal, enabling you to seamlessly integrate your Power Apps (model-driven app or canvas app) into Microsoft Teams. Since its introduction, many users have embraced this feature, incorporating their personal productivity apps into Teams. In 2021, Microsoft enhanced this experience to simplify the process of adding your existing Power Apps to Microsoft Teams even further. Hence, you see two different options to add your apps to Teams.

Option 1: Add to Teams

The "Add to Teams" option will launch the Teams application either in a browser tab or as a desktop application, and you'll see a pop-up dialog, as shown in Figure 12-22. You can either add your app to a team or a chat. I have opted for a team.

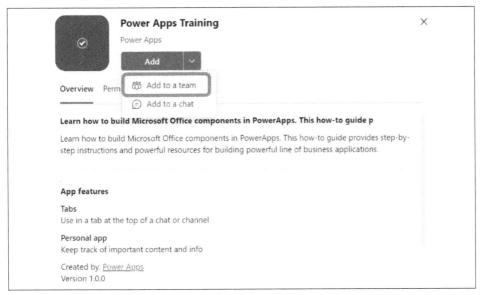

Figure 12-22. Adding an app to a team

Then you need to choose the team where you want to add the app as a new tab, as shown in Figure 12-23. Click "Set up a tab" to continue.

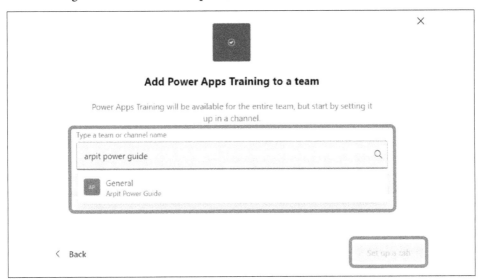

Figure 12-23. Adding an app to a team

Finally, you can view your app as a new tab in the Teams application. Click on the Power Apps Training tab to launch the app, as shown in Figure 12-24.

Figure 12-24. App added as new tab in Teams

Option 2: Download App

Another option to add the Power Apps application to Teams is to download it on a local machine. This will export the app's ZIP file to the local machine, as shown in Figure 12-25.

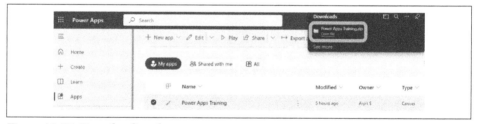

Figure 12-25. Downloading the canvas app

Then you need to upload it into Teams. Open Teams, click on Apps in the left navigation bar, click on Manage your apps → Upload an app, as shown in Figure 12-26.

Figure 12-26. Uploading an app created in the Power Platform environment

Select the exported app from the download on your machine and upload it, as shown in Figure 12-27.

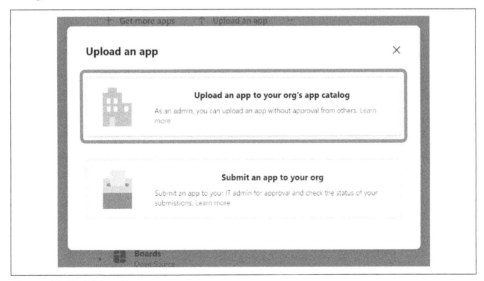

Figure 12-27. Uploading an app

Finally, click on Add to add the app to Teams, as shown in Figure 12-28. After that, follow the same steps explained in Option 1.

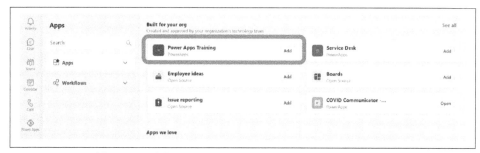

Figure 12-28. Adding a model-driven app to Teams from the Power Apps home page

Summary

This chapter covered the different ways in which Power Apps and Microsoft Teams can be integrated. This integration enables business users to create custom apps, chatbots, and flows within Teams using Power Apps, Copilot Studio, and Power Automate, all of which are built on Dataverse for Teams. Additionally, the chapter also covered the different ways in which canvas apps and model-driven apps developed in the Power Platform environment can be embedded into Teams. Dataverse for Teams is available to citizen developers with limited Dataverse capacity and capabilities and does not require an additional Power Apps premium license. For more advanced features and custom development, you should create an app outside of Teams.

Read the FAQs for Dataverse for Teams (*https://oreil.ly/i-puF*) if you have any further questions regarding when to use it.

We have covered every aspect of Power Apps up to this point, so now it is time to get hands-on with all these features by building a live project. In the next two chapters, I will take you through a real-world case study to help you understand how to use the various components and features of Power Apps along with other Power Platform components to design an end-to-end business solution.

CHAPTER 13

Model-Driven App Case Study

Until now, you have learned every aspect of Power Apps and its various features and components with real-world examples. Now it's time to stitch these components together and develop an end-to-end solution by using an example of one real-world case study.

A retail company that sells electronic devices such as laptops, mobile phones, tablets, and watches has more than 100 stores across more than 25 countries. The company receives a lot of queries regarding its products and order deliveries, as well as complaints about orders when there are defects or in case of a delayed order delivery.

The retail company is currently facing the following business challenges when it comes to offering customer service to its clients:

Manual work
Currently, most of the service-related activities are handled manually, including sending emails, issuing meeting invitations, and sending approval requests to service managers for order returns and refunds. Also, there is no way to expedite processes for premium customers.

Reporting capability
There is no centralized data repository. Instead, each service agent uses their own spreadsheet to keep track of customer data, so the company lacks the capability to get a 360-degree view of its service data.

Data security
There is no role-based data security system in place.

Mobility
Service agents who are working in the field have no access to the system or data when they are visiting customer locations.

Lack of structure or unified approach

There are no defined process flows or formal instructions for service agents to help them perform service activities or solve customer queries.

Business logic

Service agents currently use spreadsheets and often struggle to find the right data due to data ambiguity and duplication.

User interface

There is no proper user interface or application in place where coworkers can get everything related to a customer in one place with easy access to related and historical data.

Data integration

Service agents often need to find customer data in various other applications and systems, requiring them to switch applications and put customers on hold until they find the correct information.

The retail company wants to develop a cost-effective Power Platform-based low-code, no-code solution that can solve all of these business challenges. Additionally, it wants that solution to be scalable and easy to configure and maintain with minimum development effort. To this end, the company plans to develop two apps: Book My Service for service agents working in stores and Service at Home for field service agents. The company has asked me and my team to come up with this solution.

In this case study, my objective is to create a model-driven app for the service agents who are working in the stores and handling customer queries and complaints over the phone, through email, or in the stores. In the next chapter, we'll create a canvas app for the field service agents, who visit customer locations to install devices, fix issues, and collect customer feedback.

You can find the final solution app in this book's GitHub repository (*https://oreil.ly/pvoZI*).

First, we need to plan our implementation methodology. You should always start your project by planning your implementation methodology, regardless of whether you are creating model-driven or canvas apps.

Planning the Implementation

Any Power Platform or Power Apps project implementation not only requires developing a solution containing a set of features, but also needs to focus on and understand the implementation methodology to be undertaken to take the right path toward successful project execution.

Implementation Methodology

It is critical to establish an implementation methodology at the beginning of any Power Apps or Power Platform project. Planning your steps in advance puts you and your project team on the right path toward:

- Improved consistency and predictable outcomes
- Clear definitions of project phases, milestones, deliverables, and entry and exit criteria for each phase
- Clear definitions of roles and responsibilities required for the project
- Reduced risks of missing critical activities required for a successful outcome

Adhering to the right implementation methodology is like planning a vacation with your family. You first decide your destination, then decide the dates of your stay, then gather suggestions and reviews from your friends who have been there to minimize risks and expenses, then take the most efficient route to reach your destination, and finally enjoy your stay by reaching your destination on time and within budget.

Similarly, any Power Platform or Dynamics 365 roadmap to success includes the following steps:

1. Plan ahead. Make sure you have clearly defined the project scope and have all the right tools (resources, governance, methodology, etc.) and a checklist (project monitoring) before starting the project journey.
2. Know the road. Clearly define the route or solution blueprint to set clear expectations on start and end dates for milestones. This helps monitor the project progress, and the team understands what is expected from them.
3. Avoid pitfalls. Follow proven best practices that Microsoft has provided based on thousands of Dynamics 365 and Power Platform project implementations. This will help minimize risks and bugs in the final solution.
4. Get there faster. Take advantage of strategies to develop your solution that help you save time and money and also ensure that you are taking the most efficient route to reach your goal.
5. No surprises. Delight customers by delivering a solution on time and within budget.

Implementation Phases

When you follow any implementation methodology (be it Agile, waterfall, or hybrid), there are certain predefined phases that any project team needs to follow to be successful, as shown in Figure 13-1.

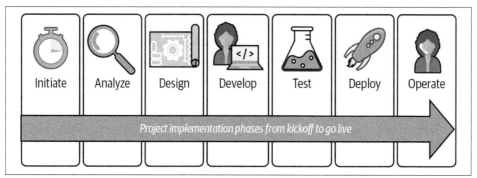

Figure 13-1. Project implementation phases

These implementation phases are:

Initiate

Initiation is the beginning of any new project, where the project team interacts with the key business stakeholders and customers to understand and evaluate their current business process and infrastructure. Based on that, the team prepares the project plan, proposals, and statement of work (SOW).

Analyze

Analysis is the stage where the project team goes a bit deeper and understands the current business model and functional/non-functional requirements from the customer, performs the fit-gap analysis, and then proposes a high-level solution blueprint to the customer. Fit-gap analysis is a detailed assessment of how a proposed solution fits with customer needs and where it leaves a gap. These analyses are documented in the functional requirements document (FRD).

Design

In this phase, the project team writes a functional design document (FDD), which contains information about how the application will behave or function for end users, and a technical design document (TDD), which contains information about what components need to be designed and how particular functionalities need to be implemented. You can find more information about FDDs and TDDs in the Microsoft documentation (*https://oreil.ly/hOpEt*).

Develop

In this phase, app makers and professional developers start doing app configurations using low-code, no-code components and, if required, write code to customize applications. Along with this work, developers are also responsible for conducting a sanity check of the feature they developed to ensure it is aligned with the proposed solution design (which was finalized in the design phase) and project timelines (which were proposed in the analysis phase).

Test

In this phase, the testing team conducts functional and feature testing of the solution. If they find problems, they assign them to the development team, which fixes the issue and assigns it back to the testing team. This back-and-forth process goes on until all issues are fixed and the testing team signs off on the project.

Deploy

In this phase, the project team finalizes the go-live checklist, sets up the production environment, deploys the solution, and migrates master/configuration data to that environment. Training end users about the new application and preparing user manuals is also included in this phase.

Operate

This is the phase where you fix the post go-live issues and provide on-going support, which includes activities that continue through any future involvement with the customer after the project is completed.

To successfully implement any project, every project team member—whether they are a pre-sales consultant, business analyst, functional consultant, solution architect, low-code, no-code developer, professional developer, tester, DevOps engineer, or support team member—needs to work collaboratively.

Implementing the App

Before commencing development work, all Power Apps developers must be aware of the implementation methodology that is being used in the project. For the purposes of this model-driven app case study, I will concentrate only on the development phase of project implementation.

As you have already learned about model-driven apps, canvas apps, and their features in earlier chapters, I will not go over how to design the app's components in this chapter. Instead, I will concentrate on what business logic is needed in each component to meet the business requirements.

Step 1: Prerequisites

To get started with the Power Apps model-driven app implementation, you need to perform the following prerequisite activities.

Create an Azure Account and Work Account

You must have an active Microsoft Entra ID account to proceed with the Power Apps implementation or learn Power Platform. If you don't have a work account, you can create a test tenant using the Microsoft 365 Developer Program (*https://oreil.ly/ XMDXq*) or manually create one yourself (*https://oreil.ly/lBYtD*).

Set Up the Power Platform Environment

Once you have set up an Azure account and work account, it's time to create a Power Platform environment to start creating resources and components for your model-driven app implementation. The Power Apps Developer Plan (*https://oreil.ly/JD2gC*) gives you a free development environment in which to build and test your Power Apps components and Microsoft Dataverse. I have already given an overview and explained the steps to create this account in Chapter 3. You can also follow the Microsoft documentation (*https://oreil.ly/GIHzq*) to get step-by-step instructions to create your developer environment.

If you already have a Power Platform environment and want to create your Power Apps developer environment there, go to the Power Platform admin center (*https:// oreil.ly/VExT9*), select Environments from the left panel, and click New from the command bar to create a new environment of type Developer, as shown in Figure 13-2.

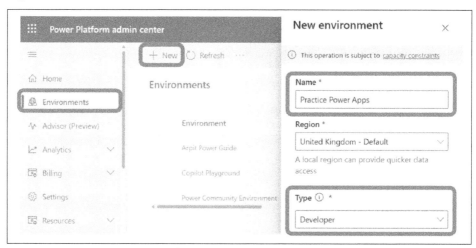

Figure 13-2. Creating a Power Platform developer environment

Once the environment is created, it can have only one Dataverse database, which serves as a container to store Power Apps, business data, flows, chatbots, security, etc. Additionally, it offers security to maintain the segregation of your components from those in other environments.

 It is advised that you set up two developer environments for this implementation (for example, Book My Service Guide and Book My Service Dev). In Book My Service Guide, you will import my version of the solution (which we'll discuss in the next step), which you can use as a guide to begin developing your own solution components. And in Book My Service Dev, you will create your own solution, app, and its related components.

Import the PowerAppsBookLiveProject Solution

I have created a solution called *PowerAppsBookLiveProject.zip*, where I have already created a model-driven app called Book My Service and its related components. You can download this solution from my GitHub (*https://oreil.ly/pvoZI*) repository and import it into the Book My Service Guide environment.

From here on, please refer to the solution in this book's GitHub repository for assistance with any configuration and customization you will do in the Book My Service Dev environment for app development.

Step 2: Create Publisher and Solution

Once the environment is set up, it's time to start creating your app components, which require a solution. To create a solution, first navigate to the Power Apps home page (*https://oreil.ly/WlAha*). Choose the Book My Service Dev environment from the list in the upper-right and select Solutions from the left panel. Then, select "New solution" from the command bar.

You can't create a solution before creating a publisher to uniquely identify your organization's specific components. So, click on "New publisher" in the pop-up window. Fill out the publisher details as per your own or your organization's choice. Consider the Prefix value carefully, as this will determine the schema name of your new components. For example, if the prefix value is "arp" then the component name will be arp_componentname, as shown in Figure 13-3.

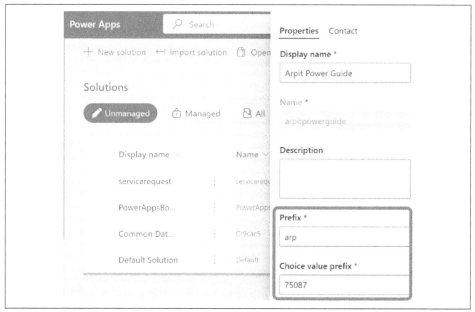

Figure 13-3. Creating a publisher

While creating a new publisher, you can also configure the "Choice value prefix," as shown in Figure 13-3. This number is used when you add options in the Choice column. For example, if you set the "Choice value prefix" to "75087" and create a new Choice column with three Option labels A, B, C, and D, then the Option values would be 750870000, 750870001, 750870002, and 750870003, as shown in Figure 13-4.

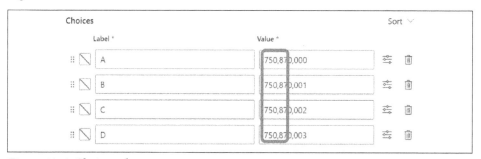

Figure 13-4. Choice values

After you create your publisher, select it in the pop-up dialog that appears when you create a new solution. Enter additional information about your solution, as shown in Figure 13-5. When you create a solution, you also have the option to set the Configuration Page (under More options). Here, you can display a custom page or HTML web resource to show information about your solution, installation instructions, or usage guidelines. This is particularly useful when you are creating an ISV solution or publishing your solution in AppSource (*https://oreil.ly/qwSoT*). For the purposes of this implementation, I am leaving it set to None. Finally, click Create to finish creating your solution.

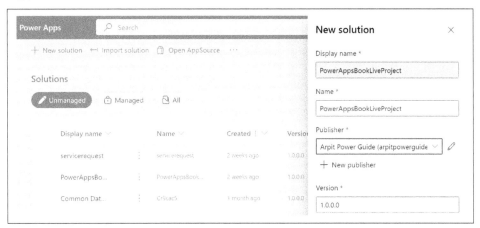

Figure 13-5. Creating a solution

Step 3: Design Data Model

Now that you are all set with the groundwork, it's time to set up the foundation for your Power Apps with data modeling. Data modeling defines the tables, columns, relationships, and metadata to store your customers' and organization's data and make relationships between them. This data will then be used further in various app components to perform various operations.

We are using the following tables in our app:

Case (custom)
> A case typically represents an incident, complaint, escalation, or feedback that's submitted by a customer and that requires an action or resolution. I have created this as a custom table, because I am not using the Dynamics 365 Customer Service app (*https://oreil.ly/vs7pH*), which has a built-in Case table and creates other customer service-related tables in the Dataverse, for my app implementation.

Contact (out-of-the-box)
> A contact typically represents an individual or a customer to whom you are providing service. Here, I will store information about customers who are reporting an incident.

Account (out-of-the-box)
> An Account table typically stores company information. Here, I will store the company information of the customer who is reporting an incident.

Knowledge Articles (out-of-the-box)
> The Knowledge Articles table stores the articles and documentation about the most common issues, product features, answers to frequently asked questions, product briefs, and more. Service agents can benefit from them to solve customer issues.

Queue (out-of-the-box)
> Queue is a centralized list of pending work items such as cases and tasks that need attention. Every user in Dataverse has a queue to which they assign work items to act on. Here I will assign or escalate cases to various team members' queues so they can take various actions like order return and refund approvals.

Activities (out-of-the-box)
> Activities are used to plan, track, and organize all your customer communications, such as take notes, send email, make phone calls, and set up appointments. I will use activities to communicate with customers, for example, setting up an appointment to meet at the customer location to fix an issue.

I've used many out-of-the-box tables in the app. To keep the app simple, I will mostly use the Contact and Case tables during implementation. And I have customized only the Case table; the rest of the tables remain as is. Several tables (like Accounts, Queue, Knowledge Articles, and Activities) are included solely for your reference; you can use these to extend the app for additional practice.

Make sure you have created the Case table and its columns before moving to the next section. You can either download the complete metadata of the Case table from my GitHub repository (*https://oreil.ly/pvoZI*) or refer to the final case study solution.

Step 4: Design Security Model

The first thing you should do after setting up a data model is to set up the security and decide who will do what in the application. There are three categories of security to configure: Power Platform environment resources, Dataverse data, and the Power Apps model-driven app.

Securing Power Platform Environment Resources

Once you create a new Power Platform environment, there are many built-in resources and components created automatically in your environment. It's important to secure them so that unauthorized users in your organization can't access them.

Environment-level security can be configured using security groups and security roles:

Security groups

Security groups will not let any user with an appropriate license log in to the environment if they are not a member of the security group designated for that environment. Security groups can't be assigned to *default* and *developer* environments.

Security roles

Security roles will not let any user create or customize any resources or components of an environment if they don't have either System Administrator (to perform all administrative actions) or System Customizer (to create various resources and components) roles.

 Environments have preconfigured security roles: Environment Admin and Environment Maker. These preconfigured security roles adhere to the security best practice of "minimum required access," providing the bare minimum of business data that a user requires to operate an app.

In an environment without a Dataverse database, Environment Maker and Environment Admin are the only predefined roles. Since we'll be using Dataverse, these roles are not applicable to our case study.

In an environment with a Dataverse database, a user must be assigned the System Administrator role instead of the Environment Admin role to have full admin privileges. And, users who make apps that connect to the database and need to create or update entities and security roles must have the System Customizer role in addition to the Environment Maker role because the Environment Maker role doesn't have privileges on the environment's data.

For this implementation, you can create a new user and designate it as the Administrator of your environment by giving it the System Administrator and System Customizer role. This will allow that user to carry out all administrative tasks and create new resources and components.

Securing Dataverse Data

Once you have configured the environment-level security, it's time to secure your organization and customer data stored in Dataverse. Dataverse data is stored in the form of tables, which can only be secured using security roles, as we discussed in Chapter 2. For this implementation, I have created six new security roles:

L1 Support User
> These users will be the initial point of contact when customers seek technical assistance. Their primary responsibility is to handle basic queries and common issues.

L2 Support User
> These users will handle the issues beyond basic troubleshooting. They have a deeper knowledge of systems and applications. L1 Support Users assign or escalate complex issues to L2 Support Users.

L3 Support User
> These users are the most advanced technical support users, who have deep technical knowledge and expertise in troubleshooting. L2 Support Users assign or escalate cases to L3 Support Users when there is a very challenging issue.

Service Manager
> This role is responsible for reviewing cases of type "order return & refund" and providing necessary approvals.

Finance Manager
> This role is responsible for reviewing order refund requests and providing approval or rejection. On approval, the payments will be processed.

Field Service Agent
> This role will only be provided to service agents who work in the field and visit customer locations to resolve their issues. These service agents will use mobile/tablet apps to access the data, which I will discuss in the next chapter.

To create these security roles, go to the Power Platform admin center (*https://oreil.ly/yVm8T*) and select Environments from the left panel. Open your environment and click on "Security Roles (see all)" from the Access panel. Search for "Basic User" in the security role list, choose the role, click Copy from the command bar, and then provide the new role name, "L1 Support User," as shown in Figure 13-6. This will create a clone of the Basic User role that you can now modify per your business needs.

Since creating a custom role from scratch is very time-consuming and potentially risky because you do not know what permissions are needed to provide access to some necessary and built-in features of Power Apps, it's a good idea to create a copy of an existing role that is similar to what you want. By creating a copy, you only need to worry about providing access to the tables that you are using in your app.

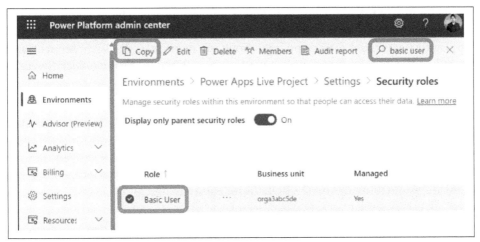

Figure 13-6. Copying the Basic User role to create a new role

Securing the Power Apps Model-Driven App

Restricting users at the app level is a common business requirement. For example, in our implementation, the Support Department and the Sales Department use the same environment, but the Support Department is only responsible for providing support-related activities for the products that are sold by the Sales Department. Each department uses the same environment and Dataverse, but they use different model-driven apps. As a result, sometimes providing security at the environment and Dataverse level is not enough to secure your app. You need to specifically decide which users or teams can access your app within the organization.

Before sharing a model-driven app with other members of your organization, it needs to be created or made available within your environment. I'll walk you through the detailed steps to share the app in the next section.

Step 5: Design the Model-Driven App

You set up your environment, created a solution, and designed the data and security model. Now it's time to design the model-driven app, Book My Service, for the service agents, service managers, and finance managers who will access this app from either desktop or laptop from stores to provide technical assistance to customers.

To design Book My Service, go to the Power Apps home page, click Solution from the left panel, and open your solution. Then click New from the command bar, select App, and select model-driven app, enter your app name (e.g., Book My Service), and provide a description (optional) in the pop-up box. When you're done, click Create to create your model-driven app.

As discussed previously, to share the model-driven app with a specific user or team, first you need to define the security role that will have access to the app at the model-driven app level. To do that, first run your app, then click on the app name from the top-left corner. A pop-up window will display all model-driven apps available in your environment. Click on the three dots (...) from the top-right corner of the Book My Service app and select MANAGE ROLES (see Figure 13-7).

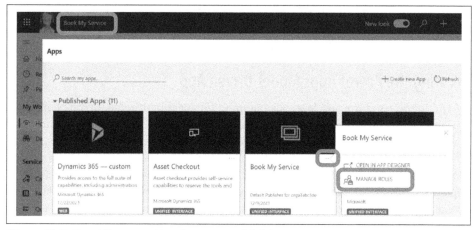

Figure 13-7. Providing security roles to a model-driven app

Choose the desired security roles from the list, as shown in Figure 13-8.

To share the app, choose the Book My Service app from the solution and click on Share from the command bar. This will open the window where you can search for the user or group with whom you want to share the app and assign them the appropriate security roles so that they can use your app (see Figure 13-9).

Figure 13-8. Assigning security roles to a model-driven app

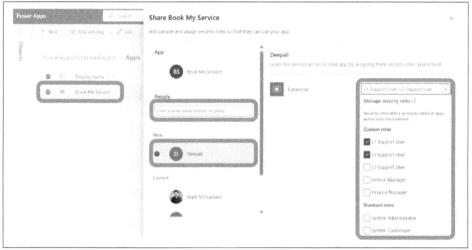

Figure 13-9. Sharing a model-driven app with other users in the organization and providing them with security roles

Step 6: Create Model-Driven App Components

Once you click Create to create your model-driven app, you will be taken to the app designer page, where you can design your app by adding pages, views, forms in the site map, and other app components. Table 13-1 provides a brief summary of the components we are going to create and their purpose in the Book My Service app.

Table 13-1. Book My Service components and their purpose

Component	Purpose
Site map	Design the left navigation panel of Book My Service.
Forms	Design a Case form to enter information about a particular incident that a customer is reporting via email, phone call, visiting the store, website, chatbot, etc.
Views	Create views for the Case table to display the list of case data and provide users with the ability to filter, sort, and search cases based on various conditions.
Business process flow	Create a business process flow to ensure that service agents are entering data consistently and following the same steps every time they work with a customer.
Business rules	Create a business rule to make the Order No field mandatory on the Case form when the case type field value is either Order Delivery or Return & Refund.
Command bar	Create custom commands (toolbar buttons) on the command bar—Resolve, Reopen, On-Hold, etc. Write Power Fx expressions to perform various operations within the app.
JavaScript	Switch business process flows on the click of a command bar button, depending on the customer's request.
Low-code plug-in	Prevent service agents from creating a contact with a duplicate email address.
Pages	Create two custom pages: a landing page for Book My Service and a dialog pop-up, where the service manager will enter request details to send to the finance team for approval.
Dashboard	Create a multi-stream dashboard called Customer Service Hub to give a broad overview to service managers and agents of customer service experience.
Web API	Read the customer type from the Contacts table on the Case form and prioritize the case accordingly.
Plug-in assemblies and steps	Create a plug-in that prevents service agents from resolving cases that have any open child cases.
Power Automate flow	Write a Power Automate flow to send approval requests to the finance team in Microsoft Teams.
Environment variable	Store configuration data that can change in the future or across environments.

Let's create each of these components in the Book My Service app.

Site Map

First, let's design the site map (the left navigation panel). I won't go into more details about how to add pages, views, and forms to the site map using the site map designer, as I have already discussed this in Chapter 6. Once the site map is designed, the app will look as shown in Figure 13-10.

You won't be able to add all the necessary components to the site map at this stage because some, such as the dashboard, haven't been created yet. So for the time being, you can set any default component to those pages, and you can update the site map with newly created components later on.

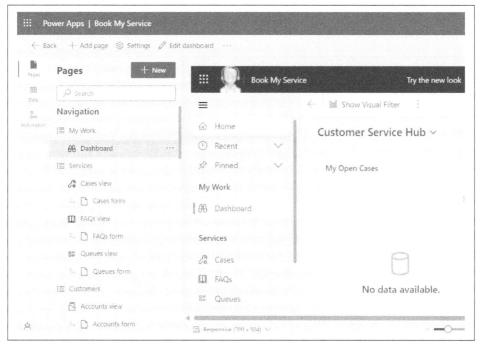

Figure 13-10. Designing the site map using app designer

I have added the groups and pages listed in Table 13-2 to the site map.

Table 13-2. Groups and pages added to the site map of the model-driven app

Group name	Pages	Component name	Page type
My Work	Dashboard	Customer Service Hub	Dashboard
Services	Cases	Case (custom table)	Dataverse table
	FAQs	Knowledge Article	Dataverse table
	Queues	Queue (OOB)	Dataverse table
Customers	Accounts	Account (OOB)	Dataverse table
	Contacts	Contact (OOB)	Dataverse table
Interactions	Appointments	Appointment (OOB)	Dataverse table
	Emails	Email Messages (OOB)	Dataverse table
	Phone Calls	Phone Call (OOB)	Dataverse table

Forms

In this section, you will design a Case form to enter information about a particular incident that a customer is reporting. Make sure you have already created the Case table and all its relevant fields (discussed in "Step 3: Design Data Model" on page 475) before you start designing the form.

For this implementation, I have updated the automatically created form called "Information (Main form)." To design this form, first open the form in the form editor and add all required form controls like Tabs, Sections, Fields, Subgrid, and Quick View on the form. I will not go into further detail on how to design the form; instead, you can view its design by referring to the completed app. The form will look similar to that shown in Figure 13-11.

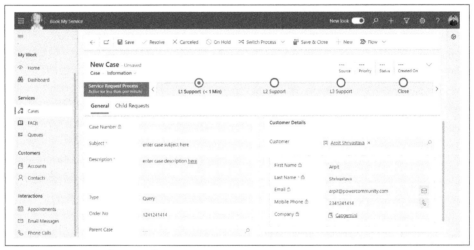

Figure 13-11. Case form in the app

Sometimes you have multiple forms or some unwanted forms of a particular table that you don't want to appear in the app despite the user having access. You can remove these (or add other forms) from your app designer by clicking on the three dots (…) next to the form name and selecting Remove (from "In this app" section) to remove the form from the app or Add (in the "Not in this app" section) to add the form in the app, as shown in Figure 13-12.

For example, if you have installed Power Pages and created additional forms specifically for the Power Pages website, and you don't want internal app users to see these forms, you can remove them from your model-driven application.

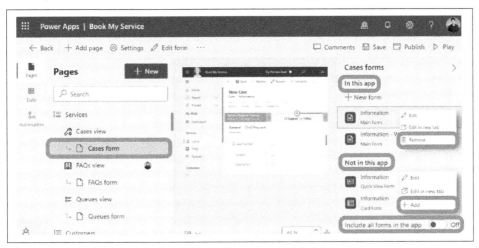

Figure 13-12. Adding or removing forms from the model-driven app

Views

In this section, you will create some views for the Case table to display the list of case data and provide users with the ability to filter, sort, and search the cases based on various conditions.

Create new views

To create a view for a Case table, first you need to go to your solution. From there, you can create a new view from scratch by clicking on View from the command bar, or you can create a new view from an existing view by opening any existing view, selecting Save As, and giving it a new name. Creating views from existing views is often helpful when you have already created views with columns, complex filter criteria, sorting, etc. and now you want to create another view with exactly the same configuration except different filter criteria with different columns.

For this implementation, you need to create the following two views by copying the Active Cases view:

- My Open Cases will display all cases with a status of In Progress, More Information Requested, On Hold, Under Approval, as shown in Figure 13-13.

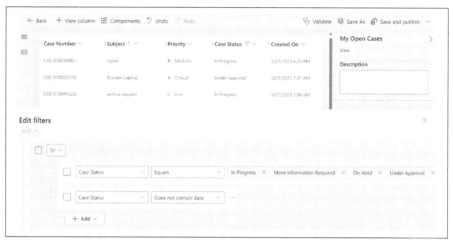

Figure 13-13. My Open Cases

- My Closed Cases will display all cases with a status of Rejected or Resolved, as shown in Figure 13-14.

Figure 13-14. My Closed Cases

As with forms, sometimes you may have some extra or unwanted views that you don't want to show to app users. You can go to the app designer and remove them as you did with the forms, choosing "Cases view" in the site map rather than "Cases form," as shown in Figure 13-15.

For example, if you have Power Pages installed and have created some additional views just for the Power Pages site that you do not want internal app users to see, you can remove the views from your model-driven apps.

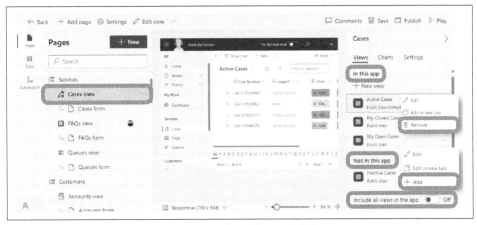

Figure 13-15. Adding or removing views from the model-driven app

Add components to the views

It would be useful for users to be able to highlight cases with different colors in the view based on their priority and status. To do that, first I need to add color codes to the Priority and Case Status columns, as shown in Figures 13-16 and 13-17.

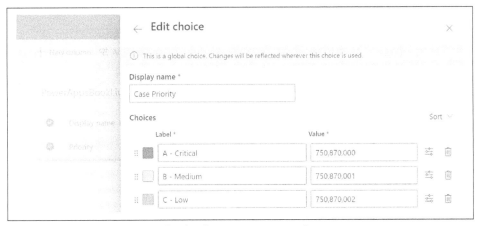

Figure 13-16. Setting color codes for the Case Priority column

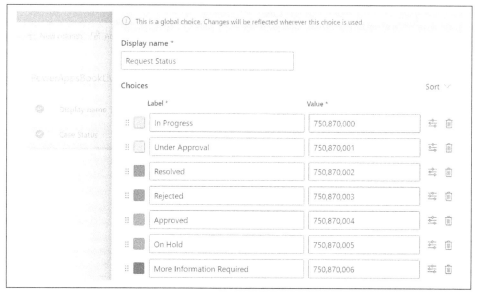

Figure 13-17. Setting color codes for the Case Status column

Once colors are added to the column, add a Power Apps grid control to the views to change the look and feel. Click on Components from the command bar in the view editor, then click on "Add a component" → "Get more components," search for "power apps grid" in the search bar, and click Add to add the control in your control list, as shown in Figure 13-18.

Figure 13-18. Adding the Power Apps grid control

Now the Power Apps grid control will appear in the list. Click on that control and select Cases in the Table drop-down and My Open Cases in the View drop-down, as shown in Figure 13-19. Additionally, you need to enable all property values to "Yes" in the pop-up box. You can find more information about the properties of the Power Apps grid control from the Microsoft documentation (*https://oreil.ly/edHrh*).

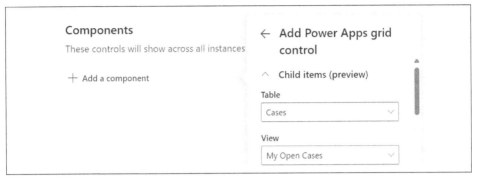

Figure 13-19. Power Apps grid control added in the control list

Once you add the Power Apps grid control to your view, run the Book My Service app. Your view should look like Figure 13-20.

Figure 13-20. Applying Power Apps grid control to the view

Business Process Flow

In this section, you will create a business process flow (BPF) to ensure that service agents are entering data consistently and following the same steps every time while working with customers. For this implementation, I have created two BPFs:

Service Request Process
> This flow will have a guided flow and steps to resolve common customer queries and issues.

Return & Refund Process
> This flow will have a guided flow and steps to resolve only those customer complaints related to the order return and refund process. This process requires an

approval from the service manager and finance manager; therefore, it requires a separate business process flow.

You could use a common BPF to handle both processes by changing the steps conditionally based on the case type. But for this implementation, I have created two flows so that later I can switch them to use JavaScript.

Create business process flow

To create a new BPF, go to your solution, click on +New from the command bar, then select Automation → Process → Business Process Flow. This will open the business process flow designer screen. Change the BPF name to Service Request Process. Then add the following four stages and added steps and fields within them, as shown in Figure 13-21. You can add more fields if you want:

L1 Support
    Add data step and add field Escalate to L2.

L2 Support
    Add data step and add field Escalate to L3.

L3 Support
    Add data step and add field Resolution Comments.

Close
    Add data step and add fields Notify Customer and Case Status.

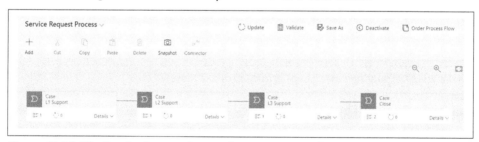

Figure 13-21. The Service Request Process business process flow

Once the BPF and its stages are created, you need to activate the BPF to use it in the app.

Similarly, I have created another BPF called Return & Refund Process and added the following fields in each stage of this BPF, as shown in Figure 13-22. You can add more fields if you like:

L1 Support
    Add data step and add field Escalate to Manager.

Service Manager
Add data step and add field Assign to Finance Team.

Finance Team
Add data step and add fields Payment Processed, Resolution Comments, and Rejection Reason.

Close
Add data step and add fields Notify Customer and Case Status.

Figure 13-22. The Return & Refund Process business process flow

Add business process flow to your model-driven app

Business process flows will not be shown on the Case form, unless you add them to your model-driven app. To do this, edit the Book My Service app in app designer, then click on Automation from the left panel. Here you can Add or Remove the business process flow, as shown in Figure 13-23.

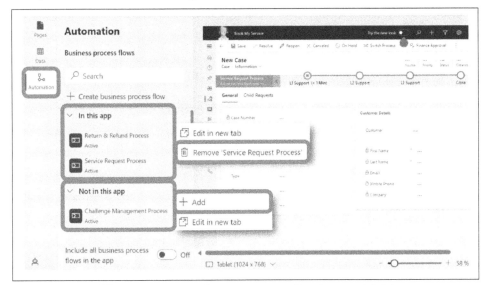

Figure 13-23. Adding or removing a business process flow in a model-driven app

Finally, if you run your app, the business process flow should look like Figure 13-24.

Figure 13-24. Business process flow in a live app

Later in this chapter, I will show you how to change the business process flows to be activated by a button click on the command bar.

Business Rules

In this section, you will write business rules to perform client-side validation. In our implementation, you need to create a business rule to make the Order No field mandatory on the Case form when the case type field's value is either Order Delivery or Return & Refund, as shown in Figure 13-25.

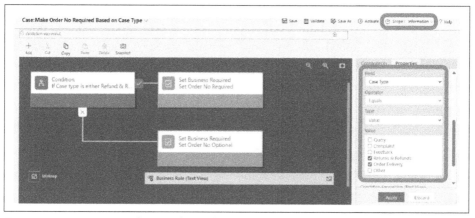

Figure 13-25. Business rule to make Order No field mandatory based on case type

Command Bar (Toolbar) Design

In this section, you will create custom commands (buttons) on the command bar and write Power Fx expressions to perform various operations within the app. For this implementation, I have created the following commands for the Case form:

Resolve
> To change case status to Resolved

Reopen
To change case status back to In Progress

Cancel
To change case status to Canceled

On Hold
To change case status to On Hold

Switch Process
- Service Request to switch to the Service Request Process business process flow
- Return & Refund to switch to the Return & Refund Process business process flow

Create commands

To create new commands, edit the Book My Service app in app designer and click on the three dots (...) next to Cases view from the site map, and then select "Edit command bar" → "Edit in new tab," as shown in Figure 13-26.

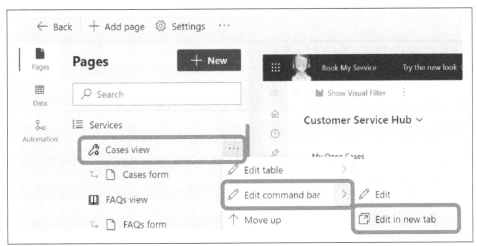

Figure 13-26. Opening the command bar designer from app designer for the Case table

Add the highlighted commands on the Main form of the Case form, as shown in Figure 13-27.

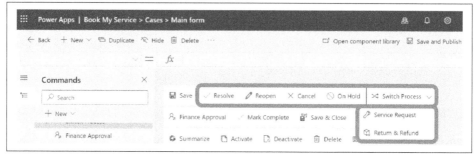

Figure 13-27. Add new commands on the Main form of the Case form

Power Fx expression to perform action on command bar

You need to write the Power Fx expressions shown in Table 13-3 to perform actions when a command is clicked by the user.

Table 13-3. Power Fx expressions for commands on the Case form

Command name	Purpose	Formula on `Action` property	Formula on `Visibility` property
Resolve	Change the case status to Resolved and the status to Inactive. Then, display a success message.	`Patch(Cases, Self.Selected. Item, {'Case Status': 'Request Status'.Resolved}, {Status:'Status (Cases)'.Inac tive});Notify("Case is Resolved",Notification Type.Success,5000);`	`Self.Selected.Item. 'Case Status'<> 'Request Status'. Resolved`
Reopen	Change the case status to In Progress and the status to Active. Then, display a success message.	`Patch(Cases, Self.Selected. Item, {'Case Status': 'Request Status'.'In Progress'},{Status:'Status (Cases)'.Active}); Notify("Case is Reopened", NotificationType.Success, 5000);`	`Self.Selected.Item. 'Case Status'= 'Request Status'. Resolved`
Cancel	Change the case status to Rejected and the status to Inactive. Then, display a success message.	`Patch(Cases, Self.Selected. Item, {'Case Status': 'Request Status'.Rejected}, {Status:'Status (Cases)'.Inac tive});Notify("Case is rejected",Notification Type.Success,5000);`	`Self.Selected.Item. 'Case Status'= 'Request Status'. Rejected`

Command name	Purpose	Formula on `Action` property	Formula on `Visibility` property

On Hold	Change the case status to On Hold and the status to Inactive. Then, display a success message.	`Patch(Cases, Self.Selected.`
		`Item, {'Case Status':`
		`'Request Status'.'On Hold'},`
		`{Status:'Status (Cases)'.Inac`
		`tive});Notify("Case is`
		`rejected",Notification`
		`Type.Success,5000);`
			`Self.Selected.Item.`
			`'Case Status'=`
			`'Request Status'.`
			`'On Hold'`

Call a JavaScript function from the command bar

Power Fx expressions are quite powerful and enable you to write business logic using low-code, Excel-based expressions. However, this feature still has some limitations and is not suited for writing advanced or complex business logic—for that we need JavaScript. In our implementation, you need to write JavaScript code to be able to switch the business process flows on the click of a command bar button. Specifically, you need to perform the following steps to call a JavaScript function from the command bar:

1. Refer to the web resource Service Request Script in the completed app or download the JavaScript file directly from my GitHub repository (*https://oreil.ly/ pvoZI*).

2. Go to your solution and create a new web resource of JavaScript type and upload this JavaScript file.

3. This JavaScript file has code for some other functionality that I will discuss in a later section. But for switching the business process flow, you need to focus only on the function `switchBPF(primaryControl, requestedProcessFlow)`. (This web resource and uploaded JavaScript file will remain the same throughout this app implementation.)

4. Call this JavaScript function from the command bar, as shown in Figure 13-28. This example shows only the Service Request command bar. You can follow the same steps for the Return & Refund command as well; just change the value of parameter 2 to Return & Refund.

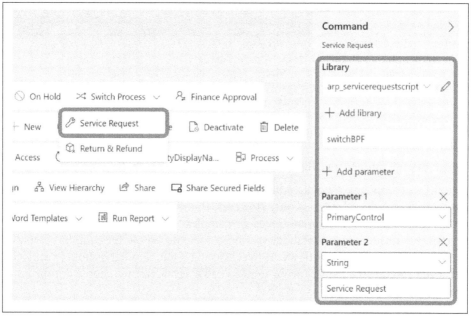

Figure 13-28. Calling a JavaScript function on the Service Request command bar

I have created one more command called Finance Approval on the Case form, which I'll use later to open a custom page as a pop-up dialog, where the service manager will enter details and send a request to the finance team for payment approval. I'll discuss this command in "Custom Pages" on page 498.

Low-Code Plug-in

As discussed earlier, data redundancy is one of the major business challenges for this retail company. To overcome this, you need to prevent service agents from creating duplicate data in the application. To do that, you'll write a low-code plug-in to prevent the creation of contacts with duplicate email addresses. This is a new feature (as of 2024) and has a lot of scope of improvement, but just to showcase the capabilities of it in our model-driven app, I have used this as well in my implementation.

Since I have already covered the detailed steps needed to create a low-code plug-in in Chapter 9, we'll just look at the plug-in configuration and business logic here. You need to register this plug-in on the PreOperation stage and trigger it on the Create event of the Contacts table, as shown in Figure 13-29.

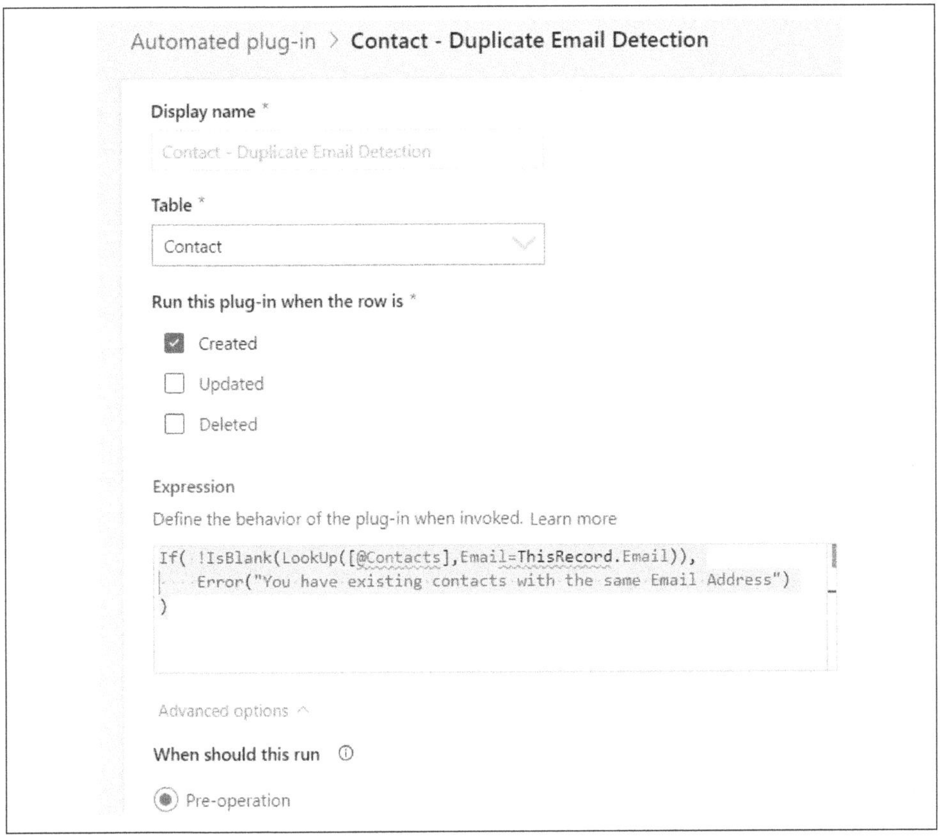

Figure 13-29. Automated low-code plug-in to restrict contact creation with a duplicate email address

I have written the following Power Fx expression to restrict contact creation when there is a duplicate email address:

```
If(!IsBlank(LookUp([@Contacts],Email=ThisRecord.Email)),
    Error("You have existing contacts with the same Email Address")
)
```

If you run the Book My Service app and try to create a contact using an already existing email address, you'll see the business process error shown in Figure 13-30.

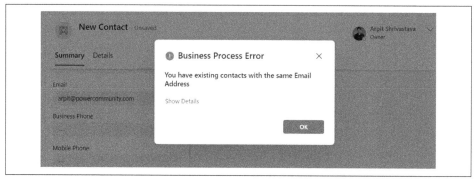

Figure 13-30. Business process error thrown by low-code plug-in

 As of this writing, low-code plug-ins (*https://oreil.ly/tiuiI*) are in preview, which means they aren't intended for production use and may have restricted functionality. If you are working on an actual project implementation, I don't recommend including low-code plug-ins in your solutions, as they may cause problems with other solution components.

Custom Pages

In this section, you will create custom pages for the following two purposes:

- A Welcome page to serve as the landing page for the Book My Service app
- A Finance Approval page, a pop-up dialog where the service manager will enter request details and send the item to the finance team for approval

Since I have already covered the steps to create a custom page in Chapter 7, I will not go into detail here; instead, I will explain the configuration of the page and the controls that I have added. You can refer to my final solution for detailed design steps to create the page from scratch.

Welcome page

The Welcome page has three screens, as shown in Figure 13-31:

Home screen
> Displays company's campaign videos (I have used Microsoft's Copilot videos for demonstration) along with Outlook emails and scheduled meetings for the logged-in app user

View Email screen
> Provides a detailed view of an email (subject, description, date) when an email is clicked from the email list on the Home screen

View Meeting screen

Provides a detailed view of a meeting (title, description, date) when a meeting is clicked from the meeting list on the Home screen

Figure 13-31. Custom page to design the landing page of the Book My Service app

Now open the Book My Service app in app designer and click on the three dots (...) next to the page name. Select "Move up" to move the page to the top, change its title to Home, and link this page with your custom page named Welcome Page, as shown in Figure 13-32.

Figure 13-32. Adding a custom page to the site map and changing its name

Finally, run the app to see the Welcome page on the landing screen of the Book My Service app, as shown in Figure 13-33.

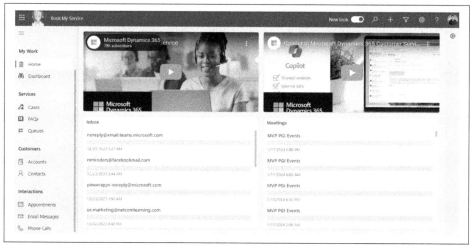

Figure 13-33. Book My Service landing page

Finance Approval page

The Finance Approval page has only a home screen, as shown in Figure 13-34. The purpose of this screen is to display a Text Input control for service managers to provide input, and a Button control labeled "Send for approval" to call Power Automate and pass as a parameter the service manager's input. This Power Automate flow sends the request for approval to the finance team in Microsoft Teams, waits for a response, and then updates the information back to the Case form whenever the finance team approves or rejects it with comments.

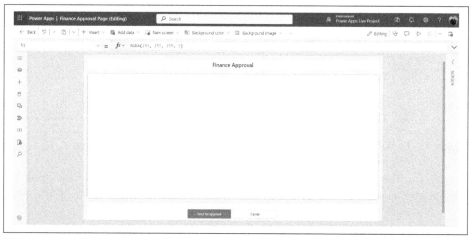

Figure 13-34. Custom page to design Finance Approval pop-up dialog page

To call this custom page when Finance Approval is clicked on the command bar, you need to perform the following two steps:

1. Go to your solution and open the web resource named Service Request Script that you created in the previous section. In this JavaScript file, you will find a function named `openApprovalPage(primaryControl)`. This function includes the name (schema name) of the custom page that you need to open from the command bar; ensure that it matches your custom page name.

2. Call the JavaScript function from the Finance Approval command bar, as shown in Figure 13-35. Here the `PrimaryControl` parameter is used to get the `formcon` text, which provides the control's information available on the form. Additionally, I have written the following Power Fx expression on the `Visible` property of the Finance Approval command to show the button only if the Case Status value is Under Review:

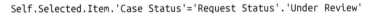

```
Self.Selected.Item.'Case Status'='Request Status'.'Under Review'
```

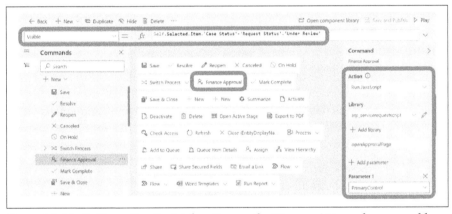

Figure 13-35. Calling a JavaScript function on the Finance Approval command bar to open a custom page

Now, when you run the Book My Service app, open any existing case whose status is Under Review, and you'll see the new Finance Approval command on the command bar. If you click on that command, you'll see a pop-up dialog in the center of the Case form, as shown in Figure 13-36.

Figure 13-36. The Finance Approval pop-up dialog

Later, we'll add functionality to call Power Automate when the "Send for approval" button is clicked.

Dashboard

In this section, you'll create a multi-stream dashboard called Customer Service Hub to give a broad overview to service managers and agents of the customer service experience as well as detailed reports on cases, appointments, and emails. To create the multi-stream dashboard, first you need to create the four charts shown in Figure 13-37.

You will get these charts in the *PowerAppsBoolLiveProject.zip* solution once you import it into your environment.

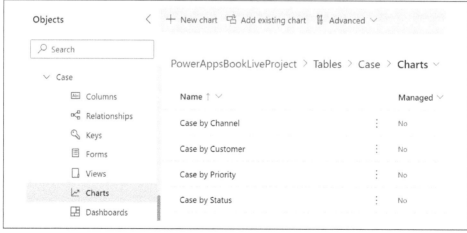

Figure 13-37. Charts created on Case table

Now, create a multi-stream dashboard (you'll find the option in the classic solution editor) and add the charts and multiple table views (streams), as shown in Figure 13-38.

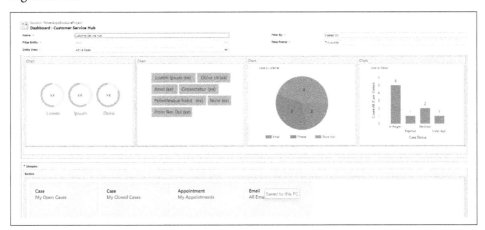

Figure 13-38. Add charts to the dashboard

Open the Book My Service app in the app designer and select Customer Service Hub dashboard on the Dashboard page in the site map, as shown in Figure 13-39.

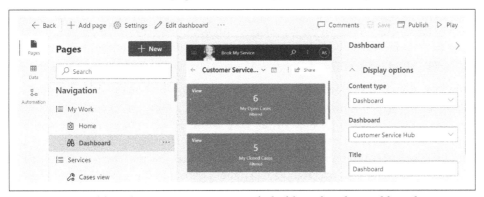

Figure 13-39. Adding the Customer Service Hub dashboard to the Dashboard page in site map

Finally, if you run the Book My Service app and click on Dashboard from the left panel, you will see the Customer Service Hub dashboard, as shown in Figure 13-40. You can filter the dashboard data using either the global filter (command bar) or the time filter (right top corner) as well.

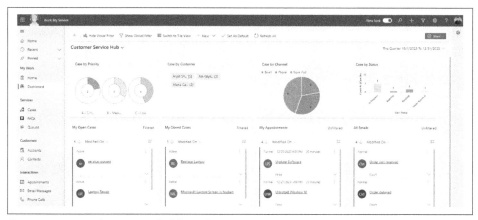

Figure 13-40. Multi-stream dashboard

Web API

One of the major business requirements of the retail company is to prioritize service for their premium customers.

To determine if a customer is Premium or Standard, I have added a column called Customer Type to the Contacts table. If the customer is Premium, I would like to notify service agents directly on the Case form so they can give priority to their customer's needs and offer benefits associated with premium service. To do this, you will need to write JavaScript code on the Case form and call the Dataverse Web API to get the value from the Customer Type column of the associated contact.

You have already downloaded the JavaScript file from the book's GitHub repository and created a web resource. Now you need to call the function `CheckPremiumCusto mer(executionContext)` on load of the Case form. To do that, go to your solution, expand Tables, expand Case, select Forms, open "Information form (Main)," and add the function `CheckPremiumCustomer` on load event of the form, as shown in Figure 13-41. I have also selected the Customer column in the Table Column Dependencies drop-down to lock the field on the form because my JavaScript function is dependent on that column, and I don't want it to be removed from the form accidentally.

Now when you run Book My Service and open any existing case record, you'll see a notification message on the top of the case's form, as shown in Figure 13-42.

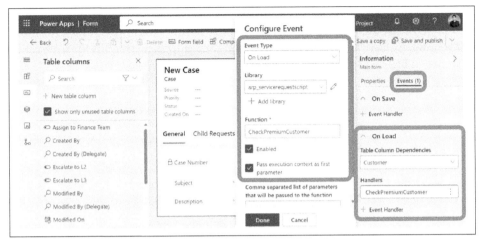

Figure 13-41. Adding a JavaScript function on load event of the Case form

Figure 13-42. Premium Customer Notification on Case form

Plug-in Assembly

Imagine the same customer raising an issue through multiple channels, such as web, phone, and email, or perhaps another customer raising an issue that has previously been raised by a different customer. Rather than capturing each issue as a separate case, you can create a parent case and link other similar cases to it (as child cases) for better tracking and maintainability. By doing this, you can reduce data redundancy and duplication. To this end, I've already made a self-referential relationship on the Case table by adding a Parent Case lookup field and a subgrid to show all child cases of any particular case.

In this section, you'll write plug-in code that prevents service agents from resolving cases that have open child cases.

I have already covered the steps to write and register a plug-in in Chapter 7. So for this implementation, you can download the plug-in code from my GitHub repository (*https://oreil.ly/pvoZI*), build it, and register it on the Update event of the Case table, as shown in Figure 13-43.

Figure 13-43. Registering a plug-in assembly

Also, select the Case Status column under the Filtering Attributes field so that it triggers only one update of that column, as shown in Figure 13-44.

Figure 13-44. Registering a plug-in on Update of the Case Status column

This plug-in will first retrieve the GUID of the case record that service agent is trying to resolve from the plug-in context:

```
Entity currentCaseRecord = (Entity)context.InputParameters["Target"];
```

Then, it adds a condition to execute the plug-in logic when the case status is changed to Resolved:

```
int caseStatus =
  currentCaseRecord.GetAttributeValue<OptionSetValue>("arp_casestatus").Value;
if (currentCaseRecord.LogicalName == "arp_case" && caseStatus == 750870002) {…}
```

Finally, write the fetch XML query (download using advanced find (*https://oreil.ly/vdUkA*)) to get all child cases of the case you got from the plug-in context. Then it checks the count and throws an error message if the count exceeds 0:

```
string fetchOpenRefundRequests = @"
<fetch version='1.0' mapping='logical' savedqueryid='11ede493-
  b00e-4fd4-89e7-592baaa46cc3' no-lock='false' distinct='true',
  <entity name='arp_case',
  <attribute name='statecode' />
  <attribute name='arp_name' />
  <attribute name='createdon' />
  <order attribute='arp_name' descending='false' />
  <attribute name='arp_casestatus' />
  <attribute name='arp_casenumber' />
  <attribute name='arp_caseid' />
  <filter type='and',
    <condition attribute='arp_parentcase' operator='eq' value='{" +
      currentCaseRecord.Id + @"}' uitype='arp_case' />
    <condition attribute='arp_casestatus' operator='in',
        <value>750870000</value>
        <value>750870001</value>
        <value>750870006</value>
        <value>750870005</value>
    </condition>
  </filter>
 </entity>
</fetch>";
EntityCollection result = service.RetrieveMultiple(new FetchExpression
  (fetchOpenRefundRequests));
int resultCount = result.Entities.Count;
if (resultCount, 0)
{
 throw new InvalidPluginExecutionException("This case cannot be closed because
   a refund request is still being processed");
}
```

 Some components, like tables, forms, views, web resources, dashboards, canvas apps, custom pages, and so on, must be published after they are created or updated. You must also publish the app if you are changing the app's components and design with app designer or editing commands with command bar designer.

Step 7: Power Automate

In this section, you'll write a Power Automate flow to send approval requests to the finance team in Microsoft Teams. When you imported *PowerAppsBookLiveProject.zip*, you got the Power Automate flow named Finance Team Approval Flow.

Power Automate Trigger and Actions

This Power Automate flow is being triggered from the Finance Approval Page custom page that we created, which will pass `CaseRecordId` and `Message` to the Power Automate flow and perform the following four actions in sequence, as shown in Figure 13-45:

1. Create an approval (using the Approvals connector (*https://oreil.ly/9hf9p*)). This step will create an approval request by providing details about the approval type, title, details, recipient, etc.

2. Post a message in a chat or channel (Teams connector). This step will send the approval request to the finance team via Microsoft Teams.

3. Wait for an approval (Approvals connector). This step will wait for the finance team to take action and either approve or reject the request.

4. Update case in Dataverse (Dataverse connector). Once a request is approved or rejected, this step updates the details in the Case record in Dataverse.

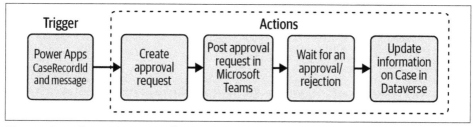

Figure 13-45. Power Automate flow trigger and actions

Trigger the Power Automate Flow from Finance Approval Page

After creating the Power Automate flow, navigate to your solution, select Pages from the left panel, and open the Finance Approval page; this will launch Power Apps Studio. Now, select Home Screen from the left panel and write the following Power Fx expression on the `OnVisible` property of the screen, to get the GUID of the case record from which the Finance Approval Page is being opened. This expression stores the Case record's GUID in the global variable named `CaseRecordId`:

```
Set(caseRecordId, Param("recordId"));
```

Now, add the Power Automate flow in the Finance Approval page by clicking on the Power Automate icon from the left panel and then clicking "Add flow." Once the flow is added to the page, call the `OnSelect` property of the "Send for approval" button, as shown in Figure 13-46.

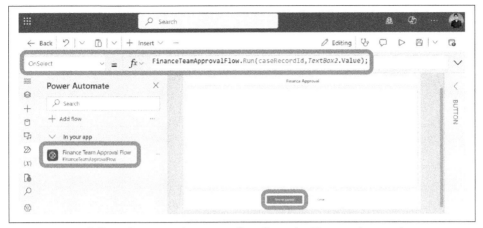

Figure 13-46. Calling the Power Automate flow from the Finance Approval page

Environment Variables

Environment variables are a great way to store configuration values in key-value pairs. For our app, the finance team email address and the URL of the Case record are good candidates for environment variables. The email address is used to send approval requests via Outlook or Teams. The URL is included in the request so that finance team members can quickly open the record to get more information.

These two details may change in the future or could be different across environments. Therefore, it's good to store them in environment variables, as shown in Figure 13-47.

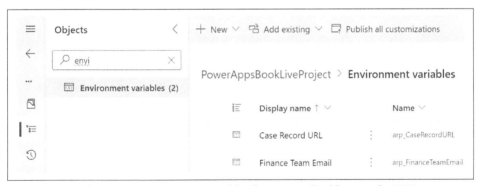

Figure 13-47. Creating environment variables for an email address and a URL

Figure 13-48 shows how environment variables are used in Power Automate.

Figure 13-48. Using environment variables in Power Automate

Summary

This chapter covered a real-world case study of a retail company and its current problem with providing customer support. You have learned different implementation methodologies to plan the Power Platform and Dynamics 365 project implementation. You have also created a model-driven app called Book My Service for the store workers, which included numerous low-code and no-code components to meet the business requirements and some code components to extend the app's functionality.

In the next chapter, I will show you how to create a canvas app called Service at Home for field service agents who visit customers' homes to resolve their problems.

CHAPTER 14

Canvas App Case Study

In the previous chapter, I walked you through the prerequisite activities and implementation steps to create a model-driven app solution for a retail company. This model-driven app was designed to assist support agents who work in stores and handle customer queries and complaints over the phone, email, or in stores.

This chapter is a continuation, where I will walk you through creating a canvas app called Service at Home for the field service agents who frequently travel to customer locations to deliver orders, set up and install electronic devices, and resolve issues. To keep this app simple, it will only have six screens:

- A Login screen to allow field service agents and service managers to log in to the app
- A Case screen to view all cases assigned to a field service agent
- A Contact screen to view information about the customer who has created a case
- A Map screen to view a map to the customer location, along with information about estimated travel distance and time
- A Case Approval screen where service managers can view all cases assigned to them for approvals
- A Success screen to display a success message once the service manager approves or rejects a case

Step 1: Prerequisites

To get started with the implementation, make sure that you have already opened the canvas app, which is available in the PowerAppsBookLiveProject solution (*https://oreil.ly/gtQld*), in Power Apps Studio.

Step 2: Create a Canvas App and Case Screen

As you learned in Chapters 3 and 8, there are plenty of ways to create a canvas app. You can create an app from a blank screen, from data, from templates, or using Microsoft Copilot. For this implementation, I will create an app from data, since I already have the data available in my Dataverse tables, as shown in Figure 14-1.

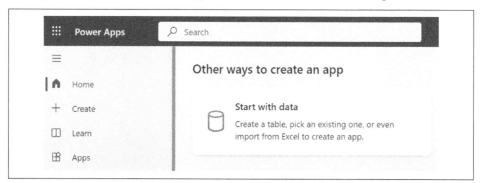

Figure 14-1. Creating a canvas app with Dataverse data

Once you click on the "Start with data" option, you will be taken to the page where you need to choose "Select an existing table," since you already have Case, Contact, and other tables in your Dataverse. Then, you need to choose your table (I have selected Case) from the list and click the "Create app" button to start creating a canvas app using data stored in the Case table, as shown in Figure 14-2.

Figure 14-2. Creating an app using the Case table

Once your canvas app is created, a new screen, MainScreen1, will be created automatically in your app connected to the Case table. Rename this screen to Case Screen, as shown in Figure 14-3.

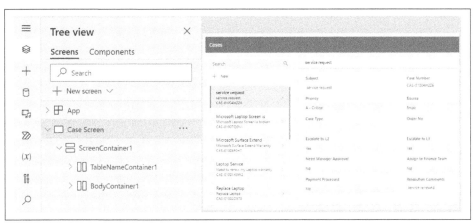

Figure 14-3. Main screen (automatically created) in canvas app

Step 3: Create Canvas App Components

I will create five more screens and a couple of controls in the canvas app to add some more features.

Contact Screen

In this section, I will add a new screen called Contact Screen to display the Contacts in the app. Service agents can navigate to the Contact screen to get detailed information like phone number, email address, and address for a contact who has initiated a case.

I want the look and feel of this screen to be similar to that of the Case screen, so I will create it by duplicating the Case screen instead of designing a new screen from scratch.

To duplicate the Case screen, click on the three dots (…) next to the screen name and select Duplicate Screen. This will create a duplicate of the Case screen, which you can then rename to Contact Screen.

Now, to connect this screen to the Contacts table, do the following:

1. Add the Contacts table to the app, as shown in Figure 14-4.

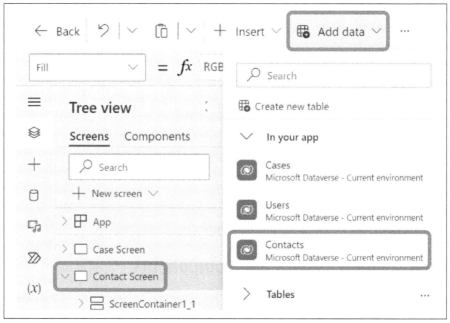

Figure 14-4. Add Contacts table to the app

2. Add the following Power Fx expression on the `Items` property of a Gallery control, as shown in Figure 14-5. This expression will search for the contact in the specified columns (firstname, emailaddress1, lastname, fullname) based on the input provided in the SearchInput control:

```
Search([@Contacts], SearchInput1_1.Text, "firstname","emailaddress1",
    "lastname","fullname")
```

Additionally, add the following expression on the `OnSelect` property of the Gallery control:

```
UpdateContext({itemSelected: true, CurrentItem: ThisItem })
```

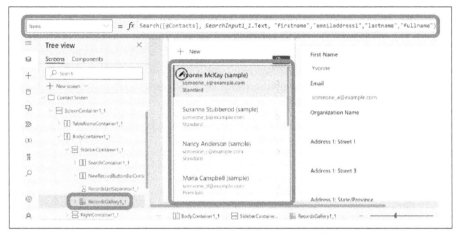

Figure 14-5. Add expression on the `Items` property of a Gallery control

3. Set Contacts on the `DataSource` property of the Form control, as shown in Figure 14-6.

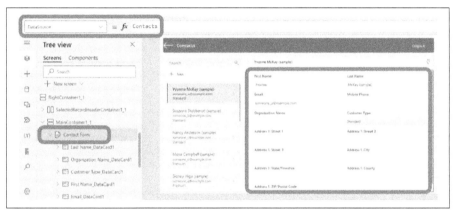

Figure 14-6. Setting Contacts on the `DataSource` property of the Form control in the Contact screen

4. Once you change the data source from Cases to Contacts, you will see an error on the form because it still shows the case columns in the DataCards. To replace the case DataCards with the contact DataCards, select the form again, click on Edit Fields from the right panel, and remove all fields one by one by clicking on the three dots (…) and selecting Remove. Once you've removed all fields, add the Contacts table's fields, as shown in Figure 14-7.

Additionally, set `'Contact List'.Selected` to the `Item` property of the Form control.

Figure 14-7. Adding Contact fields on the form

5. Now, add the following Power Fx expression on the Text property of the Label control, added on the header of the screen, as shown in Figure 14-8. This Power Fx expression is used to get the display name of the Dataverse table:

```
DataSourceInfo([@Contacts], DataSourceInfo.DisplayName)
```

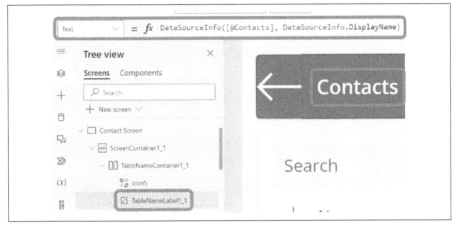

Figure 14-8. Changing the Text property of the Label control

 If you still have any error or confusion after following these instructions, refer to *PowerAppsBookLiveProject.zip*, edit the Service at Home app in Power Apps Studio, and check all the Power Fx expressions with respect to a particular control there.

Map Screen

In this section, you will create a Map screen in the Service at Home app to provide a route map for field service agents traveling to a customer location. The field service agents will be able to enter their source and destination addresses on this screen, and a map will display the route, estimated time of arrival, and estimated distance.

You must first make sure that the Full toggle is turned on under "Map and address services" in the Power Platform admin center, as shown in Figure 14-9. Otherwise, you will get error message "Routes cannot be shown. To show them, enable full map and address services in the admin center."

Figure 14-9. Enabling full map and address services

Then, perform the following steps to create the Map screen in the canvas app:

1. Add a new screen of "Header and footer" type and name it Map Screen, as shown in Figure 14-10.

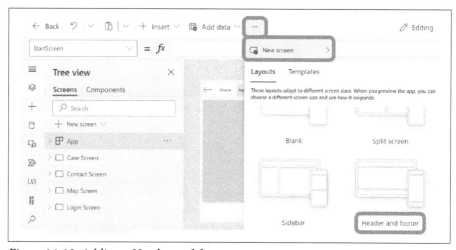

Figure 14-10. Adding a Header and footer screen

2. Add the following controls to the HeaderContainer, as shown in Figure 14-11:
   - A back arrow icon to navigate back to the previous screen
   - A Label control to display "Source"
   - An address Input control to enter the source address
   - A Label control to display "Destination"
   - An address Input control to enter the destination address

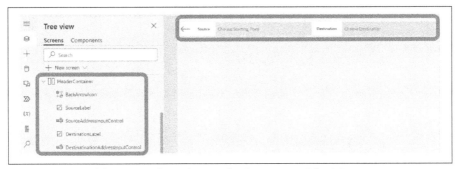

Figure 14-11. Adding controls to the HeaderContainer of the Map screen

3. Add a Map control in the MainContainer of the Map screen, as shown in Figure 14-12.

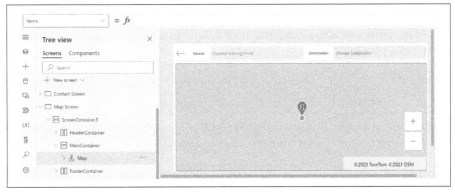

Figure 14-12. Adding a Map control to the MainContainer of the Map screen

4. Add a car icon and a Label control to the FooterContainer of the Map screen to display the distance and estimated travel time to reach the destination address. Then, add a Power Fx expression on the Text property of the Label control, as shown in Figure 14-13. This expression converts the distance from meters to kilometers and travel time from seconds to minutes. You can either refer to the final solution or download this expression from the GitHub repository (*https:// oreil.ly/pvoZI*).

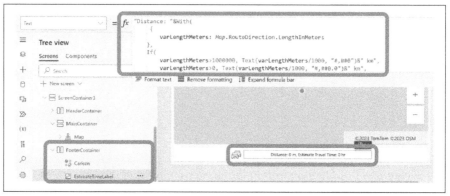

Figure 14-13. Adding controls to the FooterContainer and an expression on the Text *property of the Label control*

5. Add the following expression on the `OnVisible` property of the Case screen. This expression stores the logged-in user details in a global variable named `Current User` on load of the Case screen:

```
Set(
    CurrentUser,
    LookUp(
        Users,
        'Primary Email' = User().Email
    )
);
```

6. Add the following Power Fx expression on the `Default` property of `Source AddressInputControl`. This expression retrieves the logged-in user's address and sets it to the `SourceAddressInputControl`:

```
CurrentUser.'Other Street 1' & " " & CurrentUser.'Other Street 2' & " " &
CurrentUser.'Other Street 3' & ", " & CurrentUser.'Other ZIP/Postal Code' &
"," & CurrentUser.'Other City' & "," & CurrentUser.'Other State/Province' &
"," & CurrentUser.'Other Country/Region'
```

7. Add a waypoint icon to the Contact screen and add the following Power Fx expression to the `OnSelect` property of the Icon control, as shown in Figure 14-14. This expression redirects users to the Map screen from the Contact screen and passes the customer address that is available on the contact form as a context parameter when the waypoint icon is clicked:

```
Navigate(
    'Map Screen',
    ScreenTransition.CoverRight,
    {
        custAddressStreet1: custAddressStreet1.Text,
        custAddressStreet2: custAddressStreet2.Text,
        custAddressStreet3: custAddressStreet3.Text,
```

```
        custAddressPostcode: custAddressPostcode.Text,
        custAddressCity: custAddressCity.Text,
        custAddressState: custAddressState.Text,
        custAddressCountry: custAddressCountry.Text
    }
)
```

Figure 14-14. Adding a Power Fx expression to the waypoint icon on the Contact screen

8. Add the next Power Fx expression on the `Default` property of `Destination AddressInputControl`. This expression reads the customer address from the context variables that you have passed in the `Navigate` function in the previous step:

```
custAddressStreet1 & " " & custAddressStreet2 & " " & custAddressStreet3 &
", " & custAddressCity & ", " & custAddressState & ", " &
custAddressPostcode & ", " & custAddressCountry
```

9. Add the following expression on the `RouteWaypoints_items` property of the Map control and toggle on "Enable routing," as shown in Figure 14-15:

```
Table(
    {
        Name: SourceAddressInputControl.UserInput,
        Latitude: SourceAddressInputControl.SelectedLatitude,
        Longitude: SourceAddressInputControl.SelectedLongitude
    },
    {
        Name: DestinatinationAddressInputControl.UserInput,
        Latitude: DestinatinationAddressInputControl.SelectedLatitude,
        Longitude: DestinatinationAddressInputControl.SelectedLongitude
    }
)
```

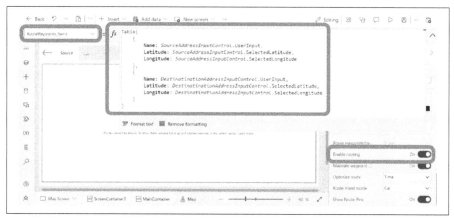

Figure 14-15. Adding an expression on the `RouteWaypoints_items` property and toggling on "Enable routing"

10. Finally, when you open the Contact screen and run the app, it will display the contact details in the right panel, based on the Contact record selected in the left panel. When you click the waypoint icon from the top right corner of the screen, it will take you to the Map screen and display the route and estimated travel time and distance, as shown in Figure 14-16.

Figure 14-16. The completed Map screen

Success Screen

In this section, you'll create a Success screen, which will be used in the Case Approval screen (which you'll design in the next section) to display a confirmation or success message. To create this screen, add a "Header and footer" screen type to the app. Then, add the following controls to the screen, as shown in Figure 14-17:

Header container (HeaderContainerSuccessScreen)
Add a back arrow icon to redirect users to the Case Approval screen.

Main container (MainContainerSuccessScreen)
Add a checkbox icon and two Label controls to display success and confirmation messages.

Footer container (FooterContainerSuccessScreen)
Add two Label controls, one to display the case number and another to display the case status on which action was taken:

- Add "Case No: "&CaseNumberVar to the Text property of the Case Number Label control.

- Add "Status: "&CaseStatusVar to the Text property of the Status Label control.

I will pass the values of the CaseNumberVar and CaseStatusVar variables dynamically from the Case Approval screen in the next section. So, ignore the error on the variable names.

Figure 14-17. Success screen controls

Case Approval Screen

In this section, I will add a new screen called Case Approval Screen to display the cases that are assigned to the service manager for approval. Service managers will land on this screen as soon as they log in to the app using their Microsoft Entra ID credentials and click "Login as Service Manager."

I want the look and feel of this screen to be the same as the Case screen. To do that, I will duplicate the Case screen rather than design the new screen from scratch.

To duplicate the Case screen, click on the three dots (…) next to the screen name and select Duplicate Screen. Rename this screen Case Approval Screen. I have added one new horizontal container, `FooterContainerForButtonControls`, and two buttons inside that container named Approve and Reject, which will be used to approve or reject the case, as shown in Figure 14-18.

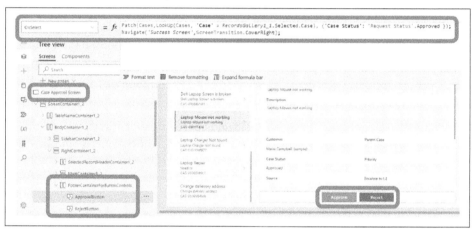

Figure 14-18. Buttons to approve or reject the case from the Case Approval screen

Add the following expression on the `OnSelect` property of the Approve button control. This expression will change the case status to Approved and redirect the user to the Success screen along with passing the variables Case Number and Case Status as context parameters. You have already used these variables in the Success screen:

```
Patch(
    Cases,
    LookUp(
        Cases,
        Case = RecordsGallery1_1.Selected.Case
    ),
    {'Case Status': 'Request Status'.Approved}
);
Navigate(
    'Success Screen',
```

```
                ScreenTransition.CoverRight,
                {
                    CaseNumberVar: RecordsGallery1_1.Selected.'Case Number',
                    CaseStatusVar: "Approved"
                }
        );
```

Add the following expression on the `OnSelect` property of the Reject button control. This expression will change the case status to Rejected and redirect the user to the Success screen along with passing the variables Case Number and Case Status as context parameters:

```
Patch(
        Cases,
        LookUp(
            Cases,
            Case = RecordsGallery1_1.Selected.Case
        ),
        {'Case Status': 'Request Status'.Rejected}
);
Navigate(
        'Success Screen',
        ScreenTransition.CoverRight,
        {
            CaseNumberVar: RecordsGallery1_1.Selected.'Case Number',
            CaseStatusVar: "Rejected"
        }
);
```

Login Screen

In this section, you will create a Login screen, which will be the first screen that field service agents and service managers see when they log in to the canvas app. This screen will navigate users to different screens of the canvas app based on the security roles assigned to them in Dataverse.

To create the Login screen, add a new Split Screen to the canvas app and rename it Login Screen. Click on the three dots (…) next to the screen name and select "Move up" to make it appear at the top of each screen. Then, add a sample image to the left container and two button controls (labeled "Login as Field Agent" and "Login as Service Manager") to the right container, as shown in Figure 14-19.

Figure 14-19. Login screen

Add the following Power Fx expression on the `OnVisible` property of the Login screen. This expression will retrieve the logged-in user's security roles from Dataverse and store them in a collection named `LoggedInUserRoles`. To check the table rows stored in collections, click on the "*(x)*" icon (which represents variables) in the left panel, then expand Collections, click on the three dots (…) next to the collection name, and select View Table, as shown in Figure 14-20:

```
>
    ClearCollect(
        LoggedInUserRoles,
        (LookUp(
            Users,
            'User Name' = User().Email
        ).'Security Roles (systemuserroles_association)').Name
    );
```

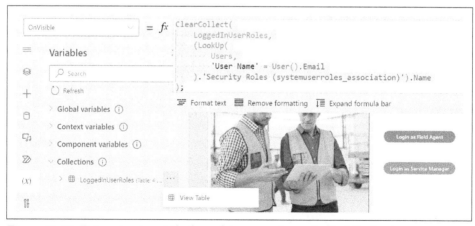

Figure 14-20. Expression to get the logged-in user roles on load of the Login screen

Now, add the following Power Fx expression on the OnSelect property of the "Login as Field Agent" button control to restrict access to only authorized users. This expression will make sure that only logged-in app users who have the Field Service Agent role in Dataverse will be able to use the features of the app that are intended for field service agents:

```
Set(
    CheckUserHasRole,
    CountRows(
        Filter(
            LoggedInUserRoles,
            "Field Service Agent" in name
        )
    ) > 0
);
If(
    CheckUserHasRole,
    Navigate(
        'Case Screen',
        ScreenTransition.CoverRight
    ),
    Notify(
        "You don't have sufficient privilege to login to the app.
        Please contact your service manager",
        NotificationType.Error
    )
)
```

Add the following Power Fx expression on the OnSelect property of the "Login as Service Manager" button control. This expression will make sure that only logged-in app users who have the Service Manager role in Dataverse will be able to use the features of the app that are intended for service managers:

```
Set(
    CheckUserHasRole,
    CountRows(
        Filter(
            LoggedInUserRoles,
            "Service Manager" in name
        )
    ) > 0
);
If(
    CheckUserHasRole,
    Navigate(
        'Case Approval Screen',
        ScreenTransition.CoverRight
    ),
    Notify(
        "You don't have sufficient privilege to login to the app.
        Please contact your service administrator",
```

```
        NotificationType.Error
    )
)
```

Logout Control

I have included a Logout option on each screen, which will redirect app users to Service at Home's Login page. This is simply a Label control that I placed in the top right corner of each screen. I then used the `Navigate ("Login Screen");` expression on the `OnSelect` property.

This control will not log you out of the canvas app or your Microsoft Entra ID account, which you used to log in to the canvas app. It will just redirect you to the Service at Home app's main screen.

Copilot Control

Imagine a field service agent is at a customer location and having trouble resolving or investigating an issue. They can quickly ask Copilot for help, and Copilot can get the relevant information from the knowledge articles or documentation provided by the company. Additionally, field service agents can ask anything about the data stored in the Dataverse table, such as "What is the current status of case no CAS-01004H2Z6?" or "What is the pin code of the customer Arpit?"

 To enable the Copilot feature in the Power Platform environment and in the canvas app, refer to "Prerequisites for the AI Features in Power Apps" on page 412.

To add a Copilot control to the Case screen, click on the plus (+) icon on the left panel and select Copilot. This will add a Copilot control to the currently opened app's screen. You can adjust its height, width, and alignment on the screen. Now, to control its visibility, I have added two icons (for Help and Cancel) on the right top corner of the screen (see Figure 14-21) and added the following Power Fx expression on the `OnSelect` property of the Help icon:

```
Set(
    CurrentUser,
    LookUp(
        Users,
        'Primary Email' = User().Email
    )
);
Set(
    ShowHelpIcon,
```

```
        true
);
```

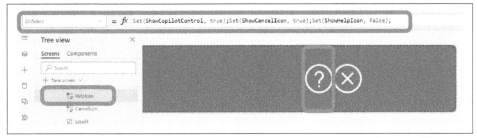

Figure 14-21. Show/hide the Copilot control and Cancel icon using global variables

This expression creates three global variables, whose purpose is to show the Copilot control and Cancel icon and to hide the Help icon, when the user clicks on the Help icon.

Then, add following expression on the OnSelect property of the Cancel icon, as shown in Figure 14-22:

```
Set(
    ShowCopilotControl,
    true
);
Set(
    ShowCancelIcon,
    true
);
Set(
    ShowHelpIcon,
    false
);
```

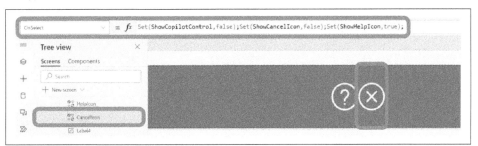

Figure 14-22. Show/hide the Copilot control and Help icon using global variables

This expression creates three global variables whose purpose is to hide the Copilot control and Cancel icon and to show the Help icon, when the user clicks on the Cancel icon.

Now set the ShowCopilotControl variable on the OnVisible property of the Copilot control, set the ShowCancelIcon variable on the OnVisible property of the Cancel icon, and set the ShowHelpIcon variable on the OnVisible property of the Help icon to automatically show/hide the Copilot control when the user clicks on the Help and Cancel icons.

To demonstrate, I added a Copilot control to the Case screen and set its Items property to Cases, enabling it to search the data in the Cases table in Dataverse. I asked the copilot, "How many cases are related to a laptop screen?" and it replied, "There are 3 cases related to a laptop screen," as shown in Figure 14-23. You can add a Copilot control on other screens as well, per your business needs.

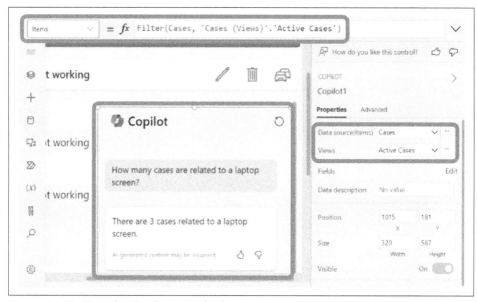

Figure 14-23. How the Copilot control takes input and generates output

Step 4: Save and Publish the App

Once all the screens and controls are created, click Save and provide the app name "Service at Home." Now, click Publish in the top right corner of the screen to publish the app. Once published, open your solution, click on "Add existing" from the command bar, and select App → Canvas app → the From Dataverse tab, then choose your app (Service at Home) and click Add.

Step 5: Share the App

Once you have created a canvas application that meets a business need, you can designate which users within your organization have access to run, modify, and re-share the application. You can designate specific users by name, or you can designate a security group in Microsoft Entra ID. If you believe that your app will be useful to everyone, you can designate that everyone in your organization has access to run it. See "Canvas App Sharing" on page 330 for instructions.

Step 6: Deploy the Solution

Finally, your solution is ready with a model-driven app, canvas app, and all related components. It's time to deploy your solution to the target environment. You can deploy your solution either manually or automatically using Power Platform pipelines (*https://oreil.ly/-5l2H*) (for citizen developers) or Power Platform Build Tools (*https://oreil.ly/lsQJE*) in Azure DevOps (for professional developers and DevOps teams).

The following high-level deployment steps are applicable to both manual and automatic deployment:

1. Ensure you have a target environment available. If not already created, then first create another trial or developer environment that you will use as the target environment.

2. Enable any additional settings and features from the Power Platform admin center that you have enabled in your source environment, such as Copilot and map and location services.

3. If you have installed any third-party solutions (DocuSign, Adobe, etc.) or any external business apps or solutions from AppSource (*https://oreil.ly/4NGiF*) in your source environment, install them in your target environment. For example, I had installed Power Pages in my source environment and created a site using a FAQ template (*https://oreil.ly/4kI4s*) that automatically installed the Power-Pages_FAQ managed solution in my environment. So I have to install this solution in my target environment as well. Sometimes Microsoft also installs some built-in managed solutions in your environment during setup that you might need to install in your target environment manually.

4. Make a backup of your target environment. This is only applicable when you are doing incremental deployment; for the initial deployment, it's optional.

5. Run a solution checker to validate your solution in the source environment. This will provide you with a detailed report that lists the issues identified and the components and code affected, along with a link to documentation that describes how to resolve the listed issues.

6. Export the solution from your source environment. It's recommended that you should always use a managed solution to deploy to the target environment. You can import an unmanaged solution only if you plan to further develop or change

the solution components after deploying it to the target environment, such as when preparing a client demo or POC, when your environment is about to expire, or for your own practice.

7. Import the solution to the target environment and change connection references, environment variables, etc. as necessary for the target environment.

8. Migrate your configuration data using the Configuration Migration tool (*https:// oreil.ly/mDq6a*).

9. If you have published an unmanaged solution, publish all customizations in the target environment.

10. Finally, assign appropriate security roles to the users in your target environment. Next, share your Service at Home app with the field service agents. If you want to limit access to the Book My Service app to specific service agents and service managers, you may also need to share the model-driven app. If access is unrestricted, anyone can access the Book My Service app without having to share it with everyone individually, unlike the canvas app.

Sometimes, you may have to perform some additional steps pre- or post-deployment, depending on your solution design and environment configuration.

Summary

This chapter describes the development of a canvas app called Service at Home for field service agents and service managers. For field service agents, you designed a Case screen to view the cases assigned to them, a Contact screen to view information about the customer who raised the case, and a Map screen to display the route to the customer location. You also designed a Case Approval screen for service managers to approve or reject the cases assigned to them. In addition, you also used the AI capabilities of a Copilot control to enable chatbot capabilities in the app.

The goal of this chapter and the previous chapter was to provide a hands-on experience using Power Apps. These tutorials demonstrate the high-level solution design and implementation steps to give you an understanding of how to kickstart, plan, design, implement, test, and deploy your Power Apps-based business solution. I would recommend you extend this solution for your own learning and practice by incorporating other components like Power Pages, Copilot Studio, AI Builder, and Power BI.

In the final chapter, I will wrap up this book by sharing some essential guidelines, best practices for creating scalable Power Apps applications, along with some useful tools, articles, and other stuff to advance your learning process.

CHAPTER 15

Power Apps Best Practices

Throughout this book, I have covered the journey of Power Apps from its evolution to implementation. You have learned the fundamentals of every aspect of Power Apps, its components, controls, and interaction with various data sources via connectors, along with its integration with other Microsoft products and applications to extend its capabilities. You have also witnessed how Power Apps enables everyone, of all skill levels, from technical to non-technical, to create end-to-end business applications in so many ways.

If you are implementing a Power Apps project for the first time, it's important to know some best practices and implementation guidelines that will help you optimize your time and effort and improve the quality of your work. As you are already aware, there are numerous ways to implement a given requirement in Power Apps, and you can choose from a variety of low-code, no-code, and pro-code components to get the job done. Therefore, it is important to know some tried-and-true guidelines and best practices to develop a bug-free solution.

In this chapter, I will discuss some key points that you should think about either in the planning stages of your implementation or during the actual implementation, rather than later on when it's too late to make changes. Let's get started.

Model-Driven Apps

Model-driven apps use a component-focused approach for app development. It provides plenty of features and components that can be extended by developers to achieve a more customized experience. While customizing model-driven apps, a developer must be aware of important guidelines and best practices. I shared the component-specific tips and tricks in Chapters 6 and 7, where I discussed model-driven app components and their extended features, respectively.

Here I am sharing best practices from an overall app configuration and customization perspective.

Solutions

The following are model-driven app solution best practices:

- You should create a solution first and start creating your model-driven app components there instead of in the default solution.

- Avoid adding "all metadata" of any out-of-the-box component unless it's absolutely necessary. For instance, if you have created two custom fields in the Contacts table, add only those two fields to your solution rather than the entire Contacts table and all of its metadata. This also applies to incremental solution deployment.

- There are known limitations (*https://oreil.ly/B9FY0*) to solutions. Keep them in mind to prevent mistakes during development.

- Changing the *solution.zip* file is not recommended and unsupported. However, sometimes you may have some dependency issues during solution deployment that can't be resolved until you remove those component references from *customization.xml* and *solution.xml* files. (Microsoft support engineers also had to do this during support activity.)

- Please read about the supported (*https://oreil.ly/sV6rR*) and unsupported (*https://oreil.ly/ghG2E*) customizations for Dataverse while doing actual implementation.

- A solution can be up to 32 MB in size; try to keep your solutions under that limit from a maintenance and performance perspective. The larger the solution, the longer it will take to export and import in the environment. If your solution's size exceeds the limit, Microsoft has offered a few options (*https://oreil.ly/39zWA*) to manage it.

Design

The following are model-driven app design best practices:

- Add a detailed description to each new component (fields, forms, views, Power Automate, workflows, etc.) you create in the solution to make it easier for other developers to understand its purpose.

- Create custom fields for existing tables instead of creating a new table. Also, rename the existing table to make the name more meaningful. For example, customize system tables such as Opportunity, Contact, and Account, instead of replacing them with custom tables so that you can use the built-in features of existing tables.

- Try to use out-of-the-box fields whenever possible; only if they don't fit your needs should you create custom fields with unique and meaningful names.

- Use appropriate data types because they can't be changed once fields are created.

- Choose the Lookup rather than Choice data type for columns if the options frequently change, the options list is very long, or if Dataverse users need to be able to add or update options directly in the app without customizing the solution. For example, if I have to create a column to store country, city, etc., I would create a Lookup type column rather than a Choice type.

- Always give preference to out-of-the-box features over customization when designing your solution. Sometimes excessive customization can be challenging, as it may degrade your app performance and may have an impact on future upgrades. The more you customize the application, the more maintenance it will require.

- If your stakeholders (for which you are building the application) cannot be convinced to use built-in controls, then your first preference should always be to use no-code components like business rules, business process flow, workflows, and formula columns.

- If something is not achievable using no-code components, then your next preference should be low-code components such as low-code plug-ins, Power Automate flows, custom pages, canvas apps, and Power Fx expressions.

- Pro-code components (JavaScript, C#, Dataverse Web API, Azure Functions, PCF Controls, HTML web resources, etc.) should be your last choice when it comes to customizing your application.

- There are situations when your stakeholder would benefit more from using ready-made apps or third-party apps (DocuSign, Adobe Acrobat Sign, etc.) available in Microsoft AppSource (*https://oreil.ly/3yQ0w*) than having them created from scratch. This not only speeds up the development process but also helps you minimize the amount of heavy customization required in your application in order to develop the complex features.

- Always check the Dynamics 365 and Microsoft Power Platform release planner (*https://oreil.ly/P26RG*), Microsoft 365 roadmap (*https://oreil.ly/VGG0p*), and official Microsoft Power Platform blog (*https://oreil.ly/YKH7g*) for new features before settling on a solution design and beginning implementation. This is because the component you are creating today might become obsolete in the near future.

- Remove unwanted forms, views, and business process flows from the app designer to improve app performance. The more controls and components you have in the application, the longer it will take to load.

- Plan carefully which columns you will use for the alternate key, because once it is created, you cannot apply column-level security to those columns. Sometimes not considering these minor details during the implementation might be painful in the future when you do not have any options to backtrack.

Client-Side Logic

The following are model-driven app client-side logic best practices:

- To improve form performance:
  - Don't write too much business logic, client-side code, or long-running logic on form load. Additionally, remove unwanted lines of code and libraries from your web resource file for faster code execution.
  - Write reusable code whenever possible. Writing the same business logic and code in multiple functions increases code execution time, which impacts form performance.
- Business rules should be your first preference for client-side validation across all the forms (and if you want to run that same validation on the server side as well). If business rules don't fit your business needs, only then go with JavaScript.
- Add the columns that you use in your JavaScript code to the Table Column Dependencies list; otherwise, your code will break if someone accidentally removes that field from the form.
- You should always create namespaced JavaScript libraries (*https://oreil.ly/84fl-*) to avoid having your functions overridden by functions in another library.
- To avoid making repeated server connections, data can sometimes be temporarily stored in the browser cache by using local storage (*https://oreil.ly/IiGkg*) and sessions storage (*https://oreil.ly/liToG*).
- Make efficient use of the Dataverse Web API when using JavaScript. Only request the data and columns that your application needs for better performance.
- Use batch operations using the Dataverse Web API (*https://oreil.ly/xOiab*) to perform multiple operations (CRUD) in a single HTTP request, instead of making multiple calls.
- Writing Document Object Model (DOM)-based scripts is not allowed or supported in model-driven apps. This is the type of script where you write code based on HTML elements of the form controls; for example:

```
document.getElementById("firstname");
```

or:

```
$("#firstname").val();.
```

- Disable the loading of the navigation bar when opening forms or views programmatically using an environment URL (*https://oreil.ly/fr9se*). Loading the navigation bar could lead to slower client performance on high-latency networks. The following code will open the form without loading the navigation bar:

```
function disableNavBarFromLoading() {
    var globalContext = Xrm.Utility.getGlobalContext();
    return globalContext.getClientUrl() + "/main.aspx?appid=7530ecfb-8891-
    ee11-be36-
    002248282d51&navbar=off&pagetype=entityrecord&etn=arp_case&id=66f0a918-
    f1b7-4176-8676-8d27d4c74fc1";
}
```

However, I always recommend using custom pages to open the form or view it in a pop-up dialog box.

- Always use the Dataverse Web API to perform operations in Dataverse from external applications. If you are creating any C#- or ASP.NET-based web or Windows applications, then you can also use XRM tooling assemblies, as discussed in Chapter 7.

Server-Side Logic

The following are server-side best practices for model-driven apps:

- Carefully decide when to use a synchronous plug-in or real-time workflow. Real-time workflows provide both no-code and pro-code (custom workflow) ways to perform operations, whereas plug-ins can only be written in C# or VB.NET code.

- Use synchronous components or logic as little as possible for writing client- and server-side code to improve app performance.

- Remove or delete plug-ins, workflows, flows, and other components from the solution if they are not being used. This will keep your solution clean and prevent unwanted components from increasing the size of the solution.

- Remove unwanted commands or buttons from the command bar to improve app performance. The more commands you have on the form's command bar, the longer it takes to load, which will also increase the form's load time.

- Remove unwanted or unused columns from the form to improve performance. The more columns you have on the form, the longer it takes to load.

- To handle localized strings in any user interface you build or display error messages, use RESX web resources (*https://oreil.ly/t9x0V*) rather than hardcoding messages or strings in your code (JavaScript, Plugin, etc.).

- Use database storage effectively to reduce the storage and improve performance.
  - Store files, attachments, and documents in SharePoint or Azure Blob storage or another cost-efficient storage instead of in Dataverse.

— Data that is not being used frequently in your app and is only being used for logging, monitoring, reporting, analyzing, mining, or auditing purposes can be stored outside Dataverse in Azure SQL Database (*https://oreil.ly/E_mjP*), Azure Data Lake, etc.

— Delete audit logs and system jobs after a particular interval of time.

— Consider using Dataverse's long term data retention (*https://oreil.ly/tU066*) to reduce storage costs.

- Don't use `ExecuteMultipleRequest` (*https://oreil.ly/c-spX*) or `ExecuteTransactionRequest` (*https://oreil.ly/_umDn*) message request classes within the context of a plug-in or custom workflow activity due to the execution time limit of two minutes. Use these batch messages where code is being executed outside of the platform execution pipeline, such as in integration scenarios where network latency would likely reduce the throughput and increase the duration of larger bulk operations.

- Make sure that you don't have multiple synchronous plug-ins registered on the same table on the same event. This can lead to model-driven apps that are unresponsive, have slow client interaction, and a broken browser. If this is still necessary, look into the possibilities for combining multiple plug-ins into a single plug-in, change your plug-in to asynchronous type, or change the plug-in order.

- Don't use multi-threading or parallel calls within plug-ins or custom workflow activities. It can cause corruption of those connections and you may get errors ("Generic SQL error. The transaction active in this session has been committed or aborted by another session.") because the sandbox service (the service running on Microsoft's server, responsible for executing plug-ins registered in sandbox mode) has been designed to execute calls in a specific order as part of a transaction.

- Limit your plug-in registrations on `Retrieve` and `RetrieveMultiple` events to avoid performance issues.

- When registering plug-ins for an Update event, be sure to use `FilteringAttributes` to specify which columns (when they are modified) should trigger plug-in execution. This will avoid unnecessary plug-in executions (such as on autosave), which cause undesirable behavior and degrade app performance.

- Manage plug-ins in a single solution in your development environment. The reason for this is that plug-ins consist of `PluginAssembly` and `PluginType` records that are associated with each other. `PluginAssembly` contains the binary contents of the plug-in assembly, while `PluginType` contains a reference to the class in the plug-in assembly that implements the `IPlugin` interface. If the same assembly is included in two solutions installed on top of each other, the type validations will fail if there are mismatched types within the assemblies.

- Whenever you deploy a plug-in solution to a target environment, always use the Upgrade (*https://oreil.ly/n-ExH*) option. For instance, if you have the *TestPlugin.dll* plug-in assembly available in both SolutionA (Managed Solution Layer1 and v1.0.0.0) and SolutionB (Managed Solution Layer2 and v1.0.0.0) in the target environment, and you update your plug-in assembly in the development environment and deploy SolutionB (v2.0.0.0) to the target environment, it will fail because the top-level SolutionA (Layer1) does not yet contain the updated plug-in assembly. Using the Upgrade option will upgrade your solution to the most recent version and roll up all previous patches in one go.

- Don't use the `SetTimeout`, `Sleep`, or `Wait` functions while making API calls within plug-in code. This may cause a long transaction times and impact other operations. For long-running operations, plug-ins are not advisable, due to the two minute timeout.

- Dataverse has a 16 MB assembly size limit that cannot be modified. If your assembly size is getting close to 16 MB, you may want to consider splitting your plug-in or custom workflow operations into multiple assemblies.

- Limit the number of custom workflow activities in a single assembly. Microsoft recommends including no more than 50 custom workflow activities in a single assembly.

- Avoid using `Columns.All` or `ColumnSet(true)` while retrieving or updating data in Dataverse using LINQ, Fetch XML, or query expressions (*https://oreil.ly/d8r-_*). Retrieving and updating all columns of a particular table can have a negative impact on app performance. Additionally, it can unintentionally trigger other components like plug-ins, workflows, and flows. For example, the following code should not be used:

```
QueryExpression contactquery = new QueryExpression
{
    EntityName="contact",
    ColumnSet = new ColumnSet(true):
};
Use this instead:
QueryExpression contactquery = new QueryExpression
{
    EntityName="contact",
    ColumnSet = new ColumnSet("firstname", "lastname", "contactid")
};
```

Integration

The following are model-driven app integration best practices:

- Use service principal or application user (app user) to perform operations on Microsoft Dataverse when there is no need to access the data by logging in to the application. A Power Apps license is not required to access Dataverse data. Additionally, you must assign only limited access to the app users. A few uses of service principals are:

— Running Power Automate

— Server-to-server (S2S) authentication

— To interact with Microsoft Dataverse data externally

— To build a third-party application on top of Dataverse

— To set up an Azure DevOps Pipelines connection

— To support and work with an organization that uses multifactor authentication (MFA)

 In Dataverse, a service principal or application user refers to a security identity that represents an application or service, rather than an individual user. It's typically used for programmatic access to Dataverse resources, such as when integrating with external systems or automating processes. Both service principals and application users provide a way for applications and services to authenticate and interact with Dataverse securely, without needing to rely on individual user credentials. They play a crucial role in enabling automation, integration, and external access to Dataverse resources.

• Use either virtual tables, custom pages, or an embedded canvas app to display external application data in model-driven apps. If they don't fit your business needs, then go with a custom component.

• Use Dataverse Web API for integrating external applications for the following scenarios:

— If no API unification is required. You can't change the API endpoint, API name, operation name, and other properties of Dataverse Web API.

— If no data transformation is required. You need to store the API response as is and no further processing is required.

— When API consumers need to generate access tokens to call the Web API.

— When there is no need to retry failure, monitoring, and API failure management.

— To support API request and response only in JSON format.

- Use Azure APIM for integrating external applications for the following scenarios:
  - API unification is required. You can change the API name, operation, and endpoint as needed.
  - Heavy data transformation is required. You are required to transform the data in the requested application format.
  - API consumers don't need to generate access tokens.
  - You need API analytics, failure management, and application insights capabilities.
  - You need support for API request and response in JSON, XML, and other formats.
  - You need to overcome API limits to cache the data.
  - You need security, such as an IP allow list.

Security

The following are model-driven app security best practices:

- Limit the number of users with the System Administrator role because this role has complete access to Dataverse data, components, and environment resources. Ideally, you should grant admin access only to people who are developing the application and controlling resources in your environment; everyone else should be assigned the least-privileged roles based on tasks they need to perform.
- Assign users to the appropriate role based on their role in the organization or job description. Create roles based on the security best practice of least privilege, providing access to the minimal amount of business data needed for the task.
- Avoid using administrative accounts for executing code because the admin can perform all types of operations on any Dataverse table. Instead, use accounts that have limited access to the data or table based on their role so that they can interact with components and data they have access to.
- Do not modify Dataverse data by any means other than the SDK or Web API because doing so bypasses the Dataverse security model. All built-in Power Apps and other Power Platform components also use Web API internally to communicate with Dataverse.
- Avoid running plug-ins under the administrator's context because this code may access information that the logged-on user does not have access to.
- Enable MFA for all user accounts and also consider using Azure's Conditional Access policies to restrict user access of Dataverse based on location, device type, etc.

Canvas Apps

Similar to model-driven apps, canvas apps also provide a wide variety of approaches for data visualization, data connection, and control creation for designing applications. However, in contrast to model-driven apps, which rely primarily on professional developers to design business solutions, canvas apps offer a wider range of low-code and no-code design possibilities, giving both technical and non-technical users the freedom to create apps. However, this flexibility can sometimes result in poorly designed apps and poor performance, so it is important for everyone—especially those without a technical background—to understand how the canvas app works in the background to display data in the app.

When a user opens a canvas app, the app goes through several phases of execution before the interface is displayed to the user:

Authentication
Users are prompted to log in with their credentials for whatever connections the app needs. Users might need to log in every time they open the app, depending on the organization's security policies.

Get metadata
Once the user is logged in, the app retrieves metadata, such as the version of Power Apps and sources from which it must retrieve data.

Initialize the app
Execute expressions written on the OnStart property of the app. (But note that writing expressions on the OnStart property can cause performance issues; see "Optimize the OnStart Property" on page 544 for more information. As of this writing, Microsoft is working (*https://oreil.ly/xkoxF*) to provide an alternative solution.)

Render the app screen
Render the first screen with controls that the app populates with data.

You need to follow best practices in each phase of canvas app execution for a better end-user experience and to improve app performance. Let's discuss some important tips and best practices to boost the canvas app's performance.

Reduce Data Flow Time

The number of connectors that can be used with the canvas app is not exactly defined. As a general guideline, an app should not use more than 30 connectors, and it is advised to keep the number of connectors as minimal as possible. This is because when an app runs, each connector requires CPU resources, memory, and network bandwidth to connect and retrieve data from its data source, which increases the time to start the app. Turning on developer tools in Google Chrome or Microsoft Edge while the app is running enables you to easily evaluate your app's performance.

For all online data sources, data requests are sent via APIM, as shown in Figure 15-1.

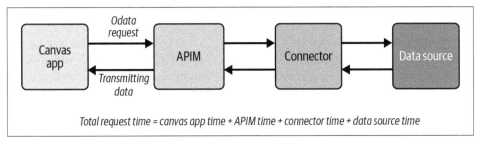

Figure 15-1. Total time taken to load canvas app while connecting to external data sources

For all on-premises data sources, data requests are sent via APIM with one additional layer called on-premises data gateway (*https://oreil.ly/nFc7_*), as shown in Figure 15-2.

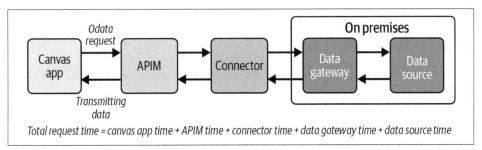

Figure 15-2. Total time taken to load canvas app while connecting to on-premises data sources

For Microsoft Dataverse, data requests are sent directly to specific environment instances without using APIM, as shown in Figure 15-3.

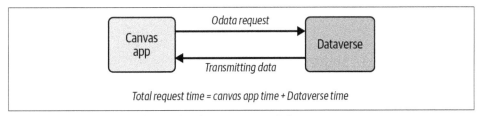

Figure 15-3. Total time taken to load canvas app while connecting to Dataverse

Now that you have a general understanding of this high-level concept of data calls traveling through various layers, you can dive into the specific layer and analyze your application's performance. To put it briefly, performance overhead can originate from any of the following sources: the client, APIM, connector, on-premises data gateway, or backend data sources.

Limit the Number of Controls

Don't add more than 500 controls in one app. This is because the canvas app generates HTML document object models for each control. The more controls you add, the more generation time the app needs. You must also be aware that some controls, like a PDF viewer, data table, and combo box, take longer to load than others. To optimize the use of controls, either divide your functionality across multiple screens or use a Gallery control, especially when you have to display multiple instances of a control on the screen, or use components or a component library to create reusable controls and then use them across your application.

If you design a canvas app with more than 10 screens and a large number of controls that are directly bound to the data source across multiple screens, you should activate the preview feature (*https://oreil.ly/2ZiKi*) for delayed load. If you don't, app performance may suffer because all of the controls in all of the screens must be populated, even when the screens are closed.

Optimize the OnStart Property

The `OnStart` property of a canvas app runs when the user starts the app. This property is often used to perform the following tasks:

- Retrieve and cache data into collections using the `Collect` (*https://oreil.ly/rHG8E*) function.
- Set up global variables using the `Set` (*https://oreil.ly/qo69y*) function.

However, writing expressions on the `App.OnStart` property can cause delays when loading an app and should be avoided. Microsoft has introduced new alternatives, such as `App.StartScreen`, that offer a better way to accomplish the same thing. Another alternative is to write your expressions on the `OnVisible` property of the first screen.

Optimize the Data Source Connection

To perform various data operations, you may occasionally need to establish connections with multiple data sources on the same screen, but it can take a long time to establish connections with each data source individually (see Figure 15-4). So, to optimize the data source connection, you can use the `Concurrent` function to load data sources simultaneously, which can cut down the amount of time an app takes to load data by half, as shown in Figure 15-5.

Expression without the Concurrent function:

```
ClearCollect( Product, '[SalesLT].[Product]' );
ClearCollect( Customer, '[SalesLT].[Customer]' );
ClearCollect( SalesOrder, '[SalesLT].[SalesOrder]' );
ClearCollect( Invoice, '[SalesLT].[Invoice]' );
```

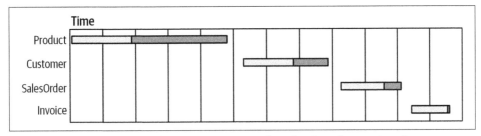

Figure 15-4. Total amount of time operations took to finish without using the Concur rent function

Expression with the Concurrent function:

```
Concurrent(
ClearCollect( Product, '[SalesLT].[Product]' ),
ClearCollect( Customer, '[SalesLT].[Customer]' ),
ClearCollect( SalesOrder, '[SalesLT].[SalesOrder]' ),
ClearCollect( Invoice, '[SalesLT].[Invoice]' )
)
```

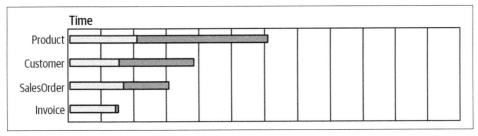

Figure 15-5. Total amount of time operations took to finish when using the Concurrent function

Cache Repetitive Data in a Temporary Database

Storing data temporarily in the canvas app cache is the best way to improve the app's performance. You can use the ClearCollect function to cache data locally in tabular format if it does not change throughout the user's session. Use the Set function to store data in global variables to avoid repeatedly retrieving data from the data source.

Avoid Control Dependency Between Screens

A canvas app should load its screens into memory only when needed to maximize the app performance. This optimization can be compromised if, for instance, screen 1 is loaded and one of its formulas uses a property of a control from screen 2, meaning that screen 2 must load to fulfill the dependency before screen 1 can be displayed.

Use Delegable Functions and Queries

The key to designing an efficient canvas app is to minimize the amount of data that must be brought to your device. The more data you bring, the more time the app will take to load, which may cause the app's screen to appear unresponsive or broken.

To handle this situation, Power Apps uses delegation (*https://oreil.ly/xlPJc*), which assigns the processing of data to the data source itself to minimize the data moving over the network, rather than moving the data to the app for processing locally, which needs a lot more processing power, memory, and network bandwidth. Let's understand this with an example.

Say I write this Power Fx expression to retrieve an account from Dataverse based on the account name entered in the Search Box input control (`SearchInput`):

```
Search([@Accounts], SearchInput.Text, "name")
```

When executed, it will not display an error in the formula bar (see Figure 15-6) because it's a delegable query and internally it will be fully translated into an equivalent query that can be run on the data source and return accurate results to the app.

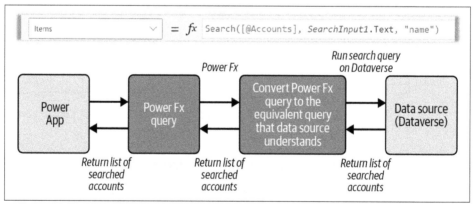

Figure 15-6. How data is processed if the query and function are delegable

However, if I write this Power Fx expression to retrieve the filtered accounts from Dataverse based on the account name entered in the Search Box control:

```
Filter([@Accounts], SearchInput1.Text, "name")
```

when executed it will display a delegation warning in the formula bar (see Figure 15-7) because it's not a delegable query and internally it will not be translated into an equivalent query that can be run on the data source. In this situation, the canvas app only gets the first 500 records from the data source locally in the app, and then the app will perform the actions in the query.

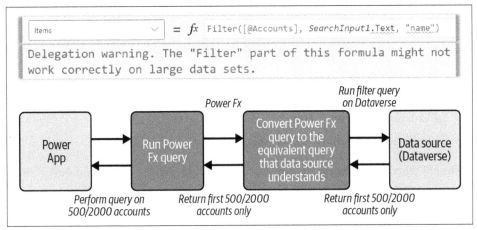

Figure 15-7. How data is processed if query and function are not delegable

You can change this data row limit (*https://oreil.ly/Ar_2o*) to any value up to 2,000. However, this limitation can be problematic because the query may return inaccurate results if the number of records in the data source exceeds the limit. For example, suppose your data source contains 10 million rows and your query needs to operate on the last part of the data (e.g., customer names beginning with Z). However, your query includes a non-delegable operator (such as Filter). In this instance, you'll only receive the first 2,000 records (or whatever you set the data row limit to), and you'll get incorrect results.

Delegable data sources

Currently, delegation is supported only for specific tabular data sources in:

- Microsoft Dataverse (*https://oreil.ly/LGG2U*)
- SharePoint (*https://oreil.ly/4ArEG*)
- SQL Server (*https://oreil.ly/K3yrK*)
- Salesforce (*https://oreil.ly/GDGjB*)

Imported Excel workbooks (using the "Add static data to your app data source" option), collections, and tables stored in context variables do not require delegation.

Delegable functions

The `Filter`, `Search`, `Lookup` (*https://oreil.ly/eV9ia*), and `First` (*https://oreil.ly/ffPN9*) functions can be delegated if you use them with the following operators and functions:

- And (including &&), Or (including ||), Not (including !) (*https://oreil.ly/JzTuU*)
- In (*https://oreil.ly/ii79M*)
- =, <>, >=, <=, >, < (*https://oreil.ly/iDKYp*)
- +, - (*https://oreil.ly/p_Q2y*)
- TrimEnds (*https://oreil.ly/Ht13y*)
- IsBlank (*https://oreil.ly/bLmWh*)
- StartsWith, EndsWith (*https://oreil.ly/Ap9yA*)

I would highly recommend that you read more about the delegation and query limits in canvas apps in the Microsoft documentation (*https://oreil.ly/qWDvp*).

Republish Your App Regularly

When you publish a canvas app, it gets updated to run on the most recent version of Power Apps. Your app benefits from all of the new features and performance enhancements that have been added since your last publication. If you haven't published an update in several months, you may notice an instant performance benefit when you republish the app.

Avoid Repeating the Same Formulas in Multiple Places

Consider setting a property once and using the result of that property in subsequent properties, if multiple properties run the same formula (especially if it is complex). For instance, instead of setting the `DisplayMode` property of controls A, B, C, D, and E to the same complex formula, set the `DisplayMode` property of control A to the complex formula, then set the result of control A's `DisplayMode` property to the `DisplayMode` property of control B, and so on for controls C, D, and E.

Another option is to run your formula just once, save the results in a local cache (Collection or Global variable), and then use the results throughout your application.

Enable the DelayOutput Property on all TextInput Controls

Set the TextInput control's `DelayOutput` property to `true` if you have multiple formulas or rules that reference the value it holds. This will prevent the formulas or rules from running as frequently and improve app performance by updating the `Text` property of the control only after a series of quick keystrokes have stopped.

Use DelayItemLoading and LoadingSpinner to Improve Gallery Performance

If you have a Gallery with complex templates, you should set the `LoadingSpinner` property to `LoadingSpinner.Controls` and the `DelayItemLoading` property to `true`. This will make the render time appear shorter, and it will also delay the rendering of the templates, which will speed up the rendering of the rest of the screen because the gallery and the screen aren't competing for the same resources.

Limit Data and Columns Retrieved

Adding more (or all) columns from the data source downloads all the data in the columns, which leads to a high number of network overhead calls and high memory utilization in the client device. Instead, it's advised to pick only the columns that are required for the application.

Don't Use Unsupported or Legacy Browsers

Make sure that users use only supported browsers (*https://oreil.ly/ebwQz*) to run canvas apps. Users who use unsupported or legacy browsers may encounter performance issues.

Set an Appropriate Environment Geographic Location

App performance can be impacted by the environment's geographic location and distance of data source from the users. Therefore, it is advised that the environment be located close to app users.

Establish Canvas App Coding Guidelines

Creating a simple canvas app is easy. But as the complexity of your app increases, care must be taken to keep your apps maintainable and performant. I suggest that you read Microsoft's whitepaper on canvas apps coding standards and guidelines (*https://oreil.ly/TJ3N-*), which are aimed at the enterprise application maker, who is in charge of designing, developing, testing, deploying, and maintaining apps in a small business, corporate, or government environment. These coding standards and guidelines are flexible and serve as a starting point for organizations to develop their own standards.

Summary

This chapter covered the key best practices and guidelines for creating Power Apps. Adherence to these guidelines will assist you in developing bug-free, consistent, performant, and easily maintainable apps. Some of these guidelines are from Microsoft, and some are based on my own Power Apps experience. There are many more such guidelines available on the internet, shared by Power Apps experts from Microsoft and by Microsoft MVPs. Once you start working on your own Power Apps project, you may also discover additional lessons that you can apply to your future implementations.

Closing Thoughts

It is finally time to write a few closing words to wrap up this book! The end of this book should be the start of your journey into the world of Power Apps. This book was intended to make you fundamentally strong and proficient in the core concepts of Power Apps. From working with Power Apps, I've learned that features may change over time, but the fundamentals remain the same. One of the biggest advantages of using Power Apps is that it has simplified development. Before Power Apps, developers were the only ones who could create any kind of software or business apps for the company. But now, with the help of low-code, no-code features, everyone can contribute to application development. Nowadays, when companies need to quickly create apps for simple tasks, they can use ready-made apps and no-code features to speed up app development if they don't have employees with coding skills. However, if a company wants the speed of low-code without compromising the scalability or customizability, and both professional developers and business users will use the apps, then low-code is the way to go.

After finishing this book, you probably have a lot of new ideas floating around in your head. So, where do you start? Well, try taking any real-world case study as an example and create your own Power Apps-based solution. You can learn more about Power Apps from the official Power Apps documentation (*https://oreil.ly/nQiZf*) and also start your journey today by exploring Microsoft learning paths and modules (*https://oreil.ly/mPJYi*). After that, you should start looking into the other parts of Power Platform, such as Power Automate, Microsoft Copilot Studio, Power BI, Power Pages, and Microsoft Copilot, and see how you can integrate them to expand the capabilities of Power Apps.

And with that, on behalf of the entire team that has worked to bring this together, I would like to thank you for choosing this book to learn about Power Apps. I wish you good luck and success on your new journey in the world of Power Apps.

Index

About the Author

Arpit Shrivastava is a Power Platform architect at Capgemini, with a passion for learning new, cutting-edge technologies. He has vast experience working with Microsoft Dynamics 365 and the Power Platform, and often shares best practices and solutions for these services on Microsoft Community forums, the Power Platform community, and on his personal blog. In addition to being a Microsoft MVP, Arpit is a Microsoft Certified Trainer and leader of India's D365 Community User Group. He is also an active speaker and organizer of community events and runs a free mentorship guide through his YouTube channel.

Colophon

The animal on the cover of *Learning Microsoft Power Apps* is a spotted bowerbird (*Chlamydera maculata*), a passerine found in eastern Australia. Bowerbirds are well known for their courtship behavior. Males build an elaborate structure, known as a bower, that they decorate with brightly colored objects in order to attract a mate.

Unlike most bowerbirds, the spotted bowerbird is monomorphic. Both males and females are reddish brown with gray-brown streaks, and have a lilac crest and black beak. Their diet consists mainly of fruit and insects. They live in dry woodland areas dominated by eucalyptus or acacia trees.

Many bowerbirds exhibit complex vocal mimicry, and the spotted bowerbird is no exception. They can mimic the calls of other birds, as well as many other sounds, including the sound of breaking branches, wood chopping, human speech, and barking dogs.

Male spotted bowerbirds build and maintain avenue bowers made of two walls with sticks and twigs. They collect various objects to display in and around the bower, such as leaves, flowers, shells, bones, and human-made objects such as glass and metal. Females appear to prefer males that collect a large assortment of items. Some males even paint the walls of their bowers with masticated grass. Some bowers have been maintained for 20 years, with various males rebuilding a portion of it in successive years.

Spotted bowerbirds are considered Least Concern by the IUCN. Many of the animals on O'Reilly covers are endangered; all of them are important to the world.

The cover illustration is by Karen Montgomery, based on an antique line engraving from *Lydekker's Royal Natural History*. The series design is by Edie Freedman, Ellie Volckhausen, and Karen Montgomery. The cover fonts are Gilroy Semibold and Guardian Sans. The text font is Adobe Minion Pro; the heading font is Adobe Myriad Condensed; and the code font is Dalton Maag's Ubuntu Mono.

O'REILLY®

Learn from experts.
Become one yourself.

Books | Live online courses
Instant answers | Virtual events
Videos | Interactive learning

Get started at oreilly.com.

Milton Keynes UK
Ingram Content Group UK Ltd.
UKHW012005050824
446578UK00003B/4